A HISTORY OF GERMANY IN THE MIDDLE AGES.

A

HISTORY OF GERMANY

IN THE

MIDDLE AGES

BY ERNEST F. HENDERSON

A.B. (TRIN. COLL. CONN.), A.M. (HARVARD), PH.D. (BERLIN)

EDITOR OF "SELECT HISTORICAL DOCUMENTS OF THE MIDDLE AGES."

HASKELL HOUSE PUBLISHERS Lᴛᴅ.

Publishers of Scarce Scholarly Books

NEW YORK, N. Y. 10012

1968

First Published 1894

HASKELL HOUSE PUBLISHERS LTD.
Publishers of Scarce Scholarly Books
280 LAFAYETTE STREET
NEW YORK. N. Y. 10012

Library of Congress Catalog Card Number: 68-25240

Haskell House Catalogue Item # 954

Printed in the United States of America

To my Friend and
Fellow Student
JOHN OSBORNE SUMNER.

PREFACE.[1]

IT may seem strange that one whose aim and desire is to be considered an American writer, should first launch his adventurous craft on the tide of English popular favour, rather than entrust it to the currents, likely to be more favourable or less dangerous, of his own native depths. This has come about in great part by accident. I happened to be on this side of the ocean when this volume reached its completion, circumstances prevented my return to America, and yet I was eager without delay to try my experiment on the public.

For it is an experiment. Apart from the question as to whether or not I am capable of putting life and spirit into the vast body of facts and events that concern the past of so enormous a political creation as Germany, I have been assured from competent side that there is not sufficient interest in the subject to warrant a work like the present.

My belief is, that if there is not, there ought to be. Not to speak of the breathlessly exciting incidents of the German Reformation, nor of the proud emancipation of the grand modern empire from the trammels of disunity and disorganization, there is that in the fortunes and misfortunes of a Charlemagne and Henry IV., of a Barbarossa, a Henry VI. and an Emperor Frederick II., which should stir the heart of any observer, no matter what his nationality. The rise and fall of the mediæval German Empire is in itself a subject boundlessly interesting, boundlessly important. Open your eyes, oh ye students of men and of institutions, and see how Europe has come to be what it is, and how near it came to being something quite different! If Italy had remained under the sway of Germany, if Frederick Barbarossa or his successors had done away with the papal power, as they often

---

[1] This volume is intended to be the precursor of two others covering the whole of German history.

seemed about to do, would the fate of England and France have been the same?

And yet what do the ordinary English or American readers know of the mediæval German Empire, or, to give it the full title it enjoyed when in its prime, of the Holy Roman Empire of the German nation? And how should they know anything about it, considering how scanty and how insignificant is the literature on the subject! Bryce's essay is almost the only very recent book to which one can point, and this is, as it was meant to be, the merest fleeting sketch. What does it tell us of the daily movements and occupations of the mediæval emperors, of the condition of things in their lands, of their legislative measures, or of their wars?

I think I am right in saying that there is no narrative history of Germany—apart from a few translations of antiquated German works, and a few compendiums which certain ladies and gentlemen have compiled in their leisure hours— in the English language. In this regard England has been treated better by German scholars. Lappenberg and Pauli's history of England is written with all the care and devotion that native historians could have shown.

The present work is the result of much labour, and of years of enforced exile from home. May all these pains not have been in vain; may the book not fall dead as soon as it is born, but rather may it live and play its part in the world vigorously. May it make its friends, and, if need be, its enemies, be hated deeply and loved warmly.

E. F. H.

LONDON, *April 15th*, 1894.

CONTENTS.

INTRODUCTION.

SINCE the comparatively recent time when, by the efforts of Wolf, Niebuhr, and Ranke, historical investigation was raised to the rank of a science, the whole of the German history has been re-written. New sources of information have been opened up, old problems in many cases solved. More than fifty thousand historical essays and other works, relating to Germany, have been reviewed by the "Jahresbericht der Geschichtswissenschaft" in the thirteen years alone between 1878 and 1890.

Not in one, but in many ways has history writing been revolutionized in our own day. In the first place, the immense importance of text-criticism has been recognized; no scholar now edits a chronicle or document of the past without distinguishing carefully between the original, or at least the oldest obtainable, manuscript and the horde of later copies with all of their accumulated errors. The study of palæography has enabled men to determine at least in what century a given text was written, and many a document or chronicle long considered very ancient has been found to be by a comparatively modern hand, and *vice versâ*.

By comparing the changes, too, and the omissions of words and clauses in a number of different manuscripts of a given work, the prototype or original manuscript from which all the others were taken can often be discovered.

What this method signifies for the truth and accuracy of a historical text may be made clear from the case of Einhard's life of Charlemagne, written shortly after the death of the great hero. Of this valuable writing there are eighty manuscripts extant, of which all but a very few are worthless copies made, in the course of centuries, not from the original, but one from the other. The later scribes and copyists, too, were men far less capable of performing such a task than are many schoolboys of to-day.

It is only modern scholars who have been able to establish the relationships of these Einhard texts to each other, and to sift the later ones of their accumulated errors and interpolations. And the case just mentioned is but one among hundreds.

It must be remembered in this connection that, in the Middle Ages, as parchment grew scarcer, or at least more expensive with time, it became the custom to contract almost every word of more than one syllable; and that the next copyist often had to use his imagination as to the real word that was intended. Many of the manuscripts of the thirteenth century seem a mere mass of signs and tokens of abbreviation. How often, too, not to speak of interpolations wittingly and wantonly made for a given purpose, have marginal remarks of a reader or commentator been attributed by a later scribe to the original author, and placidly incorporated in the new copy!

Altogether the study of palæography and of original historical sources gives one an amazing insight into the peculiarities, the follies, and the weaknesses of our forefathers. The abbot of a monastery interpolates or otherwise falsifies a charter of privileges to gain or preserve this or that right, or to raise the value of these or those relics. A chronicler does not hesitate to put down fictitious details which may add to the glory of the ancestors of a family which gives him its patronage. More than half the charters attributed to Merovingian times have been proved to be fraudulent in either one way or another.

Follow the stream back to its source, reconstruct your edifice from the very foundation, find out the original authority for every assertion; such are the watchwords of the modern school of historians. How many extravagant and yet long-credited assertions concerning Charlemagne have been traced back to the gossipy and far from veracious monk of St. Gall, who wrote more for the amusement than for the edification of Charles the Bald! And Heinrich von Sybel, now the Nestor of German historians, has shown that the chronicle on which most of the modern accounts of the first crusade have been based was never intended even by its original author to be taken seriously.

It is for mediæval times especially that most astonishing difficulties have had to be met and overcome by the modern investigator. For this the peculiarities of the old chroniclers are mostly responsible.

There was a formalism, for instance, that seemed to belong to good tone among writers of a given period. We find one author, Lambert of Hersfeld, who seems to have a regular formula for conspiracies. They all come about in the same way, and the details are repeated in almost the same words. It is most usual, too, and the blame for it attaches to Livy, who set the example for Latin writers, for chroniclers to put set speeches in the mouths of those with whom they are dealing—speeches which they never by any chance could possibly have uttered. Others will relate interviews—it is Lambert again who sins in this way—as though they themselves had been actually present, when we know for certain that the two persons concerned were absolutely alone and would never have been likely to repeat even the general tenor, let alone the actual words, of what had passed between them.

It was the custom all through the Middle Ages for one writer to tacitly embody whole passages, whole pages, and even whole chronicles, of another in his own work. There was, probably, no intent to deceive, the object was to secure a good work, and to continue it if possible, for one's own cloister library.

The historian of to-day has to distinguish what is borrowed from what is original, and, in the great modern collections of mediæval sources, the " Monumenta " of Germany, or the " Rolls Series " of England, the borrowed, so far as it can be ascertained, will be found to be printed in smaller type.

But it often seems impossible to tell who was the original author, and where he lived, who copied from whom, and whether both, perhaps, did not borrow from a third.

It is exactly in this matter of analyzing chronicles, and tracing the different parts back to their origins, that German scholars have performed their greatest services to the studious world. Every clue is followed, every similarity of style investigated; passages are often fathered without the shadow of a doubt on this or that older writer.

Perhaps the most striking case of all is that of the Altaich Annals, edited by the late Wilhelm von Giesebrecht. A number of different chroniclers of the tenth century, who could not have known the writings of each other, showed a remarkable similarity in their description of certain events. Giesebrecht came to the conclusion that they must all have borrowed from one and the same source; and, excerpting and comparing all that the different writers had in common, he edited and published the lost prototype. It is an actual fact that the original chronicle, the "Annales Altahenses," was later discovered, and that Giesebrecht's conjectural readings were found, as far as they went, to be almost absolutely correct.

Nor are text-criticism and the reconstruction of lost chronicles by any means the only branches in which modern scholarship has improved the writing of history. Not only the works of dead and gone chroniclers have been tested and searched, but their lives and opinions as well. It is safe to say that no considerable writer of the Middle Ages is without his careful biographer in the present century.

Germany especially possesses a well-disciplined standing army of investigators, recruited yearly from her great universities, and ready at a given signal to begin the fight in any quarter where obscurity or error is found to lurk.

The deeper one goes, the more one finds how important it is to know the character and tendency of a given chronicler— especially of one who is our sole authority for this or that assertion. Was he well-informed ? Did he move personally in the circles where the events that he describes were taking place, or does he write by hearsay of things that happened in some distant part of the land ?

How much more weighty is a word of blame from one who can be proved to be well-disposed on the whole towards the personage of whom he writes; how worthless, often, the verdict of a political opponent! Especially in the mediæval chronicles the number of accusations is legion that can be proved to be utterly groundless.

Our forefathers of a thousand years ago were, if possible, even more partisan in their judgments than we are to-day. They were more under the ban of fixed and formal ideas; their minds were more closely sealed against anything new or unexpected. Everything was churchly, there was no such thing as a public opinion. The prince who plundered or oppressed the monastery in which a given monk was writing —and there are centuries during which no one but monks did write—or who may only have insisted too sternly on his own just rights, goes down in the pages of history as the antichrist in person, however beneficial to the land as a whole his reign may have been. And *vice versâ*. The Frankish king, Clovis, wholesale fratricide, and breaker of every kind of sacred oath and treaty, marches forth in the pages of the pious Gregory of Tours as a God-sent champion to fight the just fight of Trinitarianism against the Arian heresy.

The historian's task would be lighter, indeed, if all chroniclers were as honest and as transparent as Luitprand of Cremona, a tenth century bishop. In his case it is comparatively easy to tell what to believe and what to attribute to wounded feelings. Luitprand informs us at the very beginning that he is going to punish the King and Queen of Northern Italy for wrongs inflicted on himself. With this end in view he calls his chronicle of the times the *Antapodosis*, or "Book of Retribution."

Apart from the characters and the prejudices of ancient writers there are certain peculiarities, the discovery of which vastly alters the trust and confidence that we are justified in placing in them. It has always been known, for example, that mediæval historians have borrowed much of their phraseology from the ancient classics: Ovid and Virgil, Livy and Sallust are the forcing-houses whence all the fairest flowers of mediæval rhetoric have been culled.

It is only within the last ten or fifteen years that this propensity has been systematically investigated. How far has the truth suffered by being crushed into this classic garb— that is the question that is now everywhere being asked and answered. Einhard's characterizations of Charles the Great are taken in great part direct from Suetonius; Ragewin, the historian of Frederick Barbarossa, describes the siege of Milan in the very words in which Josephus tells of the conquest of Jerusalem, yet applies those words with singular skill and aptitude. There is a detailed description, for instance, of an octagonal tower which we find from independent sources to tally exactly with the true state of affairs.

A famous example is Lambert of Hersfeld's vivid description of the hardships which the Emperor Henry IV. endured while crossing the Alps in winter to humble himself before Gregory VII. at Canossa. What a picture we are given of the king sliding down the icy slopes on ox-hides, of his intense sufferings from cold and hunger! yet the account is taken bodily from Livy, the name of Hannibal being altered to that of Henry.

One may say—Lambert undoubtedly did say to himself—

that the fatigues and dangers of a winter journey over the
Alps are much the same in all ages. The poet Angilbert,
whose verses deal with many of the events of Charlemagne's
time, was not so consistent in his description of Aix-la-
Chapelle. He borrows Virgil's account of Carthage and,
forgetting that Aix lies inland, boasts of her splendid
harbour !

This analyzing of the language and peculiarities of style of
mediæval authors, taken in connection with other criterions,
has led, often, to the discovery that writings were spurious.
There are expressions in the forged Isidorian decretals—that
gigantic swindle on which the popes, from Nicholas I. down,
based many of their most exalted claims—that were copied
from works which appeared three centuries after the dates
claimed for some of the several documents.

It is in great part through methods here touched upon that
the famous Florentine chronicle of Malaspini has been proved
to be a forgery, compiled at a time much later than its
professed date for the purpose of glorifying the ancestors of a
certain family.

It is this same criticism and comparison of original historical
sources that has led to the discarding of many a pleasant
anecdote, many a stirring incident that had long been believed.

Take the old German tradition of the faithful wives of
Weinsberg. You will find it told in many history books how
King Conrad III., in 1140, besieged this town and finally
took it ; how he declared the men guilty of death but allowed
the women to depart with all that they could carry on their
shoulders. Of course they carried their husbands:—a beautiful
legend, which, by the way, is claimed by nearly thirty different towns as an episode of their own past history. But
unfortunately the originator of the story has been traced, and
has been found to have had the anecdote " on the brain " as
it were. He repeats almost the same tale in connection with
the siege of Crema in 1160, on which occasion it is well known
that such wifely devotion was quite unnecessary, the whole
garrison being allowed, as it was, to withdraw in peace.

And William Tell, in spite of Schiller and the chapel
on the Lake of Lucerne, has had to step down from his high
pedestal as liberator of Switzerland. One may well believe
that Swiss patriots have searched the archives, and eagerly
sought some proof of the existence of their hero. But in vain.

No Hapsburg can be found to have interfered at this period in Uri, no bailiff Gessler appears in any local register, and no historian of the time, local or foreign, mentioned the occurrence.

One hundred and fifty years had passed before a chronicler came upon the idea of embellishing his work with this romantic story which he stated to have taken place in the fourteenth century. Nor was there anything new in the episode that he chose. It bears certainly more than a chance resemblance to an incident related by Saxo Grammaticus, a writer of the twelfth century. Saxo tells us of a certain Toko who lived in the tenth century at the court of Harold Blotan, a Danish king.

The king commands Toko to shoot an apple from his son's head. Toko prepares to obey but lays down beside him two extra arrows. The king asks him why he does this. "If the first fails I shall take vengeance on you with the other two," was the answer. The arrow did not miss, but later the king's tyranny became unbearable, and Toko, concealed in a bush, shot him as he passed by.

It must not be supposed that the modern historical method is purely destructive in its tendencies. On the contrary, never before has there been such a search as in our own generation for every available piece of historical evidence from a peculiarly shaped furrow in the ground to a series of ambassador's reports on the complete correspondence of popes and emperors. Never before have there been given to the world such marvellous books of reference, such labour-saving aids to those who are engaged in the work of research.

A digest has been made, for instance, of the subject-matter of forty thousand papal writings and decrees drawn up before the year 1300. In the case of each single document one is told in what printed collection, or in what archive of manuscripts, the original may be found.

The same work is in progress, and has been for twenty years, for the correspondence of all the early German emperors, and a number of large and carefully-edited volumes have already appeared. The whole is so arranged that one can cast the eye through the summaries of a thousand or so of letters during the course of a single day's work, and find which of them require more special investigation. The examples of such comprehensive works that save one years of labour might be multiplied to almost any extent. One enterprising writer, Gams, has published a large volume containing the names of all the Roman Catholic bishops that ever lived in any part of the world, together with references to such books as will in each case give further information. A Frenchman, Chevalier, has printed a dictionary of all the names of note in the Middle Ages, in this case, too, with full lists of the works treating of each given personage.

Wattenbach, a noted professor in Berlin, has written a critical account of each and all of the historical sources in the Middle Ages relating to Germany. Here one can find at a glance the relative scope and value of a given chronicle, and also the latest and best editions.

A great mark of progress in the present century, and a further proof of the constructive tendency of the work of modern historians, is the systematic employment of charters, deeds, and legal documents as historical sources.

Every gift, every privilege granted in earlier times, almost every transaction of any kind was duly certified by a deed signed and sealed in the presence of witnesses. Probably a hundred thousand such pieces of parchment have come down to us from the Middle Ages alone. The single monastery of St. Gall, to-day, possesses in its archives about seven hundred and fifty originals of the eighth and ninth centuries.

It is only the last two generations of scholars that have known how to make extensive and proper use of these rich sources of information, and to control by means of them the assertions of the chroniclers.

Such documents often furnish us with new and important facts. The whole history of the feudal system—indeed the whole of the constitutional history of Germany—would be a hopeless riddle did we not have the charters granted by lords to their vassals, by kings to their cities and nobles. By a comparison of the dates and localities of royal charters we can often follow the progress of a potentate from one end of his domains to the other. The mediæval German king has no fixed abode: he is always on the march. To-day he confers a privilege on this or that town, to-morrow invests a bishop or noble with a fief of the realm, and the next day hurries to a given monastery to confirm to it the jurisdiction over the thieves and robbers in the vicinity.

What were the conditions of land-holding, what the commercial relations between one district and another; what contingents did that man, or that institution, or corporate body send to the army ; what taxes could a territorial lord impose ; who were the bondsmen, who the half-free, and who the free : to all such questions, and to infinitely more, charters, if rightly interrogated, will give a full and satisfactory answer.

Enough has been said to give a faint insight into the methods and labours of modern German historians. It will not surprise the reader to find that in constructing this history the author has made it his aim to choose his authorities, other things being equal, among the most recent writers on a given period or subject.

A WORD CONCERNING THE MORE IMPORTANT AUTHORITIES CONSULTED FOR THE SUBJECT-MATTER OF THIS VOLUME.

FOR the sake of those who wish a complete bibliography of German history it may be as well to mention the work of Dahlmann (continued by Waitz),[1] the yearly report of historical science,[2] and the weekly catalogue of Hinrich.[3]

The first of these books gives a list of some three thousand works on German history arranged according to periods. All the more important writings that appeared before 1883 are here to be found.

The "Jahresbericht" is a grand co-operative work in which scholars all over the world take part, and which attempts to review systematically each year all the writings which deal with historical subjects.

By the aid of Hinrich's catalogue one can follow the new books as they appear. All those on history are in a section by themselves.

The great historical reviews of Sybel[4] and Quidde[5] give exhaustive accounts of the more important works that have been published.

The work in two staunch, closely-printed volumes which goes under the name of "Bruno Gebhardt's[6] Handbook of German History" is, in reality, one composed by twelve different well-known historians, each of whom writes on the special period for which he is considered an authority. A feature of the book is the rich literary references. The work has been of great use to the writer of the present history. It is safe to say that never have so many well-authenticated facts concerning the history of any land been contracted into so small a compass.

On the other hand the book is more than dull for the ordinary reader.

---

[1] Dahlmann-Waitz: "Quellenkunde der deutschen Geschichte." Third edition. 1883.
[2] "Jahresbericht der Geschichtswissenschaft." 1878. ff. Grote. Berlin.
[3] "Hinrich's Wöchentliches Verzeichniss der Neuigkeiten des deutschen Buchhandels." Leipzig.
[4] Sybel's "Historische Zeitschrift."
[5] Quidde, "Zeitschrift für Geschichtswissenschaft." (Appears quarterly).
[6] Bruno Gebhardt: "Handbuch der deutschen Geschichte." 2 vols. Berlin and Leipzig, 1891-92.

A book of which three volumes have already appeared, and
which in a way marks an era in history writing is Lamprecht's.[1]
It is altogether the work of a great historian, and the political
history is made to recede behind a detailed account of social,
agrarian, literary, and artistic developments. The narrative is
brought as yet down to the year 1300.

Somewhat similar to Lamprecht, and indeed the work which
seems to have given the latter his inspiration, is Nitzsch's[2]
" German History," which extends from the earliest times to the
Reformation period. It is an extremely suggestive book, but one
which suffers under the peculiar circumstances attending its origin.
Nitzsch died before it was put into proper form, and one of his
pupils compiled it from the great scholar's notes and lectures.

Schröder's[3] " Constitutional History," without possessing the
originality of the works of Waitz[4] and Brunner,[5] is the best
general handbook for the subject. It is clear and systematic, and
embraces the latest results of historical investigation. The last
part, concerning the history of modern times, is treated in too
short a compass, the author having been unwilling to extend his
book beyond the limit of one volume.

Scherer's[6] " History of German Literature " is a delightfully-
written book, by a great scholar and a great master of his subject.
It extends from the earliest times to the end of the time of Goethe.
Scherer brings the history of the literature into connection with
the general history and culture of the time.

Ranke's[7] " History of the World," which extends only to the
eleventh century, is particularly important for the masterly group-
ing of facts and the bringing of them into their proper connection.
It presupposes in the reader a considerable amount of previous
knowledge of the subject.

Kaufmann's[8] book extends to the end of the reign of Charles the
Great. Kaufmann was known for many excellent monographs on
special subjects concerning the ancient German tribes, and at last
embodied the results of his investigations in the form of a narrative
history. His work is excellent, almost exhaustive. Hoyns's[9]
book covers about the same period as Kaufmann, extending, however, to 911. It is a clear, readable, and reliable account, without,
indeed, being of great independent value.

In Mühlbacher's[10] " History of the Carolingians " we have a truly
important work. Every scrap of contemporary evidence is made

1 Lamprecht, "Deutsche Geschichte." Berlin, 1891. ff.
2 Nitzsch, "Geschichte des deutschen Volkes." Leipzig, 1883.
3 Schröder, "Lehrbuch der deutschen Rechtsgeschichte." Leipzig, 1889.
4 Waitz, "Deutsche Verfassungsgeschichte." 1880. ff. (8 vols.).
5 Brunner, "Deutsche Rechtsgeschichte." 1887. ff. 2 vols.
6 Scherer, "Geschichte der deutschen Litteratur." Berlin, 1885.
7 Ranke, "Weltgeschichte." 1884. ff. (8 vols.).
8 Kaufmann, "Deutsche Geschichte." 2 vols. 1880. ff.
9 Hoyns, "Deutsche Geschichte."
10 Mühlbacher, "Deutsche Geschichte unter den Karolingern" (in Bibliothek
deutscher Geschichte). 1894. Stuttgart.

use of by one who has known better than any living man living where to find it. Mühlbacher has for years been engaged in making a digest of letters and other public acts of the Carolingians for Böhmer's *regesta imperii.*

Giesebrecht's [1] history, which was intended to extend to 1250, and which fills five large volumes without having nearly reached its completion, covers the period from 911 to 1180. It is a favourite habit of lecturers on German history to find flaws in this work; it is nevertheless a work of prime importance, and possesses the further advantage of being written in a pleasant and readable style. It has done more than any other book to rouse a wide interest in the study of mediæval history, and also to instil thoroughness of methods of investigation. The amount of material that Giesebrecht has worked over for a period covering more than two hundred and fifty years is simply astounding.

Manitius' [2] book, covering the period from 911 to 1125, is naturally largely based on Giesebrecht, but the author has been able to make use of later investigations. Manitius is conscientious and reliable, but it must be confessed that the work is heavy, and that the mass of detail prevents one from gaining any clear picture of the time.

For the Hohenstaufen period there lacks as yet any general and comprehensive work up to the requirements of the day. Jastrow, in Berlin, is treating the period for the "Bibliothek deutscher Geschichte," and his book is sure to be excellent; but it will probably be two or three years before it is completed.

Raumer's [3] history of the Hohenstaufens made a great stir in its day, but is now completely out of date. De Cherrier's [4] history is still of value, but parts of it are also antiquated. For special reigns there are a number of useful works.

Prutz's history [5] of Frederick Barbarossa is very learned and exhaustive, and Toeche's Henry VI.[6] is the model of what such an investigation should be.

Winkelmann's works on Philip of Hohenstaufen and Otto IV.,[7] and on Frederick II.,[8] are immensely learned and exhaustive, but thoroughly to be avoided by the general reader. They also form part of the collection of year books of German history, in which the treatment is chronological.

Schirrmacher's [9] "Frederick II. and the Last Hohenstaufens" is

[1] Giesebrecht, "Geschichte der deutschen Kaiser zeit" (latest edition, 1875, ff.). 5 vols.

[2] Manitius, "Deutsche Geschichte unter den sächsischen und salischen Kaisern." (Bibliothek d. Geschichte), 1889.

[3] Raumer, "Geschichte der Hohenstaufen." Fifth edition. Leipzig, 1879. 6 vols.

[4] De Cherrier, "Histoire de la lutte des papes et des empereurs de la maison de Souabe." 3 vols   Paris, 1858-59.

[5] H. Prutz, "Kaiser Frederick I." Danzic, 1871-73. 3 vols.

[6] Toeche, "Kaiser Henrich VI." Leipzig, 1867. (One of the Jahrbücher der deutschen Geschichte.)

[7] Winkelmann, "Philip von Schwaben und Otto IV. von Braumschweig." Leipzig, 1873-78.

[8] Winkelmann, "Geschichte Kaiser's Friedrich II." vol. i. 1889.

[9] Schirrmacher, "Friedrich II. und die letzten Hohenstaufen." 1874. 2 vols.

a shorter and a later treatment of the period covered by the author's more voluminous work on the same subject. It is reliable on the whole.

Zeller's [1] "Frederick II." is more or less of a compilation, but gives all the main facts of Frederick's reign correctly, and is altogether an attractive treatment of the subject. It is one of a series of works written on early German history. Zeller is a Frenchman, and has the French grace of style.

Kempf,[2] in his history of the Interregnum, has carefully and conscientiously performed a thankless but needful task. The period from 1245 to 1272 is most utterly dreary and uninteresting, and has never before been made the subject of a separate work.

In concluding, the author may be allowed to mention a work of his own,[3] which was undertaken as a direct preparation for the present history. It is a collection of original documents translated from the mediæval Latin, and made accessible to the general reader. The author's belief is that no one should attempt to write a popular history who is not thoroughly at home in the primal historical sources.

[1] J. Zeller, "L'empereur Frederic II. et la chute de l'empire Germanique du Moyen Age, Conrad IV. et Conradin." Paris, 1885.
[2] Kempf, "Geschichte des deutschen Reichs während des grossen Interregnums." Würzburg, 1893.
[3] Henderson, "Select Historical Documents of the Middle Ages." 1892. (Bohn's Antiquarian Library.)

A HISTORY OF THE GERMAN PEOPLE.

CHAPTER I.

GERMANS AND ROMANS.

I T is as enemies of the Romans that the Germans first meet us in history ; but there was a time far back in the ages when the people of the two races were friends and brothers. The modern science of comparative philology has shown beyond a doubt that Germans and Celts, Greeks and Romans, Indians and Persians, once formed part of the same great family, and that their languages are derived at bottom from one primæval tongue.

The Indo-Germanic race.

By means of a careful sifting of roots and derivations a grammar and dictionary of this Indo-Germanic mode of speech have been constructed, and on these and on a comparison of the earliest known customs of the chief descendant tribes, a history of the habits of this primæval race has been based.

The names of the trees, flowers, and animals that were known to them suggest, as does also an old tradition, the plains of Russia as their home. They were a nomad people and lived on meat and milk, at times indulging in a fermented, intoxicating drink, which was made from honey and was called *médhu* (mead). They clothed themselves, for the most part, in the skins of wild beasts, but also knew the use of wool, plucking instead of shearing their sheep.

Customs of the race.

In summer they lived in tent-wagons, in winter in holes in the earth. If one pictures a season passed in such an abode, with its impure air and its vermin, one will not be astonished to find that words signifying " coughing " and " consumption," not to speak of itch." have been proved to exist in the Indo-Germanic vocabulary

Family life. The records of the family life of these our progenitors are far more creditable than one might expect. They have words for " father," " mother," " brother," " sister." Marriage was a well-known institution, the bride being either bought or carried off by force. If she failed in bearing offspring she was passed on to a friend. Should she, on the other hand, have properly fulfilled her vocation, hers was the privilege on her lord's decease, in common with the latter's favourite horse and his favourite slave, of seeking death on his funeral pyre, and accompanying him to the abodes of the blessed.

The Germans. The Germans—it is Julius Cæsar, however, who first calls them by this name—seem to have left their original home very much later than the Greeks, Romans, and Celts. Already in 330 B.C., nevertheless, they were firmly settled on the amber-producing shores of the North Sea. Pytheas, of Marseilles, the Christopher Columbus of Germany, visited them there in that year. On the shores of the Baltic, too, the numerous stone implements that have been found, the most perfect specimens known, tell of extensive settlements.

When, in the second century before Christ, the wanderings of the Germans brought them southward—a people dependent on agriculture, and with no knowledge of how to economize and improve land, must, as the population increases, spread out in all directions—they found Greece and Rome with a century-long history behind them, while Gaul and Northern Italy were completely peopled by Celtic tribes.

The Cimbrians and Teutons. It was the Cimbrians and Teutons who opened the long line of demonstrations against Rome, which finally were to rob that power of all her provinces. The annals of Roman history tell of two victories gained by the great Marius in the years 102 and 101 B.C., the one over the Teutons at Aquæ Sextiæ (Aix in Provence), the other over the Cimbrians in Northern Italy.

For eleven years and more these two tribes in common had been harassing the Celts, and, in spite of their naïve and probably most true assertion that they only wanted land upon which to settle, making the Romans tremble for their capital. But in Marius, with the extraordinary powers that had been bestowed upon him, in view of the impending danger, and with the army which he had been able to reorganize, they found their master.

A few details of the two battles have come down to us, which show that the barbarians were completely outwitted by the superior tactics of their adversaries, who were able to fall upon them simultaneously in the front and in the rear. The burning sun of the south helped to weaken their power of resistance, and in both cases defeat was synonymous with annihilation. *Battles with the Romans, 102 and 101 B.C.*

It is related that in both battles the women at last offered a desperate resistance from the camp of wagons, and that at Aquæ Sextiæ no combatants were finally left on the field but the dogs, who defended the corpses of those who had fallen. Poseidonias, a historian of this time, tells us that the land around Aix was so fertilized as to bear fruit in astounding quantities, and that the people hedged in their vineyards with the bones of the slain.

The next great conflict between the Germans and Romans took place in the time of Julius Cæsar on the confines of Gaul. This time on the side of the Germans we meet, not as in the Cimbrian-Teuton War, with a few shadowy heroes of whom we only know their names and that they fought hard and died, but with a real leader, the head and king of seven tribes. *Cæsar and Ariovistus.*

Ariovistus was the first organizer and the first political thinker among the Germans. His name was known far and wide, and in 72 B.C. the Celts called in his assistance against Rome. When Cæsar's troops found that they were to march against him, they were so terrified that they all but renounced their obedience. Only the threat of their commander that he would march forward with the tenth legion alone shamed them back into order and discipline. In the end the Roman skill and training conquered ; Ariovistus was put to flight and we soon hear of him no more.

Friendly
relations
between
Romans and
Germans.
The relations later became more friendly between the warriors of the north and the warriors of the south. Germans entered the Roman service—Augustus had a bodyguard of them—and learned there valuable lessons which they were soon able to turn to account in their own land.

The subjugation and reorganization of Gaul by the Romans brought them into closer contact with the Germans ; the old culture and the new courage were now of the greatest influence on each other. In the year 39 B.C. the powerful tribe of the Ubii was allowed by Agrippa to settle on the left bank of the Rhine ; here in their midst, in due time, an altar was erected in honour of Augustus, and around it German priests performed the Roman rites. It was among the Ubii that, less than three generations later, the city of Cologne was founded, Aggripina, the mother of Nero, having sent thither a colony of Roman veterans.

Augustus
and the Si-
gambrians.
The Sigambrians were the next Germans to begin a series of wars with the Romans. They had been exasperated by the oppressions of the Roman commander Marcus Lollius. In the year 16 B.C. they seized and crucified several Romans, and made an inroad into Gaul in which they were joined by other tribes. They defeated the Roman legate and even secured the eagle of the fifth legion. It is about this time that the poet Horace wishes Augustus a victory over the Sigambrians as the greatest triumph that he could have in his life.

The Sigambrians were soon induced or compelled to make peace, but Augustus determined that his provinces should never again be exposed to a similar danger. He came himself to Gaul to survey the field, and to prepare for an invasion of Germany on a large scale, but in 13 B.C. transferred to his stepson, Drusus, the direction of the undertaking.

The inva-
sions of
Drusus,
13-9 B.C.
Drusus built fortifications along the Rhine, and between the Main and the Lippe. The most famous of his fortresses are the Saalburg, near Homburg, in the Taunus mountains, and Castle Aliso, the site of which is only approximately

known. Drusus also constructed a canal that proved of great assistance in later campaigns, allowing Roman fleets to sail into the heart of Germany. It led through the land of the friendly Batavians from the Rhine to the Yssel, and from there through the present Zuydersee, then an inland lake, into the North Sea.

Every year, until his death in 9 B.C., Drusus undertook an expedition through the deep morasses and primæval forests of Germany. His bravery and perseverance won for him the highest possible marks of esteem at Rome. The Senate gave the name Germanicus to him and his offspring; a triumphal arch which still remains was erected in his honour on the Appian Way, and a monument which Tiberius raised to him on the Eichelstein, near Mayence, lasted for seventeen centuries, and was finally destroyed by the French.

Great, however, as were the successes of Drusus, he was unable to lay lasting fetters on tribes so numerous and so widely dispersed.

Tiberius, who succeeded his brother in the conduct of the war, was able in the year 8 B.C. to inflict a fearful punishment on the Sigambrians. Their chiefs were taken prisoners while on a peace-embassy to Rome, and nearly the whole tribe, bereft of its leaders, was transplanted to the left bank of the Rhine. **Tiberius and Marobod.**

We have accounts of further expeditions of Tiberius in the years 4, 5, and 6 A.D. In the latter year he determined to annihilate the power of a certain Marobod, leader of the Marcomanni, who had defeated the Boiers in the present Bohemia, and had raised up for himself a power such as never before had been seen in Germany. The most varied tribes, from the Goths in the east to the Thuringians in the west, looked up to him as their king. He had himself been in Roman service and knew the tactics of the enemy with which he had to cope.

The army that Tiberius raised for this expedition was the largest that had ever marched against any one single enemy of Rome. Twelve legions took the field, but they never came in sight of the object of their attack. A revolt in the recently subjected Pannonia broke out and detained Tiberius for three full years. By that time a more dangerous antagonist even than Marobod had appeared upon the scene.

Arminius and Varus.

On the river Weser the Cheruscans played much the same *rôle* that the Sigambriams had once played on the Rhine. But with more success. Their leader, Arminius, fell upon the Roman procunsul, P. Quinctilius Varus, in the Teutoberg forest in the year 9 A.D., and destroyed those splendid legions, the loss of which Augustus is stated to have bemoaned in the famous " *Vare, Vare, redde mihi legiones meas !* "

Varus had tried to emulate the oppressions of a Lollius, and to tread under foot the Germans as he had, in his former proconsular district, the Syrians. But he had not calculated on the organized opposition by which he had been met ; he had not expected to find a patriot like Arminius—one, too, who had been trained at Rome.

Battle in the Teutoberg Forest, 9 A.D.

When Varus finally saw that the battle was going against him, he threw himself on his own sword. Arminius sent his head to Marabod, seeking an alliance against the common enemy. Marabod, however, had already made a treaty of peace with Augustus, and felt no inclination to join hands with the victor.

The exact locality of the battle in the Teutoburg Forest, which took place, however, somewhere in the hilly district between the Ems, the Weser and the Lippe, has not been determined. Germanicus, the son of Drusus, later visited the scene of the disaster, and found there, nailed to trees, the skulls of the centurions and tribunes who had been sacrificed to Wotan. In recent times a large number of Roman coins have been found in the neighbourhood of Barenau. It is assumed, even by an authority like Mommsen, that they came from the pouches of the soldiers of Varus and remained, uninjured by time, long after the bones of those to whom they once belonged had rotted away.

In Rome the importance of the German victory which, as we even now acknowledge, was one of the decisive ones in the world's history, was fully recognized. It was even feared that the capital itself might be invaded. The bodyguards of Augustus, as well as all German visitors, were banished from the city, a stricter watch was kept by night and day.

Tiberius, having ended the war with the Pannonians, again visited the Rhine provinces, but busied himself chiefly with restoring discipline to the Roman army. Becoming emperor in the year 14, he entrusted the command in Gaul and the direction of the German war to the young Germanicus. The latter was able to carry off as captive to Rome Thusnelda, the wife of Arminius. Small credit to the Roman commander, for her own father, Segestes, head of a party hostile to the conqueror of Varus, had brought her into his hands. Thusnelda, and an infant son to whom she had given birth in captivity, graced the triumph of Germanicus, in which Segestes took part as an honoured guest. *The young Germanicus.*

The campaigns of Germanicus, although not inglorious— in a great battle that was fought on the bank of the Weser Arminius suffered heavy losses—were on the whole fruitless, and Tiberius at last recalled him (16 A.D.). For half a century no more wars were waged with the Germans.

More was gained by this policy of non-interference than by any number of petty expeditions. The Germans, bereft of a common enemy, and yet accustomed to all the excitements of war, fell to fighting among themselves. Marobod and Arminius became the centres of two rival camps, and a great but indecisive battle was fought between them. Marobod's subjects finally fell away from him, and the great king himself ended his days as an exile in Ravenna, where the emperor had allowed him to take up his abode. Roman writers reproach him with having cared to live so long. *Arminius and Marobod.*

Arminius in the end fell a prey to the spirit of faction. He was struck down by the hand of one of his own relatives.

His exploits have never been forgotten. Tacitus calls him the "*liberator haud dubie Germaniæ,*" and in our own day a grand monument has been erected to him by the German nation.

Claudius
Civilis, 68
A.D.

The Romans never again attempted the subjugation of
Germany.   A revolt broke out in 68 A.D. among the hitherto
friendly Batavii.   It was headed by Claudius Civilis, and was
joined by a number of neighbouring tribes.   The plans of
Claudius seem to have been ambitious enough, but Rome was
too strong as yet.   The storm soon passed over, and left no
lasting results.   The Batavii remained, as before, friends and
allies of the Roman people.

The Roman
Limes.

The Romans have left us two valuable reminders of their
connection with the Germans, the one of a practical the other
of a literary nature.   The first is the *Limes*, a broad fortifica-
tion-wall, flanked at intervals by fortresses and watch-towers,
to the very base of which the full tide of Roman culture once
flowed.   Its course can still be traced almost along its whole
length, and a number of scholars, supplied with funds by the
German Government, are now engaged in laying it bare.
Numerous camps and settlements, not to speak of other remains, have already been brought to light.

Its course.

The *Limes* ran along the Danube from its confluence with
the Altmühl to the monastery of Lorsch on the Wurtemberg
frontier, thence along the Rhine and the Main, and around
the Taunus mountains.   It ended at a point nearly opposite
to Bonn.

The Danube section, the so-called *Teufelsmauer*, was built
for the protection of the *agri decumates*, those lands which
were given over to Romans and barbarians alike for a fixed
rent of ten per cent. of their produce.   This *Limes trans-
dubianus* was five feet high and twelve feet broad, and was
protected for long distances by a moat and a second wall.

The *Limes transrhenanus* was higher, sixteen feet on an
average, and was provided along its whole length with a
moat twenty feet wide and ten deep.

Object of
the Limes.

Extensive as these fortifications were, they could not have
kept off a serious and organized attack on the part of the
Germans; but none such was to be dreaded for two centuries
after the wall was begun.   It was the petty plundering expeditions to which it was intended to put an end, and this ob-

ject was in the main attained. Behind their wall the Roman veterans, the soldiers and camp-followers, as well as the friendly German settlers, passed a secure and civilized existence. If danger threatened, signals were exchanged from one watch-tower to the other, and the forces concentrated at a given point.

Beyond the *Limes* a broad stretch of land was left uncultivated, the trees cut down, the shrubbery burnt away. A considerable commerce was carried on with the Germans, but the barbarian traders were only allowed to approach the *Limes* at certain points and at stated hours. They were obliged to accept and to pay for an escort of Roman soldiers, and they themselves were not permitted to carry arms. *Commerce with the Germans.*

The Roman merchants, on the other hand, penetrated far into the German lands. In the present Sweden nearly five thousand Roman denars of the first and second century after Christ have come to light, and Roman productions have been found in the most distant parts of Germany.

The building of the *Limes* was begun under Augustus, but more than a century passed before it neared its completion. The line of defence that had to be erected was more than three hundred miles in length ! *The building of the Limes.*

It must be remembered in this connection that the men who composed the Roman legions were not merely soldiers, they were also stone-hewers and builders. To them we owe many temples, baths, and amphitheatres on German ground, and many of their peculiarly-constructed roads can still be followed.

The second great heritage that we have from the Romans is the " Germania " of Tacitus. At a time for which all other sources of information fail us, the Roman historian undertook to write a comprehensive description, to paint a colossal picture, as it were, of the Germany of his day. *The " Germania " of Tacitus.*

Tacitus tells of a land " bristling with forests, or covered with ugly swamps ; " he tells of a people fresh and vigorous, with an unwritten but fixed code of law and honour, and not without their vices and weaknesses. They drink and gamble,

and pay their stakes, if need be, by becoming the slaves of
their debtor.   War is their chief occupation, the ultimate end
and object for which their youths are reared and trained.
Cowardice and desertion of the army are the crimes most
hateful to them ; the usual penalty is suffocation in the mud
of the marshes.

Manners and Customs.

The form of government varies among different tribes:
here it is republican, there a liberal monarchy.   The land is
divided into larger and smaller districts—into counties, if we
may call them so, and into hundreds.   Already there are
different classes of society ; the slaves carry on the limited
agriculture, and the chieftains, each with his select " following " of youths, lead their people to war, or administer justice in the districts allotted to them by the general assembly.
Woman is respected and honoured, but wifely infidelity is
punished by death.   Priests conduct the worship of the gods
and keep the peace in the army and in the councils.

Germans cease to be nomads.

The building of the *Limes*, and the successful defence of
it by the Romans—it was the end of the third century before
the *agri decumates* were abandoned, and the fifth before the
Rhine boundary altogether fell into disuse—worked a revolution in the inner life of the Germans.   Prevented from advancing further, the people ceased to be nomads from very
necessity.   They began more systematically to till the fields
and to lead a less arduous, less warlike existence ; but at the
same time their numbers grew apace: they were naturally
prolific, fond of family life, and untainted as yet by vice or
luxury.   In the fifth century, Salvianus, contrasting them
with the Romans, exclaims regretfully, " they increase daily,
and we decrease ! "

Amalgamation of petty tribes.

But the fertile districts in central Europe are of limited
extent.   The tribes overflowed their boundaries in all directions, one encroached on another, subdued, annihilated, or
drove it away.   A double process of suppression and amalgamation took place, which, in a short space of time, reduced
the countless little kingdoms and republics to great " stems,"
the numbers of which may be counted on one's fingers.

We know little of the habits and customs of the Germans during these early centuries, but here and there a scanty notice has come down to us. Their civilization was higher than one might expect, and they had fixed notions of right and wrong, of truth and fidelity. In one respect they were far beyond the level of an ordinary, unthinking savage. " In the kingdom of the Goths there are no unchaste men except the Romans," writes Salvianus about the year 430. The Vandals, whose name to-day is a by-word for barbarism, having conquered Carthage, compelled all the impure women to marry, and placed a heavy fine on prostitution. According to the law of the Franks,[1] reduced to writing about the year 490, the fine for groundlessly calling a woman unclean is second only to that for attempted murder.

Civilization of the Germans.

In our own day hundreds, if not thousands, of graves of ancient Germans have given up their dead. In all the chief museums of Germany one can see the skulls and bones, the weapons, adornments, and implements of these old warriors. They were evidently, as a rule, buried in full state, and some of their belts and dress ornaments have withstood the ravages of time. On their legs, arms, and fingers, and around their necks are found circlets of gold, or of bronze, iron, or copper. Utensils of glass and amber, and vases of clay, usually lie close to their shrivelled bones. Trusted pages and faithful wives often shared the death of their lord; in one of the graves the master's corpse lay stretched along on the shoulders of eight of his crouching servants.

Graves of the Germans.

The Germans had often enough looked longingly towards the land of promise over the entrance to which the Roman legions kept watch and ward. In the year 166 A.D. a vast horde of Marcomanni, Quadi, and other tribes, urged forward by the Goths, who shortly before had left their home on the Vistula to found new settlements on the Black Sea, broke their bounds and flooded northern Italy. It was the life-work of the emperor Marcus Aurelius to drive them back.

The Marcomannic war, 166 A.D.

[1] See Henderson's " Select Documents," p. 176.

He succeeded in his endeavours, but not without fearful sacrifices. The plague had decimated his army ; he filled the broken ranks with slaves, gladiators, and robbers, and such Germans as he could muster. When all other supplies failed, the silver plate from his own table was offered at public auction in the forum of Trajan.

The importance of the Marcomannic war, however, consists not in the Roman endeavours and victories, but in the fact that by the treaties of peace—the last of these was signed by Commodus on the death of Marcus Aurelius in 180—many a barrier between the Germans and the Romans was levelled to the ground. Thousands of the former were received into the Roman armies or allowed to settle on Roman lands. It was the beginning of the end.

Wars along the Limes. From the time of the appearance of the great "stem" of the Allemanni in the district between the Main, Neckar, and Danube—Caracalla was first appealed to against them in the year 213—the wars along the Limes, although interrupted at intervals, never really ceased. By the end of the century the present Wurtemberg and Baden were lost to Rome, and the region was called henceforward "Allemannia" or "Barbaria."

The Goths. The Goths meanwhile had plundered the Balkan peninsula ; in 251, after defeating and slaying the emperor Decius, they ravaged Greece, and showed their scorn of Diana of the Ephesians by laying her temple in ruins. The Emperor Claudius won a great victory over them in 269, and Aurelian drove them back over the Danube, but relinquished to them the province of Dacia—the later Lower Hungary and Transylvania.

The Goths as Arians. The Goths soon lost to a great extent their character of barbarians, and a number of them accepted the Christianity of which they had heard their Roman captives speak. In a heretical form, indeed, for from the beginning the church had been rent by schisms and the one going on at the time between the Arians and the Athanasians was to prove the most bitter of all. It was the Arian teachings that were adopted by the Goths.

At the council of Nicea, which was called by Constantine for **Ulfilas.** the purpose of restoring the unity of the faith, and which set forth the doctrine of the Trinity as it is now accepted, the Goths were represented by their own bishop, Theophilus. A few years later Ulfilas unfolded his marvellous talents as a missionary, and made that Gothic translation of the Bible which is the oldest monument of German literature. Fragments of it may still be seen and deciphered in the university library at Upsala.

It was with no ordinary difficulties that Ulfilas had to cope. He had to construct from Greek, Latin, and Runic characters the very alphabet of the tongue in which he wrote. He created a written language for his people; all the other German races took theirs from the hands of the Romans.

From first to last Ulfilas had the good of his people in view. He is recorded to have left out the Book of Kings from his translation of the Bible because it tells too much of war and bloodshed.

Already, by this time, the Saxons, the Burgundians, and **Saxons,** the Franks had appeared upon the scene. The latter, who were **Burgun-** later to become masters of nearly all of Europe, had begun **dians, and** their career in the year 257 with a grand plundering expedi- **Franks.** tion which had brought them as far south as the very foot of the Pyrenees. The Emperors Diocletian and Constantine retarded the approaching fate of Rome. They introduced farreaching reforms, reorganized the army and the administration, and once more prevented the barbarians from crossing the *Limes transrhenanus.*

But within the empire itself the process that began after **Germaniza-** the Marcomannic war went on unceasingly. Every branch of **tion of the** the administration became Germanized, and the new soldiers **Roman em-** and colonists did not hesitate to help in guarding the frontier **pire.** against those of their own race. Germans married into noble Roman families, became officers in the imperial armies, and often exercised a leading influence at court. Not many years were to pass before they were to be in a condition to raise and depose emperors at will.

Had the empire been given time it might have peacefully assimilated the German elements that poured so unceasingly into its lands. But the advent of the Huns on the Volga about the year 375 precipitated upon it an avalanche of peoples—flooded it, ruined it.

It is a grim spectacle, this final struggle of western Rome, this repopulating of half a continent. The crowding nations engage with each other in a rushing dance of death. Side by side or face to face they sweep over southern Europe ; now forward, now backward, until each falls into its own position, to have and to hold as long as it can be maintained. Within the space of a hundred and sixty years seven great kingdoms arise on the ruins of the Roman provinces. That of the Franks alone was ultimately destined to triumph and survive.

CHAPTER II.

THE WANDERING OF THE NATIONS.

THE Huns were, according to Ammianus Marcellinus, who is trustworthy in the main despite a tendency to make rhetorical effects, " savage beyond measure." He describes how they scarred and made hideous their children's faces; how they lived on raw meat which they warmed by placing between their bodies and their horses; how they ate, drank, held their assemblies and slept on the backs of their tough little steeds. Their mode of attack was terrible, their chief manœuvre to simulate flight, then suddenly to turn and charge.

Their first victims were the Alani, a nomad and apparently half-German tribe. The next were the eastern Goths, many of whom were slain, many others reduced to subjection. The western Goths were more fortunate; one of their chiefs, Athanarich, offered a brave resistance and was at last able to make an orderly retreat.

But the fear and dread of the Huns was overpowering. By hundreds of thousands the western Goths fled to the Danube, convinced that their only hope of rescue lay in the hands of Rome. When Athanarich opposed this view his camp was deserted and the people flocked round other leaders who were soon treating with the Emperor Valens. The Huns meanwhile remained in the vacated lands, in the so-called " Gothia " of the Romans. It was here between the Danube, Theiss, and Dniester, that Ruga, the uncle of Attila, established for himself that monarchy to which, on his death in 435, the " scourge of God " was to become heir.

The negotiations of the Western Goths led finally to their peaceful reception on Roman territory. Valens was oppressed with the prospect of a war against the Persians, and with the struggle against the orthodox or Athanasian Christians. He was, moreover, at odds with his nephew Gratian, who ruled in the west, and persecuted the Arians. It was, therefore, in the hope of making allies of the Western Goths, among whom Arianism had taken deep root, that Valens permitted them to cross the Danube. When, later, the remnants of the Eastern Goths asked for the same favour they were refused.

Revolt of the West Goths. Valens took precautions to secure the good conduct of his new settlers. A number of their noblest youths were surrendered as hostages, and were carried off to Asia Minor. When the revolt broke out, as it did soon enough, they were all put to death.

This revolt seems to have been called forth simply and purely by the greed and incapacity of the officials whom Valens had appointed to superintend the new colonization ; "an evil demon blinded the emperor," says a contemporary, " when he chose these rascals." The Goths, forbidden to plunder, were yet left without food and supplies. They sold their slaves, their children, and their wives, to keep themselves from starving. Before the town of Marcianople matters came to a crisis. The Germans had tried to enter the city for the sake of procuring food, and had slain some of the sentinels. The Roman official, Lucinus, caused a number of Goths to be executed, but the result was rebellion not intimida-

The battle before Adrianople, 378 A.D. tion. It was a costly proceeding for Rome. The Germans declared themselves to be no longer bound by their recent treaty. A time of fighting and plundering began, the Goths being led by their Christian chief, Fritigern. His policy was to waste no time in sieges, but to devastate the open country. " I do not fight with walls," he is said to have cried out, and therein lay the secret of his success. After a fierce but indecisive battle with troops, which Valens had at last been forced to summon from the Western Empire, Fritigern was able to

induce a number of Huns, of Eastern Goths, and of the conquered Alani, to cross the Danube and come to his aid. The
further sending of reinforcements from the west was delayed
by a fierce inroad of the Allemanni, and Valens, without
waiting for the promised troops, engaged in battle with the
Goths under the walls of Adrianople. The Roman army was
not defeated, but annihilated, and the emperor himself, to the
joy of the orthodox Christians, who saw in his fall a judgment
against the Arians, perished in an attempt at flight. It was
four years before his successor, Theodosius, was able to restore
quiet in the Balkan peninsula. But in October, 382, the
joyful news was proclaimed that "the whole nation of the
Goths have entered into a peace and alliance with the Romans."
So long as Theodosius lived the relations were friendly, and
the chief ambition of the barbarians was to gain advancement
in the imperial service.

But under Honorius and Arcadius they again threw off **Alaric.**
their yoke : a new German hero had arisen, the greatest since
Arminius. We first hear of him in 393 as a subordinate
commander in the army of Theodosius. For nearly a generation the Goths had been without a king ; they now raised
Alaric on the shield, and swore to him the oath of their
allegiance. Many of the Germans in the Roman army joined
his banner. Thrace was plundered, and even Constantinople
was in danger. Rufinus, however, the guardian of the boy
emperor Arcadius, bought off the invaders. The latter turned
to Greece, and penetrated as far as Sparta. Stilicho, the
master of the horse and father-in-law of Honorius, hastened
eastward with an army, and at last surrounded the Gothic
forces. How it happened no one knows, but Alaric was soon
free from his pursuer, and, through a treaty with Arcadius,
received a part of Illyria, with Dyracchium as his chief sea-
port. A wedge was thus placed between the eastern and the
western empire.

The campaign in Greece was but the precursor of a more **Alaric and**
desperate conflict. In Stilicho, however, Alaric found his **Stilicho.**
equal, and, after invading Italy and losing the battle of

Pollentia (402), he was glad enough when his great rival offered to close with him a not disadvantageous peace.

But for Stilicho himself there was no rest. In 404 a countless horde, consisting chiefly of Eastern Goths, but recruited from various other German tribes, precipitated themselves upon Italy under their leader Rhadagast. The barbarians were already besieging Florence when the Romans fell upon and vanquished them. Stilicho took twelve thousand Gothic warriors into the Roman service, but the rest of the captives were dragged to the slave markets, and, to add to their disgrace, were sold for the most trifling sums. Two years later a new band, consisting of Vandals, Suevi, and Alani, crossed the Rhine in search of adventure. After plundering and ravaging for three years they crossed over into Spain.

In their wake the Allemanians, Burgundians, and Franks descended upon Gaul, which was harried and desolated to the last degree. Only in the cities could the Roman culture maintain itself at all; and this only for the reason that civic life was distasteful to the Germans, and that fertile fields attracted them more than walled enclosures.

Stilicho's fall. During this time Stilicho was engaged in warding off the attacks of his private enemies, and in making warlike demonstrations in the name of Honorius against the Eastern Empire. In the year 407 he employed Alaric to lay waste the East Roman province of Epirus.

The expedition was soon countermanded, but Alaric claimed 4,000 pounds of gold for services already rendered, and Stilicho, acknowledging the justice of the demand, himself laid the claim before the senate. It was finally granted, but with reluctance, and the negotiations showed plainly that Stilicho's influence, which for years had been supreme, was at last shaken. His fate quickly overtook him. It was whispered in the ear of Honorius that his great general had designs upon the throne. By the emperor's own command the rescuer of Rome was put to death, and all his friends and allies persecuted. Everywhere the two parties in the Western Empire came into conflict.

The Roman legions rose against the barbarian auxiliaries that had fought under Stilicho, and stormed the towns and villages where their wives and children were quartered. Nearly 30,000 Germans thereupon marched to Noricum and placed themselves under the banner of Alaric. The latter with his whole army marched straight upon Rome. To the embassy that came out to meet him, and to assure him that the whole Roman people was about to rise in arms, he answered—so says the Roman historian—"the thicker the grass the more easy to mow." He demanded all the gold and silver in the city, and all the slaves of German race. To the question as to what he intended to leave them, "your lives," was the terse reply. There seems to have been in these remarks either a mere intention to intimidate, or a certain grim humour, for the truce that Alaric finally made was upon exceedingly moderate terms. He had no thought at the time of harming either the Roman Empire or the Roman people. On the contrary, he desired nothing better than to enter into Rome's service, and he bade the senate send an embassy to offer peace in his name to the emperor. He demanded the provinces of Venetia, Dalmatia, and Noricum, and the title of *magister militum*, besides a sum of gold and a quantity of grain. With his whole army, in return, he was to fight Rome's battles and maintain her glory.

Alaric as an avenger.

Alaric seeks alliance with the Romans.

Considering the state of disorganization at this time in the army, as well as in every branch of the administration, Honorius could not have done better than to accept the offer. But, although Alaric lowered his conditions, although he offered to content himself with Noricum, and to forego the sum of money first demanded, his proposals were rejected. Honorius was surrounded by intriguing courtiers who dreaded the prospect of having anyone at all in authority over them. They drove the weak and foolish emperor to swear an oath that he would never make Alaric *magister militum*.

Alaric for his own part was most anxious to come to terms and to secure for his people the blessings of the Roman civilization. He offered at last to forego the dignity that he

The siege of Rome, 410 A.D.

had demanded ; but when, even on these terms, his proffered alliance was not accepted, his patience gave way. He cut off the supplies of Rome, and compelled the people to desert Honorius and to acknowledge as their emperor Attalus, the prefect of the city. Honorius retired to Ravenna, but would neither abdicate nor, when Alaric tired of Attalus and deposed him, would he come to an agreement.

Sack of Rome.

The plundering of Rome was the last resort of a cautious and determined man, who had tried every other means of providing for the wants of the huge army under his care. From the 24th to the 27th of August, 410, the city was given over to the soldiers, who robbed and despoiled it. "My tongue falters and the words I would dictate to my scribe will not pass my lips," writes the great Hieronymus ; "the city is subjected that once subjected the universe ! "

And yet it was no absolutely indiscriminate ravaging and burning that took place in Rome at this time. The Goths were many of them Christians who reverenced the churches and the sacred relics. Alaric, too, had commanded them to spare human life, and there is every reason to believe that, in the main, he was obeyed.

The attitude of the unworthy successor of the Cæsars in this emergency is later held up to bitter scorn by Procopius, the historian of these times. The anecdote that he relates may or may not be a pure invention ; that such a tale could be told is reason enough for repeating it. "Rome has perished," announces the guardian of the poultry-yard, who had been the first to hear the news. "He has just been feeding from my hand," exclaims the Emperor in surprise. The eunuch assures him that nothing has happened to his favourite rooster !

Alaric's end and burial, 411 A.D.

Alaric's victorious course came to an untimely end. He attempted to cross over to Africa and cut off the supplies that came from there to Rome, but his ships were wrecked and he was forced to return. Before he could renew the experiment death intervened.

We have seen what importance the Germans attached to the

proper burial of their great men. Now that their leader had died in an enemy's land they outdid themselves in showing him honour. They forced their Roman captives to divert the current of the river Busento, in order that his grave should be undisturbed. Here in the bed of the stream, with rich treasures heaped around him, they laid him to rest. The water was turned back into its course, and the workmen were slain lest they should betray the secret.

Athaulf, the new king of the Goths, remained with his forces for two years in Italy, and then led them over into Gaul, carrying with him Placidia, the sister of Honorius. Here he fought first for them against the usurper Jovinus, but did not receive from Honorius the anticipated reward for his services. His demands had been very much the same as those once made of the emperor by Alaric. *Alaric's successors.*

Wallia, however, the successor of Athaulf, at last came to an agreement with Rome. Placidia was restored to her family the wiser by many experiences. She had been forced by Athaulf to wed him, and the nuptials had been celebrated at Narbonne with great magnificence. In the week of anarchy that had followed on Athaulf's death, in 415, she had been subjected to every hardship; she had even been forced to walk as a captive in the triumphal procession of a certain Sigerich, who had claimed for himself the rule of the Goths.

Wallia's treaty bound him to make war against the Vandals, Alani and Suevi, who had crossed into Spain, where they had at first been treated as allies by Rome. In this task he was successful. He completely subdued one whole branch of the Vandals who dwelt around the present Andalusia—originally Vandalusia—sending their king as a prisoner to Ravenna. As a reward for these services Wallia's people, in 419, were given settlements in Aquitaine, the land being made over to them by formal deed of gift. *Founding of the kingdom of Toulouse, 419 A.D.*

It was here that the kingdom of Toulouse was founded, here that the homeless and weary Western Goths were at last to find their needed rest. Between the years 453 and 456 they were able to extend their power over parts of Spain.

The West
Goths in
Spain.

King Eurich (466-484) brought the kingdom to its greatest
height of prosperity, but under his successor all the original
West Gothic possessions in Gaul came into other hands.

In Spain the Western Goths continued to flourish.   Under
Reccared (586-601) they gave up Arianism and became
Catholics ; their king's conversion began with a religious disputation in 586, and was finally consummated at the Council
of Toledo three years later.   We shall see how the Arabs
finally put an end to the West Gothic power.

The Bur-
gundians
transplanted
to Savoy.

Earlier even than the kingdom of Toulouse another German
monarchy had been founded on Roman ground.   Already in
409 Honorius had ceded to the Burgundians the so-called
province of Upper Germany on the left bank of the Rhine.
In 437 the Roman general Aetius, having to punish them for
unlawful efforts to enlarge their boundaries, slew their king,
Gunther, took their chief city of Worms, and transplanted
their tribe to the present Savoy.   He was aided in his undertaking by a number of Huns.

It is this rout of a whole people that is dealt with in the
last part of the "Nibelungenlied," the famous poem of the
thirteenth century, where, however, Attila or Etzel, as he is
called, is falsely made the instrument of disaster.

The Vandal
kingdom in
North
Africa, 429
A.D.

We have said that seven great kingdoms were founded by
the Germans on Roman ground.   The third in the list was
the Vandal settlement in the province of North Africa.   The
kingdoms of Odoacer, of Clovis, of Theoderick, and of the
Lombards complete the number.

The so-called Asdingian Vandals, who had crossed over into
Spain in 409, had, by agreement with the other tribes that had
accompanied them, received settlements in the north-western
part of the Peninsula, in the province of Gallicia.   In 429,
under their leader Genserich, they crossed over into Africa,
called in, as the story goes, by the Roman stadtholder, by
Bonifacius, the rival of Aetius.   Here they managed to found
an independent kingdom, and in 439 even Carthage fell into
their hands.

North Africa had been the great grain-reservoir of Rome, and its occupation by the Vandals, who were to hold it for a hundred years, was an irretrievable misfortune. And the new settlers, ambitious as they were and possessed with a love of conquest, were no pleasant neighbours for Italy. In course of time Sicily, Sardinia, Corsica, and the Balearic Isles came into their possession, while Rome itself was occupied and plundered by them for fourteen days (455).

The strength and the power of resistance of the Western Empire were meanwhile slowly ebbing away, while the fearful onslaughts of extraneous powers showed no signs of ceasing. In 449 the Roman legions were definitively withdrawn from Britain, and the Angles and Saxons began to found the sturdy race that has since done them so much honour. **Weakness of Rome.**

In 451 the Huns, led by their powerful king, Attila, and accompanied by numerous remnants of subjected German tribes, marched along the Danube and the Rhine and entered Gaul. Metz was burned and Orleans besieged; the booty from the latter place was already loaded on the waggons when a term was put to further devastations. The fading glories of Rome revived once more; once more and for the last time fortune smiled on one of her endeavours. Aetius was a worthy successor of Stilicho, whose fate, too, he was destined to share. He reinforced his army as best he could from the various German tribes in Gaul; while the Western Goths under the leadership of their king, Theoderick, fought as his allies. **Attila the scourge of God.**

In the plains of Champagne, in the so-called Catalaunian fields, there was a scene of desperate combat that was only put an end to by the closing in of night. The Gothic king lost his life, but the Roman commander-in-chief maintained the field, and Attila beat a retreat. In the following year he bore down upon Italy, storming the towns of Aquileija, Pavia, and Milan. It was at this time that Venice came into being. The oppressed people fled to the islands and sand-bars of the sea-coast, and Italy, after a season of direst travail, gave birth to the fairest of her daughters. **The Catalaunian Fields.**

Attila spared Rome, induced, we are told, by an embassy **Attila spares Rome.**

sent to him by Pope Leo the Great. Superstitious fears may have done their share; the death of Alaric had been looked upon by many as a judgment of God. The same judgment, indeed, overtook Attila in spite of his leniency. He died suddenly in the following year in the midst of his wedding festivities.

The fall of Rome. Western Rome was meanwhile entering into the last phase of her decay. The Suevian Ricimir now became the ruler of her destinies, and raised five emperors in succession upon her worthless throne. After his death, in 462, four pigmy potentates in turn essayed their fate and, on the fall of the last of them, him whose double name disgraced alike Rome's founder and her first emperor, the rule of Italy came into the hands of the barbarian Odoacer.

Odoacer, 476-489 A.D. Tired of the shameful farce, the German mercenaries had raised him to be their king. The title of "patricius" was asked for and obtained from the Eastern Emperor Zeno, but, although of some use to Odoacer in his dealings with the subjected Romans, it made him no whit dependent on the court of Constantinople. That court always regarded him as a usurper, and rejoiced at and promoted his final fall.

Odoacer's reign was a rule of moderation; he made no sweeping changes, and engaged in no adventurous undertakings. His German subjects received settlements on a plan which had long been employed when barbarian allies were allowed to encamp on Roman ground. Each soldier was quartered on a Roman, and received one-third of the latter's land as his share.

Romans and Germans in Odoacer's kingdom. It was a plan that had been adopted by many of the wandering German tribes that had settled on Roman soil. If occasion demanded the fraction could be increased. The unbidden guests were brought more intimately into connection with the culture which they strove to assimilate than could have been the case by any other method of division.

The new-comers, to be sure, were always regarded as interlopers, and reasons enough were there to prevent anything like a lasting fusion of the two peoples. The most fatal

causes of disunion were those relating to religion. The
Arianism of the Goths, and of most of the other German
tribes, was always a stumbling block to their intercourse with
the Romans. This unhallowed difference of dogma ate like
a canker worm at the foundations of the new kingdoms;
again and again do we find, for instance, the Catholic bishops
leading the opposition against their Arian rulers.

Odoacer did not greatly interfere with the system of administration that had been carried on under the empire. The
same officials remained in power, and the land seems to have
enjoyed a season of comparative prosperity.

There was no real strength, however, in the new political
creation, and its span of life was a short one. In 489
Theodoric, the king of those Eastern Goths whom the Huns
had subjected, but who had regained their independence after
Attila's death, marched to Italy at the instigation of the
Eastern Emperor. It was again not merely a warlike expedition, but the descent of one people upon another. It is
known, for instance, that a new race of cattle which has never
since died out in Italy was introduced at this time.

*Theodoric,
489-526.*

Odoacer met the advancing host at the river Isonzo, but
suffered a defeat; nor did the battle of Verona end more
favourably. Ravenna, however, proved a secure retreat for
the oppressed king, and Theodoric for three years besieged
it in vain. A treaty was then effected, and it was agreed that
the two kings should rule in common over Italy. Theodoric
afterwards found an effectual method of removing his rival
from his path; he invited him to table and ran him through
with the sword.

*Murder of
Odoacer.*

Theodoric reigned in Italy fully in accordance with the
traditions of the empire. He himself had long served the
court of Constantinople, had been made consul, had celebrated a triumph, and had been honoured by the erection of
an equestrian statue.

*Theodoric
as successor
of the em-
perors.*

It was a restoration that he wanted in Italy, a resuscitation
of the imperial power that had just died. More than once,
in the introductions to his edicts, he says himself that he

desires to rule, not like the wild kings of the barbarians, but like Trajan and the great emperors of the past. In a public proclamation the Gauls are bidden to rejoice that after their long separation they have been re-united with the Roman Empire, and the Spaniards are ordered to pay their tribute " as they had formerly paid it under the emperors."

Theodoric's foreign policy. Theodoric was the first of the German kings to look beyond the boundaries of his own lands; he developed what may be called a regular foreign policy. His object was to gain a predominating influence over as many as possible of the barbarian powers, and with that end in view he took a bride himself from a royal house, and wedded four of his female relatives to kings, or sons of kings. Over the western Goths he, for a long period, held complete sway, acting as regent for his nephew Amalrich, whom they had chosen to be their king. Their treasure for a time reposed at Ravenna, and a part of their taxes flowed yearly into the coffers of Italy.

Art and literature. Theodoric's reign was looked back upon later as a golden age for the lands over which he ruled. It was his pride and ambition to restrain lawlessness and, besides carrying out works of utility, to encourage literature and art. Cassiodorus, the famous historian and the chancellor of Theodoric, has preserved to us in one of his letters an edict of his master's allowing the senator Decius to drain a portion of the Pontine Marshes, and to keep possession of the lands thus reclaimed. An inscription on stone still exists to show that Decius carried out his good intentions, and drained the land.

It was in Theodoric's reign that Boethius—in prison, indeed, and under the shadow of the death that his suspicious king had determined to inflict on him—wrote his well-known book on the consolations of philosophy. It is a search for the grounds of human happiness, in the course of which he rises at last to the proud assertion that man is independent of the blows of fate, and that fortune and misfortune, if rightly accepted, may prove in the end to be equal blessings.

Of one phase of Theodoric's activity our own age can

judge to no small extent. There are churches and monuments still standing in Ravenna that date from his day; and the tomb that he built for himself, with its circular roof made of one colossal stone—how it was ever raised into its position remains a problem—is in a good state of preservation.

After Theodoric's death, his kingdom fell a prey to inward dissensions and intrigues. A boy was made king whose mother was so enamoured of the regency that even after her son's death she held on to the reins of power, and wedded a noble whom she hated, hoping in him to find a furtherer of her designs. He murdered her and ruled alone, but was later stabbed himself to make room for the next comer. *Theodoric's feeble successors.*

But why tarry with these petty despots? Who cares to-day for Athalarich and Theodatus, for Ildibald and Vitiges and Erarich. Enough that the weakness of the Goths raised the courage of the Eastern Emperor, and induced him to reclaim possession over Italy. His action raised all the spirit that was left in the people of Theodoric.

In 535 Belisarius was sent by Justinian to attack Dalmatia and Sicily. For five years the great general conducted sieges or withstood them in Italy and was, on the whole, successful. But under Totila the Goths regained most of their strongholds. *Belisarius.*

Up to this time, in default of a better effigy, the Goths had always stamped their coins with the face of the Eastern Emperor. The likeness of a barbarian king now shared the surface, if it did not entirely replace the customary image.

Belisarius, who had been recalled to Constantinople in 540, was sent back to Italy four years later, but accomplished little except to take the city of Rome. On this occasion the statues that adorned the castle of St. Angelo were hurled down upon the Goths, and in the general devastation twelve out of the thirteen great conduits that supplied the city with water were rendered useless. Rome was again lost on the withdrawal of Belisarius in 549.

Narses, the successor of Belisarius, defeated the Goths in 552, and their king, Totila, fell after performing wonders of *Subjugation of the East Gothic kingdom.*

heroism. The next king, Teija, shared the same fate before a year had passed; it is of him that his enemy, Procopius, relates that no heroes of the past could boast of greater valour.

But the *rôle* of the Goths in history had now been played to its conclusion. The war ended with the subjugation of Italy, and thousands of able-bodied men were marched off to Constantinople to fight the emperor's battles. Here they did excellent service, and were so highly valued as warriors, that, in a land where otherwise no heretics were endured, they were allowed to have their own Arian church.

End of the Vandal kingdom, 539 A.D. The Vandal kingdom in Africa had by this time also come to an end, leaving behind it few traces save those exasperating tombs in Morocco, which the sultans refuse to have explored on account of passages in the Koran forbidding the dead to be disturbed.

Belisarius, in 533 and 534, had taken advantage of a revolt in the island of Sardinia, for the suppression of which the Vandals had sent their best forces. He had also been able to mix himself in a dispute between two rival claimants to the Vandal throne itself, and had finally mastered himself of the land.

The last Vandal king, Gelimer, was made to walk in a triumphal procession through the streets of Constantinople. As he knelt in the circus at the foot of the emperor, he is declared to have frequently repeated the Bible saying, " Vanity of vanities, all is vanity."

Even without foreign interference the kingdom would probably have soon enough fallen to pieces. The Romans had by no means fused with their conquerors, and had been the special victims of religious persecution. It was they that had to bear the brunt of revenge for imperial measures that had been passed in general against the Arians; add to this that the Vandals, in ceasing to be a wandering and a warlike nation, had gone to the other extreme. They had been ruined by their warm climate and their life of unwonted luxury.

CHAPTER III.

THE FRANKISH KINGDOM.

IN the present Belgium, five years after the fall of the Childeric. Western Roman Empire, a child was chosen head of one of the many petty kingdoms of the Salian Franks. It was Clovis, the son of a certain Childeric, of the line of Meroveus.

Childeric had borne the title of " ally of the Roman people," and as such had fought against the Western Goths. His centre of government had been at Tournay, and here, in 1683, his tomb was found and opened ; from it were taken the famous golden bees that later adorned the coronation mantle of the great Napoleon.

Clovis it was who laid the foundation for a great united Clovis, 481- Frankish kingdom. That unity for him, indeed, meant the 511 A.D. annihilation of all possible rival powers, and one by one he wrought the ruin of all the princes in his neighbourhood. The chief account that we have of him—that of Gregory of Tours—lauds him to the skies on the one hand, but on the other does not conceal the fact that he waded to the neck in blood and treachery. He is known to have incited a Frankish prince to slay his own father, and then to have punished him with death for the deed. He bribed the nobles of a neighbour- ing people to renounce allegiance to their king, and paid his debt in jewels that were false. When his dupes protested they were laughed to scorn.

Clovis's first expedition was against the Roman governor, Clovis and Syagrius, who seems to have retained in his own hand large Syagrius. remnants of the lands which he had formerly administered in the name of the empire. A single battle sufficed to bring the

whole province, with its capital of Soissons, into the hands of
the Franks. It was an immense gain for Clovis, and the
Roman settlers at the same time were little worse for the
change; they retained their law, their lands, and their liberty,
and were even allowed later to intermarry with their conquerors.

Clovis's
conquests.

There was danger that the new Merovingian kingdom
might itself become Romanized if it were to push its conquests much further to the south; but new German elements
were constantly being introduced. The amalgamation with
the Romans of Syagrius was followed by the conquest of the
essentially German Allemanni in 496. The war with the
Western Goths, which almost drove that people out of Gaul,
brought the Franks once more in possession of lands where the
Roman civilization prevailed; but the subjugation of the
Ripuarian Franks renewed the German preponderance. Some
slight successes against the Burgundians were equalized by
the partial overthrow of the Thuringians.

These Frankish conquests were purely dynastic in their
character; they were no longer the simple descent of one
people on another. Nor did the division of the newly won
territory take place in the same way as in the other German
kingdoms. The public lands, and those which had been left
vacant by the death of their owners, came into the hand of
the king, to be distributed by him as he might please. There
was no oppression, no enslaving of a population, no hateful
quartering of man on man.

Clovis be-
comes a
Christian.

The keystone of Clovis's political arch was reached when,
in 496, he became a Christian. What was almost more important for the future of his kingdom, he received Christianity not in the form of Arianism, but of Roman Catholicism.
In the battle against the Allemanni, which was fought near
Tolbiacum, on the road between Cologne and Treves, he swore
to accept the God which his queen, the Burgundian Clotilda,
had so often recommended to him, providing that the tide of
victory should turn in his favour.

The battle was won, the oath fulfilled, and Clovis executed

thereby the master move of his life. The Catholic clergy of Gaul, with the power to influence thousands of souls, rallied round him as their head. He was baptized by the Archbishop of Rheims with great pomp and circumstance, and it is related that the prelate addressed him thus : " Bow thy neck in humility, oh, Sigambrian ! Adore what thou hast burnt, and burn what thou hast adored."

Three thousand of his nobles followed Clovis's example, and the greatest of all barriers to the fusion of his Roman and German subjects—that fusion so necessary to the vitality of the new state—fell to the ground.

Fusion of Romans and Germans.

The church itself, be it here remarked, gained nothing by the change. Its old discipline soon relaxed, church synods became less and less frequent, the discipline of the clergy sank to its lowest level. The bishops, who had hitherto been elected by the clergy and people, came to be appointed by the king, and generated too often into the mere instruments of his will.

It was as the champion of Catholicism that Clovis set out to fight the Western Goths. " I can not bear," he says in that naïve gospel according to Gregory of Tours, "that these Arians should possess a part of Gaul. Let us set forth with God's help and defeat them, and add their land to our kingdom."

Clovis as champion of Catholicism.

We have seen the result. In spite of the aid of the powerful Theodoric the Western Goths lost all their possessions in Gaul save the district around Arles, Carcassone, and Narbonne —the so-called Septimania or Gothia.

The sons of Clovis carried on his work of conquest. The Frankish kingdom, indeed, was now divided into four parts— this principle of equally sharing the heritage was adhered to as long as the dynasty lasted—but it still formed a unity in more than one respect. The bishops of one sub-kingdom might appear at the synods in another, while the chief warlike achievements, the final subjection of the Thuringians and of the Burgundians were common undertakings of the brothers.

The sons of Clovis.

The Thuringians were defeated in 531 at Scheidungen on

the river Unstrutt, the Franks being aided by 9,000 Saxons, who were afterwards given a share of the conquered lands. Three years later the land of the Burgundians fell an easy prey, and was completely dismembered. About this time, too, the Bavarians, the former Marcomanni and Quadi, became more or less a subject people of the Franks. They had but shortly before wandered into their present habitations, leaving their settlements in Bohemia to the tender mercies of the Slavs.

Franks become civilized. It is under their Merovingian rulers that the Franks step definitely out of the ranks of barbarism. Already in the time of Clovis a code of written laws [1] had been drawn up for the conduct and guidance of the people. It regulates the intercourse of man with man; each crime receives its penalty, and even the insulting expressions in common use are drawn up in order, and labelled with their appropriate fines.

Administration. A state organization was created, and gradually more and more perfected. The kings had their revenues and their officials, their marshals and their mayors of the palace. A special official, the *domesticus*, saw to the administration of the estates that had fallen to the crown in war.

The kings. The sign of kingship was the long waving hair; we can still see it on the coins and seals of the time, and proofs are there to show that an heir who had lost his locks was obliged to renounce his right to the throne until they had grown again. On one occasion a mother chose death for her young sons rather than let them be shorn.

The Merovingian kings were not crowned and not anointed. As a symbol of authority a spear was handed to them. They had no fixed abode, but moved from place to place, being obliged frequently to show themselves, and also, with their courts, to consume in rotation the produce of their various estates.

The land. The land of the Franks as a whole was parcelled out into larger and smaller districts, into counties and hundreds.

---

[1] See "Select Documents," p. 176.

Every county had its count or *graf*, who retained a fixed proportion of the tolls and taxes for his own sustenance, and who saw to it that justice was done, and that the proper contingents were sent to the army. He presided over the courts that were held in the hundreds, and at which the people as a whole were bound to appear, and to give judgment. These judicial assemblies were held in the open air; the count sat on a raised throne, his shield being hung up near him as a token that court was in session.

The administration of justice was a far simpler matter than it is in the present day. Guilt and innocence were proven by purely external means, and enquiries were not made into the intricacies of each special case. A judgment of God, or ordeal, was appealed to, and decision given according as the boiling water or the glowing iron did or did not burn the hand of the accused, or of his or her hired champion. In other cases a number of friends and relatives were allowed to give an oath which cleared the accused from the crime imputed to him. *Justice.*

Besides the courts there was the great yearly muster, the Marchfield. Here the army came together, and here, too, cases of great importance were decided, and matters discussed which had to do with the good of the state. *The Marchfield.*

The fusion of the Romans and the Germans in the Frankish kingdom progressed now undisturbed. Each gave to the other a part of the heritage of its own past. The Germans had the most to gain; they learned now to read and write, they took from the Romans their methods of taxation, the forms of their utensils, their laws as to high-treason, as to the making of wills, the sale of property, and the superannuation of claims. *Relations of Romans to Germans.*

The Romans, on the other hand, dressed their hair after the German fashion—sober and reliable investigators give us these details—and adopted the Frankish weapons, especially the battle-axe, or so-called Franziska. The German Wiergeld, too, or system of atoning for crime by a money payment to the relatives of the murdered or injured man, came into use

D

among them, as did also the judicial combat—that appeal to the decision of the god of war, which was to hold its own in European law, in the letter at least, as late as our own century.

The village communities.

In the course of the Merovingian period great changes began to make themselves felt with regard to the relation of one free man to another, and also of the distribution of landed possessions.

One may say roughly, that the Germans of the third and fourth century had been possessed individually of no landed property. The families in a given settlement, or village, enjoyed the woods and pastures in common, and each had a right to a given quantity of land for agricultural purposes. This land, however, had continued in the actual ownership of the village community as a whole, and could be withdrawn and re-distributed.

By the sixth century the Franks had come to have fixed "manses," farms, as one might call them. The common rights to woods and meadows still continued—they have continued in parts of Switzerland down to the present day—but, in addition, we find these parcels of land in absolute ownership, and the possession of them was handed down from father to son.

Social change.

It was but natural that a distinction between rich and poor should soon enough arise. Some families possessed but one "manse" in common, in other cases many came to be united in one and the same hand. The Churches especially grew to be great landowners, for many persons who died without heirs left to them their estates, wishing to provide for the good of their souls. The monastery of Fulda, already by the eighth century, possessed no less than fifteen thousand "manses."

We shall see in the course of this history how the poor came into dependence upon the rich, and were forced to become their vassals, or "men," and to do them service. To the fact of owning or not owning this or that quantity of land may be traced the evolution of the later classes of society, of serfs and freemen, of free lords, knights, and princes. The favour of the king might change a man's rank, but to support that rank he needed a territorial basis.

The last of Clovis's sons, Clothar, died in 561, after having once more, for the space of three years, united the whole kingdom into one hand. Under his sons and their descendants bloodshed and murder knew no end in the land. *Neustria, Austrasia, and Burgundy.*

Three separate kingdoms, subdivisions of the Frankish territory, take form and shape at this time, and, although sometimes two or all of them are united under one ruler, maintain themselves until the end of the Merovingian period. They are Neustria, Austrasia, and Burgundy. Austrasia later became exclusively German, while Neustria and Burgundy developed into modern France. For the time being no such differences of nationality were at all perceptible; in each of the three kingdoms Germans and Romans lived side by side, and the preponderance of one race over the other had not yet made itself felt.

Two new external enemies had meanwhile arisen for the Franks. *The Avars.*

In 565 Sigbert of Austrasia was defeated by the fierce Avars, a tribe allied to the Huns; he later induced their khan, however, to enter into a treaty of peace.

The Lombards, the last of the wandering Germanic nations that found a home on Roman ground, appeared in Italy in 568. In the previous year, in league with the Avars, they had subdued the not inconsiderable kingdom of the Gepidi on the river Theiss. By 572, almost all Northern Italy, besides the Duchy of Benevento, to which they afterwards added Spoleto and Capua, had come into their hands. Pavia submitted after a three years' siege. The Eastern Empire retained only Rome and the line of cities on the sea-coast, the Pentapolis or the Exarchate of Ravenna. *The Lombards.*

The Lombards soon commenced making inroads into Gaul, and year after year devastated Provence. The Austrasian Franks, however, at last determined to revenge themselves, and, in bond with the Eastern emperor, made a number of expeditions into Italy. From the year 590 on they remained *Wars of Franks and Lombards.*

on good terms with the new Lombard kingdom. which had enough to do to withstand the double enmity of the Greeks on the one hand and of the papacy on the other.

Pope Gregory the Great, 590-604.

It was at this time that Pope Gregory the Great was commencing to organize and consolidate the power of the see of Rome. He gave up, indeed, the claim of Leo the Great to the primacy over all the churches of the world. He is known even to have quoted the passage in Corinthians where Paul blames the disciples for saying, " I am a disciple of Paul, I of Apollo, I of Peter." But, though claiming no more for Rome than the headship over the churches of the west, he did her the greatest and most practical of services. He established officials to administer the " patrimony of Peter," those estates in different lands which had been given to the church by pious and repentant souls. He was the first pope to favour the monkish orders, which were later to become the scouts and outposts of the great church militant.

Gregory and the Lombards.

Gregory conducted in person the defence of Rome when it was besieged by the Lombard Duke of Spoleto in 592; he showed himself a diplomatist, too, and skilfully played off one of the rival powers in Italy against the other, preventing the papacy from becoming a dependency of either.

Brunhilda and Fredegunda.

The internal history of the Merovingian kingdom from 567 to 613 shows us one continued succession of deeds of horror. The names of Chilperich, of Fredegunda, and of Brunhilda would grace the annals of crime in any age or in any land.

Brunhilda was a West Gothic princess, beautiful we are told, who married Sigbert of Austrasia ; her sister, Galswintha, became the bride of Chilperich of Neustria.

Chilperich had promised to discard his numerous other wives in favour of his new queen ; but one of them, Fredegunda, was not to be put aside. She had been pre-eminent in the palace, and she soon regained her old ascendancy. She now inaugurated a terrible series of murders, Chilperich aiding and abetting her. Galswintha, Brunhilda's sister, and Sigbert, her husband, were the first to go. In order to have a choice instrument of vengeance Brunhilda married a son of

Chilperich, named Merovech. He too was ruthlessly cut down. Fredegunda also caused the death of another of Chilperich's sons, Clovis, together with the mother who had borne him.

In each of the three Frankish kingdoms there was at this time a bitter struggle going on between the crown and the nobles. Chilperich now lost his life through a conspiracy which the latter had instigated. Fredegunda herself died in 597—peacefully as far as our knowledge goes.

Brunhilda was meanwhile the leading spirit in Austrasia, and finally became the actual regent for her son Sigbert II. Hers was, also, a passionate unbridled nature, and in her efforts to keep down the pretensions of her nobles she receded before few acts of violence. But she enforced her claims and maintained the dignity of the crown. Letters are extant, written to her by Gregory the Great, in which the Pope addresses her almost obsequiously and as a powerful ruler, and begs her to protect his missionaries who were on their way to found the Roman Church in England. *Brunhilda's able rule.*

Fredegunda's son, Clothar II., continued the family enmity to Brunhilda. He answered the call of a discontented faction of her nobles and invaded her land. The queen herself, at this time between sixty and seventy years of age, was taken captive. Clothar accused her of having murdered ten kings of the Franks—a groundless charge, and one which his own blood-bespotted parent had not quite accomplished—and prepared for her a death of torture. She was tormented for the space of three days and ended her existence on the public highway, being bound to the tail of a wild horse by her hand, foot and hair. *Brunhilda's death.*

In spite of such preliminary episodes as this, it was, on the whole, a season of unwonted prosperity that the Franks enjoyed under Clothar and also under his son Dagobert. The civil wars had ended for the time being, and few foreign enemies disturbed the peace. *Clothar's charter, 614 A.D.*

It is Clothar who reunited once more the domains of Clovis in one hand. The nobles in the end seem to have gained what they had fought for, a share in the government of the land. A charter is extant which was granted to them in 614 as a reward for the services they had rendered in the war against Brunhilda. According to its provisions violence was to be checked, justice to be observed, no new taxes to be imposed. Only such men were to be appointed as " counts " or district administrators as should have considerable possessions of their own, of which they were to be deprived if they did not properly fulfil the duties of their office. The bishops were to be chosen by the clergy and the people, but the king might veto an election. At this time there were no less than one hundred and twelve bishoprics in the Frankish kingdom.

Dagobert, 629-638 A.D. Clothar died in 629 and Dagobert succeeded, being obliged however to share the kingdom with his brother Charibert. On the latter's death, Dagobert murdered the youthful heir and reigned alone.

Dagobert is known as a law-giver and a good administrator. The early laws of the Thuringians and Bavarians which we still have, were drawn up at his instigation. He favoured the Church, and issued an express command that each one of his subjects should be baptized. He protected and encouraged the followers and disciples of St. Columbanus, those Irish-Scottish missionaries to whom the Allemanni and other German stems owed their conversion.

Charters of Dagobert are still at hand to show that in Mayence, Spires, and other Austrasian towns, he saw to the building of churches and monasteries as well as palaces.

With Dagobert's death in 638 the history of the Merovingian dynasty may be said to have practically ended. And yet one hundred and fourteen years were still to pass before these originators of the type of *rois fainéants,* of do-nothing kings, were to descend the last step that led from the throne to the cloister.

Resumé. Thus far have we traced the history of the German settlements on Roman ground. We have seen the might of the Burgundians yield to that of the Franks, the monarchy of Odoacer go down at the approach of Theodoric and his Eastern

Goths. Theodoric's kingdom, too, went headlong to destruction, sharing a common and almost simultaneous fate with the Vandal rule in North Africa. The Lombards in Italy and the West Goths in Spain were to eke out a somewhat longer existence as political powers, but they too were eventually to find themselves in the path of the destroyer.

One, and one only, of the new foundations bore within it the seeds of real progress, although at the time of which we are writing the Franks, too, seemed to be sinking down, dragged under by their worthless kings into the slough of disunity and corruption.

But the right men in the Frankish kingdom stepped forward at the right juncture, and the brave and ambitious mayors of the palace, the forefathers of a Charlemagne, supplanted the worn out Merovingians.

It was the victory of the second Pipin, won at Tertri in 687, that decided the future of the Frankish kingdom and the supremacy of the Carolingian line. **The Mayors of the Palace.**

Since the reign of Dagobert the power of the mayors of the palace—the office was at that time in the hands of Pippin the Elder, the grandfather of Pippin II.—had been steadily growing. Entrusted as they were with the guardianship of the youthful kings and with the management of the royal estates, they had come to rule in all but name. One of them, indeed, Pippin's uncle, Grimoald, had actually tried to place his own son on the throne, but had atoned for his daring with his life. The people still set store by their infant kings, and wished to keep them, if only as a relic of the past.

The battle of Tertri was fought against the major-domus, Bertharius, who administered the affairs of Neustria and Burgundy, and its outcome determined the unity of the Frankish kingdom. The young king of Neustria and his treasures and his household were handed over like any other spoils of war, and Pipin, as we are told, " arranged all things and returned to Austrasia." He left his son, Grimoald, as major-domus of Neustria. **The battle of Tertri, 687 A.D.**

Tributary Peoples.   The internal wars and constant disturbances in the Merovingian kingdom had induced all the tributary peoples—the Bavarians, Allemannians, Thuringians, Aquitanians, and others—to throw off their yoke. It was the task of the new rulers to regain the lost influence as well as to round off and increase the kingdom in all directions. All the labour expended in this regard by Pippin II., by Charles Martel and Pippin the Younger, was to bear rich harvest in the time of Charlemagne.

Of Pippin II.'s deeds we are badly informed. In the so-called "annals," at first mere scanty notes, written on the margin of the Easter tables of the time, the events of a whole year are sometimes summed up in a single remark. We know that he conquered the Frisians for the time being, and that he made two expeditions against the Allemannians. His reign, if we may call it so, lasted for twenty-seven years, and on his death in 714 he left the office of major-domus, in Neustria at least, to his grandson, a child of six.

Charles Martel.   The old woes of the Merovingians under woman's rule seemed about once more to fall on the Frankish people, for Pippin's widow, Plectrude, seized the rudder, while Charles Martel, his son by another union, set to work to wrest the power from her hands. Plectrude had him seized and imprisoned, but fortune favoured him in the end by showing the utter weakness of his stepmother's rule.

The nobles of Neustria rose against their little major-domus—there was no thought any more of rising against the king—and drove him from the land. All union between the three sub-kingdoms seemed at an end, civil war was breaking out in all directions, and the greatest of all the external enemies that had ever threatened the Franks was pressing on towards their southern border.

Charles restores order.   Charles Martel at this juncture saved the tottering Frankish kingdom, restored to it peace, order, and discipline, and averted from Europe one of the greatest evils that has ever approached it. He escaped from his prison, was received with joy by the Austrasians, and gained a great victory over the

Neustrians at Vincy, in the province of Cambray (717). Two years later, having ruled over Austrasia in the meantime, and having, as the annals go, " set up his own king by the name of Clothar," he again defeated the united forces of the Neustrians and of Eudo of Aquitaine. In the latter province the people, aided by those Basques from Spain who have left their name to Gascony, had come to consider themselves an independent power. In 720 Eudo was compelled to surrender the new king of the Neustrians, Chilperich, of whom Charles showed his scorn and contempt by making him, on the death of Clothar, king of all the Franks. For that sinecure one Merovingian was as good as another. Chilperich died almost immediately, and Theuderich IV. succeeded him—so entirely a shadow-king that when he died in 737 no annals of the time mention the event. We learn of it by a chance remark in a treatise on chronology !

Charles's external policy was the same which his father had pursued. We hear of a war with the Allemannians and of two or three expeditions into Bavaria. In the latter land the power had come into the hands of the Agilolfing dukes, and these Charles brought to recognize the suzerainty of the Franks. Their relative, Swanhilda, was brought back in the train of the returning conqueror. She bore him a son, Grifo, who was later to dispute the succession with Charles's lawful sons. **Charles's external policy.**

The Bavarians were left in the enjoyment of much independence, but they acknowledged the right of the Frankish crown to levy an army, to pardon criminals, and to depose rebellious dukes.

The wars against the Saxons and Frisians were, at bottom, a conflict between Christianity and Paganism. When Charles, in 734, finally subdued the latter of these peoples, one of his first cares was to burn their gods ; while the failures and successes of the missions keep regular pace with the fortunes of war.

We are in the midst of an age of tremendous religious activity. The prophets of Allah on the one hand and the **The Arabs.**

vicars of St. Peter on the other could already count their votaries by millions, and the fanatic conversions of the Saracens were offset in a measure by the triumphs of church organization on the part of the popes.

A great and awful conflict between the two religions was bound to come. Ever since 622 A.D., ever since the flight of Mohammed from Mecca to Medina, the tide of Arab conquest had been swelling and advancing. Mecca itself had early succumbed to the growing enthusiasm for the prophet, while the conquered Persian provinces seemed destined to form the nucleus for a new world rule. The wonderful scorn of death of the Islamites, furthered by the sure promises of everlasting bliss for those who fell in defence of the faith, made their army one of almost invincible warriors.

Viewed in one light the Arab advance was but one more wandering of a nation. The race, so inconveniently numerous that the killing of a part of the female offspring had become a regular custom, had at last broken its bounds and carried all before it. It was not long before Egypt and all Northern Africa were in the hands of the Mohammedans, and in 708 the Arab leader who has given his name to the Straits of Gibraltar (Giber al Tarik) crossed over into Spain.

The Arabs in Spain. The seven days' battle of Xeres de la Frontera, fought by Tarik against the Western Goths in 711, ended in a complete defeat for the latter. Their kingdom, already a prey to inward dissensions, received its death-blow, and the whole of Spain, except Galicia, Asturia, and Biscaya, was brought under subjection. Arabs as well as Moors and Berbers streamed into the land. The newly-won territory was organized into an Arab province and was ruled by a stadt-holder of the caliph.

In Gaul. In 720 the Arabs crossed the Pyrennees and conquered Narbonne, but were defeated before Toulouse by Eudo, duke of the now almost independent province of Aquitaine. Eudo sustained for the next ten years the brunt of the Arab attack. Charles was busy with other enemies and seems not to have realized the extent of the danger. It is possible, too, that the overthrow of the Aquitanian power would not have been unwelcome to him.

Eudo finally found it more profitable to treat the new-comers as friends than as foes, and gave his daughter in marriage to the chieftain who commanded on the border. At the same time he broke the terms of a treaty that he had once entered into with Charles.

The latter made two expeditions against his recalcitrant ally, and Eudo fled before him. But the Arabs proved fickle friends, the more so as Eudo's son-in-law had meanwhile fallen in a feud.

In the spring of 732 the stadtholder Abderahmen advanced into Aquitaine at the head of a countless army. Eudo met him on the bank of the Garonne, was defeated, and sent a despairing cry to Charles for aid. It was the highest time; the religion and the civilization of Europe were in jeopardy, and had Charles failed to respond to the call there is no knowing what would have been the fate of Christendom. **Battle between Tours and Poictiers, 732 A.D.**

The battle fought between Tours and Poictiers in October, 732, is one of the most famous in the history of the world. According to a contemporary report—from the side of the excited victors, to be sure—375,000 Saracens were made to bite the dust. Abderahmen himself was among the fallen.

Although not entirely driven from the land—it was years before Narbonne and Arles were freed from their grasp—the progress of the Arabs had been effectually checked, and their greed of conquest had received a deadly blow. Torn as they were by the rivalry between their two great houses, the Abbasides and the Ommeiads, they were unable to repeat the invasion; although we shall see in the next centuries what they could do in the way of harassing the shores of the Mediterranean.

Undoubtedly a small part, at least, of the credit of Charles Martel's victory over the Saracens belongs to Boniface, the apostle of the Germans. For ten years this prince of missionaries had been busily at work among the various German stem-tribes, teaching and preaching, organizing and **Boniface the apostle of the Germans.**

subordinating. All of these stems sent their contingents to Charles's army; for the first time the full resources of the kingdom had all been drawn upon at once. The new enthusiasm for Christianity must have roused a corresponding zeal to defend the faith against its approaching oppressors.

Boniface, the Anglo-Saxon monk, had been raised to the episcopal rank by Pope Gregory II. in 722. He had taken the oath of the suburbicarian bishops, or bishops around Rome, promising to preserve the unity of the Catholic Church, and to implicitly obey the Pope. He had omitted the clause, usual at such ceremonies, of allegiance to the Eastern emperors; from whom the Popes, technically at least, as yet held their possessions. He had further sworn to have nothing to do with bishops who did not live according to the old teachings of the fathers.

The Irish-Scottish monks are here alluded to—those spiritual descendants of St. Patrick who never could bring themselves to accept certain customs and laws of the Roman Church. One of the popes, Gregory III., had dubbed them "false priests and heretics." Notably were their views unorthodox as to the proper method of determining Easter. In England the antagonism of the two parties was at times so great that the more eager adherents of the one would not sleep under one roof, or drink from one cup, with members of the other. To the Irish-Scottish monks had belonged Columbanus and Gallus and numerous other missionaries and founders of monasteries; Boniface, on the contrary, bowed implicitly to the dictates of Rome.

Boniface himself ascribes much of his success to a letter of safe conduct granted to him by Charles Martel, and directed to all the nobles of the kingdom. But Charles's sympathies were not altogether with Rome, and under his reign more influence was exerted over the heathen than over the dissolute Frankish clergy.

Charles Martel died in 741. He had reigned absolutely, although assuming no title higher than that of mayor of the palace. Since 737 he had allowed the Merovingian throne to

he Irish-cottish [onks.

nd of the .le of harles artel.

remain unoccupied, and the charters of the time are dated in such and such a year "from the death of Theuderich." Just before his own death he divided the land in truly monarchical fashion between his two sons, Carlmann and Pippin. The former received Austrasia, Thuringia and Suabia, or Alle-mannia ; the latter, Neustria, Burgundy, and Provence.

A century later it was related of Charles Martel, than whom, indeed, by his conquest of the Arabs, no single monarch had ever done or ever did greater service to the cause of Christianity—that he had been seen in hell by a certain pious bishop of Orleans, who had descended thither in the good company af an angel. The angel had declared that Charles was being thus punished for having confiscated and re-divided the Church estates. And there is no reason to doubt but that he began the process which was further developed, and finally legalized under his successors. An abbot, who presided over St. Wandrille from 734 to 738 is soundly rated by his biographer for having allowed the estates of the monastery to be rented out at a nominal sum, so that spurs, saddles, and the like might be bought with the profits of the produce. It was exactly thus that the so-called secu-larization was carried on in the later reigns—the nominal rent, the actual utilization for practical purposes. *Confiscation of Church property.*

It was the needs of the State that drove Charles to these desperate measures. The crown-lands of the Merovingians and their other sources of income were insufficient to meet the expenses of the army ; the more so as Charles seems to have found it necessary in view of future conflicts with the agile and well-mounted Arabs to largely increase, if not entirely to form anew his cavalry. It is only a conjecture that he did so, but how else can one explain the fact that at this time a new tax, the *fodrum*, or fodder tax, is introduced ; that new weapons, more suitable for cavalry contests, come in vogue, and that the Marchfield, or yearly review, is eventually changed to meet in May, in which month it may be supposed that the grass would be more plentiful for the horses. The records of St. Wandrille too, a point which must not be for- *Introduction of cavalry.*

gotten, relate that the lands of the monastery went to pay for
" spurs and saddles."

The Church and her property. Under the brothers, Carlmann and Pippin, efforts were
made by the Church to regain her lost possessions. Carlmann,
in a capitulary issued in the " Concilium Germanicum " of
742, promised unconditionally " the restitution and return of
the estranged church lands," but was obliged in a later synod
to declare that he intends " by the advice of the servants of
God and of the Christian people, on account of the threatening wars and the attacks of the surrounding nations, to retain
for a time a part of the Church estates for the strengthening of
his army, in such wise that from each " manse," or court, a
rent of one shilling = 12 denars, shall be paid to the church,
or monastery."

Pippin had long since made a similar disposition for his own
lands, with the reservation that regard should be had for the
needs of the poorer religious foundations. It was always intended to return this land—which was let out in large tracts
to powerful nobles—to its original owners, an intention which
was in part carried out under Louis the Pious.

Reform in the Frankish Church. One of the first acts of Carlmann and Pippin was to call in
Boniface, by this time an archbishop, and entrust him with
the reformation of the Frankish Church. He it was who
renewed the practice of holding synods, a practice that had,
according to Boniface himself, been in abeyance for eighty
years. Such assemblies dealt with matters concerning church
lands and church discipline, with the discarding of heathen
customs, with rules regarding marriage, with the private life
of the clergy. The latter, for instance, are bidden to abandon
the delights of hunting, and to dismiss their dogs and falcons.

Boniface and Rome. Boniface's great service—some think it was no especial
gain—was the bringing of the German Church under the
rule and discipline of Rome. He paved the way for the close
alliance of Church and State that was to characterize the reign
of Charles the Great. Boniface himself made three visits to
Rome, and kept, besides, in constant correspondence with the
Pope. He sought the latter's advice on every occasion, and

many of the letters that passed may still be read. They are not all equally edifying or important. If in one of them Boniface reports of the proceedings of a synod: "We have decreed and professed that we will hold fast to the end to the Catholic faith, and to the unity and obedience of the Roman Church," in another he asks the trivial question as to when the people might eat ham.

In response to the latter interrogation the Pope's answer is worth recording. " The Church Fathers have left no directions on that point, but since you ask me, I advise that it be eaten only cooked or smoked—not raw until after Easter."

Boniface was the founder of the monastery of Fulda, and there, in our own day, a monument has been erected to him. **Monument at Fulda.** Single voices, indeed, have been raised in protest by those who see a harm to their nation in the long continued subjection to the influence of Rome. One man, whose services to historical science have been very great, has been known to exclaim : " Not to Boniface, but to the slayer of Boniface—he was killed by a Frisian savage—a monument should be erected ! "

Carlmann and Pippin possessed now all but sovereign rights. Nevertheless, in 743, in deference to the nobles, they **Carlmann and Pippin.** again appointed a king. The feeble Childerich III. speaks in one of his charters of " the major-domus Carlmann, who has placed us on the royal throne," and Pippin, as well as Carlmann, signs himself as " him to whom the Lord has entrusted the care of the administration." In publishing their laws each denotes himself as " prince and duke of the Franks," while Pippin goes so far as to use the kingly " we " when speaking of himself, being the first of his line to adopt this custom.

Every change of ruler in these unsettled times gave the surrounding only half-subjected nations occasion for re-asserting their real or fancied rights. Under Pippin and Carlmann we have notices of bravely conducted wars with Aquitanians and Bavarians, with Allemannians and Saxons.

Upon the Allemannians Carlmann wreaked bloody vengeance at Cannstadt in 746, and to repentance for this act is **Carlmann's retirement.**

ascribed his renunciation of his share in the kingdom, and
his retreat to a monastery in the following year. It was a
step which many weary rulers of the eighth century had
taken or were to take, among them Ine of Wessex, Hunold of
Aquitaine, and Offa of Mercia.

Carlmann went to Italy and settled as a hermit on Mount
Soracte, but was too often disturbed, we are told, by visits of
admiring Germans. He latter retired to Monte Casino, where
we lose sight of him for a while.

CHAPTER IV.

THE CAROLINGIAN KINGS.

PIPPIN, after his brother's retirement, ruled alone. He put down a rebellion of his stepbrother, Grifo, who had made common cause with the rebellious Saxons. He thoroughly subdued the Allemannians and Bavarians, treating the land of the latter as a mere benefice, and conferring it on Tassilo, the son of the former duke. Tassilo, indeed, was allowed privileges that were almost royal; the fine, for instance, of thieving within his palace was twenty-seven times the ordinary penalty. High treason against him was punishable with death and confiscation. *Pippin alone.*

Pippin's false position as servant in name and master in reality, at last induced him to take a step that was to mark an era in the history of Europe. By the counsel and with the consent of the Frankish nobles he sent an embassy to the Pope—whose authority by this time, thanks chiefly to Boniface, was widely recognized—to ask his advice in his present dilemma. The Pope was the highest instance in matters of conscience, and as such Pippin represented his doubts with regard to continuing in the old path. *Pippin becomes King of the Franks. 752 A.D.*

The note of the annalist concerning this matter deserves to be given in full. " The ambassadors asked," he says, " with regard to the kings in the Frankish kingdom who at that time possessed no more royal power, whether this was right or no ; and Pope Zacchary sent word to Pippin that it was better that he who had the power, rather than he to whom no kingly power remained, should have the name of king ; and that, so that the public peace should not be disturbed, Pippin should become king by apostolical authority."

E

The Pope's consent having thus been gained, Pippin was elected by the Frankish people, consecrated by the bishops, and done homage to by the nobles. This was in November, 751. The ceremony of anointing, that old theocratic institution, was performed upon him by Boniface. Pippin calls himself *rex Dei gratia*—not king by hereditary right, but king because God, through the Pope, has recognized him as such.

End of the Merovingian Dynasty.

The last Merovingian king was shorn and sent into a monastery, and the records of St. Wandrille tell later of a monk who seems to have been the last male descendant of the line.

Einhard's introduction to his "Life of Charlemagne"—written, indeed, sixty years later, but by the most distinguished of all mediæval writers—may serve as a fitting epitaph for this most unfortunate dynasty: "The race of the Merovingians, from which the Franks were accustomed to appoint their kings, is generally considered to have ended with King Childerich. . . . Although it only became extinct with him, it was already long without vital power, and possessed no other advantage than the empty royal title, for the possessions and power of the kingdom lay in the hands of the chief court officials, who were called mayors of the palace, and who ruled the State. There was nothing left to the king but that, content with the royal name, with waving hair and long beard, he should sit on the throne and play the part of ruler; that he should receive the envoys who came from afar, and give them at their departure, as if on his own authority, the answers which had been taught him, or which he had been commanded to give."

Pippin and Pope Stephen II.

Three years after his elevation to the throne, Pippin was treated to an honour which no founder of a dynasty was since to enjoy until, in our own century, the great Napoleon laid stress upon procuring it for himself.

Pope Stephen II. came over the Alps, and was fittingly received at Ponthion by Pippin, who had sent the youthful Charlemagne to meet him as far as St. Maurice, in the Rhone valley, and consecrated and anointed the new king and his

wife and sons in St. Denis. He threatened the Frankish
nobles with interdict and excommunication should they in
future choose a monarch from any other line. On Pippin
Stephen bestowed the title of " Patrician of the Romans." It
was a dignified appellation that the Exarchs of Ravenna had
borne as stadtholders of the Eastern Empire and protectors
of the Roman Church.

Pippin, on his part, had shown every sign of submission and
reverence to the Pope, and at Ponthion had performed the
menial service of holding the stirrup for him to mount. It
was a mark of humility upon which future popes were to lay
the greatest emphasis. Four centuries later, when Frederick
Barbarossa had strongly objected to thus humbling himself,
it was pointed out to him that the custom was an ancient one,
and he reconsidered his refusal.

It was not a purely unselfish motive that had induced Pope
Stephen to visit the Frankish kingdom.

The Lombard monarchy in Italy had gone through many
vicissitudes in the two centuries since its foundation, and had
at times seemed in danger of breaking up into a number of
small and independent principalities. Nowhere was the
struggle between Arianism and Catholicism more bitter than
here, and to this struggle, directly or indirectly, may be
ascribed the murder of several kings.

With Liutprand (714-744) begins a period of order and
prosperity, although by this time the duchies of Benevento
and Capua had more or less broken loose from the rest of the
kingdom.

It was the effort to subdue these, as well as the general
desire of increasing their territory, that brought the Lombard
kings in conflict with the Pope, and, through him, with the
Franks. Already, under Gregory II., they had besieged
Rome, and the Pope had sent an appeal for aid to Charles
Martel, forwarding to him the keys of the tomb of St. Peter
as a sign that he was the Church's chosen protector. The
Byzantine emperors, through their officials the exarchs of
Ravenna, had hitherto held this proud position, but the war

The Pope
and the
Lombards.

of images and dogmatic differences were already engendering that opposition which was to divide the religion of the East from that of the West, and which was to continue into modern times. A few years more, and the consent of the Eastern Empire was no longer to be asked for the papal elections, and the mere announcement to the Frankish king took the place of the earlier formal authorization.

Liutprand's own piety and reverence for the Papal See appears to have led him to withdraw his troops, and allay the storm that had threatened Rome.

King Astolphus. But King Astolphus, who ascended the throne in 749, was made of sterner metal. He deprived the Greek Empire of its last province in central Italy, the Exarchate of Ravenna, that strip of land which stretches along the coast from the mouth of the Po to the town of Ancona. The duchies of Spoleto and Benevento were reduced to partial dependence by the Lombard, and only Rome and its surrounding duchy stood in the path of the conqueror. Pope Stephen proved, as his ancient biographer tells us, " an exceedingly courageous defender of his sheepfold." He forced Astolphus to make with him a forty years' peace, but was at the end of his resource when, after a few months, the Lombard king saw fit to break his solemn engagement. It was then that Stephen appealed to Pippin, and begged the latter to invite him to visit the Frankish kingdom ; he knew that Astolphus would not dare to molest him if he travelled as the guest and at the bidding of a powerful king.

Pippin's donation to the Pope. Pippin showed his gratitude for the kind offices of the Pope. He promised Stephen the Exarchate of Ravenna, which the Greek emperor on his own behalf had already empowered the Pope to reclaim from the Lombards, and also the Roman duchy, which practically was already under papal rule. These provinces the Pope now took over from the Eastern Empire by much the same process by which Pippin had claimed the crown of the Merovingians. Each of the two powerful allies gave his sanction to the usurpations, perfectly pardonable under the circumstances, of the other.

The matter of Pippin's donation, involving, as it did, a probable war with the Lombards, was discussed before an assembly of the Frankish nobles at Kiersy, and a deed drawn up which may be called the foundation charter of the Papal States. The document, of which the exact wording was not known, was later confirmed by Charles the Great.

Pippin sent to Astolphus, and ordered him, "out of respect for the Apostles Peter and Paul," to desist from hostilities against the Roman territory. Astolphus refused, but finding himself threatened with war, induced the former major-domus, Carlmann, to leave the seclusion of Monte Casino, and to journey on an anti-papal mission to the land over which he had formerly ruled. He was to induce his brother to leave the Exarchate in the hands of the Lombards.

Carlmann leaves his retreat.

Carlmann's intervention was a failure, and he seems to have been most emphatically reminded that he had better abide by the monastic calling he had chosen. According to the court annals he "remained behind." According to another account he "was imprisoned" in the monastery of Vienne, where he shortly after died. His sons, lest they, too, should advance inconvenient claims, were also shorn and made monks.

Astolphus refused further overtures of Pippin's, although the latter was willing to pay a sum of money—he afterwards gave it to the Pope—for the peaceful surrender of the Exarchate. Nothing remained but war, and a Frankish army was soon on its way to Italy. Astolphus was put to flight in the valley of Susa, and was then besieged in Pavia. He soon begged for peace, and accepted the terms that were offered. He was to acknowledge the suzerainty of the Franks, and to give up the provinces claimed by the Roman Pope.

War between Pippin and Astolphus.

To make promises under immediate pressure is more easy than to keep them when that pressure is removed. No sooner had Pippin returned to his own land than Astolphus renewed his old policy of oppression. In 756, aided by the Dukes of Benevento and Spoleto, he went so far as to besiege Rome, which for three months offered a courageous resistance.

Stephen sent hasty messages to Pippin urging and imploring
him to hurry to his assistance. In one of his letters he makes
St. Peter himself address the king and his sons, and all the
Franks: "Hasten, hasten, I pray and beseech you by
Almighty God, hasten . . . . before your spiritual mother,
God's holy church, through which you hope to achieve everlasting life, is humbled, betrayed, dishonoured, and besmirched
by the godless. . . . It is well known that your nation, the
Franks, was more devoted to me, the divine Apostle Peter,
than all the other nations under Heaven; and, therefore, have
I entrusted to you, through the hand of my vicar, the task of
freeing from the hands of the enemy the Church, which has
been handed over to me by the Lord."

Pippin answered this appeal by arranging a new expedition
into Italy. The campaign of 756 proved a repetition of the
previous one. Astolphus, who had again been besieged in
Pavia, submitted and consented to surrender a third part of
his treasure in atonement for his fault. To the Pope, Pippin
solemnly presented the Exarchate, with the addition, now, of
Comacchio. Abbot Fulrad of St. Denis was commissioned
to travel through the newly-won district, and to claim, besides
a number of hostages, the keys of the different cities. These
were the symbol of sovereignity; together with the donation
document of Pippin they were reverently laid on the tomb of
St. Peter.

We are told that shortly before the final overthrow of
Astolphus an embassy from the Greek emperor met Pippin
and sought by offering advantageous terms to regain the
Exarchate. Pippin answered, says the biographer of the
Pope, " that no treasure in the world could move him to take
from St. Peter what he had once given to him."

Astolphus was succeeded on the Lombard throne by Desiderius, Duke of Tuscany, who was glad enough to buy the
Pope's support against a rival claimant by assuring him the
territory promised by his predecessor, and by adding to it the
district of Bologna. Differences later arose with regard to
the actual surrender of these provinces, but they were not of

such a nature as to call for armed interference from the
Frankish king.

The last eight years of Pippin's reign—the period between
760 and 768—were almost entirely taken up with campaigns
against Duke Waifar of Aquitaine, who, among other autocratic acts, had appropriated church lands which lay indeed
in his own duchy, but which belonged to the Frankish clergy.

Subjugation of Aquitaine.

Absorbed in this struggle, Pippin allowed his vassal, Tassilo
of Bavaria, who in 754 broke his oath of fealty, and withdrew
his forces from the Frankish army, to go unpunished. It was
not till nearly a generation had passed that retribution for
his act was to fall upon the rebel duke.

The subjection of Aquitaine was the crowning triumph of
Pippin's life; the land was henceforth a Frankish province,
and submitted to Frankish laws. But the king himself
returned from the war a broken man, who felt his death
approaching. He retired to St. Denis, where he passed away
on September 24th, 768.

One of his last acts was to divide the kingdom between his
sons Charles and Carlmann. The former received Austrasia
and Neustria; the latter Allemannia, Alsace, and Burgundy,
together with Provence and Septimania.

By the order of Charles, or Charlemagne, as he is more
usually called, the correspondence of the popes with his father
was collected and copied, and is still preserved. It concerns
the Lombards, the war of images then going on in the Greek
Church, and dogmatic questions like that concerning the procession of the Holy Ghost. Presents often accompanied these
communications; on one occasion the Pope, it was Paul I.,
sent Greek books—" as many as he could bring together."
Aristoteles and Dionysius, the Areopagite, were among the
favoured authors. This shows that Pippin had certain literary
tastes—we know, too, that he interested himself in church
music, and took measures for the better training of his
choristers. With him enlightenment and political astuteness
seem to have gone hand in hand.

Correspon-
dence of the
popes.

It was Pippin's fate to have a son so infinitely greater and

Pippin's son.

more successful than himself that his own services are apt to be underrated. Whatever task he had attempted, whatever dream he dreamed, Charles brought to completion and realization. If Pippin fought against the Saxons, Charles crushed them, and moulded them to his will. What were Pippin's successes against the Lombards compared to Charles's annexation of the land to the Frankish kingdom? And Pippin's assumption of the royal title, finally, was outshone and outdone by his son's elevation to the throne of the empire.

Charles's early years. Over the history of the early years of Charles the Great hangs a cloud of mystery. His biographer and friend, Einhard, dismisses with a few words the whole period before his accession to the throne. It is not even known whether or not he was born in wedlock, the marriage of his father, Pippin, with his mother, Bertrada, being placed by two of the annalists at a date posterior to his own birth. It is highly probable, as the French triumphantly assert, that his birthplace was within the confines of the present France, for his father, when not absent on his campaigns, resided in Neustria.

Charles and Carlmann. Charles and Carlmann were anointed kings, the one at Noyons, the other at Soissons on the same day—October 9th, 768. From the very beginning the relations of the two brothers to each other were unfriendly, and when Charles, in the spring of 769, found it necessary to make an expedition against the Aquitanians, who had rebelled anew, Carlmann refused to aid or to accompany him. The campaign was carried on alone, and its successful issue could only have served to deepen the discord between the two rulers. Thanks to Bertrada, however, an open breach seems to have been avoided, and Carlmann's death in 771 freed his brother from a presence that had become irksome.

Without opposition, although to the exclusion of Carlmann's youthful children, Charles became ruler of the whole kingdom. It was by the wish, and at the invitation of Carlmann's nobles, that he did so, and the consent of the people sanctioned an otherwise irregular proceeding.

Charles's reign shows a magnificent series of undertakings which often required, individually, years for their fulfillment, and which overlapped and, at times, hindered each other. We must look at them separately, and not try to follow the indefatigable monarch in his frequent marches from one confine of his kingdom to the other. Of the forty-six years of his rule only two or three were passed in complete peace and quiet. His greatest achievements were the overthrow of the Lombard rule in Italy, the subjugation of the Saxons, the reorganization of Bavaria into a Frankish province, the annihilation of the powers of the Avars, and, finally, the acquisition of the imperial crown. We shall see, too, how in the fields of lawgiving, of education, and of art, he gained triumphs that were no less brilliant.

Charles's undertakings.

Charles had begun his reign by acceding to the wish of his mother, Bertrada, and taking to wife a daughter of the Lombard king Desiderius. Pope Stephen III. had at first been aghast at the prospect of such a union, and had written a most vehement letter to Charles and Carlmann before he even knew which of the brothers was contemplating the hateful alliance. He had spoken of the faithless and horribly ill-odoured people of the Lombards—the propagators of leprosy he had called them—and had reminded the Frankish rulers of their promise to be the friend of the friends and the foe of the foes of St. Peter, and of his earthly representative. Charles had managed to assuage the Pope's wrath, and had even given him assurances which caused Stephen to overflow in expressions of gratitude.

Charles and the Lombards.

But the Frankish monarch had soon tired of his Italian bride. After a year of marriage he had sent her back in disgrace to her father and had wedded the thirteen year old Hildegard, an Allemannian princess. No ties now bound him to the Lombards—on the contrary, Desiderius became the bitter enemy of his former son-in-law.

In 772 Pope Stephen died and Adrian I. came to the papal throne. Desiderius tried in every way, by fair means and by foul, to gain the latter as an ally against the Franks. Find-

Desiderius and Adrian I.

ing him intractable he resorted to intimidation, occupied the
cities of Faenza, Ferrara, and Comachio, and blocked the land
route of the messengers which Adrian despatched for aid to
the Frankish kingdom.

In order to have a weapon against Charles, Desiderius received at his court the widow and children of Carlmann, and
demanded that the Pope should anoint the latter as rightful
kings. He even advanced upon Rome to give emphasis to his
claims, but retreated before the threat of excommunication
which Adrian employed.

In January, 773, one of the Pope's messengers, a certain
Paulus who had managed to cross by ship to Marseilles, came
to Charles, who was in the neighbourhood of Metz. He
brought an appeal of Adrian for help against Desiderius, re-
questing most earnestly that the Lombard king be compelled
to surrender the misappropriated possessions of St. Peter.

Charles against the Lombards, 773 A.D.

Charles's decision to send an army into Italy was taken
after ripe deliberation with his nobles, and after having tried
by peaceful means to induce Desiderius to render satisfaction
to the Pope.

The Lombards retreated before the Frankish forces, and
Charles made light of the extensive fortifications that guarded
the descent from Mount Cenis. Desiderius fled to Pavia, the
siege of which occupied the Frankish troops for seven months.
Charles meanwhile busied himself with the taking of Verona,
in which city the widow and sons of Carlmann had found
refuge. They were delivered up, and probably ended their
lives, like most other inconvenient personages of these times,
in the seclusion of a monastery. No chronicler ever mentions
their name again.

Charles's donation to the Church.

At Easter, Charles made a pilgrimage to Rome where he
was received with great pomp and rejoicing. The youth of
the city came out to meet him with palms and olive branches,
and the Pope received him in state in St. Peter's. Over the
grave of the apostle they swore mutual devotion and fidelity.
A few days later Charles solemnly ratified the donation that
Pippin had made to the Church, and caused a document to be

drawn up in three copies to commemorate the occasion. The wording of this deed has come down to us—in a. changed form, indeed, for a later clause was added by some churchly scribe according to which the gift of Charles would have comprised nearly the whole of northern Italy. The extravagance of the claim has led men for years to doubt the genuineness of the whole document, but one of the latest investigators has pointed out where the interpolation begins, and how, originally written on the margin of the manuscript, it since crept into the text.

About two months after Charles's return from Rome, Pavia surrendered and Desiderius was taken prisoner as well as his wife and daughter. They were carried off as captives in the train of the conqueror, and a new era began, both symbolically and literally, in the history of Italy. The Lombard power was declared at an end, and Charles took the title of "King of the Lombards and Patrician of the Romans." Not only public but even private charters were henceforth dated according to the years of his reign. *Charles, King of the Lombards, 774 A.D.*

Charles used his victory mildly. With the treasure of Desiderius, indeed, he enriched his followers, and the crown lands were disposed of right and left to Frankish monasteries. We hear, for instance, of an island in the Lago di Garda being given to St. Martin of Tours.

Desiderius ended his life in captivity, but his son Adelchis, who had fled to Constantinople, made an effort in 776 in common with Duke Arichis of Benevento, to throw off the newly imposed yoke. In vain. *Revolt of Adelchis.*

The Pope heard of the scheme, in which was included a plan for his own imprisonment, and sent word to Charles. The latter crossed the Alps in the dead of winter and easily put an end to the rebellion, which had as yet not spread beyond the confines of Friaul. The insurgents were treated with great severity, their property confiscated and they themselves banished in great numbers. Friaul was considered the more dangerous on account of its proximity to Bavaria, and Frankish garrisons were left in its cities.

The first and last attempt to shake off the dominion of the Franks had failed. The duchy of Benevento was, indeed, as yet unsubjected and the Greeks still had footholds in Naples, Calabria, Apulia, and Sicily, but Italy was, otherwise, completely a province of the Frankish kingdom.

Pippin, King of Italy; Louis of Aquitaine. In the year 781 Charles appeared again in Rome and caused his four year old son to be baptized by the Pope, the child's name being changed from Carlmann to Pippin. Charles then arranged for the formation of Italy and Aquitaine into kingdoms; Pipin was made king of the former and his still younger brother, the future Louis the Pious, of the latter.

Charles's purpose was not to dispossess himself of any rights or privileges, but to lighten the cares of government by creating local powers which should have authority enough to ensure respect. Both for Italy and Aquitaine he continued to make laws and regulations at will. Frankish institutions, too, were gradually introduced; the letting out of church lands in return for yearly payments or services, the immunities, the custom of having counts or regular executive officials for each given district.

Charles issues laws. In order to heal the wounds of war in Italy, Charles made mild and beneficent regulations. Many freemen had been forced to sell themselves or their families into servitude or to renounce their lands for paltry prices. In certain of the districts such transactions were declared null and void, and the buyers of the lands compelled to pay their true value. From the fact that slaves had become so plentiful an extensive export of them had taken place—the trade seems to have been entered into with the Saracens as well as with the Greeks. Charles, in a capitulary published at Mantua, forbade the further carrying on of this industry, as well as to the selling of weapons to nations that were likely to prove hostile. Other laws provided for the protection of widows, orphans, and paupers, and also for the bettering of the coinage.

In 787 Charles again visited Italy, and finding that his officials were oppressing the people and demanding from them unreasonable services, he issued stern decrees against such transgressions.

Differences remained to be settled with Duke Arichis of Benevento, who had married a daughter of Desiderius and who remained in communication with his exiled brother-in-law, Adelchis. **Arichis of Benevento.**

Arichis had tried to wrest Terracina and Gaeta from the Roman Church, and Pope Adrian had urged Charles to send an army against him. Arichis, however, had no intention of braving the wrath of the Frankish king, and accepted Charles's conditions. He consented to deliver up Terracina and Gaeta to the Pope, and to pay to the Franks a large yearly tribute. Among the hostages that he was forced to give was his own son Grimoald. Arichis died in the midst of preparations for a new rebellion, in which Adelchis, with a Greek army, was to have aided him.

The people of Benevento were not wanting in courage. They demanded the release of Grimoald, who was now heir to their duchy. The original writing in which their demand was made is still existing—one of the few documents written on papyrus that has weathered the storms of the ages. Charles restored Grimoald, but took occasion to obtain the recognition of his own claims as overlord of Benevento. His name was to find a place on the coins and in the charters, and the Lombards in the duchy were to renounce their peculiar national manner of trimming their beards. **Grimoald.**

A gold shilling and two charters issued by Grimoald have been preserved. In one of the charters there is no allusion to the Franks; the other dates from the beginning of Charlemagne's new rule in Italy, while the coin bears on one side Grimoald's own name, on the other that of "the Lord King Charles." **Grimoald' charters.**

Grimoald later made further attempts to rebel, but the young King Pippin was able to cope with him alone, and, although several campaigns were fought, only once was it found necessary to send foreign troops to his aid. In 812, under Grimoalds's successor, a formal peace was entered into with Benevento, the duchy paying a large sum of money and renewing its yearly tribute.

War with the Saxons, 772-804. The history of Charles the Great's long war with the Saxons is summed up by his friend and biographer, Einhard, as tersely and strikingly as one could wish : " It is hard to say how often the Saxons, conquered and humbled, submitted to the king, promised to fulfil his commands, delivered over the required hostages without delay, received the officials sent to them, were often rendered so tame and pliable that they gave up the service of their heathen gods and agreed to accept Christianity. But just as quickly as they showed themselves ready to do this did they also always break their promises ; so that, from the beginning of the war, scarcely a year passed without bringing such change of mind."

Character of the Saxons. The Saxons were a strong and courageous people, unspoiled as yet by contact with over-civilized and waning nations. All that we can learn of them goes to prove that they stood about on the same level of culture with the early Germans described by Tacitus. The same stern morality with regard to female chastity still ruled among them. Boniface mentions in a letter to one of the Anglo-Saxon kings the cruel punishments to which the Saxons publicly subjected their fallen women and faithless wives. The Saxon laws against theft and robbery were far more severe than among other German stems, which fact explains in part the unusually heavy penalties later affixed by Charles to offences against the Church in Saxony. In his scale of crimes, those against religion were looked upon as the most heinous, and were therefore to be visited with the severest punishments.

The Saxons were still heathen ; in one of the old baptismal formulas that has come down to us the candidate promises to renounce "Donar, Wotan and Sachsnot, and all the evil beings who are their companions."

Reasons for Saxon War. Among the grounds which induced Charles to make war on the Saxons was the fact that the latter often undertook plundering expeditions into Frankish territory. The boundaries were by no means clearly defined, much less protected by any sort of defences.

It must not be forgotten in this connection that Charles possessed a love of conquest, and that he too, like Mahomet, felt a calling to convert the heathen even at the edge of the sword. Crowds of missionaries and priests accompanied his armies into Saxony, and the symbol of a conquered chieftain's submission was the cross traced upon his forehead in baptism. It was a holy war, if ever there was one, and the first sign of each new rebellion was the overthrow of the Christian sanctuaries.

The Saxons were divided into different tribes, which often showed little or no sympathy with each other. It was only towards the conclusion of the struggle that a common danger brought them more together. The war began in 772, and ended definitely in 804; between these two dates was fought out one of the most stubborn fights that ever took place for the sake of political and religious independence. **Severity of the struggle.**

In the early stages of the contest Charles seems to have deceived himself as to the gravity of his undertaking. In 777 he considered the Saxons a conquered people, and held a diet in their midst at Paderborn. Saxon nobles appeared and promised fealty to him. But, within a year, while Charles was absent in Spain, a plundering expedition on a larger scale than ever was undertaken, and the district around the mouth of the Mosel was ravaged by fire and the sword. Even Fulda was threatened, and the monks took to flight, carrying with them their costliest treasure, the bones of Boniface.

In 782 Charles again felt secure of his ascendancy, and it is probably then that he issued his famous capitulary for the Saxon land. This instrument—all of these laws are pre-served, and have been carefully edited in our own day—introduces the Frankish institutions and administrative divisions, regulates the duties of the "counts," who were mostly appointed from among the Saxons themselves, and declares that whoever breaks his oath of fealty to the king shall die the death. Capital punishment is also placed on the burning **Capitulary for Saxony.**

of churches, the slaying of a bishop or priest, on adhering to the heathen custom of burning the dead, on rejecting baptism, and even on eating meat in Lent if it be done in scorn of Christianity.

By confessing of one's own free will to a Christian priest, and by doing penance for such crimes as these, it was possible to escape the penalty.

Indignation against such rigid laws, and, even more so, unwillingness to pay the tithes exacted on behalf of the Church, fanned the rebellion into a fiercer flame than ever. The more general the measures taken against them, the more united did the Saxons become.

Massacre of Verden, 782. Charles showed himself unrelenting in the pursuance of his aim ; he had determined to break the spirit of these his most stubborn antagonists, and he took measures from which all but a few of the world's monarchs would have shrunk. After two of his commanders had been defeated near the present St. Jacobsberg, on the Weser, he caused 4,500 of the Saxons who had come into his hands to be executed in one day. This wholesale letting of blood took place at Verden, on the Aller, an awful deed of vengeance that was emulated in our own century by Charles's disciple, the great Napoleon.

The proceedings at Verden served to exasperate rather than intimidate the Saxons. The whole land rose in fierce protest, and Charles was obliged to hasten back from Metz, where he had been showing the last honours to the corpse of his Queen Hildegard. At Detmold, however, and again within a month, on the river Hase, he gained important victories.

Widukind and Abbio are baptized. The land was restored to quiet, but in 784 the rebellion broke out anew. In the year following, however, the two principal Saxon leaders, Widukind and a certain Abbio, made their submission in due form, and received baptism at Attigny. We are told that Charles acted as godfather to Widukind, and sent him away loaded with rich presents. The Pope sent a special messenger to convey his congratulations, and ordained a three days' festival of thanksgiving for the whole Frankish kingdom.

The Saxons bore their burden quietly for the next few years, but in 792, to use the metaphor of the Lauresheim annals, like a dog returning to its vomit they renewed hostilities and went back to heathenism.

It was the younger generation of warriors that now took up the fight for independence, and they waged it at intervals for twelve years, aided at times by their neighbours the Frisians and the Wends.

Charles at last adopted a measure almost more radical, if less cruel, than the massacre of these or those rebels. Thousands of Saxons were transplanted to new settlements, and their lands distributed among the king's Frankish followers. Again and again Charles resorted to this means of coercion; one of the chroniclers speaks of a "complete uprooting" of the people in a certain district beyond the Elbe. The Slavic Abodrites were afterwards allowed to settle on the vacant lands. *Transplanting of Saxons.*

Many local names in Thuringia, Hesse, and elsewhere remain to remind one of the new seats to which the Saxons were removed. Sachsbach, Sachsenberg, Sachsenheim and the like trace their origin to these times.

Besides these unwilling colonists Charles carried off numerous hostages; they were usually relegated to monasteries, whence they often returned as missionaries to their own land and their own people.

Charles modified in time his severe laws and more and more the memory of ancient freedom paled before the satisfaction at a mild and orderly rule. *Peace with the Saxons.*

The subjection of Saxony had been a horrible necessity, without it the unity of Germany could not have been accomplished either in mediæval or in modern times. Charles did his work well, and in the following century a proud dynasty of emperors was to come forth from the land that he had conquered, and to prevent the edifice that he was to found, the Holy Roman Empire, from falling to the ground.

During these years of continual warfare Charles had found time to make his numerous expeditions into Italy, to march

F

against a party of the Saracens in Spain, to conquer the Avars in the present Hungary, and also to tame the independent aspirations of Duke Tassilo of Bavaria.

Charles's Spanish Expedition, 777 A.D.

The Spanish expedition was the nearest approach to a failure of anything that Charles undertook. It was made in 777 at the request of an Arab stadtholder, who was oppressed by enemies of his own faith.

The caliphate or emirate of Cordova had been founded in 755 by the last of the Ommiads, and it was to protest against the manner in which this new power was wielded that Ibn el Arabi appeared at Paderborn. The campaign undertaken on his behalf is chiefly memorable for an attack made by the Christian Basques upon Charles's rear-guard when his army was retiring from Spain.

Roland.

It was on this occasion that a certain Roland fell, whose name later became a favourite theme for poetry and song. In the time of the crusades Charles's expedition came to be talked of as a holy war against the enemies of the faith, and Roland was taken as the type of a fearless champion of godliness. The original "Chanson de Roland" was written between 1130 and 1140, and all Christian Europe later grew familiar with the legend. It was in honour of this almost mythical hero that many of the towns of Northern Germany erected those huge stone statues in their market places—Rolands as they are still called—which were intended to symbolize civic authority. The sword was the sign of jurisdiction, and Roland was popularly supposed to have been sword-bearer of Charles the Great.

The Spanish March.

The Frankish kingdom was to suffer occasionally from petty invasions of the Arabs, but Charles henceforth left the defence of his border to the young king of Aquitaine. The latter succeeded in acquiring and fortifying a tract of territory stretching as far south as the river Ebro. It is known as the Spanish March, but was of small use, on the whole, to the Frankish kingdom.

Charles's task in Bavaria was very different from what it was in Saxony. He had to fight not against a people but against the representative of a family, a dynasty one might call it.

Bavaria had, as we have seen, been subjugated by Pippin. The Bavarian laws, drawn up about 745, expressly acknowledge the suzerainty of the Frankish king and his right to appoint, or, if need be, depose a duke. They speak continually of the land as of a " province." But Tassilo had, in 754, refused to do a vassal's service in Pippin's army and had, since 763, maintained an almost independent position. His charters omit all mention of the Frankish king, and are dated according to the years of his own " reign."

Bavaria.

With Charles the Great, Tassilo's relations had been at times not unfriendly. For a brief year the two were brothers-in-law, Tassilo having also married one of the daughters of Desiderius. In 781 Charles had sent envoys to him to remind him of his oath of fealty. Two bishops appointed by the Pope had accompanied the embassy. Tassilo had then been induced to appear at a diet in Worms, to renew his oath and to give twelve chosen hostages.

Tassilo and Charles.

In 787 Tassilo, having again offended, had again made his submission, this time renouncing his duchy and receiving it back with all formality as a fief of the Frankish kingdom. On this occasion the Bavarian people themselves had been obliged to swear the oath of fealty, and Tassilo's own son had been carried off among the hostages.

The new fetters imposed upon him were too much for Tassilo's power of endurance. He made plans and preparations for rebellion, upon hearing of which Charles had him seized and brought before a diet. The charges against him were high treason, having conspired with his country's enemies, and, finally, " heresliz " or desertion from the army. The last accusation referred to the old and silently condoned crime of more than thirty years before.

Tassilo's condemnation.

The diet, at which all parts of Charles's kingdom were represented, and where many of the Bavarians even declared against their own duke, decreed that Tassilo was guilty and spoke judgment of death against him. Charles changed the

sentence to seclusion in a monastery—it will have been seen
by this time that those houses of God were the best substi-
tutes for states' prisons.   Not only Tassilo but his whole
family, consisting of his wife, son, and two daughters, ended
their lives within cloistered walls.   Tassilo seems to have
richly deserved his fate, for he had evidently planned a rebellion on a large scale.   His allies, the Avars, made an attack
of their own accord at two points on the Frankish frontier,
but were defeated by forces under the king's officials.

Bavaria as a part of the Frankish kingdom.   In one of his charters Charles justifies himself publicly for
his recent course with regard to the Bavarian duke: "Inas-
much as the duchy of Bavaria has long been withdrawn and
estranged from our Frankish kingdom by evil-minded men,
our relatives Odilo and Tassilo (father and son), we, by the
help of God, who is the Swayer of justice, have brought it
again into our own power."   After 788 the charters date from
the year "since King Charles acquired Bavaria."   From that
time on the land became an integral part of the Frankish
kingdom, and was regularly administered by "counts."   Over
these, later, for the sake of presenting a united front to the
Avars, a "prefect" was placed.   The ducal lands went to the
fisc of the king.

In 794 Tassilo was brought from his monastery to a diet at
Frankfort, and made to acknowledge that he had been rightly
punished and to renounce all claim to Bavaria, either for himself or for his children.

The Avar War, 791-796 A.D.   The supplement to the subjugation of Bavaria was a
military expedition against the Avars.   This wild people, of
whom so little is known that the old chroniclers frequently
confound them with the Huns, had followed in the wake of
the Lombards and had settled in the plains of the Danube in
the eastern part of the present Austrian Empire.   They
possessed in the eighth century a very extended but by no
means powerful kingdom.   They lived by plunder, and the
Greek Empire was the chief sufferer from their inroads.
Their settlements were surrounded by strong walls made of
stones and trunks of trees, and these so-called "rings" were

near enough to each other to permit of communication by signals in time of danger.

In 791 Charles marched into the land of the Avars with a large army. His columns advanced along the old Roman roads on both sides of the Danube, while a fleet accompanied them on the river itself. The expedition was in vain so far as any decisive action was concerned, the Avars refusing to be drawn into open combat.

Charles made great preparations for renewing the attack, and, in 793, attempted to join the Main and the Danube by a navigable canal which should utilize the little rivers Altmühl and Rednitz. The difficulties were too great, and the canal was never finished; faint traces of it may still be seen between Treuchtlingen and Weissenburg. The Saxon war and other undertakings forced Charles to leave the final completion of the Avar war to his subordinates. In 795 Margrave Erich of Friaul took the chief Avar "Ring," the residence of the Khan, and sent treasures of incalculable worth to Aix. We hear of Charles distributing this booty in all directions; a part of it even came to England, King Offa of Mercia being presented with a sword and two silken garments. *The Storming of the "Ring," 795 A.D.*

In 796, when King Pippin of Italy renewed the campaign he found an unresisting enemy. The Khan and the chiefs of the people appeared before him and made their submission. He destroyed their "ring" and carried off the last remnants of its treasure. *Subjection of the Avars.*

No sooner was the conquest of the Avars completed than the task of converting them to Christianity was begun. A conference of bishops was called together, and came to the wise conclusion that it was better to use persuasion than force. The preaching, as we are told by Paulinus of Aquileija who drew up a report of the proceedings of this meeting, was to be "gentle and convincing and bedewed with sweetness." Charles's learned friend Alcuin bade the chamberlain, Maginfred, use his influence with the king to prevent baptism from being imposed upon the Avars by force. He also writes against a too early insistance on the payment of tithes, "which had undermined the faith of the Saxons." To his former pupil, Arno of Salzburg, Alcuin writes: "What is the use of baptism without faith? How can a man be compelled to believe what he does not believe?" Advanced views for the eighth century!

End of the Avar power. The land of the Avars was parcelled out for missionary purposes among the bishoprics of Salzburg and Passau and the Patriarchate of Aquileija. A few uprisings of the people took place, but the nation had received its death blow and was rapidly going to ruin. In 805 the Khan appeared before Charles at Aix and asked for new settlements for the remnant of his people, for they were in fear of the advancing Slavonians. The request was granted, and they were allowed seats not far from the present Vienna. In 822 the name of this once powerful nation is mentioned for the last time in history.

CHAPTER V.

CHARLES THE GREAT AS EMPEROR OF THE ROMANS.

POPE ADRIAN died in 795 after a pontificate of twenty-four years. He had been a good friend to Charles the Great, and it was by the latter's direction that the memorial tablet was engraved which may still be seen near the chief entrance of St. Peter's.

Charles and the popes.

Leo III., Adrian's successor, hastened to show his devotion to Charles, and sent him the keys of the tomb of St. Peter together with the banner of the city of Rome. A picture in mosaics of the Apostle delivering with one hand the latter symbol of authority to the Frankish king, and with the other bestowing the pallium on the Pope was later placed by Leo's order in one of the halls of the Lateran palace, where it remains to the present day. It bears the inscription: "St. Peter, thou grantest life to Leo, victory thou grantest to Charles the King."

Charles's answer to the announcement of Leo's accession shows clearly the light in which he regarded his duties towards the Church. He was its patron and protector, the censor of its spiritual head and members. "Admonish the Pope," he says in the instructions to his envoy, "to lead an honest life, and especially to observe the sacred decrees of the Church."

It may be said here in parenthesis that Charles's activity extended to every branch of church discipline, and even to the acceptation or rejection of dogmas. He was not only king but also high priest of his people. His capitularies concern themselves very much with the good order in the

Charles and Church discipline.

bishoprics and monasteries. It is prescribed among other
things that bishops, abbots and abbesses may not keep falcons,
hawks and conjurers, that nuns may not write love-ditties,
and that shoes shall be worn during the Divine Service.
Even the proper use of altar-cloths is not beneath the notice
of this unwearying legislator. In the great dogmatic disputes of the time regarding the adoptionist heresy, the war
of images, the procession of the Holy Ghost from the Son as
well as from the Father, Charles took a leading and important part, presiding over the synods where they were discussed and, in one case at least, coming to a decision opposed
to that of the Pope. The difference of opinion in question,
which concerned the war of images, had been caused by a
misapprehension, by a mistranslation from the Greek into
the Latin. It was soon explained away, but Charles had
maintained his ground with great emphasis, sending to Rome
a comprehensive refutation of what he supposed to be the
Pope's views.

**Misadven-
tures of
Leo III.**
Leo III. succeeded in making himself unpopular with the
citizens of Rome, and a far-reaching conspiracy, under the
leadership of the nephews of his predecessor, Adrian, was
formed against him. On St. Mark's day (April 25th), 799,
as he was riding in a procession from the Lateran to St.
Laurentius, he was attacked, pulled from his horse, robbed,
and otherwise ill-treated. According to a fable, widely,
almost universally believed at the time, he was blinded and
his tongue was torn out, but the Lord in His mercy restored
the missing members. Leo was carried to the monastery of
St. Erasmus, where he was kept as a prisoner. From there
he escaped by night, being let down by a rope from the wall.
He fled to one of Charles's "missi," the Duke of Spoleto,
who brought him in safety beyond the precincts of Rome.

**Leo and
Charles at
Paderborn.**
Charles, as the "Patricius" of Rome, was the natural
avenger of Leo's wrongs. To his camp at Paderborn the
fugitive therefore made his way.

A poem of the time describes the meeting. The king receives the Pope with great honour in the midst of his

assembled troops. We are in a perfect atmosphere of flutter-
ing standards and sounding trumpets. Charles, who is
described as being a head taller than all his nobles, rides on
a mighty war-horse. His armour and his golden helmet
gleam in the sunshine, but are not more brilliant than his
own radiant glance. When the Pope appears he is led by the
king into the church, after having given his blessing to the
people. The mass completed, Charles leads his guest to a
splendid feast. The hall is adorned with rich carpets, and is
resplendent with purple and gold. Falernian wine is drained
from golden beakers.

A cloud soon came over the rejoicings at Paderborn. Envoys **Accusations against Leo.**
of the Romans appeared and brought most damning charges
against the Pope. Two parties formed themselves, the one
maintaining that Leo must either cleanse himself by an oath
or be deposed, the other declaring that the Apostolic See
might judge but could not be judged. " What Shepherd of
the Church," writes Alcuin, " will remain unassailed if he be
deposed who is the head of the Churches of Christ ? "

Charles's sympathies were all with Leo. He sent the latter
back to Rome accompanied by envoys who held judgment
not over him but over the leaders of the rebellion. They
were banished in disgrace to the Frankish land.

The matter was, however, not so easily ended. The Pope's **Charles in Rome, 800 A.D.**
enemies continued to accuse him, and Charles determined
himself to go to Rome. He arrived there on November 24th
of the year 800, and, a week later, called together a great
assembly of nobles and clergy in the church of St. Peter's.
Here the charges against Leo were investigated, and he was
asked if he would be willing to clear himself by taking the
oath. It was expressly agreed that the Pope could not be
compelled to perform this act should he have scruples
against it.

Leo deigned to prove his innocence. On December 23rd,
he ascended the pulpit with the gospel in his hand and
publicly and convincingly justified himself against his
enemies.

The imperial coronation, 800 A.D.

Two days later Charles attended divine service in St. Peter's. It was Christmas Day, and, at the same time, according to the then manner of reckoning, the beginning of the new year. After the mass the king knelt to pray at the tomb of the Apostle. As he rose from his knees the Pope placed a crown upon his head, and the assembled Romans called out: "Long life and victory to Charles, the Augustus, the crowned of God, the great and peace-bringing emperor of the Romans." The scene had evidently been prepared, but Charles himself seems to have been surprised at it. According to Einhard he was at first unwilling to accept the new honour, and declared that he would not have gone to the church that day had he known of the Pope's intention. It is probable that Charles was not unfamiliar with the idea of becoming emperor, but that his plans were either not yet ripe, or that he objected to Leo's taking the initiative.

The Pope's humility.

Certain it is that the Pope acted with all humility, and not as the lofty dispenser of arbitrary favours. After the coronation he flung himself on the ground and "adored" the new emperor. Charles himself never regarded the empire as in any way a present from the Pope, nor did he later request the papal sanction for the imperial coronation of his son, Louis the Pious.

Charles and the empire.

Charles looked upon his new dignity as a very heavy responsibility. His famous capitulary, issued in 802,[1] may be taken as the programme of the young empire. In the year 789 he had made his adult subjects swear allegiance to him as a king; a new oath was now required of them, and it was clearly laid down what this oath comprised. Mere fidelity in the sense of not committing treason was no longer enough; obedience was demanded to a number of commands concerning personal uprightness of life, general justice and equity, the harbouring of strangers, the protection of widows and orphans.

One great change made at this time, and provided for in

---

[1] Published in "Select Historical Documents," p. 189.

the capitulary, was the appointment of *missi dominici* or regular envoys for the whole extent of the empire, which was marked out into districts for the purpose. These envoys were to be yearly despatched to examine into all branches of the administration. They were to call assemblies at stated times and listen to complaints against the regular officials—the counts and centenars. They were to be in direct communication with the emperor, and their reports to him formed the basis for the instructions—which in many cases may still be read—for the *missi* of the following year.

No point in Charles's career could have been more favourable for his elevation to a new rank. For more than thirty years he had been engaged in perpetual warfare, he was now crowned with the crown of peace. Along the borders of the empire, indeed, the struggle continued almost incessantly with Danes, Slavs, and Arabs ; but the emperor was only twice obliged to take the field in person—once, for a short time against the Saxons and once against the Danish king, who died, however, before a battle could take place.

Favourable time for becoming emperor.

The Holy Roman Empire had been called into being, but the old Roman Empire of the East, with its claims and its traditions, still remained to be reckoned with.

Charles and the Eastern empire.

Charles seems at first to have considered himself the direct successor of the Byzantine rulers, whose throne was temporarily occupied by a woman, the cruel and ambitious Irene. There was even question of a marriage with this abandoned creature, who, in order to strengthen her position, had consented to the blinding of her own son. But with Irene's successor, Nicephorus, we find Charles negotiating for years for recognition as emperor of the West. It was 812 before he gained his point, and that only at the price of Venice and Dalmatia, which his son, Pippin, had brought into dependence on Italy.

For the development of the little island state this surrender was of great importance, the more so as Charles assured to it free trade with Italy, as well as other privileges. The Eastern Empire was too far off to keep a strict watch on its new

Venice.

acquisition, and Venice soon came to be practically independent.

Partition of the empire, 806 A.D. In 806 Charles partitioned his domains among his three sons, Pippin, Charles, and Louis. Pippin and Louis received the lands immediately adjoining their kingdoms of Italy and Aquitaine, while the kernel of the Empire, Franconia and Saxony, fell to Charles. But the terms of the division document were never carried out. Pippin died in 810, and the younger Charles in the following year. Louis the Pious became heir to the whole empire excepting Italy. Here Pippin's son, Bernard, succeeded his father.

Charles's will. In 811 Charles the Great made his will, which we still have, disposing of his treasure, his library—which was to be sold for what it would bring—and even of his carpets, curtains, tablecloths, and cushions. The will is signed by a number of archbishops, bishops, and counts.

Of the treasure, three-fourths is left to the twenty-one metropolitan churches of the Empire; the rest is divided among his children and grandchildren, his attendants and the poor.

Coronation of Louis the Pious, 813 A.D. In September, 813, Charles held his last diet at Aix. By the consent of all present Louis the Pious was made emperor. The coronation took place in the chapel, Charles himself playing the chief part in the ceremony. It was at his command that Louis took the crown from the altar and placed it on his own head.

Charles's death and burial, 814 A.D. Charles died on January 28th, 814, and was buried within the chapel walls at Aix. Over his grave was placed an arch with this inscription : " Under this monument rests the body of Charles, the great and orthodox emperor, who gloriously enlarged the Frankish kingdom and reigned happily for 47 years. He died at the age of 70, in the year of our Lord 814, in the seventh indiction, on the 28th of January."

Charles the Great's grave has several times been opened. First by the Emperor Otto III., whose well authenticated visit was afterwards made the framework for most extravagant fables. One can to-day trace the embellishments that each succeeeding author has added to his relation of the incident.

Later Frederick Barbarossa made a pilgrimage to Aix, and caused his antipope, Paschal III., to canonize Charles the Great. It was on that occasion that the huge chandelier was presented which still adorns the chapel. Frederick caused Charles's bones to be removed from the antique sarcophagus in which he found them, and to be placed in the costly shrine where they now rest. This shrine has since been several times opened—for the last time in 1861 in the presence of a distinguished gathering. The official report of the proceedings shows that Charles's skeleton was considered to be in a good state of preservation, and that its length coincided exactly with the account given by Einhard of the emperor's size. *His canonization.*

The chapel at Aix well repays a visit to-day. The marble coffin in which Charles once lay, and which was carried off for a time to Paris by Napoleon, may still be seen there, also the marble chair on which the emperor sat, and which later was regularly used by the kings of the Romans at their coronation. Other memorials are to be found in the imperial treasury at Vienna.

It remains to say a few words about the inner workings of Charles's rule—the peculiar features that make his reign so attractive. His was a rich and magnificent court, with its many officials, its seneschal, marshal, chamberlain and cupbearer, its chaplains, notaries and scribes, its long train of brilliant scholars and wits, and of youths being trained for the service of the State. *The inner workings of Charles's reign.*

With external powers a constant intercourse was kept up. The Pope frequently sent envoys, and in 804 himself paid a visit to Charles. King Offa of Mercia, Alfonse of Asturia and Gallicia, and Haroun al Raschid, the caliph of Bagdad, often sent embassies. Haroun, the hero of the Thousand and One Nights' Tales, once sent a present that evidently set the whole Frankish kingdom agog with wonder. It was an elephant, the first that had ever been seen in the land. The chroniclers devote to it more space, as a witty writer has said, than to many a great man of the time. We know the date of its landing in the Gulf of Spezzia, where it passed the winter, when it arrived at Aix, what its name was, and when it died. There is scarcely a writer of those days who has not something to say about Abul Abbas.

A renais-sance

Charles's reign shows a reformation or a renaissance in almost every branch of the administration as well as in art, literature, and learning.

The army.

In *almost* every branch, because in one respect, the manner of drawing upon the resources of the land for military purposes, this reign must be looked upon as having brought evil instead of good. There was a movement in progress over which Charles had no control, and his efforts to force the utmost military service out of every freeman helped to foster the development of the feudal system, and the independence of the feudal lord. The ordinary man, who was unable to perform his service, or to pay the fine for not doing so, was obliged to renounce his freedom.

The courts.

The matter of criminal and civil jurisdiction is too lengthy to be entered into here. Suffice it to say that Charles lightened the burdens of his free men by decreeing that they should only be obliged to appear in court and give judgment three times in the year. Hitherto the " count " had been able to call a court at his own pleasure, and to punish with a fine those who did not appear at his summons. A fixed number of regular judges were now appointed for these extraordinary courts and—a measure which leaves much room for thought— it was ordained that they must be sober when attending to their functions !

Charles's capitularies.

Charles's capitularies go into matters with an astounding amount of detail. His directions for the management of the royal estates, which served as a model for private cultivators, tell us even the proper food to be given to hens, and the different sorts of apples that may or must be grown. The juice is no longer to be pressed out of the grapes by treading on them with the naked feet, and the gardener's house is to be made ornamental by trailing it over with green vines.

In the matter of the coinage of his realm we find Charles changing the standard that had been in use under his predecessors. Henceforward a pound of silver was to be divided into twenty shillings, and each shilling into twelve pence. England can think of no better arrangement to-day. **Coins and prices.**

Charles had difficulty in forcing his people to accept his innovation, for under Pippin the silver pound had been divided into twenty-two shillings, and the ignorant thought to lose by the change. The capitulary of 794 had to put heavy punishments on the refusal to accept the "new denarius"—slaves, for instance, were to be publicly flogged for such an offence.

The prices of food and clothing were also made subjects for legislation. The diet of 794 published a regular tariff for wheat, oats, etc., while that of 808 declared that a cloak of the best fur might be sold for thirty shillings, one of the best cloth for twenty, and an ordinary one for not more than ten.

Against usury, which was defined as " when one demands back more than one gave—when, for example, one lends ten shillings, and then claims more," strict punishments were laid down.

One of the most remarkable traits in Charles the Great was his versatility and the variety of his interests. In the midst of all his warlike and other undertakings he found time to make his court a centre of learning, and of artistic endeavour.

Even the handwriting of the time changes under his auspices. The Merovingian scrawls are the despair of the palæographist, but the so-called Carolingian minuscle which was taught in Charles's schools is as legible as one could wish. Charles himself knew how to read, but not to write. Einhard describes the monarch's efforts to acquire, late in life, the latter art. Often in the middle of the night he would rise from his bed, take the wax tablets that had been under his pillow, and practise forming his letters. But with no **The handwriting of the time.**

great success. The very effort, however, shows the deep interest Charles took in such matters.

In the written language itself a reform takes place. The study of the classic authors which was pursued so industriously had its influence, and the Latin of an Einhard is as pure as any that was written in the whole period from the fall of Rome to the Italian Renaissance.

Charles's literary friends.

The close political union with Italy was most important for the development of art and learning in Charles's empire. From here he summoned numerous scholars to lighten his own leisure hours with their talk, and to teach in the school that he founded at his court for the education of his own children, and those of his nobles. Who has not heard of the playful intercourse between Charles and his paladins, and of the fictitious names they gave each other? Charles was David, Alcuin Horace, Angilbert Homer. When the Emperor's learned friends were absent they wrote to him—mostly in verse, and often interspersing witticisms and hidden allusions. Several such letters have been preserved.

The literature of the time.

The literature of Charles's time concerned itself chiefly with dogmatic questions, or with polemics on problems of the day. We have writings on the question of ordeals, on whether it was right to wage war and to kill one's fellow men, on the position of woman, on usury, on matters of church discipline. " In spite of all defects," says a modern writer,[1] "the fact remains that this literature kept pace with all the more important phases of existence, and that the problems of life were not only set but also thought about and written about. That is the distinctive mark of a living literature and of a cultivated society."

Books.

A number of school books were compiled by the scholars who frequented Charles's court. Some of these, like the collection of homilies of Paulus Diaconus and the " Glossæ Ordinariæ " of Walafrid Strabo, continued in use during the whole of the Middle Ages.

Books in manuscript, dating from Charles's time, may still

[1] Kaufmann.

be read.   Some of them are beautifully ornamented with elaborate initials and miniatures.   The schools of Tours and of St. Denis were famous for their productions in this field. The influence of Italy may be traced here in the introduction of acanthus leaves and other designs, of dainty lamps and candlesticks.   Still more may this influence be seen in the one great illustration of the architecture of Charles's day. The chapel at Aix is modelled directly on that of St. Vitalis in Ravenna, and many of the stones and columns employed in its adornment were carried bodily from the latter city.

CHAPTER VI.

THE REIGN OF LOUIS THE PIOUS.

Evil reign of Louis the Pious.

THE reign of Louis the Pious fills one of the saddest periods of German history. No great undertakings characterize it, no improvements are made, nothing added to the edifice reared by Charles the Great. After a few years, during which the prosperity of the empire is carried along by the impetus that Charles had given it, the process of decay begins. The weak monarch falls more and more under the influence of the clergy, who become possessed with a tremendous sense of their own importance. What caste of priests that is bowed down to in all things with absolute servility, be they Christian ministers or servants of Isis and Osiris, ever has resisted the temptation to pride and arrogance? A woman finally entwines Louis in her meshes, and changes the tenor of his policy even for the worse. His reign ends in a general atmosphere of civil war, family discord, and social ruin.

External enemies.

External enemies in the meantime, like moths fretting at a garment, are rending and tearing the confines of the empire. The Bulgarians oppress its Slavic subjects in the south-east, the Saracens keep the inhabitants of the Spanish March in a constant state of disquietude, and ravage the coasts of the Mediterranean; while the Danes, Norsemen, Normans, or Vikings, as they are alternately called, are already beginning the depredatory tours that are to end with the settlement of Normandy, the conquest of England, and the foundation of a great kingdom in Italy and Sicily.

Louis's piety.

The predicate of "Pious" was given to Louis during or

mmediately after his own reign ; and he well deserved it if
piety represents numberless visits to churches and monasteries, a constant interrogating and torturing of one's own
conscience, and frequently reiterated assertions of one's own
weakness. Such an attitude of mind may be admirable under
certain circumstances, it is fatal in the ruler of a great people.
And Louis's piety, as we shall see, stood him in bad stead in
cases where his own personal interest was concerned.

Louis's first act on reaching Aix, four weeks after his **His auste-**
father's death, was to cleanse the court of the gay and, it **rity.**
must be acknowledged, licentious elements that had been
allowed to revel there in Charles the Great's time. Even the
lives of the royal princesses had not been above reproach, and
that apparently without the least interference from their in-
dulgent father. Did not the historian Nithard spring from
the unsanctified union of Berta and Angilbert ? Louis insisted that his sisters should withdraw to the respective
monasteries the income of which Charles had allotted to
them for their maintenance. The voices of the poets who
had frequently sung the charms of these royal dames became
dumb from this time forward.

Louis's reforms extended even to the public officials of the
court ; these, with few exceptions, were removed, and new
ones appointed in their stead. Among those who were
treated with the most harshness, and who afterwards were
active in various conspiracies, were Adalhard, abbot of Corvey,
and his brother, Wala. It is only a supposition, but not a
groundless one, that their disgrace in this instance hangs
together with the attitude of Louis's nephew, Bernard of
Italy. The latter delayed doing homage to the new emperor,
and only appeared in Aix after a special summons had been
sent to him.

The Pope had played no part in Louis's election. Leo III. **Louis**
was old, was bound by ties of gratitude to the Frankish **and Pope**
rulers, and did not see fit to interfere. But it was otherwise **Stephen IV.**
with his successor, Stephen IV. Two years after Louis's
accession, and scarcely a month after his own consecration,

he hastened to Rheims to meet the emperor. He had brought
with him a golden crown, apparently the one with which Pope
Sylvester was supposed to have been presented by Constan-

The Con-
stantine
Donation.

tine the Great. The so-called Constantine Donation [1] may
have been forged in this connection; certain it is that it was
in existence not many years later. It is a false deed of gift
by which the great emperor, in honour of his conversion to
Christianity, was claimed to have granted to Rome the primacy
over Antioch, Constantinople, Alexandria, and Jerusalem, a
primacy which it did not really enjoy till centuries later;
to have made the Pope chief judge over the clergy, and to
have offered him an imperial crown and dominion over all
Italy.

Louis re-
crowned by
the Pope,
816 A.D.

Four days after Stephen's arrival at Rheims, Louis was
crowned with the Pope's crown. The papacy had preserved
the fiction that the bestowal of the imperial dignity lay in its
hands. The emperor in return confirmed the gifts of his predecessors to the popes, and added an estate in his own West
Frankish lands. Under Stephen's successor, Paschal, this
gift or pact was again ratified, and a copy of the confirmation
charter is extant.

Louis and
the succes-
sion.

In the year 817 an accident took place in Louis's presence
which deeply affected the superstitious monarch, and led him
to take a step that he himself must afterwards have deeply
regretted, proving as it did an immeasurable source of woe to
the royal family and to the whole land. The wooden gallery
that joined the palace at Aix with the chapel gave way, and
injured by its fall a number of people. Having thus been
warned of the insecurity of human life, Louis prepared to
make arrangements for the succession to the empire. It was
no easy problem that was set before him. Heretofore, from
the very beginnings of the Frankish kingdom, it had been the
custom to divide the land between all the legitimate sons of
the last monarch. But the kingdom had become an empire,
and the imperial power was not divisible; had the elder sons

---

[1] See "Select Documents," p. 319.

of Charles the Great lived, that great emperor himself would
have solved the difficulty—exactly how there is no means of
telling. It is barely possible that he would have let the imperial title altogether fall into abeyance. Certain it is that
no mention is made of it in the document which he drew up
in 806, and which divided the land between the three sons
who were then living.

Meanwhile the power of the Church had been growing **Unity versus**
apace, and the Church was an ardent advocate for unity. It **heredity.**
had grown accustomed to the fact of there being one pope
and one emperor. Then, too, every partition of the land
meant dismemberment of various dioceses, for the ecclesiastical possessions had come to be scattered in different parts
of the empire. We have seen, for instance, how Lombard territory had been distributed among Frankish monasteries.

In the present case a compromise was arrived at between **Division of**
the new desire for unity and the accepted principles of **817 A.D.**
heredity. Lothar, Louis's eldest son was raised to the rank
of emperor. The two younger sons, Louis and Pippin, received each a kingdom, but were to remain in a certain dependence upon their brother. These kingdoms—Louis's centred
around Bavaria, Pippin's around Aquitaine—were not to be
further subdivided among the sons of a brother who should
die, but in each case to go to that particular son whom the
people should elect.

The act embodying these regulations [1] was drawn up with
great solemnity, and ratified by all the higher clergy. For
the latter it bore the nature of a compact entered into with
themselves, a guarantee, as it were, for the unity and future
well-being of the Church.

The name of Bernard, King of Italy, was not mentioned in **Bernard's**
the division document. That prince had apparently hoped **rebellion.**
that, on the death of his uncle, his own position would be
bettered, and that more independence would be assured to
him. That hope was now blasted; on the contrary it was

[1] See "Select Documents," p. 201.

expressly stated that Italy was to owe the same allegiance to Lothar that it had to his father.

Bernard and his followers raised the standard of revolt, but their rebellion was badly managed and failed most miserably. The emperor succeeded in guarding the passes of Italy, and himself advanced with an army to Chalons, on the Saône. Here Bernard, despairing of his cause, made his submission and fell at Louis's feet. He was placed under arrest.

In Aix a court was held and judgment passed on the chief rebels. They were found guilty of high treason and condemned to death. Louis changed the sentence to blinding, and the punishment was at once fulfilled. Bernard, however, struggled so during its infliction that he received fatal injuries. He died within three days. His gravestone is still shown in the church of St. Ambrosius, in Milan, whither he seems to have been carried.

Louis the Pious was so embittered by his first experiences of treason and sedition that he at this time caused Charles the Great's three illegitimate sons, Drogo, Hugo, and Theoderic to be shorn and placed in different monasteries. He feared everyone and anyone who might put forth a claim to a portion of the empire.

Lothar crowned emperor, 822 A.D. In 822 Lothar was sent to Italy to take over the rule of that land. Here in the following year, in the church of St. Peter, he was crowned emperor by the Pope. He had, indeed, already issued imperial charters in his own name for Italy, and this ceremony, like the former one at Rheims, is to be looked upon more as a gain for the papacy than for the empire.

Lothar's constitution regarding papal elections, 824 A.D. In the year 824 Lothar was called upon to give judgment in a conflict between the Pope and the citizens of Rome. On this occasion he drew up a "Constitution" which was considered so important in later times that it was embodied in the works on canon law in the days of Gregory VII. It provides for peaceful elections, and maintains the emperor's prerogative as highest judge. The Romans promised to allow no Pope in future to receive the consecration who should not first have taken a certain oath to the emperor. This was almost certainly the oath of fealty in which lay an acknowledgment of the emperor's right to confirm every papal election. Lothar himself, and his son, Louis II., were to enforce this claim to the full, as were also the Ottos and the first Salian emperors. Not until Nicholas II., in 1059, issued his decree placing the election in the hands of the Cardinal bishops [1] did the papacy shake off these trammels which Lothar had been the first to impose.

In 818 Louis the Pious had become a widower. Had he remained so many of the worst evils that broke over the Frankish kingdom would have been averted. But his courtiers urged him to marry again, and tried to tempt him by placing the most beautiful dames of a suitable rank " on view," as the annalist has it. The palm of victory was carried off by Judith, the daughter of that Count Guelph, the name of whose race was to become so familiar in later mediæval times.

Louis weds Judith, 819 A.D.

Judith was more than beautiful; she was already famous for her accomplishments, chief among which was the dexterity with which she played the organ. In decision of character, not to say obstinacy, she far outstripped her royal consort.

A problem of a most delicate and difficult nature was set for the ambitious wife and the yielding husband by the birth of a son. The Frankish kingdom had been solemnly and definitely, with the consent of the clergy and the nobles, divided into three parts. How was this new heir, in whom all his mother's interests centred, to be properly appanaged?

Birth of Charles the Bald.

Judith showed her real character from the time of her son's birth. Like a lioness guarding her whelp she fought for his welfare; it mattered little to her that she reduced her husband to the lowest depths of degradation, and that she plunged the land into civil and fratricidal war. The court became a hot-bed of intrigue and deceit, and one wonders whether to be

---

[1] See "Select Documents," p. 361.

more disgusted at the weakness of the emperor, the hard-heartedness and disloyalty of his sons, or the greed and relentlessness of Judith.

Evil results of Louis's piety. Louis's piety meanwhile grew apace. He soon repented of his severity against the followers of Bernard, pardoned them, and even restored their confiscated estates. At the diet of Attigny (822) he made a public confession of guilt, and did penance for the blinding of his nephew as well as for having incarcerated his stepbrothers, Drogo, Hugo, and Theoderic. This self-humiliation was, politically, almost suicidal. It increased the influence of the bishops and showed them a means of humbling their monarch, of which they were later to make excellent use.

The assembly at Attigny reminds one of the modern camp-meetings of Methodists, Baptists, and other children of the emotions. After the emperor had spoken and summed up his bad doings a similar confession was made in the name of the bishops. They declared that they had often been negligent as well in their manner of living as in their teachings and their official acts. They promised to do better for the future, but, almost in the same breath, demanded the restitution of the Church lands that had been confiscated by the earlier Carolingians. Such a restitution, indeed, was practically impossible; the mere mention of the subject was enough to throw many of the nobles among whom these lands had been distributed into a fever of excitement.

Decline of the empire's greatness. The once glorious nation of the Franks was rapidly going to ruin and destruction. All the writings of the time that exist—reports of bishops, protocols of diets, visions supposed to have been seen by saints (was not Walafrid Strabo, author of "De Visionibus Wettini," a direct precursor of Dante?), not to speak of chronicles, annals, and letters—give forth one continued wail of complaint. In these literary productions the leading personages of the time are often severely criticized. "They love bribes and not justice," says one writer, "they fear man more than God, they are deaf to the weeping of widows and orphans." The "counts" were accused of making common cause with thieves and other criminals. It was declared that the territorial lords had two kinds of weights and measures, the one for receiving, the other for giving out; while the clergy were charged with simony, extravagance, and neglect of duty. Superstitious belief in magic and in love potions, not to speak of miracles, seems to have pervaded all circles.

To add to the general demoralization came year after year of bad harvest and of plague. Einhard, the chronicler, in his account of the transference of certain relics in 827 causes a dispossessed demon to speak as follows: "I am a follower and disciple of Satan, and was for a long time usher at the gate of hell, but now for some years I have been ravaging the Frankish kingdom. Grain, corn, wine, and all other products of the soil, we have, as we were told, destroyed and annihilated; the cattle we have killed through sickness; we have spread plague and pestilence among the people. All the misfortunes and all the evils which they have deservedly endured for some time have fallen upon them at our instigation on account of the people's own wickedness and the manifold injustice of those who are set in authority over them." "Ah! how deep is our age sunken," continues Einhard himself, "when not good men but evil demons are our teachers, and we are warned to better ourselves by the instigators of crime and originators of vice!"

Bad harvests.

All the elements likely to cause an upheaval of society were present in abundance—want, oppression, misrule. Louis the Pious, indeed, promised to try and reform all the evils for which he might personally be considered responsible, and for this purpose called an assembly at Aix (828). Einhard was among those who took part in its deliberations. Here it was decided to hold a number of synods in different parts of the kingdom, and also to despatch *missi dominici* in all directions who should inquire into particular cases and bring them to the notice of the emperor, who appointed one day in the week for receiving the reports on such matters.

Efforts at reform.

The wording of Louis's promulgation in connection with

Louis's synods.

the calling of the synods is most characteristic of the man. He recognizes that the more he should not have sinned the more he has done so. He desires through God's grace to gain pardon by rendering worthy satisfaction and by doing penance. He promises to better what has hitherto, through his own tardiness and ignorance, been neglected.

The same deep self-humiliation, the same rending of the heart and laying bare of its weaknesses before the eyes of the whole world.

We have the acts of one of the synods that Louis caused to be called. The bishops soundly rate the court for the intrigues and ambitious plannings that are going on in its midst. They also beg the emperor to impress on his sons and on his nobles the power and dignity of the ecclesiastical calling, and to remind them of an alleged saying of Constantine to the effect that priests might judge men, but might be judged of no man.

Charles the Bald a brand of discord.

But Louis soon lost interest in the proposed reforms ; by the time these admonitions reached him he had become deeply entangled in matters in which the clergy were hinderers rather than allies. The Empress Judith now steps to the fore—it was probably against her that the animadversions of the synod had been directed. The time had come for creating a worthy portion for the youthful Charles—the "new Benjamin," as the contemporary, Walafrid Strabo, calls him in one of his poems.

His new kingdom.

In August, 829, the emperor, through a simple edict, presented his youngest son with a kingdom composed of Allemania, Alsace, and a part of Burgundy. This gift was made at the expense of the oldest son, Lothar, who had agreed, indeed, to help Judith in providing for her offspring, but who could not possibly have expected to be deprived of so large a slice of his own prospective heritage. He soon began to gather round him the different elements of discontent, while Pippin and the young Louis rallied to him, feeling the insecurity of their own positions should their father see fit to indulge in any more arbitrary acts of the kind.

Lothar's presence had become so inconvenient, not to say **Bernard of** dangerous, that he was dismissed to Italy, and ordered to **Barcelona.** remain there. Count Bernard of Barcelona, who had held the chief command in the Spanish March, was meanwhile summoned to court, where he soon became, as the annals tell us, "the second man in the empire, next to the emperor." In him Judith found a devoted and fearless supporter. The two had one will and one common interest, and so intimate did they become that the blackest insinuations were openly made against the fair fame of the empress. Whether with right or no will never be known. In the writings of the time the most positive accusations to the one effect are met with the most positive denials on the other.

Matters soon came to a crisis. The emperor, aware of the **Rebellion.** growing discontent, strove to give other occupation to the thoughts of his people by engaging in a foreign or at least distant war. In Brittany there had been a petty rebellion against the Frankish overlordship, and the combined forces of the empire were summoned to appear in arms. Louis himself left Aix on Ash Wednesday, the various contingents were to betake themselves to the border of Brittany in such wise that they should meet together in Holy Week. On Maunday Thursday a muster of the army was to take place. But before that time a revolt had broken out, and the troops had mutinied, calling upon Lothar and Pippin to take up arms against their father. Louis the Pious was bitterly reproached with having begun a campaign, and a useless one at that, in the sacred season of Lent.

Bernard of Barcelona soon found the court too unsafe a **Humiliation** resting-place. He escaped to Spain, while Judith sought **of Louis and** refuge in the monastery of St. Mary in Laon. Those sacred **Judith.** walls did not long protect her; she was seized and removed to Poictiers, and made to promise that she would herself take the veil, and that she would induce the emperor to become a monk.

The diet of Compiègne, at which the revolutionary party had the controlling influence, recognized Lothar as co-regent.

His name reappears in the imperial charters, in which, since his dismissal to Italy, it had been no longer mentioned.

Louis still retained the name of emperor, but as a matter of fact, to use the expression of one of his contemporaries, he was " rather honourably placed in the retired list." Every influence was brought to bear to induce him to renounce the world. Lothar kept him, as it were, in liberal custody, and appointed monks to be constantly with him, and to work upon his feelings.

The further history of Louis the Pious shows a continual succession of surprises. We have left him crushed to earth, with apparently no one to take pity on or aid him. The next moment his cause was high in the ascendant, but before long he was to sink deeper than ever in a mire of ignominy. An unhallowed fate, or rather the unbending will of the empress, drove him on and impelled him to constantly throw new brands on the discord that was smouldering between himself and his sons.

After the diet of Compiègne Lothar kept the reins of government in his own hands, but was unable to stem the public evils. He was not the man to take radical measures for the relief of the people, nor was his position an enviable one as regarded his two brothers, who were unwilling to be without share in the fruits of victory.

The whole land was meanwhile seething with discontent at the evil state of things in general. Strangely enough a reaction was started in Louis's favour, by the very monks who had been appointed to direct his thoughts away from things temporal to things heavenly and eternal. One of them went in the emperor's name to negotiate with the younger sons, Pippin and Louis, and to offer them an increase of territory if they would rally once more to their father. The mission was successful, and it was arranged that a diet should be held, not, as the revolutionary party wanted, in the western part of the empire, where Lothar had more adherents, but at Nimwegen, which was more accessible to the Saxons and to the other elements that were friendly to the old emperor.

The latter at this time showed unwonted decision, and actually imposed a certain amount of respect on his rebellious son. He even stepped forward at Nimwegen as Lothar's protector, and appeared before a threatening crowd holding him by the hand. The assembly of Nimwegen passed measures against the leaders of the recent rebellion. Judith was to be released from confinement, but was to appear at a future diet to be held at Aix. Here if any one might choose to bring accusations against her, she was either to clear herself of the charges or to submit to the sentence of the diet.

No one appeared at Aix to accuse Judith and she was soon reinstated in all her rights. At a later diet, Bernard of Barcelona offered to join in judicial combat with any one who still charged him of adultery with the empress. But the tide had by this time completely changed and no accuser stepped forward. Be it here remarked, however, that Bernard's justification of his moral character was without effect on his political career. His rôle as prime adviser had been played to the end. Lothar himself was excluded from participation in the affairs of the empire. The other conspirators were judged guilty of death, but the sentence was commuted to imprisonment in some cases and banishment in others.

Judith reinstated.

The emperor was now fully reinstated in power, but once more the old unworthy policy began. A new division of the empire was taken in hand, according to which Lothar was to be restricted to Italy, and the other lands were to be divided equally between Pippin, Louis, and Charles the Bald. Every effort was made to induce Lothar to consent quietly to this new arrangement. He was received with honour at Ingelheim and many of his former followers were pardoned.

New division and new dangers.

For the emperor new dangers were meanwhile arising. His son Pippin, so recently his ally, began to show a disobedient and rebellious spirit. He delayed answering a summons to court for so long, that when he did finally appear he was treated almost as a prisoner. Judith meanwhile was lusting after his kingdom for her beloved son. When this became clear to him, Pippin escaped from Aix and hastened back to Aquitaine, while the emperor and his councillors called together an army against him. The young King of Bavaria, Louis the German as he was later called, was ordered to march to his father's assistance, but instead of doing so he, too, unfolded the standard of rebellion, invading the kingdom of his young half-brother. Lothar, too, ceased to conceal the wrath that he had felt at the humiliations inflicted upon him.

Pippin's kingdom given to Charles the Bald.

The emperor once again showed one of those rare sparks of courage and decision that made him seem for a moment like a worthy successor of Charles the Great. Louis the German was driven back to Bavaria, and an imperial army invaded Aquitaine. Pippin humbled himself before his father, and was sent off in digrace to Treves. He was dispossessed of his land, which was at once handed over to Charles the Bald. Pippin soon escaped from Treves and returned to his former kingdom where he was able to raise an army from among his old subjects and to defeat a force sent against him by the emperor.

Interference of Gregory IV.

A civil war, and a more dangerous one than ever, was now in full progress. Lothar, Louis, and Pippin, were all three in arms and they were joined now by the strangest ally that had ever been seen in the Frankish kingdom. In company with Lothar Pope Gregory IV. had crossed the Alps, ostensibly to reconcile the sons with their father, and to preserve the unity of the empire. It is a significant mark of the small influence exercised as yet by the Roman See in Germany that German bishops were foremost among those who reproached the Pope for his unwarranted interference. A number of them refused to come to him, and declared that, should he see fit to excommunicate them, they would no longer recognize his authority.

The Field of Lies.

And, indeed, the Pope's whole conduct was neither creditable nor even honourable. It is generally believed to have been through his wiles and arts of persuasion that the disgraceful scene took place on the Rothfeld, near Colmar, which caused

that little spot in Alsace to rejoice thereafter in the name of
" Campus Mentitus " or " Field of Lies."

The army of the father lay encamped opposite to that of the
sons. The Pope crossed over and demanded to see the
emperor. He was well received, and remained for some days
as Louis's guest, discussing with him the possibility of a
reconciliation, and being allowed meanwhile to pass freely to
and fro among the soldiers. The night after Gregory's
return to the rebel camp the majority of the imperial troops
deserted their leader and went over to the enemy. Louis had
nothing to do but to acquiesce in his fate, and was soon,
together with Judith and Charles the Bald, a prisoner in the
hands of his sons.

By decree of the Pope, as we are told, and of the assembled
people, Lothar took the reigns of government completely into
his own hands. His charters of this period are dated, " the
first year of the rule of the Emperor Lothar in Francia." Louis
the German, too, omits his father's name from the public
documents issued in Bavaria, and only Pippin continues to
date in the old manner.

Lothar as ruler.

A new division of the empire was undertaken by the elder
brothers, in which no regard whatever was paid to that source
of all the discord, Charles the Bald. Three equal and independent states were formed, and we hear nothing now of
Lothar's supremacy over his brothers.

New divi-sion.

Louis the Pious, in the meantime, was taken to Soissons
and placed in the monastery of St. Medard. A writing of
Agobard, of Lyon, composed at this juncture, speaks of him
as the " emperor that was."

Lothar hastened to summon a diet at Compiègne which
should decide upon the final fate of his father. He was
determined now that the latter should drink the cup of degradation to the very dregs. The diet was attended only by
Lothar's own supporters ; Louis the German and Pippin were
both absent. The protocol of the diet of Compiègne tells us
how, through Louis's short-sightedness and neglect, the
empire has sunk to such a condition of shame and misery

Louis's humiliation at Com-piègne.

that not only do its friends mourn over it, but its enemies regard it with mockery.   Louis is declared to have forfeited the temporal rule by divine counsel and by the authority of the Church.   He is exhorted to beware lest he forfeit, too, the salvation of his soul.

Penance at Soissons, 833 A.D. From Compiègne a number of bishops proceeded to Soissons, where they induced the emperor, now utterly broken in spirit, to submit to whatever penance they might see fit to impose.   They made him appear before a large assembly in the church of the monastery, to confess, not once but four times, that he had offended God, given umbrage to the Church of Christ, and brought confusion upon the people.   He was compelled the while to hold in his hand a paper that had been given him, a paper which contained a list of the sins for which he was to ask forgiveness.   Sacrilege and murder were among them as well as every public act that was open to disapproval from the beginning of his reign.

This scene in the church of St. Medard in Soissons has few equals in history for darkness of colouring.   If Henry IV., later, bowed before Gregory VII., and confessed his sins and promised to do penance, it was a voluntary act, performed with a deep set purpose, and he rose from the ordeal still a king.   Louis the Pious, for the moment at least, gave up his will, his conscience and his crown, to the bishops of his realm.   He obeyed their commands weakly and blindly.

Revulsion of feeling. All of this had been the work of Lothar, who at this time also tried every means to induce his father to become a monk. But, through this severity and persistency, he overreached himself.   There were others in high places who were not willing that the emperor's humiliation should be so deep, and that anyone should so relentlessly seek his ruin.

Louis, the young king of Bavaria, sent envoys to Lothar to demand a milder treatment for his father.   After repeated and vain attempts in this direction he induced his brother Pippin to join with him in securing the release of Louis the Pious by force of arms.   The two were aided by a large party of nobles who were dissatisfied with Lothar's rule.   It was not long before the captive emperor was once more at liberty, and before, in St. Denis, he was solemnly reinstated in power and received back into the bosom of the Church. He appeared in public adorned with the imperial insignia.

In the case of Louis the Pious better than in that of almost any emperor of the Middle Ages one can follow the course of events in the changed wording of the public documents. The charters that he issued after his reinstatement speak of himself as " Louis, emperor through a renewal of God's mercy ! " *Louis's re- instatement.*

Abbot Rhrabanus of Fulda wrote at this time an essay " Concerning the Reverence of Sons towards their Fathers, and of Subjects towards their Kings." It was, as may be imagined, written in the interests of Louis. The whole tide of public opinion had swung round once more to the emperor's side.

It remained to reckon with Lothar. The latter gained two important victories over imperial armies, but at last, seeing that there was no hope of ultimate success, made his submission. He promised to return to Italy and to mix no more in the affairs of the empire. *Lothar's submission.*

In February, 835, a diet assembled at Diedenhofen. Here in most solemn form it was declared that the emperor's deposition and humiliation had been contrary to canon and civil law. At Metz in the same month there took place in the cathedral a scene which was the counterpart of that former one in St. Medard. Seven archbishops performed the service for the reception of a penitent into the fold of the Church. In the name of all the bishops who had been concerned, Ebbo of Rheims ascended the pulpit and declared the unlawfulness of the former proceedings against the emperor. Ebbo himself, who had played so large a share in those same proceedings was forced to declare himself unworthy of the episcopal dignity and to resign his See. *Louis's triumph.*

It would be a fitting allegory were one to represent Louis the Pious as a ship, and the popular favour of his subjects as rising and falling waves. He was now on the crest of such a wave, but how long would he remain there? He had narrowly

H

escaped stranding, would he have sense enough to avoid running near to the same breakers?

The old problem. The old problem meanwhile, the only serious one with which Louis seems to have concerned himself during the whole course of his reign, still remained to be solved. There were three kingdoms and four kings, and there was still an ambitious empress who was determined to set things right in her own way.

At the expense of Louis of Bavaria, who, in consequence of his services to his father, had been led to expect a vast increase of territory, a new kingdom was carved out for Charles the Bald. It stretched from Frisia in the north to Toul, Sens and Troyes in the south. The nobles and vassals of this vast district did homage to their new lord at the emperor's command.

Rebellion. Again the spirit of rebellion raised its head in the Frankish kingdom. The younger Louis held a meeting with Lothar near Trent, and was called to account by his father for having done so. Full of wrath and bitterness he left Nimwegen after a stormy interview with his father.

Charles the Bald had meanwhile been declared of age. Louis the Pious had girded him with the sword, and had placed a crown upon his head—a ceremony that had been omitted in the case of his brothers.

Death of Pippin, 838 A.D. In December, 838, matters were complicated by the death of Pippin. The young Louis was at this time under arms near Mayence, but was soon forced to retreat before the imperial army.

Judith determined that Aquitaine should be added to the portion of Charles the Bald, or at least that the latter should profit by his half-brother's death. It mattered little that Pippin had left behind him two youthful sons.

New Division. It was first necessary that a reconciliation should be brought about with Lothar who, since his return to Italy, had been brooding over his wrongs. He was induced to come to Worms and publicly to prostrate himself before his father. After this performance—a comedy so often repeated in these times that it must have lost its significance—negotiations were begun concerning an entirely new division. It was decided, with the exception of Bavaria, to separate the whole empire into two equal shares. Lothar was given the lands east of the Maas and of the Rhone. What Protean shapes the parts of Charles the Great's empire had been obliged to take at different times since his death!

Of course the young Louis felt himself wronged and disinherited, and prepared anew for war. In Aquitaine, too, a rebellion broke out, and Pippin's son and namesake was chosen king.

The emperor hastened from one task to the other, but his strength gave out and, after a short illness, he died at Ingelheim (June 20th, 840). He had sent the imperial insignia, the crown and sword, to Lothar, exhorting him to protect his mother Judith and his brother Charles. He sent his pardon to Louis, but wished him to remember that he had "brought down the gray hairs of his father with sorrow to the grave." The civil wars and disturbances that had taken place during the reign of Louis the Pious were but the forerunners of a fiercer struggle that was to come after his death.

Death of Louis the Pious, 840 A.D.

CHAPTER VII.

THE LATER CAROLINGIANS.

Lothar claims the whole empire.

LOTHAR, on his father's death, at once demanded for himself the whole empire. He appealed to the division act of 817, which had never been formally annulled. The old war-cry of "unity" seems to have drawn around him a large party, especially among the bishops, whom he still further won by reinstating Ebbo in the See of Rheims. The young Pippin of Aquitaine also rallied to his banner.

To Louis of Bavaria there was left no alternative except to unite with his half-brother Charles the Bald. Lothar, indeed, tried to reckon with each of his brothers separately, and managed to gain valuable time by appointing trysts and making truces that he never intended to keep.

Battle of Fontenoy, 841 A.D.

Finally, a battle that was looked upon as an ordeal or "judgment of God" was fought at Fontenoy in June, 841. Pippin of Aquitaine had by this time arrived in Lothar's camp at the head of considerable forces. The historian, Nithard, to whom we owe most of our knowledge of these times, took part in the battle as a follower of Charles the Bald. With naïve vanity he ascribes the victory in large part to himself.

Lothar's defeat.

Lothar was defeated after a hard and brave struggle, in which the losses were heavy on both sides. One contemporary writer assures us that had there been ten more warriors like Lothar himself, the empire need never have been divided.

The battle of Fontenoy was not absolutely decisive, for Lothar did not yet despair. He sought reinforcements by holding out his hand to a discontented party in Saxony made

up of freemen and leets who were opposed to the nobles.
Nor was he above taking the Normans as allies, plunderers
and enemies of the empire as they were.

Louis and Charles, meanwhile, confirmed their mutual good
faith and constancy by an oath taken at Strassburg (February,
842).

Oath of
Strassburg,
842 A.D.

In itself a not unnatural and not particularly noteworthy
proceeding—and yet the act of alliance here drawn up is one
of the most interesting documents in history. We suddenly
are made aware that the language of the western part of the
Frankish Empire had become completely Romanized, while
that of the eastern part had remained German. The political
division that was about to take place had been preceded by
one that dealt with everyday life. Charles the Bald swore
his oath in German so as to be understood by his brother's
followers; Louis, on the contrary, spoke a tongue that is
midway between the Latin and the modern French.[1]

The Strassburg oath, then, is a common monument, when
in their infancy, of the two chief languages spoken on the
continent of Europe to-day.

The allied brothers next advanced against Lothar, who
retired to Lyons. An assembly of the clergy at Aix, freed from
the influence of his presence, proceeded as they had once done
in the case of Louis the Pious at Compiègne. They declared
that Lothar was a perjurer, that he was incapable of ruling,
and that he was responsible for all the murder, adultery,
arson, and other deeds of shame that the Church had been
obliged to witness. They gave their sanction to the division
of the empire between the two brothers and bade Lothar
confine himself henceforward to Italy.

Louis and
Charles
against
Lothar.

[1] Charles's oath begins: "In godes minna ind in thes christiânes
folches ind unser bêdhero gehaltnissi . . . . sô haldih thesau mînan
bruodher, sôso man mit rehtu sînan bruodher scal, in thin thaz er mig
sô sama duo . . . ."

And Louis's: "Pro deo amur et pro christian poblo et nostro
commun salvament . . . . si salvarai eo cist meon fradre Karlo et in
aiudha et in cadhuna cosa, si cum om per dreit son fradra salvar dist,
in o quid il mi altresi fazet . . . ."

At this time the very existence of the Frankish kingdom began to be threatened by the Normans. They ran their boats into the rivers, plundering as they went. They advanced up the Seine and even took Rouen.

The need for peace was evident, and Lothar, whose task had been so much harder than he had expected, showed himself ready for a reconciliation. The brothers came together on an island in the Saône near Macon. It was the first time that they had all met since parting on the Field of Lies.

Treaty of Verdun, 843 A.D.

A preliminary peace was established and it was decided that the three claimants should keep their individual kingdoms of Italy, Bavaria, and Aquitaine, and that the rest of the territory should be divided into three equal parts. One hundred and twenty men, forty on the part of each brother, were appointed to measure and appraise the land, to calculate the income from the different estates and bishoprics, and to report at a later date.

By August, 843, the survey had been ended and the final treaty was drawn up and signed at Verdun. Lothar, who retained the imperial title, although no sovereignty over his brothers was now expressed by it, received the middle kingdom —a long narrow strip of land extending from the North Sea to the Mediterranean, from the Frisian Islands to the south of Italy. Charles the Bald was given the West Frankish kingdom, and Louis the German the provinces east of the Rhine. A district on the left bank of that river, including the town of Worms, was also given to Louis " on account of the abundance of wine " as a chronicler tells us.

For the Germans the treaty of Verdun was the birthday of their nation, although Germany long was to bear no name but that of the East Frankish kingdom.

Further disputes between the brothers.

The years which followed the drawing up of the Treaty of Verdun show at first an effort to preserve, in public at least, the appearance of unity between the brothers, and then a series of constant struggles of the one to gain this or that advantage over the other. The relations between Lothar and

Charles were at first influenced by the fact that one of the latter's vassals ran away with the former's daughter and that Lothar in some way held his brother responsible for the deed. No sooner was this dispute arranged than Louis the German, who had brought about the reconciliation, saw his two brothers forming an alliance in opposition to himself.

The enmity of the kings against each other could not conduce to the preservation of law and order in general, the less so as the Treaty of Verdun itself, dividing as it did different districts that had formerly been united, different church dioceses, and even the different possessions of one and the same great noble, gave rise to constant quarrels. "Innocent blood is shed without being avenged, the fear of kings and of laws has departed from men, with closed eyes the people are approaching hell-fire," says a writer of the time.

General confusion.

The people of Aquitaine, which Charles the Bald had succeeded in wresting from his nephew Pippin II., were not satisfied with Charles's rule and called in Louis the German. The latter first sent his son and then himself invaded his brother's kingdom, and put Charles to flight. One of Louis's charters of the year 858 is dated " the first year of the rule in West Francia."

Louis the German invades France.

Charles the Bald's secular nobles went over to the new ruler, but the bishops maintained a firm attitude and finally preserved the land to its rightful king. A synod of Quiersy, under the leadership of Hincmar of Rheims, drew up a writing in which Louis the German was warned to desist ; the strongest possible language was used, and the example was brought forward of those who had sown discord in the time of Louis the Pious.

In the end Louis, who had been looked to as a saviour but had brought no salvation, was unable to maintain his new position, and was glad enough, in 860, to sign the peace of Coblenz with Charles the Bald.

The West Frankish bishops, Hincmar at their head, had tried to make Louis do penance for his invasion of their land, and a synod sent a deputation to him to Worms for this

The West Frankish Bishops.

purpose. " But he answered from his raised throne," says the official report of the embassy, "that he could not take notice of the decrees of the synod until he should have conferred with his bishops. And so it is that that which was done in the general interest of the church and the people was without effect upon him."

Louis the German's character and rule.

Louis the German was the only one of the grandsons of Charles the Great who possessed to some extent the qualities of a great ruler. He had shown himself strong in numerous battles against the Bohemians and Moravians who had troubled his eastern boundaries.

Under Louis a number of church synods were held of which the acts have been preserved. These synods entered the lists for law and order, they placed penalties on different crimes and established a system of judicial proceeding. A free man, for instance, accused of the murder of a priest was to clear himself by the oath of twelve approved men ; a bondsman was to submit his cause to the ordeal or judgment of God and to walk barefoot over twelve red-hot ploughshares.

The synods concerned themselves, too, with the oppression of the people by the nobles, in fact with almost all the matters which had formerly been regulated by means of the capitularies.

Louis the German's chief attention between the years 862 and 873 was devoted to putting down rebellions of his own sons Carlmann, Charles and Louis III., into the details of which it is not necessary to enter. They were a repetition, on a smaller scale, of the wars of Louis the Pious with his sons, and they had to do with the same cause : dissatisfaction at the allotment of their future shares in the kingdom.

Death of Lothar I., 855 A.D.

Lothar I. died in 855, and was buried in the church of Prüm, where the casket containing his bones was found and opened in the year 1860.

Lothar left Italy to his son Louis, and the rest of the kingdom to his sons Lothar II. and Charles, of whom the latter soon died. The feeble reign of Lothar II., whose land, in honour of himself, received the name of Lotharingia or

Lorraine, caused Louis the German and Charles the Bald to cast lusting eyes on their nephew's possessions.

It was this Lothar II., whose famous or infamous divorce case, of which Hincmar of Rheims has left us a detailed and revolting account, gave an opening for the interference in foreign affairs of the first of the really great popes. Nicolas I. put through his will against Lothar in spite of the opposition of the whole Lorraine clergy.

The rise of the papal power.

While the empire had been growing weaker the papacy had been growing stronger. It was not long after the treaty of Verdun that the forged Isidorian decretals, of which Nicholas was the first pope to make use, were given to the world. They were a collection of nearly a hundred letters declared to have been written by earlier popes and giving the sanction of antiquity to many an exalted claim. The aim and object of the fabrication seems to have been to remove the higher clergy as well as their landed possessions from the jurisdiction of the State and to place them under that of the Church.

The Church for centuries was to make use of these decretals, they were the armoury from which Gregory VII. was to take many of his most potent weapons.

In 857 Lothar II. had put away his rightful wife, Teutberga, and made most shameful accusations against her. This he did for love of a certain Waldrada, whom he intended to make his queen. Teutberga submitted her cause to the ordeal; her champion plunged his arm in the boiling water and drew it forth uninjured.

Divorce of Lothar II.

Lothar, nevertheless, did not abandon his purpose. He induced two synods of the Lorraine clergy, which were held at Aix, to listen to a forced declaration of Teutberga's to the effect that she was guilty of unnatural crime, and to declare the marriage null and void. A third synod held in 862 gave Lothar permission to wed Waldrada.

Teutberga found refuge with Charles the Bald, who had his own grounds for wishing to prevent the dissolution of Lothar's marriage. That marriage had been childless and was likely to remain so, and Charles, not wishing to lose a fair heritage, did his utmost to keep the new union from being legalized by the Church. He even went so far as to invade Lorraine.

Interference of Pope Nicholas I.

Teutberga appealed to the Pope; Lothar, on the other hand, formed an alliance with Louis the German, promising to cede to him Alsace.

Pope Nicholas I. sent two legates to look into the matter of Teutberga's appeal; a synod was held at Metz at which Lothar had been ordered to appear under penalty of the curse of Rome. Again judgment was given against the hapless Teutberga, the papal legates having been won over by bribery and corruption.

Nicholas I. did not permit himself to be deceived. He went through the acts of the synod of Metz and caused a Roman synod to declare that the judgment had been false. The archbishops of Cologne and Treves, who had taken part in the Metz proceedings and had come to Rome to announce the result of the deliberations, were deposed. They laid a solemn protest against the Pope's action on the grave of St. Peter. Lothar was again threatened with the ban.

The Emperor Louis II. invades Rome.

The two archbishops had hastened to Lothar's brother, the Emperor Louis II. Louis marched against Rome, where the Pope ordained fasting and processions to the end that God might inspire the invader with respect for the authority of the Holy See. Nicholas himself took refuge in St. Peter's, where he was obliged to remain for two days without food or drink.

Fortunately for Nicholas, Louis was taken with a violent fever, which seemed to him a judgment of God. He reconciled himself to the Pope.

Temporary submission of Lothar to Nicholas.

Nicholas was able for the time to bring Lothar II. to submission. The latter was in dread that his uncles, who continually reproached him with his profligacy and unworthiness, might unite and divide his kingdom between them. In 865 he allowed twelve of his vassals to take an oath in his name to the effect that he would in future regard Teutberga as his lawful wife and queen. Waldrada was carried off by the papal legate to Italy, but escaped from her reverend gaoler at

Pavia and returned to Lorraine. In the following year she was placed in the ban by the Pope.

Lothar's hatred of Teutberga blazed forth anew, and he recommenced his intrigues against her. She was obliged to send a confession of guilt to Rome, and to declare that she would voluntarily resign the crown.

Nicholas would hear of no such thing, and used stronger and stronger language in his letters on the matter. Louis the German and Charles the Bald evidently expected that the Pope would ban and depose their nephew, and that the clergy of Lorraine would obey the sentence. They met together at Metz and swore an oath that, in the event of a division of Lothar's kingdom, one would not claim a greater share than the other.

Nicholas I. died in 867. Teutberga tried every means to induce his successor, Adrian II., to pronounce the divorce that would free her from her persecutions, but in vain. **Adrian II., 867-872.**

A synod, however, was to have the final decision in the matter, and Lothar was allowed in the meantime to come to Rome and plead his cause. He swore an oath to the Pope that he had had no intercourse with Waldrada since the time of Teutberga's reinstatement—"pretending, like Judas, to have a good conscience in the matter," as Hincmar tells us. Adrian called a synod to meet early in the following year, and legates in the meantime were to investigate the affair and to treat with the Lorraine clergy.

The divorce drama, however, had by this time been played to the end. Lothar was seized with an attack of fever, and died in Lucca in August, 869. Teutberga retired to a nunnery, and Waldrada, who for ten years had been the cause of such unending complications, did the same. **Death of Lothar II., 869 A.D.**

It is interesting to note that this Waldrada was the grand-mother of that Hugo of Italy and Burgundy, whose daughter-in-law, Adelaide, became queen of Otto I. and mother of Otto II.

At the time when Lothar's death occurred, Louis the German himself happened to be chained to a bed of sickness, while all his available forces were occupied in an expedition against the Slavs.

The treaty of Mersen, 870 A.D. Charles the Bald, by right of the strongest, seized possession of the whole of Lorraine, being aided in his endeavours by the clergy of that land. Louis the German, as soon as his health permitted, threatened his brother with war, fully intimidated the man of small courage, and finally compelled him to sign the treaty of Mersen (870). It is recorded that Louis, on his way to Mersen, had met with an accident and broken two of his ribs, but that he appeared before Charles, physically as well as figuratively, unbending, and as though nothing had happened.

By the treaty of Mersen, Lorraine was divided by a line running from north to south; as it happened the division coincided pretty nearly with the natural race distinctions. The Frisians, the Allemannians, and the Ripuarian Franks, who already spoke the German language, now formed part of Louis's share. The Rhine was at last a German stream.

Louis II. as emperor.   The imperial crown had fallen to Louis II., eldest son of Lothar I., who had received Italy before his father's death. The Pope had assumed undisputed the right of imposing the crown, a right which had never been acknowledged either by Charles the Great or by Louis the Pious. Each of those monarchs in turn had conferred the crown on his son of his own authority—the papal re-crowning that had in each case taken place had been looked upon as a kindly but not as a necessary act. Louis II.'s power was insignificant and did not extend beyond the Alps. He did good services against the Saracens in South Italy. For a time, in 871, he was a prisoner in the hands of his own discontented subjects, who plundered his treasure and threatened his life. He died without heirs in 875, having named Carlmann, son of Louis the German, as his successor.

Charles the Bald as emperor.   Again Charles the Bald tried to reap an unfair advantage, and this time succeeded. He drove one of his nephews out of Italy at the point of the sword, made a treaty with another which he never kept, and, finally, induced the

Pope, John VIII., to place the imperial crown on his own head.

Louis the German made an inroad into his brother's land, but died in the following year, 876. His three sons no longer carried out the analogy with himself and his brothers, for they remained with each other on peaceful terms. Death of Louis the German, 867 A.D.

Charles the Bald kept the honour he had coveted and won. After Louis the German's death, moreover, he tried to break the treaty of Mersen, and to possess himself of Lorraine. He even dreamt of regaining for himself the whole inheritance of his father.

He invaded Lorraine, but met with a resistance, altogether surprising and emphatic, on the part of his nephew Louis III. Charles, "the new Sennacharib," as he was called, or "the man with the heart of a hare," was put to flight at Andernach, and the young German monarch carried off a rich booty. The victory secured the unity and independence of Germany. The battle of Andernach.

Charles the Bald died in 877, and Carlmann came forward as claimant for the imperial crown, and entered Italy with an army. He was still negotiating with the Pope for the object of his desires when death put an end to all his plans (880). He left a son, born out of wedlock, Arnulf of Carinthia, the later king and emperor. Death of Charles the Bald and of Carlmann, 877 and 880.

Louis III., the victor of Andernach, died two years after Carlmann, and the whole German kingdom, together with the claim to Italy, fell to the third brother Charles III., surnamed the Fat. Death of Louis the German, 882 A.D.

Charles the Fat was a true descendant of Louis the Pious. Sickly by nature, and sunk in the petty affairs of his own conscience, he had no time left for the great questions of public utility. And yet it was into the lap of this man that fortune had determined to shake every possible honour. Charles the Fat, King and Emperor.

In 879, as Carlmann's death approached, Pope John VIII. had looked to Charles as his liberator, and had given him, with Carlmann's consent, the crown of Italy. Two years later he had bestowed upon him the imperial consecration. In 887 the nobles of the West Frankish kingdom also, on the death of the grandsons of Charles the Bald, offered him the crown of their land.

For a brief space all the domains of Charles the Great were reunited in the hand of one of his descendants. But the virtue had gone out of the Carolingian race.

Saracen inroads. As a constant background to the events of the half century following the death of Louis the Pious went the plundering expeditions of the Saracens in the south of Europe, and of the Normans in the north and west.

The Saracens had conquered Bari, in South Italy, and had settled themselves in Apulia, where they were to remain for centuries. In 842 Moorish adventurers sailed up the Rhone, and devastated the country around Arles. In 846 eleven thousand Saracens sailed into the Tiber, and it is recorded that they brought with them five hundred horses. They took the havens of Ostia and Porto, and advanced on Rome. Here they plundered St. Peter's of its silver ornaments, and of the countless gifts which had been brought by pilgrims. St. Paul's "without the walls" underwent a similar visitation.

The Leonine City. It was to avoid a repetition of the danger from this scourge that St. Peter's, together with the adjacent quarter of the city, was surrounded by a strong wall. This was completed in 852, and remains of it are still to be seen. The part thus enclosed was called the Leonine city, after Leo IV., who, at the instigation of Lothar I., carried out the enterprise. To pay for the construction of this wall, as well as for the damage which the Saracens had done to St. Peter's, Lothar ordered collections to be made from the people in all parts of his kingdom.

Norman invasions. In 841 the Normans, to mention a few of their many acts of plunder, had devastated Rouen, and two years later had taken Nantes. In 845 they captured Paris, and were only induced to retreat on payment by Charles the Bald of seven thousand pounds of silver. In the same year they carried off a rich booty from Hamburg ; an act, however, for which their king, Horich, was made to give satisfaction to Louis the German.

The annals of Xanten, under the year 849, declare that "as usual" the land had been ravaged by hordes from the north. In 851 they burned the city of Ghent, and ten years later Charles the Bald again bought them off from Paris for five thousand pounds of silver.

There was no cessation to the scourge. In 880 Bruno, the ancestor of Otto the Great, together with a number of Saxon nobles, suffered a terrible defeat near Hamburg at their hands, and himself found death on the field of battle. **The Normans a terrible scourge.**

During the year 882 the Normans rioted and plundered as never before. They made themselves masters of the Lower Rhine, of Cologne, Liège, and Xanten, of Prüm, Stablo, and Malmedy. Aix itself, the home and centre of government of Charles the Great, was for the most part laid in ashes. The famous chapel served as a stable for the Norman horses.

To Charles the Fat the people of Germany looked to rid them of their terrible oppressors ; it was but feebly that he responded to the appeal.

At a Diet in Worms it was decided that a general muster of the forces of the kingdom should be made against the Normans : even the Lombards furnished their share of the levies that were made. The object of attack was to be Elsloo, where the invaders had pitched their camp. **Charles the Fat buys off the Normans.**

Instead of driving away the Normans by force of arms, Charles opened negotiations with them, and induced them to withdraw by paying them two thousand pounds of gold. Two years later, in 884, they extorted twelve thousand more from the West-Frankish rulers. In 885 their ships appeared again in the Seine, but Paris, under its count, Odo, resisted their attacks for eight long months. By that time Charles the Fat had arrived with his army.

Again he showed his weakness and his incapacity for anything but words ; again he began negotiations, promising the **Weakness of Charles's rule.**

Normans winter quarters in Burgundy, and seven hundred pounds to pay for their retreat.

The defenders of Paris felt deceived and betrayed, and opposed the march of the Normans into Burgundy. The people, as a whole, were tired of their coward emperor, whose reign, indeed, had not lasted a year, and whose weakness was partially attributable to his health. He had inherited epilepsy and at this very time was visited by an attack of apoplexy.

Yet now, if ever, the needs of the time demanded an able-bodied and a whole-souled man.

Deposition of Charles the Fat.   Charles was deposed by a Diet at Tribur and, deserted by all, gave up the struggle, and betook himself to his estates in Suabia. Here he died in the following year.

Arnulf of Carinthia, 887-899 A.D.   Had the suffering and incapable monarch not gone willingly he would have had to go by force. Arnulf of Carinthia, the son of Carlmann, was already on the march with a force of Bavarians and Saxons, Thuringians, Franks, and Allemannians. He was now raised on the East Frankish throne, his election betokening, in the words of Ranke, " the first independent action of the German secular world." It was the nobles, eager to have a warrior at their head, and not the bishops, who brought it about.

Foundation of new kingdoms.   The fall of Charles the Fat brought about a fundamental reaction against the idea of an universal empire. The face of Central and Southern Europe breaks up now, all at once, into a number of independent kingdoms,

In Italy, in 888, Margrave Berengar of Friaul, a grandson, through his mother, of Louis the Pious, was crowned king of Pavia; at St. Maurice the Guelphic Rudolph was made king of Upper Burgundy, between the Jura Mountains and the Alps. Boso, a West Frankish count, had already founded another Burgundian kingdom—the so-called kingdom of Arles.

In the West Frankish kingdom itself two kings were simultaneously set up. One of them, Odo of Paris, maintained his ground—Arnulf was invited to become his rival, but sent him instead a golden crown—while the other, Wido of Spoleto, went to Italy, and disputed the throne of that land with Berengar of Friaul. He there, for a while, in opposition to Arnulf, wore the imperial crown.

Arnulf's was, undisputedly, the head and political centre of all the kingdoms that had just been founded. Odo, Rudolph, Berengar, and Louis, the son of Boso of Lower Burgundy, sent to him and received his sanction of their rule. Outwardly at least he was their over-lord. *The battle on the Dyle, 891 A.D.*

Against the Normans Arnulf fulfilled the hopes that had been placed in him. An army, indeed, that had been sent to Lorraine to protect that land from further ravages was fairly annihilated. An archbishop of Mayence was among the slain. But near Loewen, on the river Dyle (November, 891), Arnulf himself gained a brilliant victory. His army, thanks to the reforms instituted originally by Charles Martel, must have consisted largely of cavalry, for we are told that at the decisive moment his men leapt from their horses, and stormed on foot the fortifications of the enemy.

Shortly after this battle the plundering expeditions of the Normans came to an end. A treaty with King Alfred of England, which gave them a footing in Northumberland, seems to have furnished them with another field on which to work off their superfluous energy. In the West Frankish kingdom many fortresses had already been built against them. Flanders particularly was covered with systematic fortifications, and its Margrave, Baldwin, undertook in that quarter the protection of the continent of Europe. *The Norman invasions cease.*

In the east of his kingdom Arnulf had to cope with a new power which had assumed alarming proportions. Suatopluk of Moravia had founded an empire which had become the centre of a great Slavic league. *The Moravian Empire.*

Arnulf allied himself with Bulgarians and, above all, with the wild Hungarians against the Moravians, and in 892 and 893 invaded their land. But with no great success. The death, however, of Suatopluk, in 894, rid the Germans of all cause for fear. His sons fell to quarrel-

I

ling among themselves, and their empire gradually became powerless and ripe for the blow of fate that was awaiting it.

Berengar and Guido.

In Italy, meanwhile, Berengar and Guido had fought for the supremacy, and Guido had won the advantage. Pope Formosus called in Arnulf's aid, but was compelled, by force as it were, to give the imperial crown to Guido (891) and to the latter's son Lambert (892).

Arnulf as emperor.

Arnulf marched with an army of Germans first against Cremona, Milan, and Pavia—at which latter place he was crowned king of Italy—and then against Rome. In 896 he was crowned emperor by Formosus, and the Roman people did him homage. He was the last Carolingian to bear the imperial name.

That name, indeed, signified but little now, and no sooner had Arnulf withdrawn than Italy became the scene of a renewed conflict between Berengar and Lambert. These two opponents soon made peace and, without regard for the emperor, divided the rule in Italy between themselves.

Arnulf died in 899, and his successor was his son, Louis the Child. Another son, the bastard Swentibold, was given Lorraine, which was made into a kingdom.

Louis the Child, 900-911.

Louis was but seven years of age, and his guardian and regent was Archbishop Hatto of Mayence—a man to whom, eleven years later, the German nation was to owe the preservation of its endangered unity.

Associated with Hatto in the administration of public affairs were a number of other bishops, and the government assumed a purely ecclesiastical direction.

Rise of ducal families.

Contemporaneously with this, and partly in opposition to it, the great ducal families which were so to influence the history of the next centuries were rising into prominence: the Liudolfings and Arnulfings, the Conradines and Babenbergs. Hatto of Mayence favoured the Conradines at the expense of the Babenbergs, and the result was a fearful feud between these two Franconian families. Murder, betrayal, and civil war played their gruesome part in the conflict.

Hatto's greatest difficulty in procuring recognition for his young charge was experienced in Lorraine. The effort was successful in part, but only after Swentibold had fallen in battle against his own rebellious nobles.

It was altogether a time of political turmoil and of dissolution. In Bavaria, Arnulf, the son of Liutpold, on the death of the latter in 907, assumed the government without waiting for the royal consent. He signed himself in his charters, " Duke, by the grace of God."

On the eastern boundary, meanwhile, a new tormentor, worse almost than the Normans, had arisen for Germany. The Hungarians flooded the land from year to year. Liutpold, who finally fell in one of his efforts to drive them back, and Arnulf of Bavaria, gained a few victories over them, but nothing could stop their devastating progress. The great Moravian Empire finally received its death-blow at their hands (905 and 906), and Saxony and Thuringia, as well as Bavaria were made the scene of their destructive rioting. *Hungarian invasions.*

Louis the Child died in 911, and Reginhard, a powerful noble of Lorraine, at once tore that province loose from the rule of Germany, and placed it under that of Charles the Simple of France. *Death of Louis the Child, 911 A.D.*

There was every danger that all the separate parts of Germany would fall away, as the parts of the greater Carolingian Empire had done, into a number of independent kingdoms.

This same year, 911, which marked the death of Louis the Child marks also another important event in European history. It was then that Charles the Simple of France ceded to the Normans that province, extending from the mouth of the Seine to Caen, which still bears the name of Normandy. It was from here that the sons of Tancred de Hautville were to proceed to Southern Italy, and to found there and in Sicily their great Norman kingdom. It was from here, too, that the Normans were to cross to England and bring that land into their firm and lasting possession. The withdrawal, moreover, from their northern home of the Normans who *The founding of Normandy.*

were to enjoy the new settlement in France, gave those who were left behind room to breathe and to develop. It was not long before "Gorm the Ancient" was to found his great Danish kingdom, and Harald Haardrada was to follow his example in Norway.

CHAPTER VIII.

THE SAXON KINGS.

THE beginning of the tenth century was a time of general Demoralized condition of Europe. demoralization for Europe. There was a seething process going on out of which good was eventually to come, but for the present it seemed as though all social order were going straightway to destruction. The Magyars, Saracens, and Normans plundered at will, the central power became more and more sub-divided, the name of emperor was fast falling into forgetfulness, and popes were put up and cast down at will. Around the chair of Peter, indeed, corruption was even more rife than elsewhere. Over the corpse of Formosus, who had crowned Arnulf, the next pope had held a ghastly trial. Clothed in the papal adornments, the loathsome body had been placed on a throne, and, the mockery of a defence having been gone through with, judgment had been spoken against it. A year later the successor of Formosus had been strangled.

Literature and art had withered away for want of nourishment in the East Frankish or German kingdom. The strongest proof of this is that historical sources for the reign of Conrad (911-918) and Henry I. (919-936) were almost unknown to their own or to later ages. The court annals that had been continued during almost all of the Carolingian period come to an end, and we are dependent for information on the incidental evidence of monastic chroniclers of acts of synods and of charters.

Almost all that we know of Conrad's reign is that he made Conrad I., 911-918. a last attempt in Carolingian style to maintain the supremacy of the crown over the individual powers that were cropping up around it. He would not acknowledge the independence of the stem-duchies, although all his efforts to check that independence were in vain. Against each of the duchies in turn, against Lorraine, Saxony, Suabia, and Bavaria he waged wars which were almost universally unsuccessful. Lorraine, indeed, during his whole reign professed allegiance not to the East Frankish but to the West Frankish kingdom.

Conrad and the Church. Conrad allied himself firmly with the Church. It was through the influence of a metropolitan bishop that he had been raised on the throne, Bishop Salamo of Constance was his chancellor and chief adviser, and to the Church he granted far-reaching concessions.

That institution in turn unreservedly entered the lists for Conrad. The synod of Hohenaltheim, which was held in 916, and at which a papal legate was present, spoke a threefold curse against all who should break their oath of fealty to the king, and declared treasonable undertakings to be punishable with life-long imprisonment in a monastery. Erchanger and Berthold, of almost ducal rank, and leaders of the separatist movement in Suabia, were condemned to this penalty, but Conrad, not satisfied with its severity, later had them put to death. This act, be it here remarked, availed him little, for a more dangerous leader of the Suabians arose in the person of their new duke, Burkhard.

Failure of Conrad's policy. Conrad's efforts to create a strong monarchy that should stem the growth of the local powers had been a failure, and no one recognized this fact more clearly than himself. His last act, although a practical confession of the uselessness of his whole policy, was the grandest of his life. He empowered his brother Eberhard to deliver the insignia of royalty to Henry of Saxony, the most powerful of the stem dukes, the man who had most bitterly opposed all efforts at founding a government on autocratic principles. Instead of trying to keep the royal dignity in the hands of his own family, Conrad, himself a Frank, induced his next of kin to bring about the reversion of the throne to a Saxon dynasty.

The annals of Poehlde, a generation or more later, sum up Conrad's character in words that form a fitting epitaph for him: "This king was so bent on the good of his fatherland that he sacrificed to it his personal enmity—truly a rare virtue."

The chief problem of Henry I.'s reign, like that of Conrad, was how to keep in check the power of the stem-duchies. But Henry's method was a different one from that of his predecessor. He ceased to lean on Conrad's chief ally, the Church, and at the very beginning repulsed Archbishop Heriger of Mayence, who was about to perform upon him the ceremony of unction at his coronation. Conrad had exercised violence and repression towards the individual dukes; Henry tried negotiation and conciliation. *Henry I., 919-936.*

With Eberhard of Franconia, who had brought him the insignia, and who, in an assembly of Franks and Saxons held at Fritzlar, had secured him the election, he stood, during the whole of his reign, on the best of terms. With Burkhard of Suabia, and the almost sovereign Arnulf of Bavaria, he came in time to a peaceful agreement, and induced them to do him homage. *Henry and the duchies.*

Arnulf, indeed, was allowed to retain important prerogatives, chief among them the right to appoint bishops to the vacant sees in Bavaria. It will readily be seen what an important concession this was, a concession which no other duchy ever enjoyed. Arnulf could thus appoint to office his own particular and faithful partisans in every part of the land. They worked in his interests in their different dioceses, and were sure to take his part in any contention with the king. And their influence was not small: the bishops, as we shall often see in the future, were among the most powerful and richest political powers in the land.

Both Burkhard and Arnulf continued to call themselves "duke by the grace of God." They issued coins stamped with their own likenesses, and dated their charters according to the years of their own reign.

The result of Henry's policy was that Germany at this

time could hardly be called a monarchy. The only duties
of the dukes were to appear at the general diets and to take
part in foreign wars. All of Henry's own actual power came
to him from his position as Duke of Saxony. Here and
here only could he unfold his powers of organization and
administration.

Henry I. and Charles the Simple of France.

From Charles the Simple of France, who at first had tried
to widen his bounds at the expense of Germany, Henry
secured recognition of his own title as king of the Eastern
Franks. The two sovereigns met on a boat that was moored
in the middle of the Rhine, and closed a treaty of alliance
with each other. A Carolingian king acknowledged the
legitimacy of the elect of the people.

Lorraine won for Germany.

That same king's own position was precarious, to say the
least, and rival kings were several times set up by a part of
the French nobles. Henry was more than once called upon
to interfere, and the indirect result of his intervention was
the reacquisition of Lorraine for Germany. First, as the
ally of its duke, Gislebert, Reginar's son, then, apparently, as
his enemy, he brought the whole land into subjection, and
Gislebert acknowledged his suzerainty. In 928 the ties that
bound Lorraine to Germany were still further strengthened
by the marriage of Gislebert with Henry's daughter Gerberga.

Henry I.'s reforms.

Henry's peaceful relations with the German dukes left him
time for the important undertakings for which he is more
generally known in history. He placed a limit at least to
the greed and rapacity of the Hungarians, and gained large
provinces and tracts of land from the Slavonians. But, what
was still more, in order to attain these ends he trained and
moulded his own people.

Henry and the Hungarians.

Since the beginning of the century the Hungarians or
Magyars had been harassing Germany. What stirring accounts of these outrages come down to us in the annals of
St. Gall and other monasteries! These religious houses,
being repositories of riches as well as sanctuaries of the God
of the Christians, were especially open to their attacks. In
our own day these invasions have formed the theme for one

of the best and most popular of modern literary productions.[1]

In 924 Henry had the good fortune to secure the person of a Hungarian chieftain. The Magyars negotiated for his release, and a treaty was brought about that insured a nine years' peace to Saxony, in return for which boon Henry was to pay a yearly tribute.

Henry now set about placing his people in a condition to defend themselves. He caused numerous fortresses to be built, within which the Saxons might take refuge at the shortest notice. Such fortresses are called "urbes" in the chronicle of our informant Widukind, and hence Henry's fame as the "founder of cities." But cities they were not in our sense of the word, although on the sites of, or possibly around, individual fortresses towns were later to arise. This was undoubtedly the case with Quedlinburg, where, at his death, Henry's bones were laid to rest. *The building of fortresses.*

In the matter of military tactics Henry introduced one great reform. The peculiar nature of the Hungarian inroads made cavalry an absolute necessity, and the Saxon vassals were now trained to fight on horseback, an art which the Franks had long since learned in their wars with the Arabs. *The training of cavalry.*

Conflicts with the Wends and other Slavonians gave the necessary baptism of blood to the newly created troops. *Henry and the Slavs.*

The present Mecklenburg, Mecklenburg-Strelitz, the Ukermark and the region along the Havel were occupied at this time by different tribes, such as the Abodrites, the Redarii, Wilzi, and Liutizi. All through Thuringia, too, were Slavic settlements, and many towns and rivers such as Jena, Plaue, the Lemnitz, and the Pöllnitz still preserve their original designations. The Slavic villages were built in a circular form and were incapable of extension, which accounts for the great number of distinct settlements. In the small duchy of Saxe Altenburg alone Slavic names have been traced for three hundred villages.

[1] "Ekkehard," by Victor von Scheffel.

We hear dimly of various expeditions undertaken by Henry I. against these century-long rivals of the Germans. It was in the territory of the Dalemincians that he founded Meissen. On one occasion he advanced as far as Prague and compelled Wenceslaus of Bohemia to do him homage. Among his conquests, too, was Brennaburg, the present town of Brandenburg. These victories brought north Germany into subjection at least as far as the river Elbe.

The Hungarians defeated.
The truce with the Magyars came to an end, and on Henry's refusing to continue his tribute they renewed their attacks in 933. We hear of a successful battle fought against them in that year, and we know that Saxony was henceforth free from their invasions although Bavaria and Suabia were still to suffer for another generation.

Henry's last undertaking was a war against the Danes. We only know that it was in a measure successful, and that a tract of land between the Eider and the Schlei was won for Germany.

Henry and Athelstan.
That Henry's renown had spread far beyond the confines of his own land is proved by the almost unseemly alacrity with which King Athelstan of England entered into his proposal of an alliance by marriage. Henry sought a bride for his son Otto, and asked for the sister of the English king. Athelstan sent not one but two of his sisters, and Edith, the elder of the princesses who had come for inspection, was chosen by Otto.

Projected expedition to Rome.
It has been intimated that the contemporary history writing for the time of Henry, as well as for that of Conrad, was scanty and insufficient. Most of the details of his reign have been preserved by Widukind, who lived under Otto the Great. Widukind's chief source of information seems to have been oral tradition, and much that he relates has to be received with caution. Some statements are sorely in need of further explanation. One assertion that has given rise to endless surmises is to the effect that, at the close of his life, Henry had determined to go to Rome but was prevented by illness. Did he intend to go as a pilgrim or as a conqueror ? Was the pope's blessing or the imperial crown the goal of his ambition?

The reign of Otto the Great (936-973) may be roughly divided into three periods. During the first he tries to solve the old problem of how to reckon with the stem duchies. During the second he renews Conrad's policy of relying on the Church, not, however, as its servant, but as its head. In the third we find him as emperor and as ruler, not only over the German Church but also over the Church of Rome. Like a second Charlemagne he unites Italy and Germany under his sway ; his court, too, although less by his own efforts than by those of the distinguished women of his family, becomes a centre for the revival of letters, learning, and art.

Otto owed his throne partly to the designation of his father, partly also to the election by the nobles, which took place at Erfurt, and to the acclamation of the people.

The brilliant ceremony of enthronization which took place at Aix, shows to what a degree of unity and organization Henry I. had brought the kingdom. The nobles and vassals of the crown had been summoned from all German lands, and at Aix la Chapelle they did homage to Otto as Charles the Great's successor and as king of the Franks. Otto had laid aside his Saxon garb, for it was a recognized principle that the king, from whatever stem he might be chosen, must live according to Frankish law and custom.

The coronation was performed by the three archbishops of Mayence of Treves and of Cologne in Charles the Great's chapel, and the throne or marble chair which Otto ascended was the same on which his great predecessor had sat. It was used in turn for centuries by successive German sovereigns, and is still preserved.

In the feast which followed the ceremony at Aix the heads of the different stem duchies performed for the first time those menial services that for eight hundred years were to symbolize the submission due to royal authority. The offices of chamberlain and steward, cup-bearer and marshal, were performed by the Dukes of Lorraine, Franconia, Swabia, and Bavaria. This act was of great significance. By it, on the one hand, the dukes showed their respect for the king's position ; Otto, on the other, recognized the dukes as heads of their stems, and as second only in power to himself.

Slavonian
war.
Scarcely was Otto seated on the throne than he was called upon to suppress a revolt of the Slavic peoples to the east of Saxony, and especially of the Bohemians, who had by this time formed themselves into a state. The border tribes in general were the redskins of Germany. They too had been dispossessed of their lands, they, too, were glad of any occasion for havoc and plunder.

Hermann
Billung.
The conduct of the war against the Slavonians was entrusted to Hermann Billung, who was made margrave or count of the Saxon March, but in whose hands so much power was placed that he was looked upon with envy and jealousy by the border nobles. The latter were in the habit of drawing tribute from the Slavonians and saw their interests threatened by Hermann's measures, as also, later, by the Church Missions.

Conspiracy
against Otto.
During Otto's first years he was to be continually tried as by fire. The Hungarians renewed their attacks but were met by the young monarch in Franconia and driven back. But worse than all outward enemies were those in the king's environment and in his own household.

Eberhard, duke of Franconia and brother of Conrad I., formerly so loyal to the royal house, had been guilty of a lawless act, inasmuch as he had taken upon himself to punish one of his Saxon vassals, a certain Bruning. He had gathered a band of followers and had attacked Bruning's castle in Hessengau, killing its defenders and finally reducing the pile to ashes. Otto, who did not allow himself to be swayed by regard for any privileged person whatever in matters pertaining to justice, condemned Eberhard to a penalty which was to consist in furnishing horses to the worth of a hundred pounds of silver. His aiders and abettors were to undergo the humiliating punishment of walking a certain distance each with a dog upon his shoulders. The punishments of this time were as a rule significant. The hand that forged or that stole was cut off, the eye that lusted was put out, and the penalty of dog carrying seems to have been intended to betoken the brutal character of the undertaking that called down its infliction.

A fearful blow had been struck to Eberhard's self-esteem, it was a duel to the death now between himself and Otto. He soon allied himself with Thankmar, the bastard brother of the king, who was chafing under Otto's arbitrary disposal of certain Saxon estates to which he felt that he had a claim. A very distant one it would seem to us—they had belonged to the cousin of his mother Hatheburg, whose marriage with Henry I. the Church had declared illegal. *Thankmar and Eberhard.*

Conspiracy is a weed that grows apace if the ground be in any way favourable. Saxon nobles and others joined the malcontents, and Thankmar was soon able to attack a castle of Otto's brother, Henry, near Lippstadt, and to carry off that prince as a prisoner. Thankmar then possessed himself of the Eresburg, on the Diemel, and entrenched himself there, but Otto marched up the hill leading to the fortress at the head of such an army that the garrison did not dare to resist him. The gates were opened and Thankmar fled to the church, where he was slain near the altar by a lance hurled through the window. *Death of Thankmar.*

In the meantime a revolt had broken out in Bavaria, where the son of Duke Arnulf, who had died at this time (937), refused to do homage to the sorely oppressed king. But here too Otto was soon master of the situation. The young duke was banished, and Bavaria was given to a brother of Arnulf. Otto now took occasion to suppress some of the almost kingly privileges which the former duke had enjoyed. A new official, the palgrave, or count palatine—in this case a younger son of Arnulf—was to see that the royal rights were regarded, and the bishops were henceforth to be nominated by the king. Otto's final move in the pacification of Bavaria was the arrangement of a marriage between his brother Henry and Judith, the sister of the duke who had just been dispossessed. *Revolt in Bavaria.*

That same brother Henry, nevertheless, who, as we have seen, had been taken prisoner by Thankmar, and who had been handed over by the latter to Eberhard of Franconia, by *Otto's brother Henry joins the conspiracy.*

whom he had been released, was plotting with his recent jailor against the king. Eberhard, indeed, on Thankmar's death, had made an outward submission and profession of obedience, but it was not long before he was at the head of a new and more formidable rebellion. Duke Gilbert of Lorraine was soon won for the movement, and joined his troops to those of Henry. This combined army was met and defeated by Otto at Birten on the Rhine, and the result was that many strong places that had been in Henry's hands at once surrendered. Henry himself, after retreating to Merseburg, which fell after a two months' siege, escaped to Lorraine, where he and Gilbert began to negotiate with the French king, Louis.

Mayence joins the rebels.

Otto hurried from one scene of war to another; he was struggling with a hydra. After vainly besieging Gilbert in Chèvremont he tried to negotiate with Eberhard of Franconia, sending to him Frederick, the Archbishop of Mayence. Frederick overstepped his authority, and made a peace which Otto was forced to repudiate. The archbishop, accompanied by a number of bishops, thereupon joined the rebels, quitting the royal camp at Breisach in such haste that their belongings were left behind. The deserters were welcomed by Eberhard and Gilbert, who by this time had joined forces and taken up their position at Andernach on the Rhine.

Otto's courage.

Otto never showed himself greater than in this emergency. He is related to have remarked to an avaricious noble who wished to make capital out of his king's misfortunes, and to secure for himself the revenues of the abbey of Lauresheim: " It is written ' thou shalt not throw a sanctuary to the dogs.' If you, like the others, are going to desert me, the sooner the better ! "

Failure of the rebellion.

Soon enough the tables turned. One morning as Otto was mounting his horse to repair to church for matins, a messenger ran to meet him whose news changed the whole aspect of affairs. The counts Udo and Conrad Kurzbold, better known as Conrad the Red, had surprised Gilbert and Eberhard, who had remained with a few attendants on one bank of the Rhine, while the bulk of their army had crossed over to the other. Eberhard had attempted to defend himself but had at last fallen in the fray. Gilbert, and some of his followers, had thrown themselves into a boat which, being overloaded, had sunk in the rushing river.

After this crushing blow the rebellion languished, and soon all concerned returned to their allegiance and submitted to the light punishments which Otto decreed against them. The victory of Andernach secured the unity of Germany, for Gilbert had undoubtedly intended to make Lorraine into a separate kingdom, while Eberhard seems to have aimed at undoing the work he had once furthered, at wresting the crown from the Saxon house, and restoring it to the Franks.

Otto was now more powerful than any ruler over Germany had yet been. Bavaria had been subjected, Saxony was in his own hands, and Franconia and Lorraine were at his disposal. Over Lorraine Conrad the Red, the hero of Andernach was made duke in 944, and four years later was united in marriage to the king's own daughter. Franconia remained attached to the crown and, for the time, no new duke was appointed. Henry, the brother of Otto, was treated with the greatest leniency. He seems for a short time, previously to 944, to have been duke of Lorraine, but to have shown himself unworthy of the office. He entered into a new conspiracy, and actually plotted to take the king's life. *Otto's power.* *Henry rebels anew.*

The plan was betrayed and several persons who had been concerned in it were executed. Henry fled, but afterwards returned of his own accord and threw himself upon Otto's mercy. He was sent to Ingelheim and kept in close confinement. After a while his prison became unbearable to him, and he escaped by the aid of a priest to Frankfort, where Otto was holding the Christmas festival. The scene that followed is famous.

Early on Christmas Day while Otto was in the Cathedral and the Christmas music was being sung, a barefooted pilgrim clad in hair-cloth fell on the ground before the king and begged from his inmost soul for pardon. It was Henry *Scene on Christmas Day.*

who thus humbled himself before his brother. He was taken back into favour in spite of all his sins, and this time the reconciliation was final. The brothers lived together henceforth in perfect harmony, and Henry performed many and great services. In 947 he was made Duke of Bavaria. He made a victorious expedition against the Hungarians and penetrated to the heart of the enemy's country.

Liudolf co-regent. It had been the custom under the Carolingians for kings to associate their sons with them in the cares of government. Otto induced his nobles to declare his son, Liudolf, co-regent, and the young prince was wedded to Ida, daughter of Duke Hermann, of Suabia. In 948 Hermann died and Liudolf succeeded to Suabia. All of the duchies were now in the hands of Otto or of his immediate family.

Otto's influence. Otto had raised the German Kingdom to an unknown pinnacle of greatness, and his influence began to be felt far out over Germany's borders. In France he was the acknowledged arbiter between the king and a restless party of the nobles. A synod at Ingelheim, at which by Otto's request a papal legate was present, threatened Count Hugo of Francia with the bann should he not return to his allegiance. It was to German interference that the French king, in 950, finally had to thank his crown.

Italy since 888. The condition of Italy at this time was one of indescribable demoralization. Since the general downfall of the Carolingian Empire, in 888, there had been no less than twelve shadowy kings, almost all of whom had been arbitrarily deposed by one or another faction. Four of them were Burgundians, four Italians, three Germans, and one French.

About 930 King Hugo, a Burgundian, possessed the Italian throne, and even ventured to cast lusting eyes upon Rome. In order to strengthen his influence he wedded the most notorious, but also the most powerful, woman in Italy, a certain Masozia. She had been the concubine of Pope Sergius III., and had caused the fall and death of John X. Her favour had gained the papal throne for Leo VI. and for Stephen VIII. At last she had ventured to raise her own son by Sergius III., a youth of twenty, upon the chair of Peter. He took the name of John XI. But out of Marozia's own womb an avenger arose in the person of Alberic, whose father had been a margrave of that name. He threw his mother and his half-brother, the Pope, into prison, and drove his stepfather away from Rome.

King Hugo's son, Lothar, who was obliged to leave the lion's share of the Italian Kingdom to Margrave Berengar of Ivrea, was wedded to a princess of Upper Burgundy, Adelaide, daughter of Rudolf II. Her brother, Conrad, had stood in close connection to Otto, and had spent years at his court. No wonder that the German King was interested in Adelaide's fate, which, on the death of her husband, Lothar, in 950, promised to become tragic enough. Berengar, although acknowledged as their king by the majority of the Italian nobles, saw in her a possible rival, the more so as she had already gained the affections of the people. He strove to win her by fair means or by foul. He proposed a marriage with his own son, Adalbert, but, on Adelaide's refusal, began against her a course of persecutions. She was finally made prisoner and kept in confinement first at Como and then in a dungeon at Garda. *Adelaide and Berengar.*

The sufferings of the young queen aroused universal sympathy, especially in Germany, and it was a golden opportunity for Otto's interference. He soon determined to go to war with Berengar, to free Adelaide, to win her hand, to take possession of the kingdom of Italy, and thus to pave the way to the imperial throne. The idea of this Italian expedition won favour with the nobles, and the summer of 951 witnessed eager preparations in every part of Germany. Liudolf of Suabia, Otto's son, at this time committed the first of that series of offences against his father which were finally to lead to an open rupture. His army was first in the field, but he did not, as was fitting, await Otto's commands before descending upon Italy. His expedition was a failure, and he was obliged to withdraw. *Otto's plans for Italy.*

Otto himself soon after crossed the Brenner with an army

well equipped and of rare material. His brothers Henry and Bruno went with him, also Duke Conrad of Lorraine and Frederick, Archbishop of Mayence, besides a grand array of followers. His chief aim and object, as Bishop Rather of Verona expressly signified in a letter to Pope Agapetus, was to gain the imperial crown.

All Lombardy soon submitted to the Germans, and Berengar took to flight. Otto assumed the titles of King of the Lombards and King of the Italians. Election and coronation were indifferent to him ; he considered it his inborn right to rule beyond the Alps.

Otto and Adelaide. Adelaide meanwhile had escaped from confinement by the aid of a priest and a waiting-woman, who had excavated a way out beneath the walls of her prison tower on the Garda Lake. She had taken refuge in the Castle of Canossa, whither Otto sent to beg her hand. Shortly afterwards Pavia witnessed the celebration of their nuptials.

So far Otto had known no check in his victorious career in Italy. But now Frederick of Mayence, who had been sent to Rome to come to terms about the imperial coronation, returned with news of evil omen. The Pope, wholly in Alberic's power, refused to open the gates to the Teuton.

Liudolf's conspiracy. Otto seems to have chidden Frederick for not having better performed his mission. At any rate the archbishop, accompanied by Liudolf, who was jealous of favours shown to his uncle, Duke Henry of Bavaria, and who also chafed under the influence wielded by his new stepmother, Adelaide, left Pavia and hastened to spread disaffection in Saxony.

Conrad the Red. The two conspirators soon gained a powerful and unexpected ally. Otto had quitted Italy, leaving behind him his son-in-law, Conrad the Red, who had done such services in the former rebellion, to checkmate Berengar. Conrad, instead of crushing the ex-king of Italy, made peace with him on his own responsibility, a peace which Otto refused to ratify, although he later did of his own accord reinstate Berengar in Italy, making him do homage for the land, however, as for a fief of the German crown.

Conrad was deeply offended at the small regard paid for his mediation, and went over to the rebels. Liudolf by this time had thrown all restraints to the wind, for Adelaide had given birth to a son, and a rumour had reached him that his own rights as eldest born would be disregarded.

The rebellion began with a deep humiliation for Otto. He found himself in Mayence in the spring of 953 almost completely in the power of Liudolf, Conrad, and Frederick. They forced him to sign an agreement which was shameful and disadvantageous in the extreme. On regaining his liberty he declared it null and void.

Otto's straits, 953 A.D.

Otto was most ably aided at this crisis by his repentant brother Henry. For two months they besieged Mayence together, but in the meantime a revolt had broken out in Henry's own duchy of Bavaria. A scion of the old dynasty still lived—that Arnulf whom Otto had made Count Palatine. Around him a large party collected which had always regarded Henry as a usurper. Liudolf fled from Mayence to Bavaria, where he succeeded in making himself master of many strongholds and in driving Henry's wife and children from the land. Otto hastened to oppose him.

The year was fraught with hardships. For three months Otto besieged Ratisbon without success, and at last withdrew to Saxony. The old baneful struggle of the parts against the whole, of local interests against the crown, had broken out anew. Southern Germany seemed already lost, and the royal ascendancy was fast sinking.

At this moment relief came in a manner least expected. The Hungarians took advantage of the civil war to pour their hordes once more across the borders. The rebel German princes tried to use this invasion for their own ends, and began treating with their country's enemies. But by so doing they ruined their own cause. Enough national enthusiasm was left to enable Otto to raise a large army. Bavaria and Suabia soon returned to their allegiance, and it was not long before Conrad of Lorraine, and Frederick of Mayence made their submission. Liudolf, too, was subjected after a

Failure of the rebellion.

few more conflicts. As usual, the rebels were mildly treated. Suabia and Lorraine, indeed, were placed in other hands, but the deposed dukes were allowed to retain their liberty and their own personal estates.

Otto against the Hungarians.   The rebellion of the duchies was but the forerunner of other struggles. The Wends made an inroad into Saxony, and, although Hermann Billung drove them back for the moment, a stronger arm than his was needed to bring them into subjection. Otto was preparing fresh forces against them when a peremptory call came to him from the south. The Hungarians had overrun Bavaria, and single hordes were devastating Suabia. Never before had this plague infested the land in such numbers.

Battle on the Lech Plains, 955.   The Hungarians had formed a camp of huge proportions in the plain of the Lech near Augsburg. Ulrich, Augsburg's bishop, was bravely holding the town against them when Otto and his army approached. With the king was the repentant Conrad, ex-duke of Lorraine, leading a force of Franks.

The battle on the Lech plains was bravely fought. Otto himself headed the charge with irresistible effect, while an unexpected attack on the German rear-guard was brilliantly repulsed by Conrad. The enemy was scattered like chaff before the wind, and their camp fell into Otto's hands.

It was as victors that the Germans mustered their forces at evening, but their own losses had been severe, and many **Bravery of Conrad the Red.** of their noblest had sunk to earth. Conrad, apparently desirous to atone for the past, had fought with a lion's courage, but as he paused for rest and loosed his helmet an arrow struck him and pierced him through the neck. "A great hero, and the world was full of his fame," says Widukind the chronicler.

The fleeing hordes of the enemy found death at every turn. Many were drowned in crossing rivers, others were slain by the inhabitants of the Bavarian villages.

The Hungarians become civilized.   Never was a more decisive battle fought. Never again did this fearful enemy ravage Western Europe. In course of

time the Germans were able to push their boundary lines
further and further towards the east, and the peace and
security of the Bavarian East March, as it was called, laid
the foundation for the power and influence of the later
Austria.

The Hungarians soon gave up their nomad life. By the
year 1000 they had founded their kingdom in the present
Hungary, and they gradually became a settled and civilized
people.

Otto left the Lech plains to hasten to Saxony, where his Otto and the
margraves were holding back the Wends. Before the year Wends.
was ended he gained a brilliant though not thoroughly decisive victory. Not till five years later, not till three new
expeditions had been sent against them, was the German rule
re-established in these Slavic lands.

CHAPTER IX.

OTTO THE GREAT AS EMPEROR OF THE ROMANS.

Otto's change of policy.

IT will have been seen that Otto's cherished policy with regard to the duchies had been a miserable failure. He had hoped to found a patriarchal state, as it were, and to bring the highest temporal offices into the hands of his own relatives. The result had been a civil war. Otto's son, Liudolf, and his son-in-law, Conrad, had allowed no ties of blood or of marriage to stand in their way. The people of the duchies, too, had, in more than one case, shown their impatience under the yoke of dukes foreign to their stem.

Otto now gave up the plan of uniting local interests through a network of family ties. On his brother Henry's death, in 955, he gave Bavaria to a grandson of the old Duke Arnulf. Hermann Billung was made duke of Eastern Saxony, and native nobles held office in Suabia and Lorraine.

Favours the Church.

It was, however, almost necessary to the existence of the crown that it should be supported by a strong party, and Otto was led into a step which, however advantageous at first, was fraught with dire consequences for the German people. He made the Church that which the duchies should have been, the prop and stay of the kingly power. He encouraged new ecclesiastical foundations, and made rich gifts of lands and exemptions to the clergy, hoping in this way to bind them more closely to himself. His first care was to fill all the archbishoprics with friends and faithful servants.

Church and State.

William, Otto's own bastard son, received Mayence, Bruno was established in Cologne, and a pupil of his in Treves. For

more than a century now the history of the German Church
and of the German kingdom were to become almost identical.
The government assumes a churchly character, church rule
becomes a matter of politics. The result was to be that when
in the next century the struggle with the popes began it was
no longer possible for the princely ecclesiastics to render unto
Cæsar that which was Cæsar's, and thus to avoid the conflict
of nationality versus the Church universal.

So long as the right of choosing the bishops remained with
the king, the latter was able to constitute a body of men
whose interests were identical with his own. The bishops
were simply officials; they left no heirs, being not allowed to
marry, and at their deaths their sees reverted to the crown.
They made a splendid counterpoise to the power of the nobles,
who were already beginning to claim that their fiefs were
hereditary. Estates, honours, and riches could safely be given
to such men, and the crown lands yet suffer no diminution.

Great were the services demanded of the clergy in return. Duties of the
As fief-holders they furnished regularly their quota of vassals clergy.
to the king's army, and often took the field in person. All
the business of the court, all the charter writing, all the correspondence, was in their hands.

And Otto ruled them like a second Charlemagne. No
council might be called, no decree of the clergy passed, without his consent. Of his own accord he founded bishoprics,
and set up bishops, judged the clergy, and disposed of church
funds. The canon laws indeed, and not only the forged ones,
directly negatived such proceedings, but as yet there was no
one to call attention to such discrepancies.

The immediate result of the union of the crown with the Results of
clergy was to raise the prestige of Germany, and to pave the Church
way for the renewal of the holy Roman Empire. A time was policy.
to come, however, when the interests that joined the two were
to be sundered, and the bonds that bound them loosed. The
result was to be destructive indeed. The glory of the empire
was to be tarnished, and German unity to be trodden under
foot.

Imperial crown.

For a hundred years now the crown of the empire had been a mere bauble, the disposal of which had been for the most part in the hands of the popes. Neither Charles the Bald nor Charles the Fat, Arnulf, nor Berengar I., nor any of the other rulers of Italy seem to have regarded it as more than an empty honour. Alberic, the ruler of Rome, had not cared for the title, and had thwarted the plans of those who did. During his time, therefore—after wielding the sceptre for twenty years, he had died in 954—it remained in abeyance.

Pope John XII.

Alberic's mantle, as head of Rome, descended upon his son Octavian, a mere boy. Octavian, in spite of his youth, however, was soon made Pope under the name of John XII., thus combining in his person the sovereignty of Rome and the spiritual headship of Christendom. His great ambition was to increase his temporal power in Italy, but in this he was thwarted by Otto's old enemy and vassal Berengar. At this time Berengar and his son Adalbert were in possession of the Exarchate of Ravenna, and the dukes of Tuscany, to which the pope also laid claim, did them homage.

Calls in Otto's aid.

Pope John looked around for allies, and, finally, fixed his hopes on the German King. Otto had again broken with Berengar, and in 956 had sent his son Liudolf to Italy, promising him the crown of that fair land if he could win it. Liudolf within two years had subjected nearly the whole of the so-called Italian kingdom—the present Tuscany and Lombardy. The "path was open to Olympus," as a monk of the time has expressed it, when the heir to the German throne was attacked by fever and died. All the advantages won over Berengar were lost, and the Pope once more trembled before him. He felt himself insecure even in his own Eternal City.

It was then that John decided to summon Otto's aid and to dazzle him with the prospect of the imperial crown. Otto was won by the lure, and the first steps were taken towards that union with Italy that was to cost the nation so dear.

Otto in Italy.

Otto made hasty preparations for his expedition. His son Otto was elected and crowned co-regent, Bruno was to uphold the royal rights in Lorraine, and William of Mayence to transact the daily business of the realm. In the autumn of 961, the king crossed the Brenner.

Berenger had raised an army of 60,000 men, but at the decisive moment his troops refused obedience. Otto was able to enter Pavia unmolested and to pursue his way to Rome. In February, 962, he received the crown in St. Peter's from the Pope's hand. **His Imperial coronation, 962 A.D.**

It was not altogether without fear that Otto had entered Rome. His sword-bearer had orders to watch while the king knelt before the grave of the apostle, and to hold his weapon in readiness. The fickleness of the Romans was well known to Otto, also, to some extent, the character of the Pope. John was obliged to swear by the holy bones of St. Peter that he would never make common cause with Otto's enemies, Berengar and Adalbert.

The price to be paid to the Pope for Otto's new dignity was to be the provinces held by the two Italians. These were as yet unconquered, but a deed of gift was drawn up concerning them which is still extant. Written upon purple parchment in letters of gold, it has withstood the ravages of time. Its genuineness, long doubted, has been re-vindicated in our own day.

The " Holy Roman Empire of the German Nation " as founded by Otto the Great, was to continue for eight hundred and forty four years. Only for short intervals was the throne ever to be vacant, although in the sixteenth century the Pope's influence in the matter of its disposal was to fall into abeyance. In the time of our own grandfathers it came to an end, and the Austrian Empire, the anomalous kingdoms of Napoleon, and the North German Confederation rose on its ruins. **Refounding of the empire.**

For two weeks after Otto's coronation harmony lasted between the heads of Christendom. The Pope approved of the emperor's plan of changing Madgeburg into an arch-bishopric with many suffragan bishoprics. The details of the matter were arranged in a Roman synod and made known to the German clergy by a papal bull. But John soon found **Otto and the Pope.**

that Otto was playing by far too important a *rôle* in Italy, was winning over the bishops by rich donations, and was treating the provinces that he conquered completely as his own.

The Pope did not hesitate to commence negotiations with Berengar and Adalbert. The same messengers who brought news of this turn of affairs had much to say about John's ungodly manner of life. Otto was little affected by either of these communications, and is said to have remarked with regard to the charges of immorality: "He is a boy, the examples of good men will improve him."

But one day papal ambassadors were arrested at Capua with letters to the Greek Emperor and to the Hungarians. John confessed his treasonable intents in part, but made counter-charges against Otto which the latter condescended to explain away. The crisis, however, was not long in coming. Adalbert was received within the walls of Rome and warmly welcomed by the Pope. Otto marched against the city, which he took without difficulty. The Pope fled with Adalbert.

John XII's deposition. The Romans were made to give hostages and to swear never again to instal anyone as pope whose election should not have been confirmed by the emperor and his son. Such an influence as this did Otto win over the Roman Church! The popes became his creatures and he their judge.

A synod was summoned over which Otto presided. It was well attended. Three archbishops and thirty-eight bishops came together in St. Peter's. All the clergy of Rome and the officials of the Lateran were present, also many nobles and the Roman soldiery.

Charges against Pope John. Otto refrained at first from bringing his own causes of complaint before the synod. He wished John's ruin, but the Pope's daily manner of living was enough to condemn him. A long list of sins was brought up against him, and his contempt for the canons of the Church was clearly proven. He had drunk the devil's health, and had invoked heathen gods while playing dice. He had chosen a ten year old boy as bishop of Todi and had given a deacon his consecration in a horse's stall. He had lived like a robber-chief, and an impure and unchaste one at that.

The synod summoned John to answer the charges against him. He replied by banning the bishops who had taken part in the proceedings. A second summons was likewise disregarded.

At the third session of the synod Otto came forward as accuser and declared the pope a perjured traitor, who had conspired with the enemies of the empire. John's deposition was agreed upon and a new pope elected, but it was some months before the matter came to a settlement. John had found adherents in the city, but died just as Otto was preparing to crush him.

The Romans disregarded Otto's pope, Leo, and elected the cardinal deacon, Benedict. The result was a siege of Rome, a famine in the city, and a capitulation. Again a synod and again a triumph for the emperor. Benedict appeared before the assembly and begged for mercy. Clad in the papal robes and holding the bishop's staff he had come to the synod. He left it stripped of his pallium, his staff in pieces, himself a prisoner. He was to die in captivity at Hamburg. The last hopes for the Romans of freeing the papacy had proved in vain. One German after another now ascended the throne of Peter. *The Popes Leo and Benedict.*

Otto's last years were spent partly in administering the affairs in his own land, partly in trying to preserve quiet and to increase his power in Italy. On Margrave Gero's death, in 965, in order that no one man should again have such a preponderating influence in Saxony, his district was divided into six parts with each a separate margrave. Lorraine, too, was divided into an upper and a lower duchy, and these parts were not again to be reunited.

Otto's mere reappearance in Rome sufficed to quell an insurrection against his pope. He then proceeded to fulfil the promise once made to Pope John XII. All of its earlier possessions were restored to the chair of Peter, although the imperial rights in the ceded districts seemed to have been preserved. Otto, for instance, built a palace near Ravenna, where he often held his court.

Otto now made an effort to reap lasting fruits from all of *Otto I. and Otto II.*

his untiring labours. He wished to secure the empire to his son, to unite the latter by bonds of marriage to the still influential court of Constantinople, and, finally, to rid Italy of the Arabs who had been infesting it for a hundred years. The last of these desires was not to be accomplished either in his own or in his son's reign. The consent to the imperial coronation was easily obtained from an obsequious pope, and the ceremony took place in St. Peter's on Christmas day, 967.

The Eastern Empire. The union with the Eastern Empire was only brought about after endless negotiations and some bloodshed. Otto, determined to exert pressure on the Greeks, invaded their possessions in Apulia and Calabria and besieged Bari. He soon withdrew, however, and sent Bishop Luitprand of Cremona at the head of a large embassy to Constantinople. Luitprand was a man of letters and a skilful diplomat, but somewhat rash and fiery of temper. To him we owe most of our knowledge of these times; and among his other works is a detailed report, addressed to Otto, of his mission. It is one of the most attractive writings of the middle ages.[1]

Luitprand's mission. Luitprand found Nicephorus one of the haughtiest and most insolent of men, living in a style of great magnificence and utterly refusing to believe that any power in the world could equal his own. He demanded Rome and Ravenna as the price for the hand of a royal princess, and offered an alliance without the marriage if Otto would make Rome free.

While Luitprand was detained at the court of Nicephorus, Pope John XIII. sent an embassy to the "Greek emperor." Only the low degree of the envoys saved them from instant death, for Nicephorus considered himself the emperor of the Romans, and the only one.

Luitprand's mission was a failure. He met with insults and taunts from the Greeks, and repaid them in kind. He was absent so long, virtually a prisoner, that Otto renewed hostilities without awaiting his return. But soon a revolution

---

[1] See " Select Documents," Appendix.

took place in Constantinople. At the instigation of the empress Nicephorus was murdered, and John Zimisces succeeded to his bed and to his throne. Zimisces, surrounded Theophano. by enemies at home, was quite willing to give the hand of a Grecian princess in return for peace in Italy. Theophano, the niece of Zimisces, reached Rome in April, 972, and was wedded to Otto II. in St. Peter's. She was a gifted creature, and was destined to play a very great part in German affairs.

A number of provinces and estates were settled on the young bride, and the original of the deed of transfer, drawn up in purple and gold, is extant to-day.

In 968 Otto's favourite project of making Magdeburg an Magdeburg archbishopric, a project which had met with some opposition to be an arch- in Germany itself, was at last realized. The bishoprics of bishopric. Brandenburg, Havelberg, and Meissen were subordinated to the new creation, also two new sees, Zeiz and Merseburg, to which, later, Posen was to be added. A grand centre for carrying on the conversion of the Slavonians was at last won.

Otto's life-work was nearly done. Few German emperors Otto's death. have been able to end their days amid such general prosperity and rejoicing. He was able to take part, in 973, in a series of feasts and processions in Saxony, but died at Memleben before the year was out. He had reigned thirty-seven years, and had reached the age of sixty-two. His bones rest in the cathedral of Magdeburg.

It remains to say a few words about the social and intel- Social life lectual life in the reign of Otto the Great, and it must be under Otto I. membered in this connection that different parts of Germany differed much from each other in the degree of their culture and civilization. There was no general state organization in our sense of the word, and the duchies enjoyed a great degree of independence. The king might demand certain services of the dukes, but he could not interfere with the administration of their duchies. Here they were absolute masters, except when held in check by their local diets.

One such assembly in Saxony dared to oppose the wishes

of Otto himself, although he represented king and duke in his own august person. It is questionable whether at any time in the tenth century a royal or imperial command which was contrary to a local law would have been obeyed. The people at this time, as during the next two hundred years, were devotedly true to their dukes. How easily could one of them raise an army for his own purposes, and how many of the old German songs centre about the beloved person of a duke who, as likely as not, had been a traitor to his king!

Narrow scope of existence.

We must remember at every turn how different the people of a thousand years ago were from ourselves. Cities as centres of trade and commerce had scarcely as yet come into being, and the use of money was extremely restricted. If taxes or tolls had to be paid they were paid in kind. This or that proportion of grain or cloth was subtracted from the rest and reserved for the treasury of the king. Even the produce of the rich estates belonging to the crown was not sold. We know now why it was that the kings of the tenth century moved so frequently with their huge followings from place to place. It was necessary to consume the products of the soil, for they were perishable and not convertible. A modern historian likens the royal household to a ruminating animal that grazes up one pasture after another.

Family life.

Family life, to turn to a special phase of social existence, was a far different conception from what it is now. Among the Saxons, Thuringians, and Frisians, marriage seems to have been purely a business transaction, which was carried on independently of the wishes of at least one of the parties concerned. Fathers could dispose of their daughters at will, and regularly sold them to their future lords. The husband was master of his household in the strictest sense of the word, and the women were kept in complete subjection. Conjugal fidelity was a one-sided affair, and the marriage vows were binding only on the wife. The father had a right —how much use he made of it we shall never know—to kill his children or to sell them into captivity.

Religion.

It is possible that religious considerations tempered the

brutality of the laws. We know that Otto the Great's age was one of great piety, not to say superstition. The king himself, especially after the death of his first queen, Edith, which event was considered by him a warning to call him to good works, was untiring in furthering missions. His mother had founded several monasteries, and his daughter herself became abbess of Quedlinburg.

Otto's brother Bruno, who was his chancellor and arch-chaplain, instituted a far-reaching reform in the church affairs of Lorraine. He summoned clergy of blameless life from all parts of Germany. Monasteries which had sunk into decay were purged and regenerated. Old schools were bettered and new ones founded. The Lorraine clergy were models for Europe in education, as well as in the proper performance of their duties. Bishops without number were chosen from their midst, and Rheims raised two men from Lorraine in succession on her archiepiscopal throne. A century later Rome herself was to choose a pope from this rich nursery of prelates.

Lorraine clergy.

The religious life of Otto the Great's age was not without its anomalies. A stiff formalism pervaded this as every other phase of existence. Humility in those chosen to a high position in the Church consisted in a routine of refusing to accept the dignity, of fleeing behind the altar, of weeping copious tears, of self-deprecation. Not once but a hundred times do such performances meet us in the chronicles, and one case is known of a regular formula for the proper conduct on such occasions. Piety and charitable intent were often measured by the power to shed tears less or more copiously.

Conventional ideas.

The strange belief was almost universal that the end justified the means. We read of housebreakings and robberies, of forgeries and other crimes committed for the sake of obtaining the relics of this or that saint, and in all the literature of the time we hear no disapproval of such acts except from the side of the injured parties. On the contrary, biographers frequently praise their heroes for just such performances.

An excessive saint worship and an extreme credulity went hand in hand with such moral ideas. Miracles were thoroughly believed in, not as now merely by the ignorant, but by the best intellects of the time. The more a man could believe the higher was his piety reckoned.

Art.

In art and literature, Otto's court was the scene of a veritable renaissance. Countless miniatures or book illustrations of his time are still preserved. In St. Gall, Treves, Regensburg, and elsewhere, were famous schools for such ornamental work, and the colours used were most brilliant and enduring. Strangely enough they were used without any sense for the real fitness of things. Scarlet eagles fly through cherry clouds, yellow asses pasture in blue fields, and red oxen draw golden ploughs. Towards the end of the century the taste changed and more sombre hues crept in. It has been suggested that ascetic views, such as those which were so diligently fostered by Otto III., were responsible for the transformation.

Classical learning.

Otto the Great, although personally, as far as we know, without literary tastes, did everything to foster and encourage a revival of classical learning. We hear of an Italian who at his instigation brought a hundred manuscripts over the Alps. Virgil, Horace, Ovid, Terence, Cicero and Sallust arose from the dead as it were to a new life in Germany. They found their way into the monasteries and even into the nunneries.

Roswitha.

Who has not heard of Roswitha, Abbess of Gandersheim, who wrote comedies in the style of Terence, but with the outspoken object of maintaining the field against him? Her aim was "that the praiseworthy chastity of holy virgins should be celebrated in the same poetic strain in which hitherto the loathsome incest of voluptuous women has been narrated." Her works have been published in our own day, and fill a respectable volume.

CHAPTER XX.

OTTO II. was eighteen years old when his father died. **Otto II.** Since the age of six he had been king of the Romans, and for five years already he had worn the imperial crown. He was happily married, for Theophano had thoroughly won his affections.

No immediate disturbance marked the change of rulers, and the solemn circuit of the kingdom was made without delay. But, for many a generation, no German king was to rule without shedding of blood, and Otto's turn came soon enough. The sons of Count Reginar of Hennegau—the father had been banished from Lorraine by Otto I.'s brother Bruno for having broken the peace—came back and tried by force to regain their inheritance. The young emperor took the field in person against them, and, after besieging them in the castle of Bossut on the Hayne, put them to flight.

But in Bavaria new complications had meanwhile arisen. **Conspiracy** Here Henry, the brother of Otto the Great, had died in 955, **in Bavaria.** and his wife Judith had continued to rule in the name of her son, Henry the Quarrelsome. Judith was a most ambitious woman, and had brought about marriages between Henry and the daughter of the king of Burgundy, as well as between her daughter Hedwig and Duke Hermann of Suabia. But on Hermann's death, Otto II. conferred his duchy on Otto, son of his own deceased stepbrother Liudolf. Henry the Quarrelsome considered the Bavarian house entitled to Suabia, and, moved by this and other grievances, raised a conspiracy for the purpose of dethroning the emperor.

L

Bohemia
and Poland.

Dukes Boleslav of Bohemia, and Mesco of Poland, were won for the movement. They were always ready to rebel against their suzerain the German king, and so frequent were the conflicts with them and their successors that the pen would weary in narrating them. Bohemia and Poland were on the whole so wild and uncivilized that the German armies could penetrate them with difficulty, and the native forces could easily escape.

Downfall of
Henry the
Quarrel-
some.

The result of the present conspiracy was, eventually, the downfall of Henry the Quarrelsome. In Ratisbon a solemn judgment was declared against him, and he was deprived of Bavaria, which was given to Otto of Suabia. Not in its full extent indeed, for a new duchy, Carinthia, was sundered from it and given to a new duke, called Henry the Younger.

The Lorraine rebels had meanwhile allied themselves with King Lothar of France, and Otto was forced to make a temporary peace that was rather derogatory than otherwise to his dignity. But it gave him time to put a final end to the rebellion in Bavaria, which had been joined in his absence by the newly created duke, Henry of Carinthia. The two Henries were brought before a council of princes at Magdeburg, and declared guilty of high treason. They were banished from the realm, although Henry the Younger was soon allowed to return.

War with
France.

The peace with France was soon broken. King Lothar had revived the old claims of his house to Lorraine, and marched with an army of 20,000 men upon Aix-la-Chapelle. The unsuspecting emperor was here celebrating the feast of John the Baptist, and knew nothing of the intended invasion until the advance guard of the enemy came in sight. The very meal that had been prepared for Otto was consumed by the French, and Aix was given up to plunder. The eagle that adorned the top of the imperial palace was turned towards the west in token that the city henceforward belonged to France. The proud emblem could soon be restored to its natural position, however, for Lothar's army left Aix at the end of three days, never to return.

The French had not proceeded far on their homeward way
when an imperial messenger overtook them. He had been
sent to announce that Otto, hating subterfuge, wished to give
full warning of an approaching invasion of France. On
October 1st the king might expect him.

Otto II.
marches on
Paris.

The day appointed saw Otto under way with an army of
unprecedented size, but his expedition was as barren of lasting
results as that of the French king had been. He marched
directly upon Paris and struck his camp on the hill of Montmartre. But the city was well defended and the season was
far advanced. A siege was deemed unadvisable, and Otto
retired after avenging the gyrations of the Aix eagle by a
demonstration in kind. He gathered all his clergy together
and made them sing a *Te Deum* on the heights of Montmartre.
The mocking hymn of victory sounded down through the
streets of Paris. After the hallelujahs had ended he withdrew his troops, the French plundering his rear-guard, indeed,
as he went.

It was not long before King Lothar, at odds with his cousin
Hugo, of Francia, asked forgiveness from the emperor and
renounced his claim to Lorraine. After a successful expedition against Duke Mesco of Poland, Otto found himself at
peace with all enemies this side of the Alps. France was
kept in check by her own internal discords; Poland, Bohemia,
and Denmark acknowledged the over-lordship of Germany.

Peace with
France.

Otto, at the height of his fame and popularity, felt that the
time had come for a long-cherished project, the subjugation
of southern Italy.

Southern
Italy.

Apulia, Calabria, and Naples were still, nominally, parts of
the Greek Empire, and received their officials from Constantinople. Capua and Benevento, on the other hand, together
with Spoleto and the March of Camerino, had been conferred
as a fief by Otto the Great on Duke Pandulf the Ironheaded.
The latter had also managed to bring Salerno into subjection
to himself.

The Germans and the Greeks were alike threatened by the
Saracens or Arabs, who just at this time were greatly ex-

tending their influence along the Mediterranean. In 964 they had driven the last Greeks out of Sicily, and five years later had conquered Egypt and founded Cairo. Since 976 they had turned their attention to Southern Italy, where the Greeks were too weak to defend their provinces, and where Pandulf was their only formidable antagonist.

Greek-
Saracen
alliance.

The struggle, however, was too unequal, and Otto had long since determined to come to the aid of his vassal and to rid the peninsula from the pest of Islam.

It was feared at Constantinople, however, and not without reason, that not only would the Arabs be driven out but the Greeks also. Of many evils an alliance with the Saracens seemed to be the least. In 981 the great Arab chief Abul Kasem girded his loins for another raid, and Otto prepared to meet him. Envoys from Constantinople came and warned the emperor not to put foot on Grecian territory. He refused to recede and opened the campaign in Apulia. Greek intrigues were probably responsible for the misfortunes that followed.

Pandulph had died before the advent of his deliverer, his extensive possessions were now divided among his sons, and everywhere discontented factions arose. The emperor had no longer any firm supporters or allies.

Otto's
mishap, 982
A.D.

In the month of May, 982, Otto marched through the territory of Salerno on his way to Calabria. Near the little town of Colonne, south of Cotrona, Abul Kasem blocked his way, and a fierce battle ensued. The onslaughts of the Germans were stubbornly met, but at last Abul Kasem fell and the Arabs took to flight. But victory made the emperor less cautious. As he pursued his way along the sea-coast, hemmed in by high hills where the enemy could gather unseen, his whole army was surrounded. A scene of wild confusion followed; many sank under the sword of the Islamites, others sought death in the sea, or were captured and sold into slavery.

The escape.

The emperor escaped as by a miracle. He plunged his horse into the water and reached a ship, which, however, happened to belong to the Greeks. But on board was a friendly Slavonian, who, himself the only one to recognize Otto, persuaded the crew to steer for Rossano, where they possibly might procure a ransom for the fugitive. When the ship landed the Slavonian went on shore and procured a rescue party. The emperor was soon out of danger.

Otto's prestige had received a blow. The Greeks, who soon dissolved their union with the Arabs, remained in possession of Apulia and Calabria, while the Danes and Wends took this occasion to rise in revolt. The Milanese, too, drove out their archbishop, and only allowed him to return upon promise of great concessions.

The princes of Germany were, however, most true to the emperor at this juncture. They crossed the Alps at his bidding in great numbers, and took part in a diet held at Verona. The diet marks the close union at this time between Germany and Italy. The three year old Otto, the emperor's son, was made king of the Romans on Italian soil. Italian princes on equal footing with the Germans took part in the election. *Election of Otto III.*

Otto proceeded to make preparations on a large scale for a new war against the Arabs. The Wends meanwhile made terrible ravages in Germany. The bishoprics of Havelburg and Brandenburg were annihilated, the archbishopric of Magdeburg lost half of its provinces, and the Saxon North March came almost wholly into the enemy's hands. *Uprising of the Wends.*

Otto was in Rome at the time and was deeply moved by these occurrences. Care and discouragement combined to aggravate an illness that had come upon him. He died December 7th, 983, at the early age of twenty-eight. He was buried in an antique sarcophagues, over which was placed a vase of porphyry. That vase serves to-day as a christening font in St. Peter's. The sarcophagus is now a water-trough in the palace of the Quirinal. *Sic transit gloria mundi!* *Death of Otto II., 983.*

Upon the death of Otto II. Henry the Quarrelsome of Bavaria executed what to-day would be called a *Coup d'État.* He had been for five years an exile from his duchy and a prisoner in the hands of the bishop of Utrecht. He now *Henry the Quarrelsome.*

regained his liberty and declared himself regent of the kingdom as the nearest male relative of the youthful Otto III. He secured the person of the king and proceeded to exercise the government in his name. Nor did he stop here. He called the Saxons nobles together in Magdeburg on Palm Sunday and declared his intention of himself assuming the crown. In Quedlinburg he appeared in royal state and had himself addressed as king. Dukes Boleslav of Bohemia and Mesco of Poland swore to him the oath of fealty and became his firm allies.

Theophano and Adelaide. But Henry had deceived himself as to the strength of the opposition in Germany. Even his own Saxons disapproved of his proceedings, and the powerful Archbishop Willigis of Mayence was able to gain one supporter after the other for the king's mother and grandmother, Theophano and Adelaide. It came to blows between the two rival parties, but Henry soon saw that, having no strong adherents in any of the duchies, further efforts would be vain. He promised to surrender his youthful charge. Theophano had meanwhile left Rome, and in Lombardy had joined Adelaide, whom Otto II. had made vicegerent in Italy. The two women arrived in time for the diet of Nara, where the matter of the **Henry submits.** regency was definitely settled (June 29th, 984). Soon afterwards, at Worms, Henry, pacified by the hope of regaining Bavaria, laid his hands in the hands of the baby king and swore allegiance to him.

Henry received Bavaria in the following year after arrangements had been made for the compensation of its recent duke. The latter, also named Henry, received a new duchy consisting of Carinthia and the March of Verona.

Henry the Quarrelsome had trodden much the same path as his father, the oft-forgiven brother of Otto I. Like that turbulent noble, he, too, had come to see that fidelity to his king was the best and truest policy. He lived for ten years after regaining Bavaria, ten years of such mild and beneficent rule that his name of " Quarrelsome " gave place to "Lover of Peace " in the mouth of the people. The failure of his revolt was looked upon as a judgment of God. Thietmar the chronicler preserves a song about him to the following effect:

> "King Duke Henry fain had been;
> God in Heaven willed it not."

Theophano carried on the government with great firmness and decision. That she was gifted every one knew; the strength of will and of character that she developed was a revelation. To use the words of Thietmar of Merseburg, "she led a model life, a thing rare among the Greeks, and watched with truly manly power over the welfare of her son and of her kingdom, humbling the proud and exalting the humble." Among the "proud" may be reckoned Hugo Capet, who, to the exclusion of the last Carolingians, had swung himself upon the throne of France. He sought but never gained Theophano's recognition, and at last began to plot with the Greeks to drive the Germans out of Southern Italy.

In 988 Theophano went to Rome and conducted herself in every way as its ruler. She went so far as to call herself "the emperor" in her charters, which were dated from the year of her accession. In Rome and Ravenna she held her courts, and presided over them in person. Her officials were sent even into the patrimony of Peter.

Great things were to be hoped for from such a woman had she lived, but on the eve of a struggle with Hugo, while Germany was being harassed by new disturbances among the Wends and in Bohemia, she passed away.

Adelaide, ably seconded by Willigis of Mayence, now undertook the cares of government. Nor were these by any means light. Year after year armies had to be despatched against the Wends, until, in 996, a peace was made with them. The Swedes and Danes, too, constantly plundered the Frisian coasts, and ran their ships into the Elbe and Weser.

With his fifteenth year Otto reached the end of his wardship. He was a wonder in the matter of learning and accomplishments; but his education had only served to fill him

Theophano's rule.

Adelaide and Willigis of Mayence.

with an overweening sense of his own importance. Adelaide and Theophano are somewhat to blame for this result. They had always looked to Otto III. to complete the work begun by his grandfather. The young king's pride and insolence are said finally to have driven Adelaide from court, and she ended her life in retirement. Willigis, of Mayence, remained at the head of the royal advisers, and he it was who arranged Otto's first expedition to Italy.

Otto III. in Italy.
It was high time for interference in that quarter. The Pope, oppressed by the tyrant Crescentius, who was playing the *rôle* of a second Alberic, was clamouring for aid. In Southern Italy Capua had been on the point of throwing off the German yoke, but had been prevented from doing so by the counts of Tuscany and Spoleto.

In February, 996, the army, which was to escort Otto, assembled at Ratisbon; by Easter the expedition had reached Pavia. Here news was brought of the death of Pope John XV., and in Ravenna envoys from the nobility of Rome came to beg for a new Pope from the hand of the king. Otto named his own cousin, Bruno, who took the name of Gregory V. He was the first German to ascend the papal throne.

Otto III. crowned emperor, 996.
On May 21st, 996, the new Pope placed the crown of the empire on the head of the German king.

Otto III., who had thus been raised to the summit of earthly ambition, was possessed of two souls. The one was that of an emperor thirsting for power, longing to surpass his forerunners in glory and magnificence. The other was that of a monk, on whom the movement then going on in the Church had made the most profound impression. It was the time of the growth and prosperity of Cluny, and allied ideas had taken root in Germany. Here they had been fostered, not only in the monasteries, but also among the secular clergy.

St. Adalbert.
The man, of all others, whose absolute fearlessness and sincerity captivated the young king, was the Bohemian, Adalbert, whom he met at this time. Adalbert had been

Bishop of Prague, but, tiring of the world and of its honours, had entered a Roman monastery. Pope Gregory V. ordered him to return to his bishopric, and he crossed the Alps with Otto and his army, as they were returning from the Italian expedition.

The young emperor became devoted to the saintly bishop. We are told that he had a couch prepared for him near his own, and that whole nights were spent in confidential talk.

An inward voice was constantly calling Adalbert to great deeds among the heathen. His old bishopric, refusing to receive him back, he wandered to the Pomeranians and Prussians, on the coasts of the Baltic. Here he found a martyr's death at the hand of a heathen priest.

Otto never forgot his friend. Years afterwards he journeyed as a pilgrim to Gnesen, to the church where Adalbert lay buried. Gnesen itself was raised, by the emperor's wish, to be an archbishopric for Poland. The Adalbert church at Aix, which is still standing, was one of Otto's foundations.

If Adalbert fostered Otto's monkish tendencies, a man was not wanting who was to influence the other side of his character, to mould his intellect, and to direct his ambition. This was Gerbert, of Rheims, afterwards Bishop of Ravenna, and finally Pope. At odds with the court and with a party of the bishops in France, Gerbert willingly accepted an invitation of Otto III. to come to his court. Otto wrote that he wished to be cured of the rawness of his Saxon nature, and to have the flame of Greek knowledge fanned to life within him. Contempt for the culture of the Germans could not have been more openly expressed. *Gerbert of Rheims.*

Gerbert came to Otto's court at Magdeburg in 997, and found the young emperor surrounded by men of science and of wit. The old hall of the imperial castle was the scene of learned disputations, and Otto himself took pleasure in giving knotty subjects for discussion.

These harmless encounters were soon interrupted. Otto was forced first to make an expedition against the Wends, and then to hurry to Italy. Pope Gregory V. had been *Second Italian expedition.*

driven from Rome. Crescentius had again become master of
the city, and had begun to make levies on the revenues of
the Roman church. He soon placed an antipope upon the
chair of Peter.

Otto responded as promptly as he could to Gregory's
appeals for aid. In February, 998, having been joined by
the fugitive Pope, he appeared with an army before the gates
of Rome. They were quickly opened to him. The antipope,
who had sought refuge in a strong tower outside of the city,
was soon taken captive and mutilated. Crescentius had fled
to the castle of St. Angelo, but that huge fortress did not
long protect him. St. Angelo was stormed and soon surrendered, and the tyrant was beheaded on the castle roof. His
remains were flung to the pavement below.

**Otto's asceti-
cism.**
A year after these events Pope Gregory died, and Gerbert
took his place as Sylvester II. By this time the monkish
side of the emperor's character had grown more and more
pronounced. Grief over Adalbert's death, fear of the approaching end of the world, which had been foretold for the
year 1000, as well as other causes, combined to drive him
into extremes of asceticism. As a pilgrim he neared the holy
places where Adalbert had been. Barefoot he approached
the cloister of St. Michael on Mount Gargano. At Gaeta he
stopped to pray with the hermit Nilus ; in Rome he retired
for a fortnight to a cave near the church of St. Clement.
About at this time the names, " Servant of the Apostles,"
" Servant of Jesus Christ," were added to the imperial
title.

**His thirst
for glory.**
It seemed as if the only thing left was for Otto himself to
become a monk. But the other side of his nature asserted
itself in time. He began to make the greatest plans for the
extension of his power ; nothing short of a world-monarchy
seemed likely to satisfy him.

In order more firmly to unite Italy and Germany, he placed
the chanceries of the two lands in one hand, that of the
Archbishop of Cologne. The imperial titles become more
pretentious. The leaden seals of documents issued shortly

after the fall of Crescentius, bear the emperor's image, and the words, "Restoration of the Roman Empire." In his palace on the Aventine Otto began to unfold an oriental magnificence. Wondrous were the garments in which he decked himself, no name was too high-sounding with which to address him. He was "emperor of all emperors," "Saxonicus," "Romanus," "Italicus." Countless officials, with strangely sounding titles, surrounded him. Even a naval prefect was appointed, although no fleet was at hand.

The memorable visit to the tomb of Charles the Great, which took place on Otto's return to Germany, hangs together with these new foibles of Otto III. He wished to feed his eyes on the form of his great and worthy predecessor. The visit made a great impression on the writers of the time ; the wildest reports of what the emperor had seen were gravely circulated, and many fictitious details have been believed in our own day. But any careful historian will assure you that Charles did not sit upright on a golden throne, that his finger-nails had not burst through his gloves, and that Otto did not repair his nose with a point of gold. *Visits tomb of Charles the Great.*

Otto's dream of glory was destined not to come true. In 1001 he returned to Italy, to find the southern half of the peninsula in open rebellion. Capua and Benevento, Salerno, Naples, and Gaeta shook off the German rule. Even Rome was no longer a safe resting-place for the emperor, whose palace on the Aventine suffered a three days' siege. He withdrew to Ravenna, and from here made several attempts to retrieve his losses. *Revolts in Italy.*

Meanwhile in Germany the nobles were becoming highly discontented with the exclusively Italian policy of their emperor.

In the German Church, too, matters took a turn that threatened to bring about such a schism with Rome as already existed in France. Archbishop Willigis, of Mayence, and Bishop Bernward, of Hildeshiem, were in feud concerning Gandersheim. The former refused to be bound by the Pope's commands, and treated his legate with scorn. *Condition of Germany.*

**Death of
Otto III.,
1002.**

Otto did not survive the outcome of the struggle ; a fever, aggravated by the climate of Italy, carried him away in January, 1002. His dying wish had been that his bones might rest near those of Charles the Great, and a number of bishops and nobles determined to fulfil his last desire. It was no easy task ; the Italians blocked the way, and seven days were passed in continual skirmishes. At Easter, finally, the remains of the last male descendant of Otto the Great were laid in the Cathedral of Aix-la-Chapelle.

Under the line of kings that had just ended a national consciousness had developed among the people. Germany then first was spoken of and regarded as a finite conception ; the word " deutsch " begins to appear in the contemporary chronicles.

**Influence of
Italy on
Germany.**

The connection with Rome, so carefully fostered, was to prove disastrous in some ways, but it served to lift Germany from the depths of barbarism, and to make her heir to the culture of the past. One should go to the town of Hildes-heim to-day and see the bronze column, the iron doors, and the other evidences of Italian art as copied or worked over by old Bishop Bernward, the friend of Otto III. They are of a beauty that is simply astonishing. And not only to art but to literature, agriculture, civic life, as well as to religion, a new impulse was given. Roman refinement was grafted on Teuton sturdiness, but Germany stamped her acquisitions with the mark of her own individuality. Even the Chris-tianity which Rome gave was to assume a loftier character, and was finally to be freed from its trammels.

**Condition of
Germany.**

We have arrived, with the death of Otto III., at a time of great change, at a time when feudalism had swallowed up almost all the free tillers of the soil ; when knights and warriors had raised themselves to a plane above that on which ordinary men resided ; when a population hitherto purely rural had begun to be enclosed by cities and fortresses within their walls.

The vassals who had helped Henry I. and Otto the Great to victory had been richly rewarded. Fief upon fief, soon

about to become hereditary in their families, had been added
to their possessions, and many a fair estate from the crown
lands had fallen to their share.   The bishops, too, the firm
allies of the crown, had not been forgotten; their churches
were appanaged by vast grants of land, of immunities, and of
privileges. Otto III., at last, had placed whole counties under
their jurisdiction.   Had the sacrifices thus made attained
their object?   The supremacy which Otto I. had won over
the border nations was lost, step by step, by his descendants.
The Danes had withdrawn their allegiance; the majority of
the Wends had thrown off the German yoke; Hungary was
fast becoming independent, and Otto III., by raising Gnesen
to an archbishopric, had separated the Polish from the jurisdiction of the German Church.   Poland itself was soon to
engage in a ten years' war with its suzerain.

In France the Carolingians had always sought aid and
advice at the German court, but they had now been supplanted by the Capetians.   At the time of Otto III.'s death,
too, all Italy was in revolt, and an Arduin of Ivrea stood
ready there to play the *rôle* of another Hugh Capet.

CHAPTER XI.

Three pretendants. SCARCELY had Otto III. been consigned to his grave when three men stretched out their hands for the crown. Henry of Bavaria, son of Henry the Quarrelsome, was the nearest male relative of the line that had ended ; but heredity alone was not enough, although son had followed upon father for more than three quarters of a century. There failed him the designation by his predecessor, as well as the consent of the nobles. His rivals were Eckart of Meissen, known as a brave warrior, and Hermann of Suabia. Henry was cool and decided in pushing his claim, He it was who received Otto's corpse when it arrived in Germany, and arranged all the details for the burial. He seized the insignia of royalty, and placed under arrest the Archbishop of Cologne who had withheld the holy lance.

Eckard of Meissen. Eckard's candidacy had been much discussed, especially in Saxony. It was felt that a great blow was threatening the Saxon predominance, and that Bavaria should not be allowed to come to the fore.

Eckhard himself felt sure of the election. The Bishop of Hildesheim received him with royal honours, although Paderborn refused him entrance, and an ever-increasing party of bishops and nobles declared against him. He was murdered in the monastery of Pöhlde, where he had taken refuge for the night. There were not wanting those who accused Henry of Bavaria with complicity in the deed, but history can only say "not proven."

Election of Henry II. Hermann of Suabia had raised an army to oppose Henry, but the latter gained the mastery at every point, and, little by little, all the powers in Germany bowed before him. On June 7th, 1002, he was elected at Mayence, and, on the same day, anointed and crowned by Archbishop Willigis. The Saxons had not participated in the election, but, in return for various concessions, made their submission six weeks later. The Thuringians were won by the remission of a tax on swine, which they had been paying ever since the time of the Merovingians—ever since the days of Theuderich, the son of Clovis.

Hermann of Suabia made his formal submission in the autumn of 1002, and was treated with leniency. He was allowed to retain the duchy of Suabia, as well as his fiefs of the crown.

His position on the throne once secured, Henry II. took up with zeal the tasks incumbent on a mediæval sovereign, and strove to carry them through with patience and perseverance. In addition to the cares of administration, there was a Polish duke with Pan-Slavic aspirations to be warred with repeatedly, Italy to be reduced to subjection, and a number of struggles to be carried on with recalcitrant vassals and tributary princes. There was, moreover, the crown of the empire to be gained, and, finally, a reform in the Church to be carried through. Like a second Charlemagne, Henry marched to and fro in his kingdom, now on his eastern, now on his western boundary, always on the alert, yet sparing time to pass and enforce various salutary measures. *Henry II. and the problems of his reign.*

On a seal issued in the first year of Henry's reign stand the words "Restoration of the Frankish Kingdom." Inwardly and outwardly he strove to gain this end. He attempted to govern on legal principles, to strengthen the crown by wise institutions. Protection was granted the lower classes; a law was passed providing against the sale of slaves to Jews or heathen. *Restores order.*

The Ottos had failed through a too great absolutism. Henry made his measures dependent on the consent of his nobles—hence the unusual number of diets and other assemblies that took place in his reign. Not that his will was subservient to theirs; when occasion demanded he could be stern enough, and could let his princes know, as a chronicler expresses it, that they " must bow before the fountain of justice." Numerous are the feuds which he put down, and the disturbers of the peace whom he reduced to order. The first examples of the so-called " Landfrieden," or " peace of the land "—local regulations for the restraint of feuds—date from his reign; the faint beginnings of written law are here to be found.

Wars against Boleslav of Poland.

In Duke Boleslav of Poland Henry found a powerful and indefatigable enemy. Although a man of violent and tyrannical nature, Boleslav had compelled his people to accept Christianity, and with it something of German culture. He had introduced to some extent an army organization into Poland, and had protected the kingdom from the attacks of the Russians on the one hand, and the Bohemians on the other. He had conquered Pomerania and Prussia, Silesia and Moravia, and, on the death of Eckart of Meissen, who had always strongly defended his boundaries, had possessed himself of Eckart's Mark, and even of the town itself of Meissen. A party of the Bohemians had invited his interference in the affairs of that land too, and, in the end, he had caused himself to be solemnly proclaimed Duke of Bohemia. He had felt himself so powerful that, without troubling his suzerain the king of the Germans, he had sent to the Pope and asked that he might be presented with a royal crown.

These wars inglorious.

Henry's wars against Boleslav were, on the whole, inglorious, for he never really subjected his great vassal, although again and again returning to the charge. One measure of his that shocked the clergy, and might have lost him their goodwill, had he not thrown a sop to them by his zeal in the matter of restoring the bishopric of Merseburg, was an alliance against the Poles with the heathen Lutitii, a tribe of Wends to whom he expressly allowed the practice of their rites. He showed in this way a political wisdom such as we do not again meet before the time of Frederick II.

By this alliance not only were bounds set to Boleslav's **Alliance** aggressions, but direct furtherance was given to the cause **with the** of Christianity. The bishops of Brandenburg and Havel- **heathen.** burg who had long been kept from entering their dioceses were allowed to return in peace. By the peace of Bautzen, closed in 1005, Boleslav was bereft of one at least of the fruits of his victories. He seems to have renounced Bohemia, where indeed he was no longer wanted, and the possession of which he never regained.

In 1007 Henry sent an unsuccessful expedition against Poland; in 1009 he led one, with like results, himself. In 1013 a new peace was concluded, as Henry was eager for an Italian expedition, Boleslav for a war against the Russians. Boleslav did homage at Merseburg.

Two years later a new series of wars was begun which lasted until 1018, when a peace was concluded at Bautzen which was highly favourable to Boleslav. He was even allowed to keep Lusitania, the latest of his conquests.

His project, indeed, of founding a great Slavic empire had **Decline of** failed, although shortly before his death he assumed, un- **Polish** opposed, the dignity of King of Poland. **power.**

Henry II.'s successor, Conrad, be it here remarked, took up the struggle with Boleslav's sons. He was more successful than Henry had been, and in 1031 a peace was concluded by which Mesco of Poland gave up Lusitania. Mesco died three years later, after having renounced the title of king, and having done homage to Conrad. His son Casimir was unable to cope with the different factions in Poland itself, and was driven from the land. Boleslav's once powerful kingdom had by this time lost all its prestige; the supremacy among the Slavic lands on Germany's border was to pass to the Bohemians.

Arduin of Ivrea, to return to the reign of Henry II., proved **Henry II.** a far less formidable enemy than the Polish duke. He had **and Arduin** taken the crown of Italy at Pavia in February, 1002, and **of Ivrea.** Henry, almost immediately after his own accession, had dispatched Otto of Carinthia with a small army against him.

M

Otto was defeated, his army being surprised and put to flight.

It was more than a year before Henry, who was occupied in putting down one of the inevitable conspiracies with which each German king in turn had to cope, could proceed to the chastisement of Arduin. But by April, 1004, his army had reached Trent; it soon stormed a pass leading to the valley of the Brenta, and succeeded in spreading panic among Arduin's troops.

Henry, King of Italy.

Brescia, Bergamo, and Pavia opened their gates to Henry, and in the latter place he was crowned King of Italy. He was the first of the German kings to insist on this ceremony, the right of the Lombards to bestow their crown having never hitherto been acknowledged. Pavia had to suffer for harbouring the new King of Italy. A revolt which broke out against the Germans was put down with a hand of iron. The city was reduced to ashes, and thousands perished in the flames.

These events cowed the Italians, and the cities of Tuscany sent in their submission.

It was nine years before Henry again entered Italy. By that time conflicts with his own nobles had led him to feel that the prestige to be gained by winning the imperial crown would strengthen his position in Germany, while an understanding with the Pope might further his influence with the clergy. Arduin of Ivrea, moreover, although no longer at the head of a large following, was stirring once again; not to mention a minor revolt under the Archbishop of Ravenna.

Henry made emperor.

Henry found a strong party among the lesser prelates, as well as among the cities, which at this time were rising into prominence. Pisa, Venice, and Amalfi vied with each other in extending their commerce. Florence was just starting on her grand career, while Genoa took the lead in developing the institutions which brought about civic freedom. These new-formed powers, fearing for their existence if they should fall into the hands of the nobles, declared for the German king.

From the Pope there was little to fear. Benedict VIII.

was too unsure of his own position, oppressed as he was, on
the one hand, by the sons of Crescentius, who had hitherto
disposed of the tiara at will, on the other by the Greeks, who
had awaked to new aggressions in Southern Italy. Benedict's
only wish could be to welcome Henry should he come as a
friend. No sooner had the king recognized him as the true
Pope, than he offered to throw open the gates of Rome and
to present him with the imperial crown.

All this had been arranged before Henry's advent. In **Coronation ceremony.**
1013, then, the latter crossed the Alps, and advanced in
triumph as the acknowledged champion of the Church. At
Ravenna Benedict met him, and a synod was held by Pope
and King in common. A new era of prosperity seemed in
prospect; evils were condemned, old wounds healed, and forgotten ordinances called to remembrance. From Ravenna
the Pope hastened to Rome to prepare for the reception of
his exalted guest. On February 14th, 1014, the coronation
ceremony was performed in St. Peter's, the queen also being
anointed and crowned.

The new emperor returned triumphant to Germany, and by **Arduin sub-mits.**
Whitsuntide was already in Bamberg. Arduin, to be sure,
had not been subjected, and continued to unfurl the standard
of revolt; but he soon saw that his cause was hopeless, and,
sick in soul and body, retired to a cloister, and became a
monk. His sons tried in vain to prolong the fight, but were
unable seriously to trouble the king's peace of mind.

Henry now ruled Italy in peace by means of his officials **Henry's rule in Italy.**
Disputes among Italian nobles were settled at the German
court; on German ground Italian bishops were invested with
their office, and did homage for their fiefs. Many Germans
were promoted, too, to these rich and popular sees. Seven
years after his coronation as emperor Henry again entered
Italy. Pope Benedict had long been struggling with the
Greeks and Arabs. He had been aided in 1016 by forty
Norman knights returning from the Holy Land. For the
first time the future lords of Southern Italy had set their
foot on the land which was to become their own.

There was urgent need of Henry's presence; Salerno had withdrawn from the obedience of the empire, and the golden key of Capua had been sent as a token of submission to Constantinople. The two principalities were recovered, but the Greeks were not dislodged from Southern Italy and the expedition as a whole cost far too dear. The plague broke out, and many of the Germans were carried away.

Efforts to reform the Church. The intercourse with the Pope had again been most friendly, and a grand project of reform had been drawn up. How seldom in the course of history shall we meet again with such unity of interests between the heads of Christendom!

Chief among the evils that had crept in to the Latin Church at this time were simony and marriage of priests. The buying and selling of Church offices had become an habitual practice in high as well as in low places, while the clergy, in Lombardy especially, openly took unto themselves wives and provided for their children out of the Church lands. Heresy and schism, too, were rampant at this time, and there were prelates both in Italy and in Germany who had practically seceded from Rome.

Henry furthered the Pope's efforts with might and main. The decrees issued against the marriage of priests at a council held in Pavia were supplemented by laws pronouncing secular punishments against those who disregarded them. Freeborn women who married unfree priests were to be publicly whipped and banished.

Henry II., "the Saint." It was Henry's merits as a reformer as well as his general attitude of benefactor towards the Church that caused him to be called "the saint" by his contemporaries, and, twenty-two years after his death, to be actually canonized by Pope Eugene III.

Seldom was a monarch more conscientious in performing his religious duties, more punctilious in following out the prescriptions of the Church. He was thoroughly pious by nature, and was strongly imbued with the strict principles of Cluny. Abbot Odilo was his constant adviser, Abbot Poppo of Stablo his right hand in church administration.

With astonishing liberality Henry acceded to the demands of his bishops. Rents, tolls, and mint-monies were given over to them in plenty. But he was determined to have reform, and never were synods held in such numbers.

Henry drew the clergy closer and closer to him. They were his allies, political as well as spiritual. They were the bone and sinews of his government. He, for his part, entered into their brotherhoods and communities, fell on his face at their feet, and entreated them, if need be; but at the same time showed them more clearly than any king, since the time of Charlemagne, that he expected them to do their duty both to Church and State. He did not hesitate on occasion to annul charters of his predecessors, or to curtail their deeds of gift. The monasteries, especially, felt his chastening hand. In 1004 Hersfeld was deprived of estates and privileges, and many monks were banished; a new and sterner abbot brought the rest to submission. Reichenau, Fulda, and Corvei were also severely disciplined, while St. Maximin, near Treves, was made to surrender 200,000 acres of land to the crown. When Bamberg was founded in 1007, five abbies lost their independence in a single day.

Henry and the clergy.

Founding of Bamberg.

This bishopric of Bamberg is the spot, of all others, that is most intimately associated with the memory of Henry II. to-day. The splendid cathedral, which now stands there, was built by him, and the two great bells that surmount the edifice have been named for him and his queen, Henry and Kunigunde. By the foundation of this See, the country around was transformed from a scarcely inhabited waste, to a flourishing and populous district. Forests were cut away, the land tilled and cared for. Here, too, art and science found a congenial home.

The founding of a bishopric, a suitable diocese for which could only be formed by curtailing the possessions of surrounding bishops, was no easy matter; but a synod at Frankfort was finally induced to give a written pledge of consent to the project. The Bishop of Wurzburg, indeed, persisted in his opposition for a year, but was finally brought to terms. The consecration of the cathedral in 1012 was solemnized with the utmost magnificence.

Henry was never weary of bestowing gifts and privileges on his new creation. A number of manuscripts from the library, which he founded at Bamberg, have been preserved.

Struggle with Aribo of Mayence. One great hindrance to Henry's project of a great reform on Cluny principles, was the attitude taken towards the movement by no less a personage than the Archbishop of Mayence. The struggle with Aribo darkened the last years of the monarch's life, and prevented many of his measures from being carried through. Aribo wanted reform, indeed, but he wanted it brought about in his own way. His high-handed actions brought him into conflict with the Pope, as as well as with the emperor. In 1023 he called together a synod at Seligenstadt, where, among other decrees, one was drawn up to the effect that no one should appeal to Rome without consent of his bishop ; that papal absolution, indeed, was invalid, so long as the delinquent had not fulfilled the penance which that bishop had laid upon him.

It seemed as though the proud archbishop, full of personal grievances against the Pope, who had withdrawn his pallium, were about to draw a large part of the German church away from its obedience to the See of Rome. Aribo went so far as to summon a national council, which, however, degenerated into a synod of the diocese of Mayence.

Henry's death, 1024 A.D. Death put an end to all these complications. The year 1024 saw pope and emperor both consigned to their polished tombs, and the struggle was not continued by Aribo against their successors.

Conrad II., 1024-1037. Henry II. left no male heir. Once more it devolved on the nobles to elect a king. Their choice was a singularly fortunate one.

Conrad II., although he performed no one great deed, and engaged in no one great struggle, brought the mediæval German empire to a high—some think to its highest—pitch of greatness and prosperity. He was capable and cool-headed, diplomatic, and ready to take advantage of every opportunity that offered.

His personality, we use the words of a modern historian,[1] "is seen in its true light, if we compare it to that of his immediate predecessors. This Rhenish freeman remained entirely untouched by the power of the priestly ideas which had seized upon the dynasty of the Ottos, with a force which went on increasing from member to member. In Conrad II. there appears again at the head of the nation, for the first time after a long pause, a true German character, the warlike and justice-dispensing layman, as he had developed up to this time. He himself is one of the most remarkable representatives of this class; brave, skilled in the law, a master in negotiation and in oratory, a protector of the church, yet as king mistrustful against her, self-confident and relentless. A French observer betokens him as a man of intellectual boldness, of mighty bodily power, but of wavering fidelity." As Hercules and Ulysses in one, the same writer goes on to describe him. *His personality.*

Conrad was able to display his talents in the very assembly that raised him on the throne. (Sept. 4, 1024.)

He himself was a descendant of Otto I.'s daughter and of that Conrad who, finally, had atoned for a series of wrong-doings by his bravery and death on the plains of the Lech. But there was another descendant of Otto, called Conrad the younger, who also appeared in the meeting at Gamba (on the right bank of the Rhine, near Mayence), as candidate for the throne. The elder Conrad had managed to come to an agreement with his rival before the voting took place. Exactly what promises he made will never be known. Certain it is that he induced his cousin to acquiesce peaceably in his own election. Equally certain is it that he later did not keep his promise. *The two Conrads.*

The first, and practically the decisive vote for Conrad, had been given by Archbishop Aribo, of Mayence. We find the *Influence of bishops.*

---

[1] Nitsch.

bishops henceforth playing the leading part in every election. Aribo showed his independence—he had shown it, as we have seen before—by refusing to crown Conrad's queen, Gisela, on the ground that her marriage was not valid. She was bound to her husband by ties of blood closer than those which the Church allowed.

The Archbishop of Cologne was induced to perform the desired function. Conrad seems to have borne no malice to Aribo, who proved his ally in many ways.

A favouring providence seems to have watched over Conrad II.'s reign, and to have allowed him to complete the undertakings of his predecessors. We have seen how he succeeded in bringing the Polish difficulties to a happy conclusion, whereby the disunity and weakness of the Poles themselves played no inconsiderable part.

Conrad II. in Italy. In Italy Conrad ruled as no German prince had ruled for many a long day. Immediately after Henry II.'s death a reaction had here taken place, and a number of nobles had headed a rebellion. The palace of the German emperors in Pavia was laid in ruins, and the crown of Italy offered to King Robert of France, who, although hostile to the Germans, refused it, and then to William of Aquitaine.

Conrad was detained at first by an easily quelled insurrection on his western border in which the French king, Baldwin of Flanders, Odo of Champagne, the dukes of Upper and Lower Lorraine, Conrad the younger and Ernest of Suabia, Queen Gisela's son by a former marriage, were concerned. He was able, however, early in 1026 to appear in Italy, and he devoted more than a year to restoring order and discipline. On reaching Milan, he was crowned by Archbishop Aribert with the Lombard crown.

Imperial coronation, 1026 A.D. Pavia was besieged and taken, and the citizens of Ravenna reduced to subjection. In Rome, Conrad was well received by Pope John XIX. who placed upon his head the crown of the empire. Magnificent was the coronation ceremony, and the occasion was graced by the presence of Odilo of Cluny, of Rudolf of Burgundy, and of Canute of England. Canute,

already lord of two great kingdoms and soon to be lord
of a third, had been willing and eager to close an alliance
with the German king. The bonds of friendship were later
to be drawn still tighter by the marriage of Gunhild, Canute's
daughter, and Henry, Conrad's son.

It is true Conrad renounced some of the rights and possessions of Germany in order to gain this new friend. The Mark
of Schleswig was ceded to Denmark, which was to hold it
until in our own days, and the Danes became absolutely independent of Germany. But on one border at least Conrad's
kingdom was now secure from invasion.

While Conrad was in Italy, Ernest of Suabia, who in character was a second Lucifer, again raised the standard of
revolt. Conrad the Younger aided the movement. Although
Suabia was soon a hotbed of rebellion, Conrad's reappearance
after his successful expedition served at once to restore quiet
and order. Duke Ernest surrendered and was taken to the
castle of Giebichstein on the Saale. Conrad the Younger was
called to strict account, his best fortresses rased to the
ground, his property confiscated, and he himself placed under
arrest.

Ernest of Suabia.

It was the tragic and loyal death of Ernest of Suabia three
years later, which has endeared him to German hearts and
rendered him so popular a hero of German song. Conrad had
released him from Giebichstein, and even reinstated him in his
duchy of Suabia. But when, in 1030, the emperor required
him to pursue, as a state enemy, his own close friend the
adventurous Werner of Kyburg, the fiery duke promptly refused. Conrad determined on Ernest's ruin. His goods were
confiscated, the ban of the church and that of the empire alike
were spoken against him. Ernest was soon at the end of his
resources ; he retired to that rocky fortress of Falkenstein,
the ruins of which are so well known. Thither he was tracked
and made to turn at bay. He came forth to meet the troops
of the emperor and fell fighting in their midst. Future generations forgot that he had been a rebel and only remembered
his unswerving devotion to his friend.

Ernest's tragic death.

Conrad joins Burgundy to the empire.   Conrad II.'s chief title to fame rests on the fact that under his reign the rich and fertile kingdom of Burgundy was joined to the Holy Roman Empire, in the possession of which it was to remain for centuries. Burgundy extended from the sources of the Saone to the Mediterranean, and from the Jura mountains to the Western Alps. It controlled several of the great passes into Italy, and contained cities such as Lyons, Marseilles, Basle, and Geneva, important then as now.

Retrospect as to Burgundy.   Henry II. as the son of Gisela, oldest sister of Rudolph III., considered himself the prospective heir to the Burgundian throne. But the nobles of that land clamoured for the right of electing whom they pleased should the throne become vacant. There were candidates enough, among them Ernest of Suabia, who also could show descent from the royal Burgundian house. It was these unacknowledged claims that eventually had first brought Ernest into conflict with Conrad II.

All the real power in Burgundy seems to have been in the hands of the nobles and not of the king. Rudolph saw himself so oppressed in 1016 that he concluded to abdicate in favour of Henry II. The act was fulfilled at Strasburg at Whitsuntide and one party of the nobles did homage to the new king. But another party, under Otto William, the grandson of that Berengar who had ruled Italy in the time of Otto I., flew to arms and held its own against Henry for many months. To add to the difficulties of the situation Rudolph, weak and vacillating, retracted, renewed, and again retracted his deed of gift. Henry then turned his weapons against his untrustworthy uncle and the war, begun in 1018, dragged on until 1023 when Henry seems to have dropped his claim to immediate rule, but not that to the ultimate succession.

Conrad and Burgundy.   When Henry II. died and Conrad succeeded him, Rudolph and his nobles considered the compact as to the succession dissolved. Rudolph declared that he had intended to leave Burgundy to Henry as his nephew, not as emperor of Germany. Conrad, however, had no intention of looking at matters in this light. He hastened to Basle, took the city, and even held a diet there.

King Rudolph died in September, 1032, and the insignia of royalty were sent to Conrad. But a large party of the Burgundians preferred a weak French noble to a powerful German emperor and called in Odo of Champagne.

Conrad's adherents formally elected him King of Burgundy in Basle in 1033. He had already succeeded by negotiation in turning away from Odo the sympathies of the French crown, which at this time was in the hands of the feeble young king, Henry. Therewith the outcome of the struggle was decided. The fight with Odo continued for two years, but at the end of that time the proud noble was brought to terms, and the union of Burgundy with Germany was consummated.

Since Charles the Great, no sovereign had possessed such power as Conrad II. In addition to Germany, Burgundy and Italy were under his sway, and no rival any longer threatened his borders.

And not only by acquiring territory did he aid the development of the empire. He carefully watched the signs of the times and acted accordingly. Instead of opposing the growing desire of the lesser nobles to have their fiefs made hereditary, he encouraged it. He established for all time in Germany the principle that the son might quietly succeed to the fiefs of the father if he were willing and able to perform the duties which the possession of those fiefs implied. In this way he won to a high degree the love of his vassals, and gained a new support for the crown, the value and importance of which cannot be over-estimated. The most humble vassal could henceforth appeal against an unjust lord without the fear that that lord might vent his anger by dispossessing him. *Conrad's internal policy.*

In some ways Conrad was far from being as devoted a son of the Church as Henry II. or the Ottos had been. He ruled the clergy with a rod of iron. The bishoprics were filled from purely political motives, while the missions in the north were either entirely neglected, or left to the more zealous care of the king of Denmark. *Conrad and the Church.*

But Conrad built churches of a size and magnificence hitherto unknown in Germany. The cathedral of Spires was begun by him, and was completed mainly in accordance with his plans. The abbey of Limburg, too, dates from his time.

The final episode of Conrad II.'s reign was the struggle with Archbishop Aribert of Milan. Aribert had been foremost among the Italians in his loyalty to the emperor. He it was who first urged upon Conrad the necessity for an expedition to Italy. He had crowned him with the Lombard crown, and had accompanied him to Rome. He had personally assisted in the Burgundian war.

Conflict with Aribert of Milan.

But Aribert wished above all things to secure for his see and for the teachings of St. Ambrose a boundless sway in Italy. His ambitious plans caused him to unite with the *capitanei*, or greater vassals of the crown in Lombardy, against the valvassores, or sub-vassals. The same conflict here was going on as in Germany, the same desire for heredity of fiefs was everywhere apparent. Aribert and his allies opposed the movement ; dispossession was their favourite means of coercion.

Conrad's laws for Italy.

Conrad II., who is said to have announced that "if the Italians were thirsting for laws he would immerse them in them," published a series of regulations which, fortunately for our understanding of these matters, may still be read in their original form. The valvassors were granted the protection of the law against their oppressors. Fiefs were to be hereditary, and might not be withdrawn from anyone save by sentence passed in an assembly of his peers. The right of direct appeal to the emperor was expressly emphasized.

Failure of Aribert's conspiracy.

Aribert was called to account for certain high-handed measures, and was required to restore some fiefs already confiscated. He refused in scorn and anger, and was taken prisoner by Conrad. Escaping from his captivity he raised all Milan in rebellion against the emperor. The result was a siege of Milan, a bloody battle, and the deposition of Aribert. The latter retaliated by instigating a far-reaching conspiracy. Italy was to be entirely freed from the German yoke, and the

crown was offered to Odo of Champagne who accepted it and
hastened to his favourite game of war for the purpose of
making secure his new acquisition.   He lost his life, however,
in a skirmish with the Lorraine contingent that was levied
against him.

The leaders in the conspiracy were sent into exile, and
Aribert lost all of his allies.   His faithful Milanese, indeed, **Aribert**
still held out, but were no longer formidable, and were not **and the**
deemed worthy any more of the emperor's personal attention. **Milanese.**
They did not desert the proud archbishop even when the Pope,
in 1038, publicly excommunicated him.   Aribert it was who
first organized in Milan a city militia into which all classes of
the population, all the male inhabitants of the surrounding
district, were drawn.   The institution soon spread to the other
cities of Lombardy.   Aribert, too, first gave the Milanese
their *caroccio*, a car with a mast, and on it a crucifix and a
standard, which was to be the rallying point in desperate
battles, and was to typify civic liberty.

In the midst of the demonstrations against Milan word was **Death of**
brought that Conrad II. had died (June 4th, 1039) and that **Conrad II.,**
Henry III., a youth of twenty-two, who already during **1039.**
Conrad's life-time had been elected king, had succeeded to the
throne.   The hostilities were at once suspended, for it was
known that Henry's views differed widely from those of his
father in all church matters, and especially as regarded the
struggle with Aribert.   And the latter, to be sure, was soon
pardoned and reinstated in his archbishopric, and in all his
dignities.

Henry III.,
1039-1056.

NEVER had a king of the Romans fallen heir to such power as was Henry's on his accession. He succeeded without even the customary conspiracy of nobles to the royal power in Italy, Burgundy, and Germany. Never were the princes, although only for the time being, more subject to the crown and the clergy more dependent on it. The duchies seemed to have lost their old predominance ; Bavaria, Suabia, and Franconia were all in the hands of the crown, while in Saxony Henry possessed an all-powerful ally in the person of Archbishop Adalbert of Bremen.

Of neighbouring powers none was strong enough to excite a fear. Canute of Denmark had passed away, and his sons were fighting among themselves over their inheritance. France was suffering under the weakest of kings, while in Rome a vicious and insignificant Pope sat on the chair of Peter. Only on the eastern boundary were complications to arise, and these were to be settled without all too great difficulty, except in the case of Hungary. Seventeen years later, when Henry III. died, all was changed. The empire, as is now generally recognized, was then already on its downward way. Henry had succeeded in estranging his nobles, the lesser as well as the greater, while his policy had raised the self-confidence of the clergy, and had tended to increase immeasurably the power of the Pope. His piety, too, had induced him to give up simony, and to renounce the not inconsiderable revenues that had regularly accrued to the crown from the sale of ecclesiastical preferments. The latest authorities for the history of these times see in this a weakening of the kingly authority, a triumph for the Church.

And yet Henry III.'s reign has hitherto been considered one of the most glorious in the history of mediæval Germany. This is partly owing to the fact that the writers of the time belonged to the clergy, and that the prosperity of the Church had indeed reached its culmination. Never did it rejoice in such broad possessions, or in such far-reaching privileges. The bishops of Italy exercised undisturbed the regalia, or royal rights, which were soon to go over to the cities. The richest sees of Italy were filled by German bishops, and for twelve years German popes sat on the throne of Peter.

It was a time of prosperity for the higher classes, although the peasants seem to have been oppressed by the nobles, and to have suffered severely from a succession of years of famine. That a certain amount of luxury and magnificence was displayed at the royal court may be gathered from an anecdote from one of the chronicles. The Bavarian Count Udalric left the advice in his will to his sons never to rebel against the emperor, and also, which would cost them about as dear, never to ask him to become their guest. To properly entertain him would mean the ruin of their property. *Condition of Germany.*

Germany was at this period beginning to learn the benefits of a more extended trade. The highroads of commerce began now to turn in towards the Rhine and the Elbe. A new class of men, the merchants, rose into prominence, and one city after another became a trading centre. Conrad II. had greatly furthered this development, and had bestowed extensive market privileges and rights concerning the coinage of money. The Cologne merchants of the time were noted for their gay and extravagant manner of living, which fact presupposes a considerable amount of prosperity. The Saxon cities of Bremen, Magdeburg, and Goslar traded with the Wends and with the Scandinavian North, while the commerce with England had already become considerable. King Ethelred had allowed the Germans to enter their wares free of toll. The especial objects of German activity were the *Germany's commerce.*

manufacture of cloth, the weaving of linen, the preparation
of leather, and the forging of weapons.

It was not long before the cities, to the development of
which trade had given such an impulse, were to attain
political importance which had utterly failed them up to this
time. They were soon to be able to aid their helpless master,
Henry IV., and to support his tottering throne.

Henry III. and the peace of the land.

Henry III. did everything in his power to establish a firm
basis of national prosperity by preserving peace and putting
down feuds. He entered into combat with an evil against
which the Church, especially in France and in Burgundy, was
now fighting with might and main.

In Aquitaine, as early as 1031, the idea of a general peace
under the Church's banner had arisen; several synods were
held which ordered a cessation of wars and a general condition of brotherly love. These decrees were received with
boundless enthusiasm, but the scheme was too general, and
therefore impracticable.

The Treuga Dei.

A new plan was thought of, and in 1041 the *Treuga Dei*,
or Truce of God, was promulgated. The act which passes
under this name determined that regularly, from Wednesday
evening until Monday morning, all feuds should cease. All
who accepted the truce and kept it were to be absolved from
their sins; all who infringed it were to condone their offence
by a pilgrimage to Jerusalem or to be excommunicated.

The efforts of the French Church were widely successful.
A Burgundian synod adopted the regulation and extended it
to the periods between Advent and Epiphany, and between
Septuagesima and the first Sunday after Easter. Abbot
Odilo of Cluny was zealous in recommending the truce.

The peace in Germany.

In Germany no formal act was passed and no special days
designated, but Henry III. brought the whole weight of his
personal influence to bear on his nobles. In Constance he
himself ascended the chancel of the cathedral, declared that
he personally forgave all those who had committed wrongs
against himself, and urged each of his hearers to pardon his
own particular enemy. At a diet in Treves, and again on

the eve of a battle at Menfö, the same exhortation was repeated.

The growing wealth in Germany, as well as the general feeling of security, are shown by the number of buildings which arose in Henry III.'s time. Stone churches took the place of wooden ones ; in some cases even the city walls were torn down to furnish material for the new cathedral. When Pope Leo came to Germany in 1049 a number of splendid buildings were ready to be consecrated.

We have spoken of complications on Henry III.'s eastern boundaries. Here, at the time of Conrad II.'s death, Bretislav of Bohemia, chafing under the conviction that his land was far from holding the position it had held in other days, and anxious to raise his people to a greater height than they had yet attained, determined on attacking disruptured Poland and forming a Slavic empire with Prague for its capital. The Bishop of Prague, too, considering it beneath his dignity to continue dependent on the see of Mayence, sent to Rome and asked for the pallium to be given him directly from the Pope. Bretislav's inroads into Poland met with no opposition. Krakau, Posen, and Gnesen fell into his hands. In the latter place lay the relics of St. Adalbert, the friend of Otto III., and once, as we know, a Bohemian bishop. Bretislav made himself master of them, and carried them in triumphal procession to the cathedral of Prague. More than a hundred wheeled vehicles full of booty and a number of Polish nobles in chains graced the occasion. {Henry III. and Bohemia.}

Henry III. could not let such high-handed actions pass unnoticed ; but the first expedition sent against Bohemia met with disaster and defeat. In 1041, however, two armies, better organized and more numerous than the first ones, reduced Bretislav to great straits. Exhausted and discouraged he agreed to give up his conquests and make his submission. Poland was vacated, and its exiled duke, Casimir, the son of Mesco, was allowed to return.

Bretislav was treated by Henry with leniency, being allowed to keep Silesia. He, as well as Casimir of Poland, became the firm ally of his conqueror, and supported him in all his later wars.

Henry III. and Hungary.

There remained a third power to be reckoned with—Hungary. Hungary had become a kingdom, about the year 1000, under Stephen, or rather St. Stephen, for he was later canonized. He was succeeded in 1038 by Peter, who, however, was driven from the kingdom and sought refuge at the court of Henry III. A Hungarian magnate named Aba was installed in his place on the throne, but Aba's policy, inasmuch as he allowed full sway to the former religion of the people, and the old ravaging expeditions of the Magyars were actually renewed, was displeasing to the Germans.

Wars against Hungary.

In 1042, Henry, advancing along the left bank of the Danube, gained a victory over Aba, and the next year brought him to terms. The conditions included the surrender of a large tract of western Hungary. In 1044 Aba again became recalcitrant, and a new army under Henry's own leadership marched against him. A decisive battle was fought on the Raab, and the Hungarian army was scattered like chaff before the wind. Aba escaped, but was declared to have forfeited the crown, which was given back to King Peter. Later, Aba was put to death by order of the restored king, who himself entered into the closest relations of alliance with and subjection to the German sovereign. Before the face of the Hungarian people he surrendered the golden lance, the symbol of rule, and the people themselves did homage to Henry and to his successors.

But this happy harmony did not last long. Henry's *protégé* was soon driven out, and a noble named Andreas raised in his stead. The wars with this new prince fill up the darkest period of Henry III.'s life. His campaigns proved disastrous, he was unable to retain his new acquisitions or to regain his influence in Hungary, while his ill success gave courage to other enemies of the crown which had meanwhile begun to raise their heads.

Chief among these were Duke Godfrey of Lorraine and his friend Baldwin of Flanders.

In 1044 Duke Gozelo of Lorraine had died after having Godfrey of Lorraine.
united, by Conrad II.'s permission, both Upper and Lower
Lorraine under his sway. His eldest son, Godfrey, who already
during his father's lifetime had managed the affairs of Upper
Lorraine, considered that he had a claim to the whole duchy.
Henry, however, willed otherwise. He determined again to
separate Lorraine, and gave the lower duchy to the younger
Gozelo, surnamed the coward. A most unfortunate step, far-
reaching in its consequences, for Henry himself was involved
in a long series of contests, and under his descendants the
throne itself was made to totter.

Godfrey rebelled and lost his duchy together with all his Godfrey's rebellion.
fiefs of the crown. He became the central figure in all conspiracies against the king. Now a captive in the rocky Giebichstein, now restored for a time to his duchy, he could not
forget his real or fancied wrongs ; by every kind of alliance he
tried to undermine the royal power. In 1049 Henry called in
Denmark and even England against Godfrey and against
Baldwin. Pope Leo IX. hurled the ban of the church against
them.

Deserted by their friends the two rebel leaders yielded and
were treated by Henry III., as was his wont, with leniency.
After Henry's death, Godfrey again rose to power and influence, having married Beatrice, widow of Boniface, margrave of Tuscany. From this union sprang the Countess
Matilda, heiress of those vast Tuscan estates which for
centuries were to prove a bone of contention between the
papacy and the empire.

Henry III.'s greatest triumph remains to be recorded before Henry III. reforms the papacy.
we pass to the misfortunes of his successor.

We have seen how Otto I. rid Christendom of a vicious
Pope and succeeded for a time in reforming the papacy. But
only for a time. The year 1046 saw matters in a more disgraceful condition than they had ever been ; the papacy had
turned into a three-headed monster which needed the hand of
a new Hercules to slay.

Benedict IX., engaged in matrimonial schemes, had first Three popes at one time.

renounced, then reclaimed the holy office ; but Silvester III. had meanwhile been elected by the Romans. Benedict, by the aid of his relatives, the counts of Tusculum, drove out his rival; but finding his own position too precarious, determined again to retire. Not empty-handed, however ! By a formal bill of sale he transferred the papacy to his godson, John Gratian, for the sum of one thousand pounds of silver. John, strange as it may seem, a disciple of Cluny and a would-be reformer, took the name of Gregory VI.

Benedict afterwards repented of his bargain, and—if we can believe the later account of Otto of Frising, a famous bishop and uncle of Frederick Barbarossa—the three popes lived together in Rome, one in St. Peter's, another in the Lateran, and the third in Santa Maria Maggiore !

Synod of Sutri, 1046 A.D.

But there were not wanting in Rome the voices of prophets denouncing loudly the shame and disgrace of this state of affairs. Above all the eloquent Peter Damiani, whose writings are among the most treasured remains of these times, turned his gaze to Henry III. Henry had often enough declared against all forms of simony : here was a chance for him to strike a blow at this vice and to make an example before all Christendom.

Hurrying to Italy, Henry held a synod at Pavia and another at Sutri. The latter was a stately assembly ; the entire Roman clergy had been summoned to appear, and a number of German prelates had accompanied the king. Silvester was deposed and banished to a monastery ; Gregory VI. confessed his guilt while protesting his pious purpose in buying the papacy. He went into exile in Germany being accompanied by Hildebrand, the future Gregory VII.

At a third synod held in Rome, Benedict IX. was stripped of his dignities and the Roman clergy and people left the choice of a new pope to their deliverer.

Adalbert of Bremen refuses papacy.

Adalbert, Archbishop of Bremen, was first offered the chair of Peter, but his northern see was too dear to him. Bremen had come to form a centre for all the Slavic missions and Adalbert seems to have dreamt of making it a second Rome.

His plan was to found twelve new bishoprics and to make them, as well as Denmark, Scandinavia, the Orkneys, Iceland, Greenland, Livonia, and Esthonia, subject to his own ecclesiastical authority. The plan was to fail, of course, but Adalbert was to find another field for his talents, and was to play a political *rôle* second to no one in Germany.

When refusing the papacy for himself, Adalbert turned the choice on Bishop Suidger of Bamberg who took the name of Clement II. **Clement II.**

Peter Damiani is never tired of celebrating the triumph of the German king in having put down three bad popes and raised up a just one. He likens him to the Saviour who cast out the money-changers from the Temple. In the words of the Psalmist, he breaks out : " Thou hast broken my bonds, O Lord ; I will consecrate unto thee the sacrifice of my praise."

On Christmas Day, 1046, the new Pope was consecrated, and on the same day Henry and his queen, Agnes of Poictou —Gunhild, the daughter of the Danish king had died in 1038— received the imperial crown. Moreover, in the boundless enthusiasm of the moment, the Romans conferred on the new emperor the patriciate, and the right in future to select a pope. The next pontiffs were in fact chosen by him, and it was not until 1059 that the right of disposing of the crown of Peter was denied his successor. **Imperial coronation.**

Henry III.'s last years were full of sorrow and vexation, and wars with his border neighbours as well as struggles with discontented nobles filled his time. A conspiracy headed by his own uncle came to light ; the rebels had aimed at nothing short of the murder of the king.

Henry died in 1056, and his youthful son succeeded him as Henry IV. The boy had already been crowned and consecrated during his father's lifetime. **Henry III.'s death, 1056 A.D.**

The crown of the kingdom and of the empire had by this time become practically hereditary. Some formulas for the royal consecration, and for the imperial coronation, have been preserved. They run as follows : " O Lord, let the kings of

the future come forth from his loins to rule this whole kingdom." And, again : " Keep the place thou hast received
from thy fathers, and that has fallen to thee by inheritance."
Finally : " Receive the crown that was destined for thee by
the Lord God ; hold it, and leave it hereafter in honour to
thy sons, by the help of God ! "

And yet the princes in electing Henry IV. at Tribur, in
1053, had done so with the express reservation, " provided he
shall prove a just king."

CHAPTER XIII.

HENRY IV. AND GREGORY VII.

ONE of the mightiest of emperors had passed away, and a little boy of six was King of the Romans and future emperor. The regent for the young monarch was his mother, Agnes, a weak woman, a prey to the jealousies and intrigues of her advisers, who were, for the most part, bishops intent solely on the advancement of their several sees.

Just at this time a rival power was rising in Europe, a second claimant to the world-monarchy, a priesthood that was to play fast and loose with all the traditions of kingship. The monk Hildebrand, afterwards Gregory VII., who had received his training in the rigid school of Cluny, was the soul of the movement. He was already the *Deus ex machinâ*, the power behind the Papal throne, and was to be the central figure in European history for thirty years to come. Future popes, inspired by his example, were to reiterate his claims, and to trample in the dust a whole proud dynasty.

Hildebrand's first public act was seemingly committed in favour and support of the empire he was afterwards so bitterly to oppose. On the death of Pope Stephen IX., in 1058, the Romans, encouraged by the weakness of the German crown, elected their own pope, Benedict X. It was Hildebrand who now insisted on the rights of Germany; he caused the heads of the reform party in Italy to assemble and to elect a pope according to precedent. In bond with Duke Godfrey of Tuscany, a devoted vassal of the empire, he caused a synod to assemble at Sutri in 1059; here Benedict X. was deposed. The new pope, Nicholas II., soon won universal recognition.

Hildebrand's two allies.

The victory just won was a victory over the Roman nobility, at that time the greatest enemy of a reformed papacy. Hildebrand had used the empire as a means of gaining his immediate end ; he next proceeded to free himself from his ally, associating himself instead with two new powers that had appeared in Italy—powers already more or less hostile to Germans and to German institutions.

The "Pataria."

The first of these was the " Pataria," a party which had originated in Milan, but had won followers in the other cities of Lombardy. The Patarians, so named originally from a word meaning "rags," were anarchists, if one may so call them, who were irritated at the riches and magnificence of the prelates ; at the same time they were Italian patriots bound to shake off, if possible, the yoke of Germany. Inflamed by enthusiastic preachers, especially by a certain Deacon Ariald, whose sermons were directed against simony and the marriage of priests, they had risen against the Ambrosian clergy, whose ritual and observances differed from those of Rome. In Milan they had driven the archbishop from the cathedral, and had plundered the houses of his subordinates.

The Normans in Italy.

Hildebrand's second alliance was with the Normans of Italy. These, originally a small band of knights who fought for pay, had gained a firm hold in the land during the preceding twenty years, had grown rich and powerful by robbery as well as by diplomacy, and were henceforth to play a *rôle* in Italy second only to that which their fellows were playing almost simultaneously in England.

Robert Guiscard.

Robert Guiscard, the " sly-head," had come into possession of all Apulia, over which he ruled as count. Richard of Aversa had made himself Prince of Capua, and it was to him that Hildebrand stretched out the hand of fellowship. Richard became a vassal of the Roman See, being the first prince to enter into this relation with the Papacy. Three hundred Norman knights marched to Rome to aid the new pope, and to destroy the castles of the Roman nobility.

Robert Guiscard followed Richard's example, and was re-

cognized as a vassal for the fiefs of Apulia, Calabria, and
Sicily. He and Richard were declared rulers of their new
possessions " by the grace of God and of St. Peter." In
Sicily, where his family were to rule for the next century
and a quarter, and to heap up an immense treasure, Robert
had not as yet a foot of land ; but Gregory well knew the
adventurous spirit of the race with which he had allied
himself.

The knights sent by Richard of Aversa had their share in   Lateran
Council of
1059.
driving Benedict X. to make a formal abdication. At the
Lateran council of 1059, the deposed Pope was then forced to
publicly confess his wrong-doings, and to give up altogether
his clerical vocation. Hildebrand prepared in every way for
the struggle that was imminent between the papacy and the
empire. In this same council of 1059 a notable document
was drawn up,[1] placing the power of electing the Pope in the
hands of the cardinals. The confirmation by the emperor
was still held necessary, but the passage concerning it was
couched in ambiguous terms. Indeed, this passage was
omitted altogether in the version of the document that was
sent to the different courts of Europe.

Could we believe Bishop Benzo, of Alba, who was present,   The two
crowns.
an event occurred at this council of 1059, which shows more
clearly than anything else what magnificent claims the papacy
was now prepared to set forth. We have no reason to doubt
the anecdote itself, except that Benzo is known to have
occasionally played havoc with the truth when it served his
purpose.

Benzo declares that Hildebrand placed upon the Pope's
head a double crown, which bore upon its lower circle,
" Corona regni de manu Dei," and upon its upper, " Corona
imperii de manu Petri!" The crowns of the kingdom and
of the empire were thus declared to be the Pope's, bestowed
upon him by God and Peter. The Pope, in turn, might
confer them on whom he would.

[1] For this and for all the correspondence concerning the War of the
Investitures, see "Select Documents."

The strongest argument in favour of the bishop's assertion is, that the custom of crowning popes is known to have originated at this time. We hear of no crowned pope before, no uncrowned one after.

Estrangement with Germany.

The transactions of the council of 1059 could not but be displeasing to the German nation. Not one German bishop had been present, and yet measures of world-wide importance had been taken. The estrangement with Rome became greater and greater. A second Lateran synod seems to have declared more plainly that the king's sanction was not necessary to the validity of a papal election. A German synod, held at Worms in 1060, pronounced Pope Nicholas deposed.

Election of an antipope.

Nicholas died in the following year, and Hildebrand's party elected Anselm, of Lucca, who had been the leader of the Pataria. The Lombard bishops, enraged at this choice, brought it about that a council was summoned to meet at Basel. The regent, Agnes, determined to preserve to the empire its influence in Italy, attended. She consented to, nay furthered, the election of an antipope, Cadalus of Parma, who took the name Honorius II. He was a more welcome candidate to the Lombards, unfortunately, than to the majority of the German bishops, who showed themselves unwilling to make any sacrifices in his favour.

Cadalus in Rome.

Had Germany been united at this time, Hildebrand's party would undoubtedly have suffered a crushing defeat. As it was, Cadalus was able to enter Rome and to force his way to the very doors of St. Peter's. He was in a fair way to become master of the whole city, when Duke Godfrey of Tuscany appeared with an army, and ordered him to desist, declaring that the proper place to settle the dispute was at the German court. It is probable that Godfrey had already received news of events which had taken place in Germany, and which altered the whole aspect of affairs.

Abduction of the king, 1062 A.D.

There had been a revolution, a bloodless one it is true; and at Kaiserwerth, then an island in the Rhine, the royal boy had been enticed by the heads of a party among the princes on board a gaily-decked vessel, which had at once set sail. The young king, wild with fright, had sprung from the ship into the rushing stream, but had been rescued by one of the conspirators, Ekbert of Meissen.

At one blow the influence of the empress had been annihilated, and the reins of government seized by a powerful party of the nobles, of which party Anno of Cologne was the head.

The new regents instituted an inquiry into all the circumstances attending the papal election. The result was the abandonment of Cadalus, and the practical renunciation of Germany's old claim to have the last word in the matter of choosing a Pope. This right, the acknowledgment of which Henry III. had wrested from the Romans in 1046, was thus sacrificed in 1062 by Anno of Cologne. *Abandonment of Cadalus.*

Agnes submitted quietly to the blow which bereft her of her power. Her one thought was to take the veil, a project which she carried out some years later.

It was decided that the cares of the regency should be divided among the bishop-princes, who should exercise their office alternately. Within a year, however, all the power had come into the hands of two men, Anno of Cologne, and Adalbert of Bremen. *Anno and Adalbert.*

The one, the archbishop and arch-chancellor Anno, for a time all but the actual ruler of Germany, was a stern censor to the youthful king. A man of principle, but a strong defender of the rights of the bishops, in whose interests he is accused of having tried to permanently weaken the power of the crown.

Adalbert, on the other hand, was boundlessly vain and open to flattery; but deeply respected the royal prerogative. He was as tender and yielding with the boy, as Anno was stern and harsh. Both men were greatly ambitious for their bishoprics, and many are the records of land-grants wrung from their young charge.

In 1065 Henry was technically, although not actually, freed from his tutelage, and was solemnly girded with the sword. His first thought was Italy and the imperial crown; but *Henry IV. prevented from going to Italy.*

Hildebrand and Pope Alexander, although the latter's rival, Cadalus, who was supported by the Roman nobility, had not yet given up his opposition, were far from wishing the advent of a German army. They seem to have endeavoured to dissuade the king from interfering in Italy.

The effort was successful—to Adalbert's shame be it said. Twelve years were to pass before Henry was to cross the Alps —to cross them not as an arbiter between two popes, but as a humble penitent—and not until seven years later still was he to bear the imperial name.

Adalbert's pride and fall. Ambition for his see had induced Adalbert to play into the hands of the hierarchy; hoping to make Bremen the Rome of the north he had sought for support at the Rome of the south. But the reckless way in which he pursued his object, the unbounded influence which he won over the young king, as well as his many proud and overbearing acts, estranged and offended the rest of the princes. He spoke openly of them as fools and avaricious men; their king had raised them from the dirt, he said, and they were unfaithful to him.

Such language could not fail in its effect; the princes finally proceeded to a deed as radical as that committed at Kaiserswerth in 1062. At the diet of Treves they stormed the king with demands for Adalbert's dismissal; it was all that Henry could do to prevent actual violence against the person of his adviser, who made a hasty and shameful exit from the town.

Henry under Anno's influence. The result of Adalbert's removal was that Henry, nominally of age, but in reality too young to rule alone, again came under the control of Anno and his party. A monk of Stablo, who frequently visited the court, gives a sad picture of the king in the presence of these princes: "The king makes no replies, sitting as it were dumb and astonished; but in his stead the archbishop replies at will." And again: "Like a common slave he (Anno) possessed him."

Henry's marriage. No wonder that the boy's life was embittered for him; no wonder that a marriage forced upon him by the princes remained a dead letter in all but outward form. The virtuous and devoted Berta was hateful to Henry so long as he saw in her the ally of the party that oppressed him. By 1069 matters had come to such a pass that he used every endeavour to gain a divorce from the object of his aversion. He bribed the archbishop of Mayence with a promise of the tithes from Thuringia, and even made war against that land to secure their payment.

But Peter Damiani appeared as apostolic legate and threatened the Mayence archbishop with the ban should he fulfil the divorce. Had Henry insisted he must have renounced the long-looked-for imperial crown, and incurred the enmity of the Pope. He yielded completely, and, fortunately, soon came to know the true worth of the woman he had tried to put away; in the days of his darkest trials she was to aid him in bearing his burdens.

The time came when Henry outgrew his leading-strings, when Anno's power declined, and the long-banished Bremen archbishop was allowed to return and sun himself undisturbed in the royal favour. **Henry's emancipation.**

A double task met the king on the threshold of manhood: to reduce to subordination the great secular princes and to compel obedience from the unruly Saxons, who had done nothing but foster rebellion since the death of Henry III.

The anger of the Saxons had especially been inflamed by Henry's action against Otto of Nordheim, Duke of Bavaria, whom he summoned to the ordeal of battle on a charge of high treason, and who on failing to appear was proscribed and raised a rebellion. Otto, besides having large estates in Saxony, was the bosom friend of the young Magnus Billung. **Henry and the Saxons.**

Altogether the Saxons had never forgotten that theirs had once been the ruling race in Germany; they deeply resented Henry's coolness to these same Billungs, whose ancestors had filled the ducal office for more than a century. The wrath of the people was aroused to the utmost when the king commenced building mighty fortresses in the Harz Mountains, and in Thuringia. Everywhere arose ramparts, walls, and towers, and it was no longer believed that they were meant to serve simply as a defence against the Slavs. The garrisons, too, seem to have made themselves thoroughly detested.

Saxon Rebellion, 1073 A.D.
The rumour soon spread that Henry had allied himself with the Danes the better to oppose the Saxons. Moreover, when, in 1072, Duke Ordulf died Henry refused to bestow the duchy on the young Magnus, whom he had placed under arrest for having aided Otto of Nordheim in his rebellion. It was whispered about that the Saxons would soon be slaves, and their lands be given to the Suabians.

In 1073 a large army was mustered by the king against the Duke of Poland, who had begun intriguing in Bohemia and Hungary ; the heated imagination of the Saxons foretold that their own hour had come, and a rebellion broke out such as had not been known since the foundation of the German kingdom.

Power of the papacy.
While Henry IV. had been engaged in raising up for himself enemies in his own land, Hildebrand, his rival in all projects of world-rule, had not been idle. Between the years 1059 and 1073 the influence of the papacy had made gigantic strides in all directions. The banner of Rome had been carried to Sicily by the victorious Roger, brother of Guiscard, to England by William the Conqueror, to Spain by loyal French crusaders. Hildebrand had even ventured to prefer a claim of ownership to the whole of the last named land ; it had belonged, he said, of ancient right to the chair of Peter.

Beatrice of Tuscany.
In Italy itself new and powerful friends had joined the cause of the reformed papacy. Chief among them were Beatrice, Countess of Tuscany, and her daughter Matilda, next to Robert Guiscard, the mightiest of the Italian potentates.

Various and confused were the titles by which the countess held her possessions ; fiefs of the empire and of the papacy were interspersed with numerous " allods " or estates held in absolute ownership.

Nicholas II. and Alexander II. were more at home in the **The** **Countess** **Matilda.**
Tuscan bishoprics than they were at Rome, and Hildebrand
held absolute sway over mother and daughter alike. Matilda,
especially, shared his plans and his confidences, and to her is
due much of his success. In St. Peter's her monument stands
among those of the popes. Urban VIII. erected it in the
seventeenth century, and engraved upon it, "Champion of
the Apostolic See." A high-sounding title for one who in her
lifetime signed herself, "Matilda, who, if she is anything, is
so by the Grace of God."

The papacy, having long fought for sacerdotal celibacy **Beginning of** **war of the** **investitures.**
and for the suppression of simony, was now to enter upon
a struggle for nothing less than supremacy. Its resources
at this time were far ahead of those of the empire; Henry IV.,
too, weak and inexperienced, had a much too powerful opponent in Hildebrand.

The great conflict, the mighty proportions of which can be
guessed at by the bitter partisanship of the chronicles and
letters that have descended to us, began in a dispute regarding the election of a Milan archbishop.

As early as 1059 a Roman council had forbidden anyone to **The Milan** **dispute.**
receive a bishopric or other spiritual office from the hand of a
layman. When, in 1068, the Milan see became vacant through
the voluntary withdrawal of its archbishop, Wido, Henry IV.
appointed and invested a certain sub-deacon, Godfrey by
name. Hildebrand had already given to understand to
Erlembald, the leader of the Pataria, that he would consider
such an act on the king's part as contrary to the regulations
of the Church, and had ordered him to bring about a canonical
election. The matter had been temporarily settled by the
withdrawal on Wido's part of his resignation.

In 1072, Wido having meanwhile died, Erlembald procured the election of a young man named Atto, who was
singularly unfit for the position, and who won no favour with
the Milanese. Hildebrand, however, supported this creature
of the Pataria, and supplied Erlembald bountifully with gold
from Rome.

Henry maintains his right of investiture.

Henry considered his former candidate, Godfrey, as the rightful archbishop, and paid no heed to a letter of Pope Alexander's begging that he would give him up. The king felt, and rightly, that the whole question of his influence in Lombardy, and indeed of his whole royal power, was at stake; it was impossible for him thus quietly to resign the right of investiture.

The right of investing presupposed the right of bestowing; were the rich sees of Italy and Germany, with all their landed possessions, their fiefs and their privileges to be thus calmly abandoned to those whom Rome might choose? It would have been possible for a hostile pope to fill all the chief positions in Germany with outspoken enemies of the king.

Henry remained firm, and in 1073 the consecration was performed by his command on Archbishop Godfrey. This was the signal for war to the knife; the Pope replied by banning a number of the king's advisers. Henry held fast to his advisers as well as to his new archbishop.

Hildebrand becomes Pope, 1073 A.D.

It was at this juncture of affairs that Alexander II. died, and Hildebrand himself ascended the papal throne. It was at this very time, too, that the rebellion broke out which had so long been smouldering in Saxony.

The Saxon rebellion.

The rebellion was headed by Hermann, the brother of the defunct Duke Ordulf, by Otto of Nordheim, who had been forgiven his former misdeeds, but had been angered by the failure of his intercession for Magnus, and by Bishop Burkard of Halberstadt. It was joined by almost all the bishops and nobles of Saxony.

By August 1st, 1073, Henry found himself besieged in the Harzburg, near Goslar. The Saxons demanded the immediate destruction of the new fortresses as the only basis of negotiations for peace; this Henry could not and would not grant.

Henry's flight.

Cut off from his allies in the kingdom at large, nothing remained for him but surrender or flight. He succeeded in escaping by night from the Harzburg with a few chosen followers. The rebellion had meanwhile made rapid pro-

gress; the king's estates in Saxony had been seized, and
Thuringia had joined in the movement against him.

Shameful as had been Henry's flight, further humiliations
remained in store for him. Near Hersfeld he was met by a
number of bishops and nobles from different parts of the
kingdom; but all his entreaties—one annalist with a desire
to be graphic relates that he actually grovelled in the dust
before them—could not rouse them to take any immediate
action against the Saxons. They saw, indeed, that their
interference was needful, and they agreed to be present at
a general muster to be held two months later. More than
this Henry could not wrest from them.

It was at such a moment as this that Henry, sick at heart
and with all the world against him, stooped so low as to
write to Pope Gregory VII. a letter full of submission, and
such as neither the king himself nor one of his predecessors
had ever written to a Roman bishop. "We have sinned
against heaven and before thee," he says to the Pope, "and
are no longer worthy to be called thy son." In the Milan
affair Gregory might act as he pleased. Henry's courage was
broken.

Henry cringes to the Pope.

The Saxon princes, with whom Henry opened negotiations,
showed no signs of yielding. Their one effort now was to
blacken the character of the king in the eyes of all Germany.
The vices of a Tiberius or a Nero were laid to his charge.
The clergy were urged to excommunicate and depose so great
a monster. Henry was summoned, to answer the charges
against him, to a diet to be held at Gerstungen.

Henry summoned to a diet.

The king naturally refused to submit his royal person to
the judgment of a handful of his subjects, and is accused of
having adopted the dangerous policy of calling in the
enemies of the kingdom, the Danes and the Luititian Slavs,
against the belligerents. This expedient, if it ever was
seriously adopted, failed through lack of spirit on the side of
the new partisans.

A meeting of the German princes in general was called at
Wurzburg, where the king had taken up his abode. The

Rudolph of Suabia.

Saxons, meanwhile, had assembled at Gerstungen, and negotiations were begun between the two camps. It was at this
that Rudolph of Suabia and others abused their position as
chosen mediators, and plotted with the Saxons for the king's
downfall and the election of a new monarch.

In order to deceive Henry, they drew up a treaty, by which
the Saxons promised to submit before the following Christmas, if the king would grant them indemnity and redress for
their grievances. Completely mistaken in the character of
his emissaries, Henry accepted and ratified the treaty, and
dismissed the army he had raised against the Saxons.

Regenger's disclosure.
It was at this crisis that a certain Regenger disclosed the
fact, a figment of the imagination, that the king had hired
him to murder Rudolf of Suabia, and others of the princes.
In the intense excitement of the moment, the disclosure was
considered genuine, and a number of the nobles left the court
and took to arms. Henry himself saw in the matter, probably with justice, a plot of Rudolph's, and, forgetting his
royal dignity, offered to fight the Suabian in single combat.
It was with difficulty that his followers restrained him.

Help from the Rhenish cities.
Meanwhile, the king's position was becoming desperate.
Abandoned by his followers, there seemed no alternative to
him but to descend from the throne. But help was at hand
from an unexpected quarter. The Rhenish cities, grown rich
by commerce and traffic, declared for Henry. The citizens of
Worms overthrew their bishop, their spiritual and temporal
head, and others followed suit. The neighbourhood of
Mayence became so hostile, that the princes, who had called
a diet there, which should decide on the future of the kingdom, were afraid to risk their persons, and the meeting was
not held.

Regenger's death.
Henry, for his own part, called together the princes of
South Germany, and tried in every way to conciliate them.
The idea of a duel, or judgment of God, was once more
broached, and it was finally agreed that Udalrich of Godes-
heim, should be the king's champion against his false accuser,
Regenger. Should Udalrich conquer in the combat, the

princes declared, on oath, that they would be henceforth faithful and obedient.

Regenger died a raving maniac before the day that had been appointed for the duel. God was believed to have spoken by thus striking him down, and there was at once a great revulsion in Henry's favour. When the Saxons sent an urgent summons to the other German princes to meet them at Fritzlar, none came at their bidding.

The Saxons, indeed, were still formidable enough, and it was not until February, 1074, and after long negotiations, that the peace of Gerstungen was concluded with them. The peace was humiliating enough for the king; but it preserved to him his crown, and prevented the secession of Saxony. The hardest condition of all was, that the fortresses in Saxony should be razed to the ground, and, after long discussions, it was arranged that the work of destruction should be left in the hands of the people themselves. *Peace of Gerstungen, 1074 A.D.*

Had the Saxons been content to use their victory with moderation, all might have been well. They had permission to destroy the forts, but not the churches, and in the storming of the Harzburg the Minster, too, fell before their onslaught. Nor did they even spare the royal tombs. The bones of Henry's brother and of his infant son were dragged to the light and wantonly desecrated. *Saxon outrages.*

The news of this unhallowed outrage drew the German princes closer to Henry's banner. The deeply incensed king thought that even the Pope would now take his part. He wrote and asked Gregory to take action against the violators of sanctuaries, but received little satisfaction.

Henry now induced the princes to make preparations, under pretence of a war against the Hungarians, for the punishment of the Saxons. In a battle fought near Homburg, on the Unstrutt, the latter were worsted, and are said to have lost eight hundred of their men. Negotiations were begun, and, on the 26th of October, Henry had the satisfaction of seeing his enemies walk submissively between the drawn-up ranks of his own army. The triumph was com- *Saxons reduced to submission.*

plete, and he was able to impose, instead of submitting to galling conditions. It was not long before the Harzburg and others of the fortresses were rebuilt, and supplied with royal garrisons. In the midst of the enthusiasm roused by his victory, the king was able to gain the consent of the princes to the appointment of his son as his successor.

One ray of sunshine had flashed across the path of this much-tried king, but only for an instant. Never, all in all, was crown to be worn by a more uneasy head than that of Henry IV.

Conflict with the papacy.

We have arrived at a stage in the history of Germany where the political sky becomes fairly lurid, and the great conflict with the Papacy breaks out in full force. It was a conflict in which unreasoning wrath was to do its utmost, and where the warring principles as first laid down were to prove fully irreconcilable.

While the Saxon War was in progress, Gregory VII. had waited impatiently, hoping still that the king would fulfil the promises made in his submissive letter. In the interval he had waged a bitter war against simony and the marriage of the clergy, and five of Henry's councillors had been excommunicated on the former charge.

Meanwhile the papacy had been somewhat losing ground in Italy. The Normans had boldly encroached on territory claimed by Rome herself, and a break with them seemed imminent. The Pataria in Milan had been worsted by a party which favoured the Ambrosian rites, and which, in the pride of victory, turned to the king and demanded an archbishop from his hands.

The Milan See.

Again Milan became the apple of discord. Henry disdained the Pope's creature, Atto, and discarded his own former choice, Godfrey, placing a third prelate, Thedald, on the archiepiscopal chair. This proceeding certainly gave the Church reasonable grounds of offence. Atto might have been disregarded, for the king had never recognized him; but Godfrey had been already consecrated, and should not have been removed without a formal trial of the matter according to Church usage.

Thedald was summoned to Rome, and forbidden to undergo consecration until his claims should have been properly judged before the Pope's tribunal. At the same time Gregory took a step which for ever separated him from the king. He sent three envoys with a letter full of bitter reproaches; disregard of the ban placed on his five councillors, and non-fulfilment of his own promises of submission were the formal charges against Henry, together with disobedience to a sweeping command issued at the beginning of the year against every form of lay investiture. This last decree seems at the time of its promulgation to have been intended by Gregory as a tentative measure, which he hoped later to reduce to a form more palatable to the king by means of negotiations. Those negotiations, however, had never taken place. Gregory begins hostilities.

Gregory's envoys used strong threats to the king, stronger far than those employed in the document which they bore. Henry stood at this moment in the full glamour of his victory over the Saxons, and these men dared to tell him to his face that he deserved excommunication and dethronement for his vices. No wonder that the king was aghast, no wonder that his followers shared in his indignation, and that it was decided to proceed to the extremest of measures. Henry III. had deposed three erring pontiffs, Henry IV. determined to emulate his father. The fact was in his favour that Hildebrand's elevation in 1073 had been irregular and tumultuous, and altogether little in accord with the election decree of 1059. The king's consent had neither been formally asked nor formally given. Gregory's envoys.

At the beginning of 1076 Henry summoned the German bishops to a council, which was opened at Worms on January 24th. Of the six German archbishops, only two were present, but more than two-thirds of the bishops answered the summons. In the council the wildest accusations were brought against the Pope, many of them the merest inventions of hatred. They found credence in the excitement of the moment, however, and the bishops decreed that Gregory, having wrongfully ascended the throne of Peter, must descend from it in Council of Worms. Gregory deposed.

haste. They composed a writing to " brother Hildebrand,"
as they now called him, in which they renounced their
obedience. He had, they said, spread the flames of discord
which had been lighted at Rome over all the churches of
Italy, Germany, France, and Spain.

Charges against Gregory.

Point by point all the possible accusations against Gregory
are taken up : he had in the days of Henry III. sworn never
himself to become Pope, nor to recognize anyone else who
should be chosen without the consent of the emperor and his
son ; this oath he had broken. The election decree of 1059
had repeated this engagement; it had been disregarded.
Charges against the Pope's manner of life close this remarkable document, which may be read to-day in all its pris-
tine bitterness. Another writing, still more crushing, accompanied it to Rome, and bore the superscription : " Henry,
king, not by usurpation, but through God's holy ordinance, to
Hildebrand, not Pope, but false monk." The letter ends with :
" I, Henry, king by the grace of God, together with all my
bishops, do call to thee, descend, descend ! "

The envoys of the king set out at once for Italy ; in Piacenza a synod was held, and the Lombard bishops accepted
the decrees of Worms.

Synod at Rome, 1076 A.D.

In Rome itself the matter was viewed in another light.
Henry had addressed a writing to the Romans, accusing
Gregory of being the worst enemy of the kingdom and of his,
the king's person. " We ask you not to shed his blood," he
said, " for life after his deposition would be a harder punishment than death." But the sympathies of the populace
turned to the Pope, and it was not without danger to their
lives that the emissaries of the king penetrated to Gregory's
presence as he sat in council in the Lateran. An angry storm
broke loose in the assembly as the Bishop Roland and his
companion fulfilled their mission. Swords were drawn, and
it was Pope Gregory himself who, by the intervention of his
own person, saved from injury those who bore the tidings of
his dethronement.

Henry de-posed.

When the synod met again on the following day, it was to

answer in kind the harsh measures of the king. All the
bishops who, of their own free will, had furthered the schism,
were suspended from office ; the ban was hurled against the
king, his royal power declared forfeit, his subjects loosed from
their allegiance.

Gregory's old allies rallied to him in this emergency. The
Pataria in Milan again raised its head, Robert Guiscard renewed relations for the moment, and the Countess Matilda,
who had now entered on her inheritance in Tuscany, showed
herself as devoted a handmaid as ever in the service of the
papacy.

{Everything depended on what reception the decree of the **Effect of bar**
Roman synod would meet with in Germany. A generation **in Germany.**
earlier they would have roused nothing but indignation. But
Henry IV. had been too unpopular ; the stories, too, which had
been fabricated by the Saxons had been believed by many.
Moreover, the influence of the papacy had widely spread under
Gregory's careful management ; the new Cluniac monasteries
deeply revered the Pope, and worked for him among the
masses. Of the bishops, too, who had signed the denuncia-
tion of the Pope there were many who on riper thoughts
repented of their action and strove to palliate their error.

{ On the news that the king had been placed in the ban,
Saxony again became unquiet and the princes of South Germany entered into a new conspiracy. A strong national feeling had not yet come into being, and loyalty to principle
vanished before the petty dictates of self-interest.

Gregory knew the value of such allies as these. His next **Gregory's**
step was to write a long communication to the bishops, dukes, **German**
counts, and all "who in the German kingdom defend the **allies.**
Christian faith." The course of the quarrel is reviewed from
the beginning, the Pope's actions are justified and an appeal
is made for aid in sustaining the honour of the Church. A
prospect of forgiveness is held out to the king should he show
signs of repentance. The first attempt, however, of conciliation on Henry's part showed that the Pope would be satisfied
by nothing short of absolute submission.

Failure of Henry's measures.

Henry now proceeded to call together a new national council at Worms. It was intended in due form to institute judicial proceedings against Gregory and, having once more deposed him, to elect a successor. This successor the king in person was to escort to Rome. But few bishops and none of the princes of South Germany answered the summons, and rumours of disaffection became rife. The council was postponed and transferred to Mayence, and a number of bishops did in the latter place again denounce the Pope and declare him excommunicate. But no steps were taken towards a new election, no arrangements made for a march on Rome.

Henry now tried conciliatory measures with his enemies at home. The hostages of the Saxons were released, and were promised great rewards if they would make their people return to their allegiance.

Claims of the papacy.

All such efforts were now in vain; Saxony by this time was practically lost, and the princes of Germany were meditating nothing short of the removal of Henry and the election of a new king. Should it come to this, a consummation which he did not desire so much as Henry's voluntary submission, Pope Gregory VII. demanded the right of approving the choice of the new ruler.

Slowly the papacy was lifting itself into the universal position once held by the empire. One by one claims were put forward which never could have been maintained for a moment had not Germany been rent by civil discord, and had not the king been grossly misused by his subjects.

Henry humbles himself before the princes.

No one can fail to pity Henry in his powerless distress, but no more is one called upon to admire his attitude in misfortune. A meeting of the German princes was held at Tribur, in October, 1076 ; together with legates and lay envoys of the Pope they discussed the proper methods of a king who had become embarrassing to them. Henry had taken up his position at Oppenheim, separated only by the Rhine from the arbiters of his fate. He was ready for any humiliation, and daily sent envoys to Tribur begging his enemies to impose such conditions as they would, but to leave him his royal name and the

insignia of the kingdom.   He would better his mode of life,
he would be answerable to the princes, if need be, for every
act of government.

Henry's promises of reform made no impression, and the
princes declared themselves about to elect a new king.   But
reasons which we cannot to-day fathom induced them to re-
consider this intention and to render an ultimatum, severe
enough, indeed, but stopping short of deposition.   Within a
year from the time when the ban had been published, Henry
was to promise due obedience to the Pope, and to gain absolution from him in person.   Should he fail to obtain it, and to
clear himself of the charges against him, or do penance for
them, the throne was to be forfeit.   The Pope was furthermore
to be invited to come to Augsburg to discuss with the princes
the affair of their king, and altogether to consult for the future
of the Church and of the empire.

As a further humiliation Henry was to give up the faithful
city of Worms to its bishop, and to protect the latter from the
possibility of a new revolt of the citizens.   The king himself
and the queen were told to take up their abode in Spires.
Henry was not to choose his advisers and not to administer
any affairs of government until the absolution should have
been granted.   As an eventual reward for his obedience and
good conduct the princes promised their support in an expedition to Rome which should be undertaken for the purpose of
gaining the imperial crown and of driving out the Normans,
whose encroachments had become dangerous to the Italian
possessions of Germany.

Henry for a time submitted to his fate.   He lived in Spires
almost as a prisoner, avoiding all intercourse with the world
and deprived of all the consolations of religion.   But in quiet
he worked out a plan by which something might be saved
from the general wreck of his fortunes.   Above all was it
necessary to sunder the close union of the Pope and of the
German princes ; the meeting in Augsburg would be likely in
all probability to lead to the taking of permanent measures
for diminishing the glory of the German crown.   Things had

*The ulti-
matum.*

*Henry's
debasement.*

His plan.

indeed gone far enough when the princes of Germany invited a foreign power, the deadly enemy too of their own national independence, to come into their midst and sit in judgment on their king !

Henry in Italy.

Henry determined at any risk to put a stop to Gregory's alliance with the princes, to grovel in the dust before him if need be, but not to return without the required absolution. He sent an envoy to Rome to announce that he was coming as a repentant sinner. Gregory promptly rejected his advances and started on his journey to Augsburg. In Mantua he was met by the news that the king had already crossed the Alps. In doubt as to Henry's intentions, and suspecting that he intended to gain his object by force of arms, the Pope retraced his steps, and took refuge in a fortress of Countess Matilda, the famous castle of Canossa, near Reggio.

Canossa.

Canossa stands on a high and precipitous rock, and was at that time well defended by art as well as by nature. A threefold wall surrounded it.

When Henry arrived at the foot of the hill he sent and asked for an interview with Hugo of Cluny, and with Matilda, both of whom had accompanied the Pope. They consented at the king's request to intercede for him, but all their entreaties were in vain.

It was then that the German monarch stooped to the lowest depths of self-abasement. The moral sentiment of Europe would have utterly condemned a Pope who should have refused absolution to a sinner ready to make the fullest atonement for the wrongs he had committed. The whole teaching of the Church was that grace was obtainable for him who sought it by the proper means. The high priest of all Christendom could not afford to be wanting in mercy.

Henry as a penitent.

Barefoot in spite of the winter snows, and in a penitential garb, Henry appeared before the door of Canossa. That door was closed against him. The next day he came again ; the third day too saw a repetition of this most miserable of spectacles.

At last the Pope, induced, we are told, by the tears of the

Countess Matilda, and of the Abbot of Cluny, relented. Gregory declared that he was willing to remove the ban if certain pledges, partly in the interest of Rome, partly in that of the German princes, could be given. A meeting was held between members of the Pope's household and a certain number of the king's followers, and a writing was drawn up, the wording of which has been preserved. Henry was to give full satisfaction to the German princes in such manner, and at such time as the Pope should appoint, and whenever Gregory might choose to undertake his journey to Germany the king was to ensure the safety of his person. Any envoy of the Pope was to enjoy similar protection.

This writing was drawn up with all form and solemnity, and was signed, among others, by the Countess Matilda herself.

These preliminaries having been arranged, the doors of Canossa were thrown open, and Henry entered, accompanied by his excommunicated councillors, who had also been included in the amnesty. As the penitents came into Gregory's presence they threw themselves weeping on the ground before him. The members of the Pope's household were melted to tears, and Gregory's own eyes moistened at the sight. The absolution was administered in due form, and the apostolic blessing crowned the work of peace. *The pardon of Canossa.*

Henry IV. rode away from the castle of Canossa having gained what he had sought. He had won, indeed, a great diplomatic victory, although he had undoubtedly somewhat tarnished the honour of Germany. No humiliation could have been deeper than that which he had undergone, and even in our own day the bitterest possible scorn and hatred of concessions to Rome have been summed up in those stinging words, spoken in the diet of 1872, and engraved now on a marble monument on the Harzburg: "We won't go to Canossa!"

The compact so solemnly entered into by Gregory and Henry was not long kept by either party. Henry's action was by no means approved of by all of his own supporters, *Henry and the Lombards.*

and the Lombard bishops, who were still in the ban, looked
upon the king as a betrayer of their cause. Black looks and
a discontented silence met him when he appeared in Reggio.
In the time of Henry's distress they had aided him, and he
seemed now to be about to abandon them utterly.

Henry and the Pope. Such was not the case, however. Early in 1077 the Bishop
of Piacenza took prisoner a papal legate who had come to
encourage the Paterian rabble against the higher clergy.
Gregory at once demanded that Henry should procure the
release of the captive, a demand to which the king did not
accede. The heart of the Pope soon began to fill with dis-
trust towards the man to whom he had so recently restored
the hopes of Paradise. Henry, for his part, must have had
his own doubts against a Pope who still continued in close
negotiation with the German princes. Papal legates were
present at an assembly held at Forchheim for the express
purpose of dethroning Henry, although they took no active
part in the proceedings.

Election of an antiking. It was the 13th of March, 1077, when the assembly at
Forchheim came together, and, after a trial of Henry's cause,
and a declaration that, in spite of his absolution, they would
no longer obey him, the princes proceeded to elect his bitterest
enemy, the man whom he had once challenged to mortal
combat, Rudolph of Suabia. The papal legates did not dispute the election, but made Rudolf promise to allow the
bishoprics to be filled by free canonical election. Rudolf renounced this right of appointing bishops for which Henry IV.
had fought and was to fight so stubbornly; the antiking, in
his present emergency, was willing to make any and every
sacrifice.

Rudolph's adherents. It was chiefly the Saxon princes who had carried through
the election of Rudolf, and it was only among the Saxons
that he was ever fully acknowledged. Even Suabia, his own
duchy, refused him obedience, and his progress there, which
was intended to be a triumph, was hindered by ceaseless
conflicts. It was to Saxony that he withdrew, on the news
that Henry had found unexpected allies, had brought to-

gether an army, and was about to make a struggle for his rights.

Pope Gregory—and for this Henry had to thank the bitter experiences at Canossa—remained neutral in the conflict that now ensued, although untiring in his efforts to effect a peace. He had from the beginning demanded that the matter should be submitted to his arbitration. Gregory's neutrality.

Henry's power now grew from day to day. With forces amounting to 12,000 men he left Ratisbon in May, 1077. In Ulm he held a diet which passed sentence of death on Rudolph of Suabia and his supporters, Berthold of Zäringen and Welf of Bavaria. But these three princes had determined to make a bitter fight for their lives and dignities, and they raised an army which Henry with his heterogeneous and as yet untrained troops was careful to avoid.

In November the princes prevailed upon the papal legate again to pronounce the ban against Henry and to declare Rudolph the rightful king; but the Pope refused, for the time being at least, to ratify these proceedings.

Henry within the course of a few months forced Bavaria to subjection, held his own in Suabia, gained the support of the lower classes in Franconia, and won Bohemia as a faithful ally. Not without bloodshed were these results gained; on the Neckar and on the Danube the lands were laid waste, and everywhere the civil war spread panic and dismay. The rival kings.

The years 1078 and 1079 were passed in struggles vain as they were bloody between the rival kings and their adherents. An indecisive battle was fought near Melrichstadt on the Streu, and at the same time an army of peasants which Henry had collected was annihilated on the Neckar. Suabia was again devastated by Henry without result.

There were two claimants to the last-named duchy at this time. Berthold, the son of King Rudolph, stood over against Frederick of Büren, or Hohenstaufen, whom Henry made duke in 1079, affiancing him to his own daughter Agnes.

It was a time of utter demoralization for Germany; the land was writhing under the constant plunderings of the

opposing armies.   Gregory VII. was constantly in communication with both parties, constantly commanding the one or
the other king to send envoys to this or that council.   The
envoys were occasionally sent, but without arriving at any
agreement.

Renewal of the ban, 1080 A.D.

In 1080 Gregory, encouraged by a victory of Rudolph's
won at Flarchheim and urged by the supporters of that king,
took the decisive step of renewing the ban against Henry.
The charge was preferred that Henry had prevented the
assembling of such a council as would have restored peace
and quiet.   Rudolph was declared to be the rightful king;
the royal power was accorded to him " on account of his
humility, his obedience, and his uprightness."

The anathema against Henry was embodied in the form
of a prayer to the apostles Peter and Paul, who are declared
to have the power of giving and taking away kingdoms and
principalities at will.   Kings and princes are therefore warned
that they should dread to disregard the commands of the
Church.   The claim of papal supremacy in temporal as well
as in spiritual matters could not have been more plainly
formulated.

Effect of the ban.

Contrary to all expectations Gregory's second ban proved
as harmless as the first had been effective.   Not one of
Henry's supporters fell away from him at this crisis.   On
the contrary his following increased both in Northern Italy
and in Germany.   The general indignation against the Pope
knew no bounds.

Election of an anti-pope.

In Mayence nineteen archbishops and bishops declared
Gregory again deposed; in Brixen a synod was held where
Germans and Lombards alike appeared, and where the
spectacle seen at Worms in 1076 was repeated anew.   Twenty-
seven bishops here signed the bull for Gregory's deposition.
They went further; they elected as antipope Wibert of
Ravenna, who took the name of Clement III.   Henry IV.
agreed to escort the new head of Christendom to Rome.

There were now two kings on the German throne, two
popes on the chair of Peter.

All Gregory's efforts at this crisis to raise a strong coalition against Henry were in vain. William the Conqueror, once strongly under papal influence, could not be induced to interfere. Robert Guiscard, who had been under the ban for depredations against the estates of St. Peter, was absolved in view of the present emergency, but was too much occupied with a quarrel against the Eastern Empire to be able to give any assistance.

Gregory was forced as a final resort to fix his hopes on the antiking in Germany. But all that was mortal of Rudolph was soon lying buried in the cathedral at Merseburg. A bloody battle had taken place between the two kings near Hohenmölsen on the Grune. Henry's forces had been worsted, but Rudolph had paid his debt to nature. He had been carried from the battlefield maimed and dying; his right hand had been cut off in the fray.

Henry IV., though beaten, won a great moral advantage that day. It was a time when justice was administered far otherwise than in our own day, when portents decided what was right and what was wrong. For the winner of a combat God was considered to have spoken, and in this fight between Henry and Rudolph the latter's death was a fatal blow to his cause. The loss of Rudolph's right hand, too, seemed to the superstitious to be full of dark meaning. A contemporary, Ekkehard of Aura, reports that the Suabian said as he died: "Look, this is the hand with which I swore fealty to my king!"

Gregory VII.'s glory, too, was greatly dimmed by the outcome of this struggle; more than once he had promised victory and life to Rudolph, death and destruction to Henry.

Henry IV., with no longer a rival, for the moment at least, to fear, now hastened to Italy at the head of an army, to try and drive out Pope Gregory, and to lead his own Pope, Clement III., to Rome. Germany was far from being pacified as yet, but Henry hoped that having gained the imperial crown, he could return in triumph and crush his enemies.

Rudolph's death, 1080 A.D.

Henry before Rome, 1081 A.D.

In May, 1081, Henry appeared before Rome, to find that
city strongly fortified against him.   He had expected a
friendly reception from the Romans.   He found, instead, the
mighty walls and their innumerable towers, well armed and
defended.   Various attempts to take the city failed, and
Henry found himself involved in a task which took years to
accomplish, years of great hardship and of enforced absence
from Germany.

Hermann of Luxemburg.   In the meanwhile, chiefly as before by the Saxons, a successor to Rudolph had been chosen, a rich prince of the house
of Luxemburg, Hermann by name.   Hermann had begun his
career brilliantly, and had won no small advantage over the
supporters of Henry, who were discouraged by the king's
reverses in Italy.

Henry enters Rome, 1083 A.D.   But these reverses were atoned for, in 1083, by a successful
entry into Rome.   The whole Leonine city came into Henry's
hands, and the antipope, Clement, was solemnly conducted to
St. Peter's.   Within a few days Henry was able to withdraw
from Rome, and to disband his army.   He had gained what
he wanted.   The Roman nobles had pledged themselves to
procure him the crown that he coveted.   Should Gregory
refuse to bestow it, they bound themselves to elect a Pope
who would.

Lateran council.   Gregory, meanwhile, had summoned a council in the
Lateran, and Henry permitted it to take place, being careful,
however, to place obstructions in the way of those of his own
particular enemies, who attempted to attend.   The legates of
the antiking, Hermann, for instance, were taken captive
between Viterbo and Sutri, and the cardinal-bishop of Ostia
shared their confinement.

Henry had hoped that the council would declare in his
favour, but found himself disappointed in this hope, and
again called his army together.   He demanded the imperial
crown, and clergy and laity alike now urged Gregory to grant
the request.   But the Pope wished to make conditions.
Henry was to do penance, and be loosed from the ban, before
he should undergo the ceremony of coronation.   On any other

terms, the apostolic curse, and not its blessing, would go with the crown.

The nobles were anxious to fulfil their compact, but the Pope remained inexorable. A compromise was actually proposed, by which the crown should be lowered by a string from Gregory's refuge, in the castle of St. Angelo. Henry was to place it on his own head, and dispense with the consecration. Henry's star in the ascendant.

But Henry's star was for the moment in the ascendant, and he was able to make his own terms. He was in no mood to accept a crown thrust at him as a morsel would be thrown to a beggar. The Emperor of the East had joined him in a league against Robert Guiscard, the ally of the Pope, and furnished him abundantly with supplies. The prince of Capua and other nobles had also joined his standard.

The Romans, tired of the uncertain state of affairs, and vexed with Gregory for not more readily yielding to their entreaties, at last abandoned the Pope, whose cause they had so long supported. They allowed Henry to enter the city, and to take possession of the Lateran. On the day on which this happened, a synod was held, which formally deposed and excommunicated Gregory VII. Clement III. was acknowledged as the rightful Pope; and, on Easter Day, 1084, in St. Peter's, he placed the imperial crown on the head of Henry IV. and of his queen. Gregory abandoned by the Romans. Henry emperor.

Gregory was, meanwhile, all but a prisoner in the castle of St. Angelo. He was eventually rescued by Robert Guiscard, whose march on Rome Henry IV. had neither time nor sufficient forces to oppose.

In the end Henry IV.'s Pope prevailed, and Gregory, hated now by the Romans he had served so long, withdrew to Salerno, and died in the following year. His last words, which were true enough, according to his own criterions of right and wrong, were: "I have loved justice and hated iniquity, therefore I die in exile." His party chose as his successor, Desiderius, Abbot of Monte Cassino, who, however, accomplished nothing of importance, and died after a very short pontificate. Gregory's death.

P

It was reserved for the successor of Desiderius, Urban II., to again raise to honour the idea of a reformed and powerful papacy. Urban, indeed, had to carry on a long struggle with Clement III., but in the end he was to stand out as the acknowledged leader of Europe, and head of Christendom.

CHAPTER XIV.

CONTINUATION OF THE CONFLICT BETWEEN THE EMPIRE AND THE PAPACY.

HENRY IV. had abandoned Rome to Robert Guiscard Henry in Germany. in 1084, and had returned to Germany. He found the magic of the imperial crown far less potent than he had anticipated. He returned only to be involved again in a tangle of wars and intrigues. The antiking Hermann and Pope Gregory VII.—it was the year before the latter's death —still had their warm upholders.

A number of councils and synods were called, some by King Henry, some by his adversaries. At Quedlinburg the ban was hurled at Clement III. and at his German supporters; at Mayence the dethronement of Gregory and the elevation of Clement were expressly ratified, and Hermann of Luxemburg was declared excommunicate.

Side by side with the attempts to put an end to the civil Rebellion of Ecbert of Meissen, 1085 A.D. war by reasonings and disputations, musterings and marches were in progress. In July, 1085, Henry entered Saxony with an army, and, without striking a blow, reduced the land to submission. No sooner had the royal army been dismissed, however, than the king's cousin, Ecbert of Meissen, rebelled against him, and deprived him of all the fruits of his recent expedition.

Again the stern duel of earlier days was renewed, again Saxony was devastated year after year. Bavaria, too, was filled with feuds. Duke Welf held to King Hermann and to Ecbert, and in union with the latter gained a victory over Henry at Wurzburg.

The Saxons submit. Of great advantage to Henry was the death of Bishop Burkard of Halberstadt, who had more than any other man to continually nourish the Saxon opposition. Thirteen times he himself had marched against the king in battle. The Saxon bishops were thus left without a leader, and several of them at once submitted to Henry. King Hermann withdrew to his own hereditary lands in Lorraine, and died, in 1088, while trying to wrest an insignificant castle from one of his own vassals. Ecbert was outlawed, and was killed in 1090 while fleeing some Saxon nobles whose lands he had devastated.

Returns to Italy. Whatever were Henry IV.'s faults, want of energy was not one of them. Not yet discouraged by the uphill fight he had been waging for so many years, he left Saxony even before Ecbert had been captured, and turned to more sights of blood and more bitter struggling in Italy.

Marriage of Matilda. The Countess Matilda had, in the meantime, shown her devotion to the papal cause by marrying, at Urban II.'s instigation, the son of Henry's enemy, Welf of Bavaria. The bride was forty, the bridegroom but seventeen years of age. The ill-assorted pair had but one interest in common, to drive Henry from the German throne, and thereby to secure the future of Italy and of the papacy.

The Welfs had already been active in rousing Suabia to rebellion, so that Henry's power was threatened simultaneously on both sides of the Alps, and he was obliged to divide his forces accordingly.

The war in Italy. The war in Italy was one of those slow, harassing ones that Henry had grown to know so well. Every element was there to try his soul. The Pataria had again raised its head in Lombardy. The citizens of Milan, Cremona, Lodi, and other municipalities had formed a confederation for twenty years for the purpose of defending themselves against the emperor. It was the first of these coalitions that were eventually to prove so fatal to Germany's rule in Italy.

Defection of the empress, 1093 A.D. All of these unhappy combinations, however, were as nothing to the misfortune that fell upon Henry in 1093. It was then that the empress, the Russian princess Adelaide—Berta had died in 1087—turned against him. His son Conrad at the same time threw off his allegiance, declared himself king, and became a rallying-point for the emperor's enemies.

It was said at the time that Henry sought death on receiving this news, but was persuaded by faithful friends to continue and bear his burdens.

And heavy enough they were! The defection of Conrad and the empress—the latter, in addition, took care to spread the worst rumours, and make the most damning charges against her husband—induced many to abandon the imperial cause. The young Conrad, through the efforts of Welf and Matilda, was now crowned King of Italy by Archbishop Anselm of Milan; a marriage was arranged by the Pope between Conrad and the daughter of Roger of Sicily. Conrad against his father.

It was at this time that Urban II. began to stand forth as promoter of a movement that was to stir Europe to its centre. The followers of Clement might continue to hold the castle of St. Angelo,—as they did until 1099,—but it was to Urban that the eyes of all were turning. The first crusade.

The same council of Piacenza, which in 1095 heard shameless accusations of Adelaide to the effect that the emperor had directly driven her to commit adultery, heard also the stirring call from the Greek court for aid against the all-conquering Seljukes. The Council of Clermont, held shortly afterwards, witnessed that incredible scene of enthusiasm where, amid deafening cries of " God wills it! God wills it! " thousands thronged around the Pope to record their crusading vow.

Henry IV.'s courage had been nearly broken by the blows of fate. He remained in Italy until 1097 without an army, and seeking in vain for help from every quarter. Italy abandoned, 1097 A.D.

In the end Welf tired of his elderly spouse, who had carefully instilled into him the fact that he could never become heir to her possessions. He made a public declaration to the effect that the marriage with Matilda had never in reality been consummated, and renewed his allegiance to Henry.

By this time, however, northern Italy was practically lost,

and Henry was not in a position to attempt its recovery. It remained in the hands of the great Countess and a papal legate shared with her the cares of government.

Interest in the Crusade.

The interest in Italian affairs had waned and disappeared in Germany, and the Crusade was the all-absorbing topic. The Germans at first had kept aloof from the movement and had pointed the finger of scorn at the ragged followers of Peter the Hermit as they passed through the land. But the tide of feeling soon turned, and there were successful efforts in many districts to bring together crusading armies.

Henry V. crowned king, 1099 A.D.

Henry IV.'s return to Germany after six years of absence created little or no excitement. He was able, however, to reconcile many of his old enemies and to win from the princes their consent to regard his second son, Henry, in place of the rebellious Conrad, as king. The young prince, in 1099, was solemnly crowned at Aix-la-Chapelle.

Anarchy in Germany.

Germany by this time was in an almost hopeless state. Especially in the bishoprics were anarchy and schism rife ; the war of the investitures still continued, and Gregory VII.'s command for free elections had led to the raising up of rival bishops in many sees. As a natural consequence numberless petty struggles ensued.

Men's idols had indeed been shattered in these dark days. The nation at large had intermittently renounced and obeyed its king, who, indeed, was still in the ban. Christians had been and still were in doubt as to which Pope held the true keys of heaven, and many of the separate flocks knew not who was their shepherd.

End of the Schism.

Death at last came to the rescue as far as the rival popes were concerned, and Urban II. and Clement III. went to their graves within a year of each other. Urban's successor was Paschal II., and he put an end to two attempts to perpetuate the schism by promptly imprisoning, one after the other the hastily elected antipopes.

Henry IV. unpopular with his nobles.

The last years of Henry IV.'s reign were to prove no more quiet than the first had been. Sincere as were his efforts to restore law and order they failed signally. He did, indeed succeed in making the most prominent bishops and nobles swear to observe a prolonged truce, a so-called "peace of the land" during which all feuds should cease.

But all feuds did not cease, and jealous nobles began to murmur and to reproach the emperor; all the more so as he seemed very much to favour on the whole the lower classes. A perfect storm of indignation was roused by the fact that a well-known count, Sieghard of Burghausen, was murdered by the mob of Ratisbon almost under the emperor's very eyes, and Henry either had not wished or had not been able to hinder the deed.

Henry had publicly announced an intended pilgrimage to Jerusalem for the time of duration of which his son Henry was to be his regent. Busied with other matters the emperor delayed his crusade, much to the chagrin of those princes who longed for his absence.

The discontent in Germany was fanned by the new Pope Paschal II., who had renewed the ban hurled by his predecessors, and had openly urged Robert of Flanders and Welf of Bavaria to persecute "Henry the head of heretics."

But all the various elements of discontent would have been separately little to be feared had not an acknowledged leader risen from an unexpected quarter. The discontented princes induced the newly elected Henry, the emperor's second son, to rebel against his father as the first had done. They seem to have persuaded the young and ambitious monarch that his own future was at stake, and that, the emperor being still in the ban, an antiking would soon inevitably be elected. *Defection of Henry V.*

Henry IV. had raised an army for the purpose of punishing a certain Dietrich of Katlenburg who had imprisoned envoys from Magdeburg, where the matter of a schismatic election was being decided. The younger Henry, who had accompanied the expedition, secretly left the army at night and placed himself at the disposal of the emperor's enemies. He received the Pope's sanction for his treasonous act.

Once more the wasted land was plunged into all the horrors of a civil war. The same old story was repeated of petty *Civil war.*

sieges and fruitless negotiations, of shameful flight on Henry
IV.'s part, of bitter humiliations, and of cunning treachery.
The climax was reached in 1105 when the young king, after a
seeming reconciliation with his father, and having made a
promise to conduct the latter to Mayence, where a diet was in
progress, decoyed him instead to the castle of Böckenheim,
near Bingen. Here he was kept as a prisoner; his dignity
and his ordinary wants were alike disregarded.

Henry IV.'s abdication. Fear and discomfort did their work. Henry agreed to abdicate and to surrender the insignia of the empire. Life and
liberty were all that he asked, but before even these were
granted him, he was forced to confess to a Roman legate, at
Ingleheim, that from first to last he had sinned against the
Roman Church. Even after this confession, into which he was
fairly tortured, absolution was refused him; only in Rome
could he be free from the ban.

The Church's triumph. In thus treading under heel the luckless grey-beard who
had so long been its opponent, the Church gained a new out-
ward triumph, second only to that won at Canossa. It was
only rendered possible by the incredible selfishness and
treachery of a band of princes who might easily have restrained themselves and awaited the natural death which was
already hovering over the head of their emperor.

The younger Henry was formally recognized by the diet of
Mayence, where, at the same time, the evils in the Church were
placed under discussion, and an embassy was despatched
to Rome to beg the Pope himself to come to Germany. In
the German sees the bishops, installed by the emperor, could
no longer hold their own; they either renounced their offices
or sought refuge in flight. The corpses of those who had died
at enmity with Rome were dug up and banished from the
churches.

Henry IV.'s last effort. Henry IV. made a last effort to raise himself from the
depths to which he had fallen, and to regain the crown he
had been forced to abdicate. Liège, where he had sought
refuge, became a rallying point for all his partisans, who were
still numerous enough to make the new ruler tremble, and to

cause him to hastily levy a large army. A force of about 20,000 men was despatched against Cologne, which had also proved faithful to the dispossessed emperor, and which now successfully withstood an attack.

Death at last put an end to sorrows and misfortunes with- **Henry IV.'s** out a parallel in the history of Europe. Henry IV. passed **death and** away at Liège on the 7th of August, 1106, mourned only by **burial, 1106** the lower classes of the people, to whom he had ever been a **A.D.** generous and devoted master.

No man was ever more thoroughly hated by his political enemies, and their revengeful spirit pursued even his lifeless flesh and bones. His corpse had been buried before the altar in the cathedral at Liège, but the Archbishop of Magdeburg placed the building thus desecrated under an interdict, and the dead emperor's friends were charged with the burden of his unhallowed remains. Twice more was he buried, and twice exhumed before he at last found a resting place in the unconsecrated chapel of St. Afra, in Spires. Here he lay for five years before Rome saw fit to remove the curse from his ashes. His remains were then, with all due pomp and magnificence—oh, mockery of filial devotion!—transferred to the imperial vault.

Henry V. before his father's death had been humble before **Henry V.** the bishops, yielding towards the princes, and obedient to Rome. He soon displayed himself in a different light.

Henry IV.'s claim to the right of investing German bishops, a very natural claim, which had for two centuries been undisputed under his forerunners, had precipitated the war of Church and State. Henry V. had ascended the throne as champion of the Church, but no sooner was his position secure than he determined not to renounce this ancient privilege of German kingship.

Paschal II. had shown himself lenient in the matter of the **Henry V. and** investitures to the extent of recognizing such bishops as had **Paschal II.** been ordained during the schism provided they were otherwise above reproach. But he was determined for his own part to carry out in future the decrees of Gregory VII.

These decrees, it will be remembered, were not at all directed exclusively against Germany, and in the very year in which Henry V. came to the throne a nominal victory was won over England, where the investiture with ring and staff was abandoned by the crown. The King of Hungary, too, had given up this right.

Henry V. and the investitures. Henry V., supported by a number of his princes and bishops, paid no heed to a renewal of the commands against lay investiture. At the council of Troyes, held in 1107, his envoys fully explained his position to the Pope. Henry claimed the right of approving the nominee to a bishopric; the canonical election and consecration might then take place, the royal investiture with ring and staff was to follow; the new bishop was to do homage to the king and to take the oath of fealty. Under no other conditions were the lands, cities, castles, rents, and privileges of any see to be conferred.

The Pope sent answer that the acknowledgement of such rights meant slavery to the Church, that the investing with ring and staff was a church sacrament with which the king should have no concern, and that the clergy disgraced their calling when, in taking a vassal's oath, they laid the hands which had been consecrated to the service of the altar in the blood-stained hand of a layman. The two points of view were clearly antagonistic, and years were to pass before a compromise could be effected.

Italian expedition, 1110 A.D. Busied as he was with wars against the Poles and Bohemians—they turned out on the whole by no means greatly to the advantage of Germany—it was not until the year 1110 that Henry could seriously turn his attention to Rome and to Rome's ruler. It was then that he announced an expedition for the purpose of obtaining the imperial crown, and the project found favour with the princes.

Henry had just formed an alliance with the court of England, wedding that Matilda who was later to play so great a part in the history of her native land.

While Henry was preparing for his expedition, Paschal took occasion to renew the threats of excommunication against all who hindered the filling of Church offices by canonical elections, and against all clergy who should allow themselves to be uncanonically chosen.

It was the beginning of the year 1111 before Henry, who had crossed the Alps with a very large army, approached Rome. He had sent envoys before him to demand the imperial crown, and to express at the same time his willingness to settle by negotiation the disputes concerning the investiture.

Henry before Rome, 1111 A.D.

The envoys arrived at a time when the Pope was almost friendless. Paschal had looked around for the traditional allies of the Papacy, but had found that the Roman nobility were not to be trusted, and that the Normans for the most part preferred the wars and adventures of the Orient to a renewal of the struggle with the empire.

It was under such circumstances as this that Paschal proposed an arrangement absolutely revolutionary in its character. The wording has been preserved to us of the charters which were mutually drawn up on the occasion. The Church was to give back all the landed possessions and rights of the empire which had come into the hands of the clergy since the time of Charlemagne. Whole counties were thus to be surrendered, and priests were to be no longer princes, no longer to hold fiefs and jurisdictions. On the contrary, the clergy were to content themselves with tithes and pious offerings. The king, in return, was to relinquish the right of investiture; things temporal were to be wholly separated from things spirtual. On the day of the coronation the mutual renunciations were to be made, and Paschal was to compel the German bishops to submit peaceably to the loss of their fiefs.

The Church's renunciation.

Sunday, February 12th, had been fixed upon for the coronation ceremony. Magnificently escorted Henry V. entered St. Peter's, and the proceedings began. The king caused a charter to be read in which he confirmed the Pope, the bishops, and the abbots in the possession of their several churches, and declared that he had no wish to rob them of their belongings. His aim and object was that the

The coronation day.

whole odium of what was to follow should fall on the Pope.

When the charter containing the latter's concessions was read a scene ensued of tumult and confusion. Paschal was loudly accused of heresy. Bishops and abbots, princes and knights, were wild with excitement; the one feared that he would lose the fiefs he held from the Church, the other those which he held from the empire. The day was spent in confused disputes; Henry V. declared that the Pope had broken his compact, and demanded now the full and free right of investiture; the coronation ceremony could not continue.

Pope and cardinals taken prisoners.
When night came the Pope and the cardinals found themselves prisoners in the hands of the Germans, and were removed to a neighbouring hospice; all thought of compromise was abandoned. Henry was determined that the captives should not be released until after his right of investing bishops had been acknowledged.

The Romans rose in a body to rescue the Pope, but the Germans held their own, and were able to retire from the city, carrying with them Paschal and his fellow-captives. After weeks of imprisonment the Pope, moved by the wretched condition of Rome and the Romans, and also by the fear of a new schism, yielded to all of Henry's demands.

Pope abandons investiture.
The right of investiture was abandoned—that right in defence of which Gregory VII. and Urban II. had filled all Europe with war and turmoil. The king might enjoy it now, fully and freely, as his predecessors had done. In the camp before Rome, on April 12th, 1111, the precious document containing the renunciation [1] was placed in Henry's hands, and on the following day the coronation ceremony was performed. Henry withdrew from Rome as emperor, carrying with him hostages of the Pope.

As may well be imagined, the measures taken by Paschal met with strong disapproval in many quarters. The majority

[1] See " Select Documents," p. 407.

of the cardinals bitterly opposed such a termination as this to the war of the investitures, and the Gallican clergy were proceeding to take radical steps against the Pope when the learned Ivo of Chartres restrained them. He assured them, from the fullness of his knowledge of canon law, that Paschal, having acted under compulsion, was not bound to keep his agreement.

A Lenten synod held in the Lateran in 1112 at last persuaded the Pope to repudiate his compact, and a party of the Gallican clergy, under the leadership of Archbishop Guido of Vienne, showed themselves willing to take up the struggle against the emperor. A synod held at Vienne in 1112 declared lay investiture to be heresy, and the privilege wrung from Paschal to be null and void. The ban was laid upon Henry, who, like a second Judas, had by treachery, perjury, and desecration forced the Pope to sign the deed. *Pope repudiates his renunciations.*

It was strange that Henry V. should have found himself much in the same position, with regard to the ban, as the father whom he had, with the aid of the Church, deposed. But the parallel was to be carried still further. At the moment when the emperor most needed devoted adherents disaffection showed itself among the princes in general, and a rebellion broke out in Saxony.

Henry had offended in different ways various influential nobles, chief among them the powerful Saxon duke, Lothar of Supplinburg, who united in his own hand the former possessions of the Billungs, of Otto of Nordheim, and of Ecbert of Meissen. The fidelity, moreover, of the great Adalbert, Archbishop of Mayence, began also to be doubted by the emperor, the more so as Adalbert was known to be in sympathy with those of the Gallican clergy who so strongly favoured the abandonment of lay investiture. *Rebellion in Germany.*

Henry V. maintained later that Adalbert had been privy to a conspiracy formed at Erfurt to murder him. Be that as it may, he took the decisive step of arresting the primate of Germany. An emperor, a pope, and an archbishop had now in turn been his captives! *Arrest of the archbishop.*

For the time being Henry's move was successful, and a
victory gained in the following year by a Count Hoiers
placed Saxony once more in his hands. The rebellious
princes submitted; some were pardoned, others placed under
restraint.

But the peace was of short duration. In 1114 the citizens
of Cologne, seized with a sudden mistrust of the emperor's
motives, deserted their places in an army that he was leading
against the Frisians. They found allies, and for a long time
war devastated both banks of the Rhine. Again the Saxon
rebels raised their heads; once more Henry was obliged to
march against them. In February, 1115, he suffered a
stinging defeat at their hands.

Henry V. in the ban. It was at this time that a legate of the Pope, acting on
his own authority, indeed, ventured, upon German ground,
to renew the curse against the emperor. It was of great
advantage to the rebels that they could claim the authority of the Church for their hostile acts; once more the
cause of the Saxons was that of the opponents of lay investiture.

Everything depended on a reconciliation with the Pope, and
Henry, who in 1116 left Germany to its disunion, and entered
Italy as claimant of the estates of Matilda—the great countess
had died in the previous year, having come, it is believed, to
an agreement with the emperor—recommenced negotiations
with him. Paschal had never himself spoken the ban against
Henry, although he had approved in general terms the action
of his legate.

Death of Paschal II., 1118 A.D. But if the emperor had expected to find the Pope ready to
make peace he must soon have found out his error. The
negotiations failed, and when, in 1117, Henry came to Rome
and wore his crown, Paschal excommunicated the bishop who
had set it upon his head. The Pope had succeeded in raising
an army, and was proceeding to more active hostilities, when
death overtook him (January, 1118).

Henry V. and Gela- sius. Henry V.'s first step on hearing that a new Pope, Gelasius,
had been elected, was to hasten to Rome, where he hoped to

come to terms with the future head of Christendom before the consecration could take place. But Gelasius took fright at his approach, and fled from Rome. Henry, in concert with the Romans, sent envoys to demand his return, promising that he should be personally unmolested, but requiring an oath to the effect that the questions at issue between the papacy and the empire should at last be settled.

Gelasius sent an unsatisfactory reply. He intended, he said, to hold a council at Milan or Cremona ; the matter of the investitures could be settled there if the emperor were willing. But the emperor was not willing, neither were the Romans, who considered Rome the proper place for concluding matters of such prime importance.

The result was the election of an antipope, Burdinus, and the beginning of a new schism. More and more was the reign of Henry V. becoming the reflected shadow of that of his father ! There only failed a few ungrateful sons to make the analogy complete.

Election of an antipope.

Gelasius now formally spoke the anathema over Henry V. and over the latter's pope, and finding Rome too unquiet for himself crossed over into France.

Henry V. now returned to Germany, from which he had been absent for the space of two years. He had left the land a prey to civil war, and civil war had done its work. To use the words of a chronicler who wrote in the year 1117 : " Men rage against each other with bestial delight ; to the clergy scarcely their bare lives are left ; the fields lie waste, the villages are in ruins ; many districts and cities are completely devastated, and in many churches the service of God has altogether ceased."

Henry prevents Würzburg diet.

It was well that Henry came. The legate of the Pope had been active in promulgating the ban, and preparations were being made for a diet at Würzburg, which might have cost the emperor his throne. His deposition had already been seriously discussed, and had been made contingent upon his appearing to answer the charges against him.

Henry's presence was enough to dissipate the clouds of

treasonable intent, and to set bounds to the growing disaffection ; the Würzburg diet never took place.

Calixtus II., 1119-1124 A.D. Early in the year 1119 Gelasius died, and was succeeded by
Calixtus II., that same Archbishop Guido of Vienne, the head
of the Gallican clergy, who had been the first to proclaim the
ban against Henry after the transactions with Paschal in 1111.
He was the very man of all others with whom an eventual
agreement must have seemed impossible. Yet, strangely
enough, he showed himself, in the end at least, more peace-
loving and conciliatory, above all more amenable to reason,
than any of his predecessors.

In Germany there was a universal desire for quiet and
order consequent on the utter desolation of the land, and
all looked forward to the council of Rheims, where it was
hoped that the question of the investitures would be finally
settled.

Council of Rheims and renewal of ban, 1119 A.D. At this council, which met in 1119, documents on both
sides had been actually drawn up when a sudden mistrust
seized both parties. The emperor found reason to fear that a
penance like that which Henry IV. had undergone at Canossa
was about to be inflicted upon himself ; the Pope, that Henry
had in the neighbourhood a large army, and intended to secure
by intimidation a more favourable treaty. Idle rumours these,
so far as we know, but they served their purpose, and resulted
in the breaking off of negotiations.

The council ended with a solemn renewal of the ban against
Henry and against Burdinus ; all Germans were to be loosed
from their oath of allegiance should the emperor continue in
his evil ways. Hundreds of candles were lighted in the assembly and suddenly and simultaneously extinguished—the
usual symbolical way of casting into outer darkness the
wretch who was burdened with the curse of Rome.

Abandon- ment of Burdinus. The renewal of the ban did not greatly harm the emperor ;
indeed, in the months that succeeded, his power and influence
seem rather to have been on the increase than otherwise. He
either could not or would not, however, make great sacrifices
to uphold his puppet pope. Calixtus finally took Burdinus

prisoner, paraded him on a camel through the streets of Rome, and then incarcerated him in a monastery.

Hostile as the proceedings at Rheims had been, the discussions of that council had opened men's eyes, strangely blinded in the heat of this long struggle, to the fact that a fair compromise of opposing interests was possible : that bishops and abbots might be canonically elected, and yet still remain servants of the emperor, answerable to him alone for their estates and their privileges.

Thoughts of compromise.

It was three years before such a compromise was really effected, years of continued strife between the emperor and all who thought as Rome did among his subjects. But the right moment came at last, came at a time when two hostile armies were encamped over against each other in the vicinity of Mayence, and when the bloodiest of battles seemed about to take place.

An arrangement was hit upon which found favour with both sides. Twenty-four princes were chosen—twelve to represent the emperor, twelve the Church party; to them was left the final voice in the matter.

Arbitration.

At Würzburg in 1121 the arbiters came together and drew up a treaty of peace that was agreed to by all parties. The actual question of the right of investiture was to be decided in a council which the Pope was to summon ; the princes promised to see that at that council the honour of the empire should be upheld.

Meanwhile the emperor was to be acknowledged, and even bishops might frequent his court. An embassy was soon afterwards sent to Rome to express Henry's ardent desire for peace ; Calixtus was quite as anxious for such a consummation, and the final results of all negotiations were embodied in the famous Concordat of Worms, issued September 23rd, 1122.

Concordat of Worms, 1122 A.D.

The emperor renounced the investiture with ring and staff, and gave to the Church the right of appointing and electing her servants. But the elections were to be held in the royal presence, and the temporal fiefs and privileges were to be conferred by a special investiture with the sceptre. In Germany such investiture was to precede, in Burgundy and Italy to follow the Church's consecration.

The original document drawn up on the part of the emperor is still preserved in the archives of the castle of St. Angelo at Rome.

The kiss of peace.

In the Rhine meadows near Worms, in the presence of a crowd so great that the city had not been able to contain it, the peace of the Church and the State after their war of nearly fifty years was solemnly concluded. The papal legate extended to the emperor the kiss of peace, and administered to him the holy Eucharist. The ban was thereby loosed, and Henry received back into the lap of the Church.

Concordat a triumph for the Church.

The Concordat of Worms, although in every sense a compromise, was, nevertheless, a triumph for the papacy. What Gregory VII. had claimed, indeed, freedom from the state and dominion over it, had not been gained. But, all the same, the spiritual principalities were greatly emancipated from the authority of the crown. The emperor's right of approving of a nominee of the Church was very different from having the nomination of a candidate in his own hand.

The Church undoubtedly gained a tighter hold on the clergy of Germany, for it was able to place its best men in the several sees, and thus to carry out more fully its great aims of sacerdotal celibacy and abolishment of simony.

Charles the Great, Otto the Great, and Henry III. had striven to purify the Church, but had kept their mastery over it. Henry V., in one important respect, at least, had acknowledged that Church's independence. Moreover, the fact that during the struggle pope after pope had gained recognition in spite of the royal or imperial opposition had given the last blow to the theory that the consent of the German monarch was necessary to the validity of a papal election.

Death of Henry V., 1125 A.D.

The signing of the Concordat was the last great act of Henry V.'s life. His remaining days were spent in trying to keep peace among his unruly subjects and in preparing for an invasion of France in the interests of his father-in-law,

Henry I. of England. The invasion never took place, and the emperor died in 1125.

Henry was buried in the magnificent cathedral of Spires, the first of the great triumphs of church architecture on German ground. The building had but shortly before reached its completion.

CHAPTER XV.

THE RISE OF THE HOHENSTAUFENS.

Frederick of Hohenstaufen as candidate for the throne. THE history of the Hohenstaufen rule in Germany, that history which shows the culmination and then the temporary fall of the mediæval empire, would have begun with the year 1125, instead of fourteen years later, had it not been for the efforts, not to say intrigues, of Archbishop Adalbert of Mayence.

The chief candidate on the death of Henry V., and the man whom that king had designated as his successor, was his nephew Frederick, Duke of Suabia, son of that Hohenstaufen to whom Henry IV. had given the duchy just mentioned in 1079. Frederick was the nearest of kin to the emperor who had just passed away, and, together with his brother Conrad, heir to the private Salian possessions. He had married the daughter of Henry of Bavaria, leader of the Guelphs, and seemed best fitted to reconcile the differences which had already begun to grow up between that house and his own. But he had led the anti-papal party under Henry V., and it was feared that a continuation of the old Salian policy of antagonism to Rome might bring about the ruin of the Church.

Lothar of Supplinburg elected. Adalbert of Mayence, on whom it devolved to call together the electoral assembly, succeeded in influencing a number of princes, and in excluding the elements that were likely to oppose his plans. He then put through the election, which took place in somewhat tumultuous fashion, of Lothar of Suplinburg, Duke of Saxony, a man who had been noted in his own duchy as a just ruler and a careful administrator.

Three candidates, Frederick, Lothar, and Leopold of Austria, had been designated as eligible to the throne by a committee of forty, which had been chosen from the four stems. Lothar and Leopold had each promised to submit to the result of the voting, even though a third should be elected. The same demand was made of Frederick, but in a slightly different form. He was asked to consider himself as not having been designated, in order that the election might be an entirely free one. Adalbert had intended to place him in a dilemma, and he succeeded. Frederick asked for time to consider the proposition, and withdrew from the assembly to consult with his friends. But his action was represented to the princes as an attempt at asserting a hereditary right to the throne, and it was this claim of heredity that these same princes were bound to oppose. To show its baselessness in the present case, they gave the throne to Lothar.

There was one powerful prince, Duke Henry, surnamed the Black, of Bavaria, the father-in-law of Frederick of Hohenstaufen, whose voice had not yet been heard in the matter, and who had not been present at the election. Should Bavaria unite with Suabia against him, Lothar's position would be anything but secure. But a bribe was thought of, which proved sufficiently desirable to induce Henry to go over to the rival camp. *Henry of Bavaria won over by Lothar.*

Lothar, at this time sixty years old, and without male heirs, had a daughter, Gertrude, whose husband would fall heir eventually to huge estates in Saxony, and was not unlikely to be ultimately chosen to the throne of the empire. A marriage was now arranged between Gertrude and Henry the Proud, Duke Henry's son and heir, in whose person the Guelphic dream of uniting Bavaria and Saxony in one hand, was to be realized a few years later. The young Henry himself, through his mother, was heir to half the Billung estates.

Frederick of Hohenstaufen made his peace immediately after Lothar's coronation; but a question soon arose with regard to the Salian estates, his heritage from Henry V., *Conflict with Frederick of Hohenstaufen.*

which involved him in deadly conflict with the crown.   The
question concerned the lands of felons, which had been confiscated by the late king.   Were they to be considered as
private royal possessions, or as belonging to the empire?
Kings had hitherto disposed of crown lands at will; but
either they had left no near male heirs, or those heirs had
succeeded to the throne.

A court, held by Lothar at Ratisbon, rendered judgment in
a sense unfavourable to Frederick, and the latter was ordered
to make certain restitutions.   He refused, and, inasmuch as
he prepared to defend his claims with the sword, was
promptly declared guilty of high treason, and the ban of the
empire was spoken against him.   Lothar was fettered at first
in his attempts at coercing Frederick, by an unfortunate war
in Bohemia.   He had taken sides in an internal conflict that
was there going on, and had suffered a crushing defeat, being
able, however, in consequence of developments in Bohemia
itself, to make a not disadvantageous peace.

Guelphs against Hohenstaufens.   It was at this time that the fatal hostility between
Guelphs and Hohenstaufens, which was to be inherited by
the Italian Guelphs and Ghibellines, the adherents of the
popes and the adherents of the emperors, may be said to have
begun.   Henry the Proud, the Guelph, joined with his
father-in-law in the struggle against Frederick the Hohenstaufen.

Conrad as antiking.   Frederick, for his part, was able to raise a strong party,
which was greatly encouraged by Lothar's reverses in
Bohemia.   It soon felt itself strong enough to take a step,
warranted, alas, by precedent, both in the history of Germany
and of the papacy.   An antiking was elected in the person
of Conrad of Hohenstaufen, Frederick's younger brother.
Conrad's first act was to hasten to Italy, where he hoped to
put himself in possession of the estates of Matilda, and to
gain powerful adherents.   But the Hohenstaufens were
already to begin to feel what papal enmity could accomplish
against them, and the antiking was met by the ban of the
church hurled against him by Honorius II.   It helped him

little that the Milanese received him with open arms. He
met with loss upon loss, and allies and means alike failed
him.

The whole clergy of Germany, in the meantime, had de- Clergy for
clared for Lothar, for the sanctity of an election approved by Lothar.
Rome, and of a coronation fulfilled by the Church. The
young Henry of Bavaria, too, was most zealous on his behalf.
He surprised Frederick of Hohenstaufen in a Suabian monastery, and set fire to the edifice, hoping to smother his enemy
in the flames. But Frederick escaped to a fire-proof tower of
the minster, and Henry was soon obliged to withdraw. The
war with the Hohenstaufens, although on the whole little
blood was shed, lasted for four years. The sieges of insignificant towns were conducted on such primitive principles,
that months were often spent in useless endeavours. But
Spires and Nuremburg, those old Salian strongholds, at last
fell into Lothar's hands.

It was not, indeed, until 1134 and 1135 respectively, that Peace with
Frederick and Conrad made their submission to the king. the Hohen-
Lothar showed himself magnanimous in the extreme. Both staufens.
his former enemies were left in possession of their hereditary
lands and privileges, and Conrad was later made royal banner-
bearer on an expedition to Italy.

It was the results of Lothar's church policy, results which Lothar
did not show themselves until much later, that made his favours the
reign an unfortunate one for Germany. We must leave aside Church.
the oft disputed questions, as to whether or not he renounced
the right of investiture at his coronation, and whether, when
he afterwards twice urged the Pope to acknowledge that
right, he referred to the procedure instituted by the Concordat
of Worms, or to the state of things previous to that treaty.
Proof enough, however, remains to show that he more than
once sacrificed the ideal of imperial glory to the enjoyment
of a passing privilege.

The German Church, indeed, looked upon his reign as a
golden age. According to the annals of Pöhlde, " he left
behind him such a memory of his time as will be blessed

until the end of the world ; for in his days the Church rejoiced
in peace, the performances of divine service increased, and
there was a blessed abundance of all things." And a Saxon
monk writes : " In Lothar's time a new light began to shine ;
not in Saxony alone, but in all Germany quiet and abundance
prevailed, and peace between Church and State."

Monastic orders. Lothar's right hand man in the kingdom was Norbert,
founder of the Premonstratensian order, and later archbishop
of Magdeburg. He was a man of wide influence, and a
powerful spreader of missionary ideas. It was a time when
monastic orders were in their prime, and when their leaders
were able to control in a measure the politics of Europe.

Bernard of Clairvaux. Pope Honorius II. died in 1130, and it was Bernard of
Clairvaux, the head of the Cistercians, and the reformer in all
of more than one hundred and eighty monasteries, who won
over Kings Louis VI. of France and Henry I. of England for
the more pious Innocent II., as opposed to the antipope
Anaclete who had been chosen by the Roman nobles.

Norbert won Lothar also for Innocent, and a meeting, at
which St. Bernard was present, took place between the new
Pope and the German king at Liége. Lothar performed the
service of marshal for the Pope, and led his horse by the
bridle after holding the stirrup for him to mount. He established herewith a precedent, for no German king for centuries
had thus humbled himself save Conrad, the rebellious and
disinherited son of Henry IV.

It was here at Liége that Lothar demanded the right of
investiture as the price of his support. St. Bernard, who
completely controlled the Pope, hereupon interfered, declared
the king's wish to be " unbecoming," and prevented further
negotiations. Lothar, none the less, was won for the stricter
Church party ; he agreed to lead an army to Rome, where he
was told that the imperial crown awaited him.

Expedition to Rome. It was a hazardous undertaking, for Lothar could raise no
suitable forces. The Hohenstaufens were not yet subjected,
and an expedition had to be sent against King Niels of
Denmark and his son Magnus, the latter having killed a

Slavonian prince who was under Lothar's protection. In the end Niels and Magnus were made to do homage and to pay tribute.

It was with only 1,500 knights that the German king in 1132 crossed the Alps, and he was able to accomplish no great undertaking, although ably supported by Innocent and St. Bernard, who met him at Viterbo. The Pope had already won for himself the support of Cremona, Brescia, Pavia, and Piacenza.

Early in 1033 the Pope and the emperor marched into Rome. Anaclete was in possession of St. Peter's, and of the castle of St. Angelo, nor was it possible to dislodge him with the forces at hand. But Lothar was determined to have the imperial crown, and the ceremony of coronation was gone through with, contrary to custom, in the church of the Lateran. The oath which the new Emperor swore to the Pope has come down to us, and differs little from that taken by his predecessors. But a patriotic artist later painted the scene in the audience hall of the Lateran, and the following inscription was placed under the picture: "The king comes before the gates, first swearing due honour to the city. He then becomes the vassal of the Pope, and takes the crown which he bestows." *Coronation in the Lateran, 1033 A.D.*

Picture in the Lateran.

Frederick Barbarossa made a valiant and effective protest in later days against the wording of this inscription; the odious terms were explained away, and the aggressive work of art removed.

Lothar is said at the time of his imperial coronation once more to have asked the Pope for the right of investiture as exercised of old by his predecessors, and Norbert of Magdeburg is said to have sided against his own sovereign. Be that as it may Innocent was induced at least to confirm that provision of the Concordat requiring that the investiture in Germany should only be bestowed after the king had approved the candidate, had conferred upon him the secular privileges pertaining to his office, and had received his due profession of obedience. This charter of confirmation is still extant.

Estates of Matilda.

Another charter marks an event which may have given rise to the impression that Lothar became a vassal of the Pope. Innocent conferred on him for life the use of the estates of Matilda, of Gregory VII.'s great ally. Henry V. had regarded himself as heir to these lands, maintaining that Matilda had had no right to will them to the Church; Conrad, Lothar's rival, had gone to Italy hoping to gain possession of them as Henry V.'s successor, but the cities of Tuscany had refused to receive him as their lord.

Lothar was to pay a hundred pounds of silver for the use of the estates which, at his death, were to be conferred for life on his son-in-law, Henry of Bavaria, who was to swear homage and fealty to the Pope.

Lothar's acceptance of the estates from the hand of Innocent, his acknowledgement that the Pope had a right to bestow them, was a concession of far-reaching import—a concession that can only be explained on the supposition that there was danger of the estates falling, either by sentence of the Pope or otherwise, into the hands of the Hohenstaufens, who had claims to them that were not unfounded.

Roger of Sicily.

Three years after his imperial coronation, Lothar again returned to Italy with an army, ready to help the Pope against Anaclete, who was still unconquered, and against Roger of Sicily, a prime mover in the matter of the schism. Roger was nephew of that Robert Guiscard who had been the conqueror of Southern Italy. He had shown himself worthy of his uncle, and had maintained the possession of Calabria and Apulia, not to speak of numerous possessions of the Greeks in Africa. A king's crown had been bestowed upon him by Anaclete as the price of his support.

Such a power as Roger's in the south of Italy was a constant menace to the empire which, too, still had a nominal claim to Apulia, Salerno and Capua. Henry III., indeed, had been the last to exercise sovereign rights over these provinces.

Lothar's triumphs in Italy.

Lothar's progress through Italy in 1136 and 1137 was a succession of triumphs. A few cities, indeed, refused him allegiance, but he met with no organized resistance, and there was probably no one town in which more than a faction of the citizens was hostile to him.   He was soon the acknowledged master of Lombardy and the Romagna.   After leaving Bologna he divided his army, entrusting a portion of it to Henry of Bavaria who was joined by Pope Innocent.   When the two divisions met, each after its own career of conquest, it was to besiege the strong fortress of Bari, which, together with Salerno, soon capitulated.

Innocent returned to Rome, where, in 1138, on Anaclete's death, he won general recognition.   The relations between the Pope and the Emperor had become somewhat strained at the last, although each in turn had shown that he was willing to make concessions in case of necessity.   *His relations with the Pope.*

Innocent was under the impression that the emperor was subjugating the recalcitrant cities solely for the advantage of St. Peter, whereas his chief aim was to gain glory for the empire.   More than one misunderstanding arose.   Viterbo being forced to pay a fine of £3,000, the Pope claimed it as feudal lord, Duke Henry as conqueror of the city.   In this case, and in a dispute regarding the election of an abbot of Monte Casino, Innocent was compelled to yield.

In the important question as to who should confer the duchy of Apulia a curious compromise was effected.   Both had agreed that Rainulf of Alife was the proper person ; but the question was who should invest him, for the Pope and the Emperor each claimed to be feudal lord of Apulia.   As a final expedient the standard or token of investiture was bestowed by both in common, the Emperor holding the shaft, the Pope the point of the banner.   *Curious compromise with the Pope.*

In peace and concord, outwardly at least, the two potentates parted, and Lothar prepared to return to Germany.   Death overtook him on the journey through Tyrol.   *Lothar's death, 1137 A.D.*

Innocent II., bereft of his strong adherent, soon found himself in sore straits, for Roger of Sicily was able to retrieve his losses and to pursue his ambitious plans.   The Pope, to the surprise of Europe, finally took up arms in his own behalf, and marched out to meet Roger. The result was that the warlike pontiff and his chief supporters fell into the enemy's hands and were held as prisoners of war. Innocent at last was allowed to depart in peace, but not until he had ratified the measures of his rival Anaclete, and recognized Roger as head of a great Norman kingdom in south Italy.

A Guelph as candidate, 1137.

How often has it happened in the history of mediæval Germany that the chief interest centres on two men instead of on one—on him who holds the throne, but also on him who claims it!

At the time of Lothar's accession, in 1125, a Hohenstaufen had been the rejected suitor; at his death a Guelph was to hold that unenvied position. And the mutual relations of the two houses were not to be bettered by the new complications.

Henry of Bavaria.

Henry of Bavaria had every reason to expect the crown. He had been present with Lothar at the last, and the dying king had designated him as his successor. His power and wealth, too, seemed to signal him out above all others for the highest position in the land. Already Duke of Bavaria and of Saxony and heir to Lothar's private estates, he was about to enter upon the enjoyment of the estates of Matilda which, according to agreement, were to be his for life. Had the goal of the German princes been a purely national one, had their one ideal been to strengthen the empire and to free it from the shackles imposed by the Church, they could have attained it by electing Henry.

Objections to Henry of Bavaria.

But it was not. Many were jealous of Henry's position, and many were bound by ties of loyalty and of self-interest to the house of Hohenstaufen. To the Church, moreover, so powerful a man as Henry—one, too, who while in Italy had firmly stood his ground against the papal demands—was not likely to prove acceptable.

Archbishop Albero of Treves, who owed his advancement to that see to the personal intervention of Innocent II., prevented Henry from being chosen. To him belonged the first vote and the conducting of the election, for the see of Mayence was temporarily vacant and the Cologne archbishop had not yet received his pallium from Rome.

The object of Albero's choice was none other than that Conrad who, for a brief period, had already worn the royal crown in opposition to Lothar. The election took place at Coblenz on the 7th of March, 1138, and the crown was placed on Conrad's head by a legate of the Pope. Neither Saxony nor Bavaria was represented, and the greatest haste and irregularity characterized the proceedings. But Albero knew that the choice of Rome would be the choice of the German clergy, and that the princes would approve a measure which rid them of the fear of Henry's supremacy. The event proved that he was right, but Conrad's election was a blow to the progress of Germany. His reign was the reign of a faction and nothing good or lasting came of it.

Conrad II., 1138-1152.

Henry at first bore his disappointment with a good grace, and, either by promises or by threats, was induced to resign the insignia of royalty which had come into his hands at Lothar's death. But Conrad was not satisfied with this. Henry was far too powerful a subject for a mediocre king, and causes of dispute were not wanting. The reports that we have of the quarrel are vague and contradictory, but we know that Conrad raised objection to the holding of two duchies in one hand, and that he eventually conferred Saxony on Margrave Albrecht the Bear, a descendant of the Billungs. Henry was declared in the ban, and war between the king and his mightiest vassal became inevitable.

War with Henry of Bavaria.

Conrad left no stone unturned to gain allies for the coming struggle, and we hear at this time of his conferring upon Genoa the right of coinage—a right so valued that for centuries to come the name " Conradus " was to be stamped on Genoese coins.

In Saxony the rival dukes had already begun to despoil each other's lands. Albrecht was at first the more successful, taking Luneburg, Bremen, and other important places, and at one time holding nearly the whole duchy in his power. But in 1139 the tide turned, and Henry gained such an ascen-

Fighting in Saxony.

dancy that Conrad, when he appeared in Saxony, found the land too hostile, and did not dare to remain. His withdrawal had much the aspect of a flight, and only served to strengthen Henry's cause.

Before leading an army against Henry, Conrad retired to Bavaria, which he conferred on Margrave Leopold of Austria, his half-brother, and own brother to Otto of Frising, the clear-headed historian of these times, and of the early part of Frederick Barbarossa's reign. Otto, although a bishop, helped his brother valiantly to defend his duchy.

In the summer of 1139 Conrad's forces and those of Henry the Proud stood over against each other, prepared for the final struggle, at Kreuzburg, near the Werra. It was agreed, however, instead of fighting, to make truce, and the Saxons expressed their willingness to renew their allegiance to Conrad and to submit their complaints to a general diet to be held in Worms. The day ended, not, as everyone had expected, in havoc and bloodshed, but in a mild carouse, the Archbishop of Treves being discovered to have opportunely brought with him as baggage a considerable quantity of wine.

Death of Henry of Bavaria.
The negotiations, strangely enough, had been carried on with the Saxon nobles and not with Henry the Proud, and the latter determined to carry the war into Bavaria, which he intended to wrest from its new duke. But a sudden and fatal illness befell him; he died at the age of thirty-five. Many of his contemporaries believed, or professed to believe, that he had been poisoned.

Weinsberg besieged, 1140.
The opposition in Bavaria against Duke Leopold and Otto of Frising continued to be carried on by Henry the Proud's relative, Count Welf. He defeated them in the Mangfall Valley in August, 1140, and Conrad himself was fain to come to the help of his half-brothers. He besieged Welf's stronghold, Weinsberg (near Ulm), which fell after an eight weeks' siege. Two famous traditions attach to this victory, neither of which, however, can be said to be historically well founded. It was here that the women were allowed to depart with what belongings they could carry, and each left the city bending

under the weight of her husband. Here, too, the great cries, "Ho Welf," and "Ho Waiblingen" (Ghibelline), are said first to have been uttered.

Conrad was detained in Bavaria for more than a year, but by May, 1142, the greater part of the Welf faction, although not Count Welf himself, was ready for peace ; and a large assembly was held at Frankfort for the purpose of bringing about a general reconciliation. Saxon and Bavarian princes were present in great numbers, as well as Gertrude, the widow of Henry the Proud, and her young son, Henry the Lion. Gertrude here promised her hand to Leopold's brother and Conrad's half-brother, Henry of Austria, surnamed Jasomir-gott, from the oath which was always on his lips (" *Ja so mir Gott helfe* "). The wedding festivities were celebrated with great pomp, and lasted a fortnight, and it was hoped that the enmity between the two chief houses in Germany was about to be finally laid at rest. Saxony was given to Henry the Lion, who renounced Bavaria, which, Leopold having died a few months before the peace-meeting at Frankfort and the duchy having remained until then in the hands of the king, was given in 1143 to Henry Jasomirgott. *[margin: Truce with the Guelphs.]*

But this advancement of a member of the Hohenstaufen family to the head of a duchy that had so long belonged to the Guelphs, aroused Count Welf to new action. He now claimed Bavaria in his own right, and, strange to say, in this new struggle the youthful Frederick Barbarossa took part not with his uncle, King Conrad, but with the new claimant.

Henry Jasomirgott, however, remained master of the situation in Bavaria, and was able to take Dachau, the strongest fortress of the Guelphs.

The opposition was crushed for the moment, and Conrad was able to turn his attention to other matters. After long and oft-interrupted negotiations an alliance with the court of Constantinople was brought about, an alliance directed against Roger of Sicily, who is said to have bribed Welf to fan the discordant elements in Germany, so as to prevent Conrad from appearing in Italy. Certain it is that Welf played most ably *[margin: Alliance with Con-stantinople.]*

into Roger's hands, for his enmity to the Hohenstaufens, which infected other noble houses also with disloyal impulses, prevented anything like decisive action on the part of the king.

General demoralisation in Germany.

Who can doubt but that the failure to win the imperial crown was owing to the general disorganization and demoralization, which kept the king from crossing the Alps in spite of the Pope's urgent invitations to do so? Intestinal feuds called him now here now there, and obliged him to dissipate his strength in petty undertakings.

The prestige of the throne was sinking lower and lower. Conrad had, indeed, in 1142, made a successful inroad into Bohemia, and established his own candidate in that duchy; but since then he had accomplished nothing worthy of record. In 1146 his attempts at interference in Poland signally failed, while his influence in the lands on his south-eastern border was almost annihilated by a victory of the Hungarian king Geisa over Henry of Bavaria.

The second crusade.

In the midst of all these mishaps and dissentions the news came that a great crusade was in progress against the Turks, who had taken Edessa and were otherwise holding high carnival in Syria. The second crusade was in some ways a godsend to Germany; men laid aside their own disputes to unite in a great and common cause. Welf himself took the cross.

St. Bernard, fresh from unheard-of triumphs as a preacher of the crusade in France, appeared in person before Conrad, and, after several attempts to make the king take the cross, was at last successful. On the feast of St. John the Evangelist (December 27th), 1146, the monk rose up in the cathedral at Spires and gave vent to a burst of eloquence that carried all before it. As Bernard himself expressed it, a wonder of wonders was accomplished, and Conrad was moved to tears, declaring that the Lord himself had spoken. Bernard seized the standard from the altar and bestowed it on the king as leader of the crusading host.

Crusade against the Wends.

The zeal for the crusade became as general throughout Germany as it had been throughout France; but the Saxons were allowed the privileges of those going to the Holy Land, if they would undertake to subject the neighbouring Wends, a task which they only partially fulfilled in the following year.

Conrad's expedition left Germany in June, 1147, choosing the route through Hungary. A month later King Louis, of France, with an immense army, followed in his wake. A number of crusaders from the neighbourhood of Cologne had already joined a Flemish-English fleet, which was soon, on behalf of the hospitable king of Portugal, to conquer Lisbon from the Saracens. **Conrad's expedition.**

Great as were the preparations, and wild as was the enthusiasm for the second crusade, no one of these great expeditions ever resulted quite so miserably.

Conrad's army braved successfully the dangers that threatened it, from the fears and suspicions of the Greeks ; but on the road from Nicea to Iconium provisions gave out, the army became disheartened, and further advance was impossible. It was decided to return to Nicea, and 30,000 Germans are said to have fallen during this retreat, want and fatigue being aggravated by continual attacks of the Turks. From Nicea Conrad sent home the greater part of the troops that remained, being convinced that nothing was to be done with such untrained forces. With the rest he joined Louis of France at Lopadium, but was soon obliged by illness to return to Constantinople. **Disaster.**

The French continued their expedition, but were no more successful than the Germans had been. The greater part of them fell under the sabres of the Turks, or were dragged into captivity, while sickness and hunger completed whatever the enemy left to be accomplished.

The blame of all these disasters has often been laid to the faithlessness of the Greeks, who undoubtedly did make compacts as to means of transport, supplies, etc., which were never fulfilled. But the Greek emperor was aghast at the flood of nations that had been let loose against him, and he feared, not without some reason, that the French, at least, **The Greeks.**

R

were lusting to conquer his own capital of Constantinople. No wonder that provisions and guides were difficult to obtain, and that the wish to furnish them often failed. On the whole the Germans were better treated than the French, and Conrad, whose sister-in-law had married the emperor, was for long periods Manuel's guest.

Siege of Damascus, 1148 A.D.

Conrad again left Constantinople in the spring of 1148, and, accompanied only by his retinue, sailed for Ptolomais. From there he hastened to Jerusalem, where he succeeded in raising a new army from the crowds of pilgrims who had gathered there. In common with Louis of France, who had also gathered new forces, and with Baldwin, king of Jerusalem, it was decided to besiege Damascus, and thus by one great action to wipe out the shame of the previous disasters.

Treason in the Christian army.

The siege opened in the most promising manner, and it was hoped that, within a fortnight, the cross would be seen waving above the walls of the city. But disunion and treachery were at work in the Christian army, and the contingent from Jerusalem began treating in secret with the vizier of Damascus. The accusation of bribery was later openly brought against King Baldwin and the Templars. Certain it is that the withdrawal of the Jerusalem forces resulted in the abandonment of the undertaking against Damascus. The same cause, too, brought about the failure of an attempted siege of Askalon. Sick at heart, and feeling that they had been betrayed by the very people for whose sake they had undergone such bitter privations, the two kings set sail for their respective lands.

Conrad's return to Italy.

In May, 1149, Conrad landed near Aquileija, and prepared to take up arms against Roger of Sicily, having made a compact to that end with the Emperor Manuel. He dreaded, doubtless, a return to Germany without first having performed some feat of arms, which should make the people forget the miserable outcome of his expedition.

Count Welf VI.'s rebellion.

But Roger had not been idle. He had met Count Welf, who returned before Conrad from the crusade, and had entered into a new compact with him. Welf again stood at

the head of a rebellion in Germany, and Conrad hastened
back to take the reins of Government from the hands of his
youthful son Henry, whom the princes had chosen king at
the beginning of the crusade. This same young king soon
inflicted a signal defeat on Welf's army, near Flochberg.
Welf made his submission, and did not again disturb the
peace of the kingdom. He remained faithful to Conrad, even
when Henry the Lion, now of age, renewed his claim to
Bavaria, and prepared, as was the wont of these passionate
Guelphs, to move heaven and earth to attain his object.

But the struggle had only just commenced, when the hand
of death was laid first upon the young King Henry, and then
upon his father Conrad. The latter died February 15th,
1152. Conrad's death, 1152 A.D.

At the time of Conrad's death, hard blows of fate were
falling not only on the empire, but also on the papacy. The
Church, impregnated with St. Bernard's principles, and full
of mystic and extravagant ideas of its own greatness, had
suffered an irretrievable loss of prestige through the failure
of the second crusade. And from on all sides enemies were
now attacking it. Abelard had already engaged in his great
philosophical contest with St. Bernard, in which he disputed
the foundations of hierarchical influence. The Waldensian
heretics were raising their heads, while the boldest, as yet, of
all reformers, the great demagogue, Arnold of Brescia, had
formulated a teaching that struck at the root of the Church's
temporal power.

Arnold demanded that the clergy should renounce their
connection with the things of this world, and devote themselves to their spiritual duties. They were to renounce their
secular possessions, and to content themselves with the gifts
of the pious. Arnold of Brescia.

Arnold was banished from Italy by the Lateran Council of
1139, and went to France, where he supported Abelard in the
latter's disputation with St. Bernard at Sens. Bernard procured his expulsion from France, and he went to Zurich.

In 1143 and the following year the people of Rome tried

to throw off the yoke of their pontiff, who was alike their spiritual and their temporal head. The revolution assumed immense proportions, and Pope Lucius II. fell while defending the Roman capitol. His successor, Eugene III., was forced to reside in Viterbo.

Arnold in Rome.

At this time Arnold reappeared in the city and became its master. Rome was to have a new communal government modelled partly on that of the Lombard cities,—which were republics in all but name,—partly on antique principles with a senate and consuls. It was a movement such as the history of Rome has to record more than once; Arnold of Brescia was the successor of Crescentius and the forerunner of Cola di Rienzi.

Conrad III. was about to come to the help of the oppressed hierarchy, having refused, perhaps unwisely, the invitation of the "republic" to become its ally, when death overtook him.

Papal claims and pretensions.

In spite of all reverses and attacks the papacy did not cease to put forward the most far-reaching claims as to the prerogatives of the see of Rome. Towards the end of Conrad's reign these claims found a lasting form in the "Decretum Gratiani," a collection of canons which soon superseded all other works on ecclesiastical law, and which was to control the life of the Church for centuries. It is filled with sentences from Pseudo-Isidor, and with assumptions of papal omnipotence.

And, indeed, more and more the popes were striving to become not only the chief bishops of Christendom, but also the first princes. They commenced to surround themselves with retinues of nobles as well as of clergy, and the imperial diadem with which Hildebrand is reported to have crowned a pope in 1059 was now regularly worn together with the mitre. It professed to be the crown mentioned in the forged donation of Constantine as having been presented by that emperor to Pope Sylvester.

It was well, indeed, for the prestige of Germany that a brilliant and determined man now came to the throne. The empire was to succumb in the end to the papacy, but it would have succumbed miserably and weakly had it not been for Frederick Barbarossa and his descendants. The nation was to suffer defeat after a long and heroic defence against overwhelming odds, but the war of the Hohenstaufens and the popes was to be one of Titans against gods!

CHAPTER XVI.

Frederick Barbarossa, 1152-1189.

FREDERICK of Suabia was designated by the dying king Conrad, to the exclusion of his own remaining son, who was only eight years old, as that one of the Hohenstaufens who was best fitted to reign. The election took place at Frankfort on March 4th, 1152, and all the great peace-breakers of Conrad's reign, having laid aside their old enmity, were there: Albrecht the Bear, Welf VI. of Bavaria, Henry the Lion.

Frederick was the only candidate, and but one dissenting voice, that of the Archbishop of Mayence, who was the last upholder of St. Bernard's strict hierarchical ideas in Germany, was raised against him. Henry the Lion was undoubtedly won over by the assurance of favours which we shall soon see granted to him.

Frederick and the Pope.

It is significant of the position that the new king intended to take towards the papacy—Frederick's views were known to the Archbishop of Mayence, whence the latter's opposition —that immediately after the election he informed Eugene III. of his intention to restore to its old influence and glory the empire " bestowed upon him by God." He promised, indeed, respect and love for the Pope's person, and protection for the whole Church; but, unlike his predecessors, he demanded no papal sanction or confirmation of the election.

Frederick's personality.

Frederick at the time of his election was about thirty years of age. He was small, fair-complexioned, with reddish hair and beard. He was endowed by nature with great capacities, and was extremely ambitious. He possessed a keen sense of justice, and, on the very day of his coronation, refused to pardon a suppliant who knelt before him, declaring that he had been duly and lawfully sentenced. And all through his reign we shall find him placing justice before mercy.

Frederick's first care was to make the circuit of his kingdom and to receive the homage of the duchies; nowhere was his royal authority impugned. His next step was to enter into a solemn treaty with Pope Eugene, by the terms of which the imperial crown was to be bestowed upon him in return for aid against the turbulent Romans, against the Norman king of Sicily—Roger died in 1154, but his son William continued his policy—and against the Greeks, should they attempt to lay claim to any portion of the Italian soil. *Treaty with the Pope.*

At the same diet of Constance, where this treaty was finally drawn up, appeared two citizens of the little Italian town of Lodi, who had moving tales to relate of the oppressions they and their fellows had been made to suffer from their powerful neighbour, Milan. The two supplicants, unknown to the rest of their fellow-citizens, who were too cowed even to approve of such a step, had fled to Frederick for aid. *Fugitives from Lodi.*

We have arrived at a time when certain of the Italian cities, especially Milan, Venice, and Pavia, had developed into great communal powers. The citizens—in whose midst, and not, as in Germany, on the surrounding heights, the great nobles had built their castles—had drawn the jurisdictions and revenues, the market, toll, and coinage monies into their own hands; had conquered stretches of surrounding territory, and were on the alert for further conquests. Lodi, and Como as well, were victims of this new lust for power. *The Lombard cities.*

Frederick sent a written warning to Milan to desist from her persecutions; but the letter when it arrived was received with scorn, and the royal seal trampled under foot. The envoy barely escaped with his life. There was sure now to be a conflict, and thus early did Frederick come into contact with a power that was to be to his kingdom what Carthage had been to ancient Rome. And not unlike the fate of Carthage was to be that of Milan.

Intent upon the expedition which was to gain him the imperial crown, Frederick hastened to strengthen his position by negotiating for an alliance by marriage with the court of Constantinople, and by completing the transformation of Henry the Lion from an enemy into a friend.

Marriage with Beatrice of Burgundy, 1156 A.D. The negotiations with Emperor Manuel with a view to wedding a Grecian princess to the new king of the Romans finally failed, and Frederick eventually (in 1156) married Beatrice, daughter of the count of Macon, whose house, next to that of the Zäringens, the founders of Berne, was the most powerful in Burgundy. Beatrice brought with her a magnificent dowry. The extent of her lands may be judged from the fact that Frederick became feudal lord of 5,000 new vassals able to perform military service. The marriage, too, had great political results, for Burgundy had become estranged from the empire during the reigns of Lothar and Conrad, but Frederick from now on was able to draw tighter the bonds that bound it to Germany. In 1157 he made a triumphant progress through the land, confirming the possessions of ecclesiastical foundations, and bestowing the *regalia* on newly elected bishops.

Henry the Lion. Henry the Lion's affair was settled by the decision of a Diet at Goslar to the effect that his claims to Bavaria were just, and should be regarded. For the present he was given the royal right of investing, as Duke of Saxony, the bishops of Oldenburg, Ratzeburg, and Schwerin, and any new Slavic bishoprics with their temporal possessions. The former **The Duchy of Austria.** Duke of Bavaria, Henry Jasomirgott, remained to be reckoned with; but, in 1156 he was conciliated by the gift of the newly formed duchy of Austria. On September 17th of that year he renounced at Ratisbon the duchy of Bavaria, giving up the seven standards which were the signs of his sway according to the feudal usage. The standards were then conferred on Henry the Lion, who gave back two in token that two provinces, those lying between the Enns and the Inn, were henceforth to belong to the newly formed duchy, and not to Bavaria.

The wording of the charter which Frederick conferred on Henry of Austria is preserved. The duchy was to be hereditary and, contrary to all custom, daughters were to have the right of succeeding as well as sons. The duke was to have the sole jurisdiction in the land; his duties towards the empire were to be merely nominal.

Great as these concessions were they did not suffice for some of the later dukes of Austria, and a successful forgery distorted, after two hundred years, the original terms of Frederick's grant. The later greatness of the House of Austria was founded to a great extent on a basis of lies.

It was altogether Frederick Barbarossa's policy to favour the secular princes, and thus to gain support against the Church. He gave Suabia to his own cousin, Frederick of Rotenburg, he won the Zäringens with promises concerning Burgundy, and the South German Guelphs by granting them fiefs in Italy, among others the estates of the Countess Matilda. Frederick's general policy.

The mutilation of Bavaria for the sake of satisfying the claims of Henry Jasomirgott was, all the same, the first step towards breaking the power of the great stem duchies; the last step was taken when, in 1180, Saxony was subdivided.

It was the autumn of 1154, to return to the Italian expedition, when Frederick crossed the Alps. He held a great muster of his army in the Roncaglian fields near Piacenza, and those princes of Germany, notably the archbishop of Bremen, and the bishop of Halberstadt, who had been ordered to join the emperor, and had not done so, were declared to have failed in performing their duties as vassals, and to have forfeited their fiefs of the crown. Italian expedition, 1154 A.D.

In the Roncaglian fields Frederick received ambassadors from the Lombard cities, some of which also sent propitiatory gifts; silks, ostriches, lions, and parrots are mentioned as the offerings of Genoa. All of the cities, Milan included, seem to have taken the oath of allegiance.

The attitude of the Milanese was submissive enough. At the king's command they promised to desist from a war Frederick and the Milanese.

against Pavia, and offered to pay the sum of 4,000 marks of silver if they might not be compelled to rebuild the devastated cities of Lodi and Como—a proposal which Frederick for the present neither accepted nor rejected. He was anxious to press on towards Rome, and he demanded guides from the Milanese, and an escort which should be headed by two of the consuls of their city. These were intended, doubtless, to be hostages for Milan's good behaviour.

The German army was led through regions where food and provender failed. Frederick began to suspect the Milanese consuls of treachery, and ordered his army to retrace its steps. An embassy from Milan came out to avert his wrath, but Frederick declined now to enter into any negotiations except on the basis of a complete restoration of Lodi and Como to their civic rights. The ban of the empire, the carrying out of which was postponed till a future time, was soon spoken against Milan.

Fall of Tortona.

The rich city of Tortona, which refused obedience to Frederick, now endured a long and wasting siege, and fell in spite of aid sent by the Milanese. The city was levelled to the ground, and its punishment proved a warning example to all Italy. The news spread of the Suzerain's vigour and determination: of his sternness and justice, too, for a long train of clergy and monks that had come out from the city to beg for mercy, if not for the inhabitants as a whole at least for themselves, had been promptly sent back to suffer with the rest.

The fate of Tortona cleared the way to Rome.

Frederick and Adrian IV.

The preliminaries of the imperial coronation had already been arranged by envoys, which had several times passed to and fro between the king and the new Pope Adrian IV., the only Englishman who ever sat on the chair of Peter. Adrian sorely needed Frederick's aid, determined as he was to put down the insurrection in Rome, and to overcome the new king of Sicily. The Pope had by this time declared Arnold of Brescia in the ban, and had laid Rome under an interdict just before the Easter season—a proceeding which had broken the will of the Romans for the moment, and caused them to bow humbly before their spiritual head as he made his entry into the Lateran on Maundy Thursday.

Adrian was soon obliged to withdraw from Rome, however, not feeling safe in those unquiet precincts; he advanced to Sutri to meet Frederick.

At Sutri a disagreement arose between the two heads of Christendom because of the king's refusal to hold the stirrup for the Pope, who had ridden up before the royal tent, to dismount. Adrian refused the kiss of peace until Frederick should have performed this service, and finally withdrew in anger. The question was hotly discussed, and several cardinals left the camp; but Frederick yielded on ascertaining that precedent, especially in the case of Lothar III., was in favour of the papal claim.

Holds stirrup of Pope.

Arnold of Brescia had meanwhile, at the time of Adrian's brief triumph, fled from Rome, but had found refuge with some nobles of the Campagna. One of Frederick's first acts, one of the conditions indeed of the coronation, was to seize him and surrender him to the Pope. Arnold was afterwards, without the knowledge either of the Pope or of the new emperor, taken from prison by his personal enemy, the prefect of Rome, Pierleoni, and hanged. His body was burnt and his ashes were thrown in the Tiber.

Death of Arnold of Brescia, 1155 A.D.

The rebellious Romans had tried to draw Frederick over to their own side, and had asked him to recognise their republic. They themselves had offered to bestow on him the imperial crown and the rule, as they expressed it, over the city as well as over the whole earth. In return, the emperor was to recognize all their privileges, to protect them against all their enemies and, incredible as it may seem, to pay them 5,000 marks of silver.

Frederick and the Romans.

Frederick declared the Roman claims and assumptions to be preposterous, and received the crown from the hand of the Pope. We have a circumstantial description of the ceremony. Frederick donned the coronation mantle in the vestibule of St. Peter's, and then proceeded to the new chapel of Santa

The Coronation, 1155 A.D.

Maria in Turri, where he knelt before the Pope and promised to protect and defend the Holy Roman Church. Returning to St. Peter's he was met by two bishops in turn who called down the blessing of heaven on the imperial rule that was about to commence. Frederick was then led to the subterranean vault where the bones of the apostles Peter and Paul reposed ; while he lay here outstretched in prayer a litany was sung in the church above. He was afterwards anointed by the Bishop of Ostia and was led to the altar where the Pope awaited him. Here he was adorned with the imperial crown and girded with the sword of Peter. High mass followed, during which Frederick sat on a throne some steps lower than that of the Pope.

The coronation ceremony had been performed almost in secret in the midst of a hostile population ; a guard of German soldiers surrounded the participants. A bloody encounter ended the day and 800 Romans are said to have fallen, 200 to have been taken prisoner.

The emperor quitted Rome almost at once, leaving it still in the hands of the rebels, but like a new Jason he had snatched from the enemy the prize which he coveted.

Return to Germany.

Frederick returned to Germany, delaying only long enough to devastate Spoleto, which had refused him the *fodrum* or customary tax for an expedition to Rome, and to overcome the forces of Verona which opposed him in the valley of the Adige. On his march through Lombardy he had taken care to announce to all the cities still faithful to him that he had withdrawn from Milan all privileges, tolls, and jurisdictions, as well as the right of coinage.

Milan's boldness.

No sooner, however, had he left Italy than Milan recovered from her fright, formed an alliance with Piacenza, and later with Genoa, inflicted dire punishment on Lodi, Como, and on other cities which had supported the emperor, and assisted Tortona to rise from her ashes.

It was not till 1158 that Frederick, detained by the cares of administration and by various minor conflicts, was able to return to the charge against Milan and to fit the subjugation and reorganization of Italy into his plans for forming such a world-monarchy as represented to himself, and indeed to all the mediæval rulers, the true ideal of the Holy Roman Empire. Rome of old had ruled the world from Italy as a centre; without Italy the empire was nothing—a mere anomaly.

Frederick had, in the interval, succeeded in restoring such peace to Germany that, in the words of his biographer Ragewin, " men had changed, the land had become a different one—yes, the very heavens seemed milder and more friendly." Nor was it the peace of inanition. Frederick had been unceasing in his efforts, at last successful, to end the strife between Henry the Lion and Henry Jasomirgott; he had induced the Bohemians to promise help for the next Italian expedition by allowing their duke to wear a royal crown on great feast days; he had reduced Poland to subjection, and had 'practically brought back Burgundy to the fold of the empire. *Peace in Germany.*

The emperor's great aider and abettor in all these matters had been his chancellor, Rainald of Dassel, a man of untiring energy and of great diplomatic talent. A contemporary calls him, "the beginning, middle, and end of the emperor's honour." *The chancellor, Rainald of Dassel.*

When Frederick finally did cross the Alps, it was with one of the largest armies that ever the head of the Holy Roman Empire had led into Italy. Rainald of Dassel and Otto of Wittlesbach, Count Palatine of Bavaria, had been sent ahead to pave the way and to negotiate with the different cities; so well did they perform their task that almost all the towns of north Italy sent aid and contingents to the German army. They had even treated with the once scorned republic of Rome, anxious to have an ally if need be against the Pope. Rome now sent its prefect and a number of senators. *Italian expedition, 1158 A.D.*

The Milanese, frightened at the approach of Frederick's forces, tried to make terms, but for the present without success. The city was besieged, and its defenders, falling a prey to the heat and to the pest, were soon ripe for submission. The German army had suffered too, and Frederick was glad *Milan submits.*

enough to come to an agreement. Milan was to permit the
rebuilding of Lodi and Como; the citizens were to swear
allegiance to Frederick, to pay a large fine, to permit the
building of an imperial castle within their walls, and to
furnish three hundred hostages, fifty of whom were to be carried off to Germany. The consuls of Milan—that administrative body, made up originally from the capitanei, the valvassores, and the ordinary burghers, but now simply chosen by
the citizens from the six quarters of the city—were to have
their election confirmed by the emperor.

Milan is humbled. The submission of Milan was made with all the dramatic
formalities usual in the middle ages. The twelve consuls of
the city humbled themselves before Frederick, who awaited
them in his camp, seated on a throne. They approached
barefoot and with ropes around their necks, through two
long lines, formed by the German soldiery, and delivered up
their swords, declaring that this act symbolized the surrender
of all the weapons in Milan.

Frederick released the city from the ban, and caused the
imperial banner to be unfurled from the top of the
cathedral.

Roncaglian diet. With the fall of Milan, Frederick's mission in Lombardy
was not yet fulfilled. He was determined to establish the
relations of the Italian cities to the empire on a firm and
lasting basis, and with that purpose in view he summoned a
great diet to meet in the plains, near Roncaglia, on the 11th
of November, 1158. This diet is notable for the fact that
here laws were made for the regulation of the position of the
Lombard cities towards the empire.

The study of law. Law, as a science, was just then having its renaissance.
The eager study of it was awakening once more the memories
of ancient Rome, and of her rule over the universe, and the
Justinian code represented more than anything that ever was
written, the absolute power of the emperor, and his office as
fountain of justice. Frederick was determined to wield this
office like a new Constantine or a new Justinian; but he had
to reckon with other times than they, and the result was to

be a desperate conflict with the newly developed civic powers. It was a conflict between fixed precepts, on the one hand, and a number of cases that had never been thought of, when those precepts were drawn up; between an iron rule and a historical progress that for generations had defied that rule.

It was at Bologna that the new school of law had its centre, and it was to the doctors of Bologna, whom he afterwards rewarded by granting their university free jurisdiction over its members, that Frederick submitted the task of finding out exactly what were the imperial rights, the so-called *regalia* in Italy. He intended to begin his reforms with the communes, and afterwards to adjust his relations to the Normans and the papacy; but those communes had reached a degree of independence of which he had never dreamed. **Bologna law school.**

The result of the labours of the Bologna doctors, who were aided by twenty-eight judges, chosen from among the representatives of the different towns, is fortunately preserved to us. To the throne were adjudged to belong the public roads, rivers, and harbours, with their tolls and taxes, mines, salt-works, etc., the estates of felons, and the half of treasure-trove. The appointing of civic magistrates was the emperor's, and the right of rebuilding imperial palaces in cities where such had formerly stood. He could call in an emergency for horses, transport-waggons or ships, and even levy an extraordinary war-tax. **The " Regalia," or royal rights.**

In very many cases the income from the *regalia* had been deeded away to individuals, or to corporate bodies, as a reward for services rendered, and all such who could produce a genuine charter, were allowed to remain in possession. But there were cities which in former days, even in a former century, had wrested their autonomy from the hands of the bishops or other lords to whom the original grants had been made, and which could show no deed of gift. In all such cases Frederick confiscated the *regalia*, and eventually a large yearly sum, more than a million marks of modern money, was gained for the royal treasury.

Imperial edicts.

The next step of the emperor was to issue a general peace-proclamation for Italy, which forbade all feuds, and also all associations of individuals, or of cities. It was to be sworn to every five years by all male beings, between the ages of eighteen and seventy. Finally, Frederick issued an edict regarding fiefs and the transferance, subdividings, and forfeiture of them.

Roncaglian decrees.

The Roncaglian decrees were a mighty effort to make Northern Italy submit to leading strings; but the effort, which was to continue for twenty-four years, was ultimately to fail.

The Lombard cities, with the exception of Genoa, had given their consent to the measures passed at the great assembly. The Archbishop of Milan had addressed the emperor with high-sounding phrases, and had quoted the institutions of Justinian: "Know that all the right of the people to make laws has been vested in thee. Thy will is law, according to what is said, 'What pleases the prince has the vigour of law.'" But the cities had been under a misapprehension. They had failed to see what a weapon they were putting into Frederick's hands, and to them the report of the Bologna legists and of their own representatives, had been a mere formality. Nor had they ever dreamt of the practical consequences that were later to be drawn. It was a different matter, however, when they were called upon to renounce rights which they had exercised for centuries unopposed.

Frederick's views as to Lombardy.

Had Frederick been able to carry out to the full his views in Lombardy he would have established a rule there more absolute than that which he enjoyed in Germany. But every effort in this direction necessarily drew down upon him the unbending opposition of the three great factors in Italian politics: of the cities themselves; of the Pope, who would be hemmed in by a power so much greater than his own; and, finally, of the Norman kingdom of Apulia and Sicily.

Opposition in Genoa.

Genoa was the first of the cities to oppose Frederick's new ordinances. The people maintained that, having frequently warded off the attacks of the Saracens, they had completely fulfilled their duties to the empire.   The emperor should remember the small amount of imperial territory that Genoa possessed; it was through her shipping that she had grown rich, not through her fiefs of the crown.   In the end a compromise was effected, but Genoa took care to strengthen her fortifications in case they should later be needed.

More serious were the complications in Crema, where the imperial envoys were ill-treated and barely escaped with their lives, and where the emperor's command that all fortifications more than twenty feet high should be torn down was disregarded.

In Milan, too, the people refused to accept the podestas, **Milan.** the new officials imposed by the emperor, declaring that the treaty of 1158 had expressly permitted them to have their own consuls, which was true.   But Frederick, somewhat arbitrarily, considered that treaty cancelled by his new decrees; he prepared now to make a final and relentless struggle for the rights which he claimed in Italy.

The dispute with Crema led to a siege—a siege which **Cruel siege** shows all the worst features of mediæval warfare.   No **of Crema,** **1160 A.D.** element of horror was wanting to it, no means left untried of subduing the valiant little city.   One detail alone will suffice.   Frederick caused one of his movable besieging towers, the advance of which had thus far been checked, to be literally festooned with the persons of hostages and captives from Crema, who were let down in baskets and thus exposed to the missiles of their own friends.   The manœuvre failed, for patriotism and civic pride proved superior to all tenderer feelings; and when the tower was moved back but few of the unfortunates were still living.

For seven months this terrible siege lasted, to end as all such unequal contests must always end.   Crema fell at last, after a memorable and heroic defence, and the inhabitants were forced to surrender unconditionally.   In a long and mournful procession they withdrew from the city, which was given over to pillage and flame.

S

Punishment of Milan, 1162 A.D.

It was more than a year later before Frederick, who had sent to Germany for reinforcements, could proceed to the final punishment of Milan. Even then he did not attempt a regular siege, but contented himself with devastating the outlying fields and vineyards, and by cutting off every possible avenue of supply. The effect was slow but sure, the more so as Milan was overcrowded with those who had taken refuge from without.

The beginning of the year 1162 found the Milanese utterly discouraged and face to face with starvation. On the first day of March eight of the consuls, carrying the keys of Milan and the tokens of their own dignity, appeared before the emperor and made a complete surrender.

Milan's humiliations.

The bold city was now made to drink the cup of humiliation to the very dregs, and no ceremony was left unperformed which could show the utter abasement of the inhabitants. Hundreds of the proudest nobles were made to approach in the pouring rain, barefoot, with ashes strewn upon their heads, and to kiss the emperor's feet and cry for mercy. The mast of the *carrocio* was lowered before him, and the banner of the city removed, while all the standards that had belonged to the army were laid at his feet. The very trumpets were given over to him with a blast from which the citizens had been wont to preface their legislative functions.

The fate of the city hung in the balance for a while, but the scale was turned by the representations of those towns which had formerly been made to writhe under Milan's oppressions. It was decided finally by Frederick and his nobles that the city should be blotted out from the face of the earth, and that the inhabitants should be allowed a week in which to withdraw. Four places were appointed in the vicinity in which they might make new settlements.

The work of annihilation soon began, and Cremona, Lodi, and Como were allowed to riot in Milan's ruins and to lay the torch to the houses of their old enemies. " A second Troy has perished," writes Godfrey of Viterbo at the time.

The fate of Milan completely paralysed for the moment all opposition in Northern and Central Italy. Frederick steps forward now in all the pride of victory, and signs himself as Charlemagne once had done: " Roman Emperor crowned of God, great and peace-bringing; glorious Triumpher and continual Increaser of the Empire." In all the cities, except in those which for their services were allowed to choose their own consuls, the Podestas exercised henceforth in the imperial name an almost unlimited power. They preserved peace in the land, but by raising old taxes and imposing new ones made the people groan under their oppressions and long eagerly for occasion to revolt.

Submission of North Italy.

CHAPTER XVII

FREDERICK I. AND THE PAPACY.

Long struggle with the papacy.

FREDERICK meanwhile had engaged in another quarter in a new and more terrible contest; but in order to understand the full meaning of the long struggle between the popes and the Hohenstaufens it is necessary to go back a few years and to trace the growing estrangement of the heads of Christendom.

Whenever these great rivals came in any way in contact there was danger of an outbreak; the more they raised themselves above the surrounding powers in Europe the more sensitive became the surface which they exposed to each other.

We have seen the vexation of Adrian IV. in 1155 at Frederick's refusal to hold the bridle and the stirrup of the papal charger. A further cause of annoyance to the Pope was the fact that Frederick was prevented by the force of circumstances from fulfilling the very task for which he had been summoned to Italy and as a preliminary reward for which he had received the imperial crown. The revolt of the Romans had not been checked, and William of Sicily had not been subjugated.

Adrian IV.'s hostility.

Adrian's whole policy changed when he found that the emperor could no longer help him in Italy. He made overtures to the Sicilian king and received his homage as a vassal of the See of Rome, investing him himself with his lands of Apulia and Sicily and granting him the kiss of peace.

Besançon episode, 1158.

Frederick was greatly angered and embittered by this change of tactics, and an incident which occurred at Besançon served to deepen the unfriendliness of the relations. Eskil, Archbishop of Lund, had been captured in Burgundy by highwaymen, and Frederick, with whom Eskil stood in disdisgrace, had taken no measures to secure his release. The Pope finally sent two cardinals, Bernard and the chancellor Roland to press the matter.

Frederick received the envoys graciously enough in the presence of his nobles. But when the papal letters were read and translated with all due emphasis by Rainald of Dassel a scene of wild confusion ensued. Adrian spoke of the imperial crown as a " benefice " that he had " conferred " upon Frederick; and the indignation aroused by these expressions increased to fury when one of the legates—it is generally assumed that it was Roland—called out, " From whom then has the emperor the empire except from the Pope ? " Otto of Wittlesbach drew his sword to defend his royal master's honour, and all the emperor's authority was needed to protect the envoys from violence. The latter were sent back to Rome by the most expeditious route, and Frederick, not knowing what proportions the struggle with the papacy might now assume, hastened from Burgundy to Germany and issued a manifesto in which he proclaimed to the whole world the dignity of the empire. " Whoever shall say," he writes, " that we received the imperial crown as a benefice from the Lord Pope contradicts the divine institutions and the teaching of Peter and shall be guilty of a lie. . . . We ask you as one to condole with us over such ignominy inflicted on us and on the empire, trusting that the undivided sincerity of your faith will not permit the honour of the empire which, from the foundation of Rome and the establishment of the Christian religion "—one sees that Frederick considered himself the direct successor of the Cæsars—" up to your own times has remained glorious and undiminished to be lessened by so unheard-of an innovation." [1]

Spirited defence of imperial rights.

Almost the entire clergy of Germany shared the emperor's

[1] See " Select Documents," p. 412.

views in this matter and boldly declared their opinion to the Pope, who was fain in the end to explain away the objectionable utterance by means of a convenient sophistry. By *bene-ficium* he had not meant the technical feudal term for benefice, but simply a benefit, and surely a pope was conferring a benefit on an emperor by crowning him! The explanation, crude as it was, sufficed, and peace was established for the time being. But the Pope was filled with dismay at the emperor's growing influence in Italy, and the Roncaglian decrees embittered him more than all else, affecting, as they in a measure did, the possessions of ecclesiastical princes.

Adrian IV.'s death, 1159 A.D.   Everything pointed to an approaching struggle. Adrian refused to confirm the imperial candidate for the archbishopric of Ravenna; on one occasion he wrote to the emperor addressing him in the second person singular and placed his own name before that of Frederick; on another he caused a letter to be delivered by the hand of a minor official.

Terrible offences against etiquette these, which were speedily answered in kind. The hostilities were about to mature when Adrian died (1159). At the last he had made demands which would, if fulfilled, have deprived Frederick of all the benefits of the Roncaglian decrees as well as of the possession of the Matilda estates to which those decrees to some extent applied. He had even gone so far as to make an alliance with Milan, Brescia and Piacenza, promising for his own part to ban the emperor within sixty days; and his cardinals had agreed in the event of his (Adrian's) death, only to elect such a man as would continue his policy against the Hohenstaufen.

Alexander III.   It was now that the man came to the papal throne who was to force the proudest prince in the world to make an almost abject submission after eighteen years of ceaseless conflict.

Alexander III. was elected by a majority of the cardinals; but a minority, in the interests of the empire, chose Victor IV. Alexander was that same chancellor Roland who had once so angered the emperor and his people at Besançon; he was, moreover, known to be at the head of the party which sought in William of Sicily a counterpoise to the imperial power.

Such a man was highly unwelcome to Frederick, who was with difficulty prevented by Henry the Lion and other nobles from hanging the envoys whom Alexander sent to him.

For the sake of appearances, however, the emperor declared himself willing to submit the matter to a general council, and an assembly was summoned to meet at Pavia, January 13th, 1160. In order that Frederick should seem to exert no compulsion in the matter, none but clergy were to take part in the proceedings and the rival popes were to defend themselves in person. **Schism in the Church.**

Alexander scorned to submit his cause to any such tribunal; the more so as in the summons he had been addressed as " Chancellor Roland " while Victor had been called Pope and head of the Church. Alexander, moreover, had already commenced negotiations with England and France, with Hungary, Castile, Jerusalem and even the Greek Empire, which were to end in his recognition by all of those powers.

Victor, on the other hand, had no hope but in the might of the emperor, and willingly appeared at Pavia. Here the whole question of the election was reviewed. Witnesses asserted that a conspiracy had existed to keep Victor from being elected; furthermore, that Alexander was known to have been in collusion with the Milanese and other enemies of the empire. Finally precedent was appealed to, and it was found that in similar cases of schism the Church had always declared for him who, " by demand of the people, at the wish and with the consent of the clergy" had first been raised upon the chair of Peter by the cardinals. Victor had, in fact, after an actual hand to hand fight with Roland for the possession of the papal mantle, been the first to leave the conclave and to enter St. Peter's, where he had received the cries of praise and adulation of the multitude, who were unaware as yet of the double election. He had then succeeded in keeping Roland prisoner for nine days, but the latter on his release had been treated as a martyr by the Romans. **Synod of Pavia, 1160 A.D.**

The council of Pavia, which finally declared, as might have been expected, for Victor, was nothing but an assembly of about forty German and Lombard bishops, although England, France, and other countries had been invited to take part. In his opening address the emperor vindicated his right to hold the council by appealing to the examples of Constantine, Theodosius and Justinian, as well as to those of Charlemagne and Otto the Great.

Frederick's antipope.

After the fateful decision had been passed, Frederick received Victor before the door of the cathedral of Pavia, held the stirrup for him to dismount, and led him to the altar. The strong Emperor and the weak Pope rustled up the aisle together, with all the pomp of a cause that needed emphatic vindication. All present, beginning with Frederick, then kissed the feet of the vicar of God. Candles were brought and the anathema hurled at Roland and at the bishops who had consecrated him. The usual extinguishing of the lights followed this grim ceremony.

It was natural that Frederick should visit with his displeasure those of the German clergy who would not subscribe to the decrees of Pavia. We hear of numbers of Carthusian and Cistercian monks refusing obedience to Victor and wandering across the borders into France. The cause of Rome now became the cause of Milan, and a papal legate spoke the ban over Frederick from the cathedral of that city, the sentence being soon afterwards confirmed and renewed by Alexander himself at Anagni.

England and France for Alexander.

Had England and France sided with Frederick, as at various times there were prospects of their doing, the outcome of the struggle would have been very different. But Henry II., although the struggle with Thomas Becket, who was upheld by Alexander, later drove him to seek an alliance with Frederick, was on the whole jealous of the latter's power and soon repudiated his promises.

The *rôle* played by Louis VII. of France in the whole matter was a pitiable one ; so much so that his brother-in-law, the Count of Champagne, who had tried to win him for Victor, showed his disgust at his king's vacillation and final declaration for Alexander by becoming a vassal of the emperor.

At the time of the final reduction of Milan Frederick hoped that a victory over that powerful enemy would scatter the gathering clouds of opposition. And indeed Alexander now made an effort to win the emperor over to his side. He promised to forget the past entirely and would rejoice, he said, at an opportunity to love and honour so great and glorious a prince. But Frederick, especially in the moment of victory, was not inclined to simply let fall his Pope, and no other basis of compromise was possible. Alexander now felt himself so insecure in Italy that he passed over into France, although Louis VII. had not yet declared for him.

Victor IV. died in April, 1164, and Rainald of Dassel, who had meanwhile been made Archbishop of Cologne, brought it about that immediately after the burial ceremony a new pope was elected by the anti-Alexandrian cardinals. Frederick at the time was busy in opposing a petty coalition which had sprung into being, and which was headed by Verona and encouraged by Venice. The election had taken place without his authorization and even without his knowledge, but he was constrained to approve the act of his chancellor. *Paschal III. as antipope.*

The elevation of Paschal III. denotes a new stage in the history of the schism ; for many, even in Germany, who had supported Victor were not willing to acknowledge his successor. The archbishops of Mayence and Treves, among others, went over to the enemy—a step for which the former of these two prelates was soon afterwards deposed. And every defection was of the greatest importance to Alexander, who was now slowly gathering into his own hand all the different threads of opposition.

Frederick meanwhile had summoned a great diet at Würzburg for May 23rd, 1165. Here Rainald of Dassel made a stirring speech, and pointed to the presence of two English envoys in proof of his assertion that Henry II. and fifty of his bishops were ready to support him, an assertion which was not borne out by future events. The emperor in person, followed by many of his clergy and nobles, then took a solemn oath never to acknowledge Roland or a pope elected by his *Oath of Würzburg, 1165 A.D.*

party, but to remain true to Paschal and his successors. The diet engaged itself, should Frederick die, to elect no one as king who was not willing to take the oath that had just been uttered. The spiritual and temporal lords, moreover, were to impose a like oath on all their vassals and subjects, and all recusants were to be considered enemies of the empire.

A fatal proceeding. Frederick himself swore that he would never ask for absolution from the oath of Würzburg, nor accept it should it be offered. He soon afterwards caused a prayer for Paschal to be included in the Church service, induced nearly all the bishops of Germany who had not been present at Würzburg to subscribe to the measures passed there, and began a rigid course of persecution against all the supporters of Alexander.

The day at Würzburg was one of the most unfortunate of Frederick's life. Fetters were there laid not only on the emperor himself and on his nobles, but on the whole German people as well.

Canonization of Charles the Great. At the time, indeed, the new Justinian felt very sure of his cause; he seemed to himself at the zenith of his power. It was now that he determined to glorify the empire by the canonization of its founder, Charles the Great. The ceremony was performed with pomp and magnificence at Aix-la-Chapelle; the bones were raised from the grave and placed in a golden shrine in the presence of a large assembly. The great chandelier which still adorns the chapel was presented by Frederick in memory of this occasion, and the town of Aix itself reaped a harvest of privileges and exemptions.

Frederick's March to Rome. In the autumn of 1166 Frederick again crossed the Alps with a large army. A diet which he held at Lodi declared in favour of marching without delay upon Rome, whither Alexander had just returned after an absence of four years. The Greek Emperor Manuel, a man of great plans and small talents, was at this time preparing a gigantic scheme, by which he himself was to be made king of the Romans and protector of the papacy, and the king of Sicily was to become his son-in-law.

The Verona coalition which had opposed Frederick two

years before was still unsubdued, and the latter, too, might
well have occupied himself with redressing the crying wrongs
of the Lombard cities as he was repeatedly implored to do.
But it was thought that by striking at Rome the heart of the
opposition would be reached and that the other enemies could
then be readily overcome.

Christian of Mayence and Rainald of Cologne were the **Defeat of the**
first to approach the Eternal City. The two archbishops **Romans.**
arrived in time to take sides with the people of Tusculum,
who were warding off from their town an attack of the
Romans. Rainald's clear eye had seen how important Tusculum
would be as a strategic post for the Germans. The Romans
suffered an overwhelming defeat—a second Cannæ the battle
was called. Five thousand were slain or taken captive, and
an immense booty was harvested.

Frederick meanwhile had been busied in besieging Ancona,
—which stronghold of the Greeks he forced to capitulate,—
and in attacking a band of Normans. This one vain skirmish
with the forces of the king of Sicily was, in spite of the
numerous wars that had been planned, the only engagement
that had taken place since the time of Lothar.

On July 24th, 1167, Frederick appeared before Rome; an **Frederick**
army which came out to meet him was driven back, and a **before**
part of the Leonine city fell into his hands. The next day **Rome.**
St. Angelo was besieged—upon how many scenes of blood has
that grim fortress looked down!—and four days later fire was
set to the Church of Santa Maria in Turri, which immediately
adjoined St. Peter's. An entrance was thus forced into St.
Peter's itself, and its defenders, after a brief skirmish in those
holy halls, ceased their efforts. The Church of the chief of
the apostles was soon in possession of the emperor.

On the day following the siege Pope Paschal was solemnly
enthroned on the chair of Peter and was able to confer on the
emperor the patriciate of the city and on the empress the
consecration that had failed her until now.

Alexander meanwhile escaped; a fountain where he rested **Rome sub-**
on his flight has borne the name from that day to this of **mits.**

"fountain of the Pope." The Romans, bereft of their leader and terrified by a Pisan fleet which appeared in support of the emperor, were driven to make their submission. The senate took the oath of fealty, and Frederick's conditions were accepted by the city. Alexander was to be abandoned and Paschal acknowledged as the only true pope.

The pestilence in Rome.

But in the very moment of his triumph Frederick was struck by the hardest blow of fate that he had ever experienced, a blow that was to mark the turning point of his career. On the first day of August, amid general rejoicing, he and his empress had worn their crowns in a grand assembly at St. Peter's. On the day following the weather changed; a violent thunderstorm was succeeded by a deadly heat. A pestilence broke out in the camp and in the city, and death was wafted on every current of air.

Frederick's losses.

The emperor withdrew to the Tusculan hills with a portion of his army, but many of his soldiers were too ill to be moved, and remained, most of them to die, in the neighbourhood of Rome. The emperor's losses were enormous; it was calculated by a contemporary that twenty-five thousand men were struck down in a week. High and low, nobles and serving-men bowed their heads before the scourge. Among the dead were the emperor's cousin the young Duke Frederick of Suabia, Welf VII. of Bavaria, and, last but not least, Rainald of Dassel, Frederick's chancellor and leader of half of his forces.

There was mourning in Cologne when the news of Rainald's death was known there. He it was who had borne thither the relics of the "three holy kings," the three Magi from Milan—relics which brought to Cologne almost as much fame and prosperity as the bones of Charles the Great did to Aix-la-Chapelle.

A judgment of God.

The people of the twelfth century saw in Frederick's mishap nothing less than a judgment of God. Thomas Becket, in one of his letters, breaks forth, as it were, into a hymn of praise. He likens the emperor to Sennacherib who was struck down while opposing Ezekiel: "The Lord has crushed the hammer of the godless, and, if they do not come to their senses will shortly crush the rest" (meaning his own king) ; and John of Salisbury implies that Frederick had better henceforward consider Italy as a lost land.

It was natural that the courage of Frederick's enemies should rise in proportion to the greatness of his misfortune, and he soon found himself engaged in a bitter strife with the Lombard cities.

We have seen what a terrible vengeance Frederick took upon Milan in 1162.· During the five years that followed the sufferings of the banished Milanese were intense. Even upon them, in their newly appointed settlements, rested an intolerable burden of taxation, and relentless officials pressed all but the life-blood out of the wretched people. Every rod of land, every hearth, every span of oxen was taxed; hundreds of swine and poultry were required for the tables of the officials themselves. No wonder that the book which contained the list of lands and the sums that were to be raised from them is called in the annals of Milan "the book of pain and mourning!"

Wrongs of the Lombard cities.

Nor were the Milanese the only sufferers. Numbers of the Lombard towns groaned under their weight of taxation. Each mill that was situated on a navigable river was made to pay a yearly sum, each fisherman was forced to surrender a third of what he caught. Heavy restrictions were placed on hunting.

The wonder is not that a coalition should have been started by Verona, but that the great majority of the Italian cities should for years have kept aloof from such a movement. But there was a feeling of reverence for the emperor and it was believed, probably rightly, that the exactions of his servants were carried on without his consent or knowledge.

It was unfortunate that these grievances should first have been formally presented to him at a moment when he was straining every nerve to reach Rome and to measure his forces with those of the Greeks, the Pope and the king of Sicily. Never was there a time when the reduction of taxes must have seemed more impossible to him.

No redress for grievances.

But it was none the less galling to the Lombards to see their just complaints disregarded ; an unusually cold winter, too, added to their discomforts, making it still more difficult to find means of subsistence.   An effort was at last made to better a condition of things to which slavery would have been preferable.

The Lom-bard league.   No sooner had Frederick passed through North Italy on the way to his triumph and ultimate humiliation in Rome than the formation was begun of that greater Lombard League which was to prove so terrible and invincible an enemy. Cremona was, according to the emperor's own account, the prime mover in the matter.   Mantua, Bergamo, and Brescia joined with that city, and bound themselves to mutual protection.   The league, which was to last for fifty years, was not openly hostile to the emperor ; fidelity to him, indeed, was one of the articles of its constitution.   But only such duties and services were to be performed as had been customary in the time of Conrad III. ; so the cities practically renounced the Roncaglian decrees and declared themselves in revolt.

Return of the Milanese.   From the beginning, too, the league took sides with Alexander.   But its most daring act of insubordination was the leading back in triumph of the Milanese to the scene of their former glory.   The outer walls of Milan had not been entirely levelled to the ground and the city arose as if by magic from her ruins.   Bergamo, Brescia, and Cremona lent her efficient aid in the work of restoration.

A sculpture executed in 1171 by order of the consuls and showing the return, accompanied by their allies, of the exiles, is still to be seen in Milan, near the Porta Romana.   How few of those who look on it to-day realize what that return meant to the long-suffering citizens, and what premonitions of evil to come must have gone with them.

Extension of Lombard league.   The Lombard League spread rapidly.   Lodi, after much demur and after being surrounded by an army, was forced to join it.   Piacenza needed no constraint, and Parma yielded after some opposition.   Including, Milan there were soon eight cities in the confederation.   The imperial officials were dis-

avowed, and the old consular rule re-established, while everywhere Alexandrine bishops replaced those that had been
invested by Victor and Paschal.

Returning almost in disgrace from Rome, Frederick took
up the struggle against the revolted cities, sending an appeal
for reinforcements to Germany.   But an attack on Milan
proved fruitless, as did also one on Piacenza, and the emperor
was soon forced to entrench himself in Pavia.   His position
became more and more desperate, the more so as the new
archbishop of Milan, Galdinus, unfolded a great activity in
favour of Alexander.   The Pope named him apostolic legate
for the whole of Lombardy, and it was doubtless due to his
influence that at this time the Verona coalition formally joined
the Lombard League.

Frederick's failures.

Sixteen cities were now banded together against the emperor
who remained helpless in their midst.   Pavia soon ceased to
be a safe refuge, and he retired to Novara and then to Ver-
celli; but both cities were even then planning to join the
confederation.

In the end Frederick prepared to leave Italy as a fugitive,
and with but a small train of followers.   In Susa, where the
road begins which leads over the Mount Cenis pass, he was
told that he must give up the few remaining hostages he was
leading with him.   All exits were found to be closed against
him, and it came to his ear that an attempt was to be made
upon his life.

His flight.

The emperor fled from Susa disguised as a servant, while
his chamberlain, Hartmann of Siebeneichen, who bore him a
striking likeness, continued to play the part of captive monarch.
A band of assassins actually made their way into the royal
chamber, but seem to have spared the brave chamberlain on
learning their mistake.

The real object of their attack was meanwhile hastening on
towards Basle, which he finally reached in safety.

It was to be expected that a man of Frederick's iron will
would soon return to avenge the humiliations he had suffered,
and the League hastened to strengthen itself in all directions.

Founding of Alessandria, 1168 A.D.

Alexander was invited to take up his residence in their midst, and he, although obliged to refuse, continued to work for the rebel cities. The latter showed their gratitude by founding a new town, which was to be a common fortress for the whole league, and naming it Allessandria in honour of their ally. The citizens took an oath of fealty to the Pope and agreed to pay him a yearly tax. The new foundation, although laughed at at first by the imperialists and called Allessandria della Paglia, from its hastily constructed straw huts, soon held a population of 15,000. It continues to-day to reflect credit on its sponsor.

Frederick delays his return.

Contrary to all expectations it was six years before Frederick returned to Italy, and the Lombard League was meanwhile left master of the field. This delay is undoubtedly ascribable to the fact that the emperor found it impossible at once to raise another army. The recent blows of fate had been too severe, and no enthusiasm for a new Italian war could be called into being. When, later, Frederick did recross the Alps it was with the mere shadow of an army; the nobles had seized every possible excuse to remain at home.

Affairs in Germany.

No doubt but that the enforced rest was of benefit to Germany; there at least the emperor's power was undiminished. Indeed, the lands of many of those who had been carried away by the pestilence had fallen to him by inheritance, or lapsed as fiefs of the crown. Frederick is the first of the emperors who really acquired great family possessions. These helped him to maintain his imperial power without having to rely too much on the often untrustworthy princes of the realm. The Salian estates, to which his father had fallen heir on the death of Henry V., formed a nucleus, while, by purchase and otherwise, he acquired castle after castle, and one stretch of territory after another, especially in Suabia and the Rhine Palatinate.

By the emperor's influence feud after feud was settled, and the princes were induced to acknowledge his second son—why not his eldest has never been explained—as successor to the throne. The internal prosperity and concord were not without their influence on the neighbouring powers, and Hungary, Bohemia, and Poland were forced to acknowledge and fulfil their feudal duties.

Meanwhile Tuscany and a part of the Romagna had remained true to the empire. Frederick's emissary, Christian of Mayence, who was sent to Italy in 1171, was able to play a leading *rôle* in the hostilities between Pisa and Genoa, and, in 1173, to again besiege Ancona, which was still a centre for Greek intrigues. Christian was able to assure the emperor that some allies at least were left in Italy. Affairs in Italy.

In one way time had worked a favourable change. So long as an immediate attack was to be feared the Lombard cities— between thirty and forty of which, including such towns as Venice, Bologna, and Pavia, had finally joined the League— were firmly united and ready to make any effort. But as the years went on and the danger became less pressing, internal discord crept in among them. Venice, for instance, helped Christian of Mayence in besieging Ancona; and Pavia, true to its old imperial policy, was only waiting for an opportunity for deserting its latest allies. The League feared, too, that Alexander might leave it to its fate and make an independent peace with the emperor.

As a matter of fact, in 1170, strong efforts had been made to bring about such a consummation. But Frederick was bound by the Würzburg decrees and his envoy could not offer the submission that Alexander required. Frederick and the Pope.

John of Salisbury tells us that the emperor made a proposition to the effect that he himself, for his own person, should not be compelled to recognize any pope " save Peter and the others who are in Heaven," but that his son Henry, the young king of the Romans, should recognize Alexander, and, in return, receive from him the imperial coronation. The bishops ordained by Frederick's popes were to remain in office. Alexander answered these proposals with a certain scorn, and the imperial ambassador, Eberhard of Bamberg, returned from Veroli, where the conference had taken place, with nothing to show for his pains.

T

The Pope
and the
League.

Alexander's next move was to send an account of the interview to the heads of the Lombard League, and at the same
time to consecrate, as it were, that organization. He declared
that it had been formed for the purpose of defending the
peace of the cities which composed it, and of the Church,
against the " so-called emperor, Frederick," whose yoke it had
seen fit to cast off. The rectors of the confederation were
taken under the wing of the papacy, and those who should
disobey them threatened with the ban. The Pope recommended a strict embargo on articles of commerce from Tuscany, should the cities of that province refuse to join the
League.

At this same time Alexander showed his friendliness towards
the Eastern Empire by performing in person the marriage
ceremony over the niece of the Emperor Manuel and one of
the Roman Frangipani.

Siege of
Alessandria,
1174-1175
A.D.

Frederick's first act on entering Italy in 1174 was to wreak
vengeance on Susa, where he had once been captive ; no half
measures were used, and the town was soon a heap of ashes.
Asti, also, the first League town which lay in the path of the
imperial army, was straightway made to capitulate. But,
although the fall of these two cities induced many to abandon
the cause of the League, the new fortress of Alessandria,
situated as it was in the midst of a swampy plain and surrounded with massive earth walls, proved an effectual stum-
bling-block in the way of the avenger. Heavy rains and
floods came to the aid of the besieged city and the imperial
tents and huts were almost submersed, while hunger and
other discomforts caused many of the allies of the Germans to
desert. The siege was continued for six months, but Frederick
at last abandoned it on learning that an army of the League
was about to descend on his weakened forces. He burned his
besieging implements, his catapults, battering rams, and
movable towers, and retreated to Pavian territory.

Peace nego-
iations.

The forces of the allied cities were sufficient to alarm
Frederick, but they did not follow up their advantage. One
is surprised to find negotiations for a peace begun at a time

when a decisive battle seemed imminent. What preliminary steps were taken, or why the Lombards should have been the first to take them, is not clear; although some slight successes gained by Christian of Mayence at this juncture in the neighbourhood of Bologna may have been not without effect.

A commission of six men was appointed to draw up the articles of treaty, three being chosen from the cities, three appointed by the emperor. The consuls of Cremona were to decide on disputed points—points, namely, as to which it was impossible to arrive at a mutual agreement. A truce to all hostilities was meanwhile declared, and at Montebello both sides bound themselves to concur in whatever arrangement should be made by the commission and the consuls. The Lombards meanwhile went through the form of a submission, knelt at the emperor's feet, and lowered their standards before him. Frederick thereupon received them into favour and dismissed the greater part of his army, the League doing likewise.

Naturally enough the disputed points were the most important ones, and had to be referred to the consuls of Cremona. But the rage and disappointment of the Lombards went beyond bounds when the different decisions, which, indeed, were remarkably fair, at last were made known. The emperor was to exercise no prerogatives in Northern Italy that had not been exercised in the time of Henry V.; he was also to sanction the continuance of the League. But no arrangement was made for a peace between the heads of Christendom, although the League had made this its first demand. Then, too, Alessandria, which Frederick considered to have been founded in scorn of himself, was to cease to exist, and its inhabitants were to return to their former homes. *Failure of negotiations.*

The report of the consuls roused a storm of indignation; in many cases the document embodying it was torn in shreds by the mob. The Lombards altogether refused to be bound by the terms of the treaty, and reopened hostilities. Frederick hastily gathered what forces he could and sent a pressing call to Germany for aid.

Henry the Lion's desertion.

It was now that the greatest vassal of the crown, Henry the Lion, rewarded twenty years of trustfulness and favour by deserting Frederick in his hour of need. The only cause that is known, a strangely insufficient one, was a dispute concerning the town of Goslar, which the emperor had withdrawn from Henry's jurisdiction. The details of the meeting, which took place according to one chronicle at Partenkirchen, to another at Chiavenna, are but vaguely known to us, but Frederick is said to have prostrated himself at the feet of his mighty subject and to have begged in vain for his support.

Henry's power.

We have seen how Frederick, at the beginning of his reign, had caused Henry, who was already in possession of Saxony, to be acknowledged Duke of Bavaria in place of Henry Jasomirgott, who was conciliated by the gift of the new duchy of Austria. From that moment Henry the Lion's power had steadily grown. He increased his glory, and above all his territory, by constant wars against the Wends, developing a hitherto unheard of activity in the matter of peopling Slavic lands with German colonists. The bishoprics of Lubeck, Ratzebürg and Schwerin owed to him their origin, while he it was who caused the marshy lands around Bremen to be reclaimed and cultivated.

When, on various occasions, conspiracies were formed against Henry by other Saxon nobles, the emperor had boldly and successfully taken his part, helping in person to quell the insurgents; in 1162 he had prevented the Duke of Austria and the King of Bohemia from trying to bring about their rival's downfall.

A marriage with Matilda, daughter of the King of England, had increased the great Saxon's influence; and during the continued absences of the emperor in Italy his rule was kingly in all but name. In 1171 he affianced his daughter to the son of King Waldemar of Denmark, and by this alliance secured his new colonies from Danish hostility.

In actual extent and productiveness his estates fairly surpassed those of his imperial cousin, and the defection of such a man signified the death-knell of the latter's cause.

The battle of Legnano, fought on May 29th, 1176, ended **Battle of** in disaster and defeat. Frederick himself, who was wounded **Legnano,** and thrown from his horse, finally reached Pavia after days of **1176 A.D.** adventurous flight, having meanwhile been mourned as dead by the remnant of his army.

All was not yet lost, indeed, for the League, not knowing what reinforcements were on the way from Germany—the small army of Christian of Mayence, too, was still harvesting victories in the March of Ancona—did not follow up its successes. Cremona, moreover, jealous of Milan, began to waver in her allegiance to the cause of which she had so long been the leader, and eventually signed a treaty with the emperor.

But Frederick, although he at first made a pretence of **Prelimi-** continuing the war, was soon forced by the representations of **naries of** his nobles to abandon the policy of twenty-four years, and to **peace.** make peace on the best terms obtainable with Alexander III., and, through him, with the Lombard cities. The oath of Würzburg was broken, and the two treaties of Anagni and Venice put and end to the long war.

At Anagni the articles were drawn up on which the later long and wearisome negotiations were based. The emperor, the empress, and the young King of the Romans were to acknowledge Alexander as the Catholic and universal Pope, and to show him all due respect. Frederick was to give up the prefecture of Rome and the estates of Matilda, and to make peace with the Lombards, with the King of Sicily, the emperor of Constantinople, and all who had aided and supported the Roman Church. Provision was to be made for a number of German archbishops and bishops who had received their authority from the antipopes.

There is no need to dwell on the endless discussions that **Negotia-** ensued with regard to these matters; more than once it **tions.** seemed as though all attempts at agreement would have to be abandoned. But both parties were sincerely anxious for peace, and at last a remarkably skillful compromise was drawn up at Venice.

Frederick had objected strongly to renouncing the rights

of the empire regarding the estates of Matilda; he was to be allowed to draw the revenues of those estates for fifteen years to come, and the question was eventually to be settled by commissioners. The form of the peace with the Lombards was a still more difficult matter, but the Pope made a wise suggestion which was adopted. A truce of six years was declared, at the end of which time it was hoped that a basis would have been found for a readjustment of the relations between the emperor and the League. With Sicily, too, hostilities were to cease for a term of fifteen years.

It will be seen that all the great questions at issue, save the recognition of Alexander as Pope, were thus relegated to a future time; to a time when the persons concerned would no longer be swayed by passion, and when the din of war would be forgotten.

Peace of Venice, 1177 A.D. During the negotiatiations the Pope had remained for the most part in Venice, while Frederick had not been allowed to enter the city but had remained in the neighbourhood in order that the envoys might pass more quickly to and fro. The terms of the treaty were finally assented to by the emperor at Chioggia, July 21st, 1177. Alexander now prepared to carry out his cherished project of holding a mighty peace-congress at Venice; and there, at the news of the approaching reconciliation, nobles and bishops and their retinues came together from all parts of Europe.

Now that the peace was to become an accomplished fact, Venice outdid herself in preparing to honour the emperor. The latter, too, was determined to spare no expense that could add to the splendour of the occasion. He had negotiated for a loan with the rich Venetians, and he now imposed a tax of 1,000 marks of silver on his nobles.

Frederick's entry into Venice. Frederick's coming was announced for Sunday, July 24th, and by that time the city had donned its most festive attire. Two tall masts had been erected on the present Piazzetta, and from them floated banners bearing the lion of St. Mark's. A platform had been constructed at the door of the Church, and upon it was placed a raised throne for the Pope.

When the emperor landed on the Lido he was met by cardinals whom Alexander had sent to absolve him from the ban. The Doge, the Patriarch of Grado, and a crowd of lesser dignitaries then appeared and furnished a brilliant escort with their gondolas and barks. Having reached the shore Frederick, in the presence of an immense crowd, approached the papal throne, and, throwing off his purple mantle, prostrated himself before the Pope and kissed the latter's feet. Three red slabs of marble mark the spot where he knelt. It was a moment of world-wide importance; the empire and the papacy had measured themselves in mortal combat, and the empire, in form at least, was now surrendering at discretion. No wonder that later ages have fabled much about this meeting. The Pope is said, with his foot on the neck of the prostrate king, to have exclaimed aloud, "The lion and the young dragon shalt thou trample under thy feet!"

Prostrates himself before the Pope.

As a matter of fact Alexander's letters of this time express anything but insolent triumph, and his relations with the emperor after the peace had been sworn to assumed the friendliest character. On the day after his entry into Venice Frederick visited him in the palace of the patriarch, and we are told that the conversation was not only amicable but gay, and that the emperor returned to the Doge's palace in the best of moods.

A year after the congress at Venice the antipope—Calixtus III. had succeeded Pascal in 1168 without in any way altering the complexion of affairs—made a humble submission to Alexander at Tusculum. Therewith the schism ended, and a year later, in 1179, Alexander held a great council in the Lateran where it was decreed that a two-thirds majority in the college of cardinals was necessary to make valid the choice of a pope. There was no mention of the clergy and people of Rome, none of the right of confirmation on the part of the emperor.

End of the Schism.

CHAPTER XVIII.

END OF THE REIGN OF FREDERICK I.

Vengeance on Henry the Lion.

IT was not to be supposed that Frederick would ever forgive that act of Henry the Lion by which the whole aspect of the war in Italy had been changed. Yet it is probable that technically Henry had committed no offence against the empire; for no charge of desertion or herisliz, as refusal to do military service was called, or even of neglect of feudal duties, was ever brought against him. He probably possessed some privilege, like that bestowed on Henry Jasomirgott, rendering it optional with him to accompany the emperor on expeditions out of Germany.

But the circumstances had been so exceptional, so much had hung in the balance at the time of Frederick's appeal for aid, that no one can blame the emperor for now letting Henry feel the full weight of his displeasure. Nor was an occasion lacking by which his ruin might be accomplished. For years the Saxon nobles and bishops had writhed under Henry's oppressions, and the emperor had hitherto taken sides with his powerful cousin; he now lent a willing ear to the charges of the latter's enemies.

War with Henry the Lion.

The restitution to Udalrich of Halberstadt of his bishopric, a restitution that had been provided for in the treaty of Venice, gave the signal for the conflict. Henry the Lion refused to restore certain fiefs which, as Udalrich asserted, belonged to the Halberstadt Church. Archbishop Philip of Cologne and others came forward with similar claims.

Henry was repeatedly summoned to answer his accusers but did not deign to appear. On the contrary he prepared to raise up for himself allies and to besiege the castles of those who would not join him. His own lands were thereupon laid waste by his private enemies, and that with the emperor's consent. But Halberstadt, which took part in one of these plundering expeditions, suffered a terrible vengeance at the hand of the enraged Guelph. In one destructive blaze the city, churches and all, was reduced to ashes. In the war that he was now waging Henry did not hesitate to call in even the Wends to his aid, but Westphalia was soon lost to him, and only in East Saxony was he able to maintain himself.

At a diet held in Würzburg in January, 1180, the emperor laid the question before the princes what was to be done to one who had refused, after having been three times summoned, to come before the imperial tribunal. The answer was that he was to be deprived of all honour, to be judged in the public ban, and to lose his duchy and all his benefices. Thus was final sentence passed on the chief man in Germany next to the emperor himself. *Henry's sentence, 1180 A.D.*

An imperial army was now raised and several fortresses were besieged. No battle took place, but the fact that Frederick had a large force at his command was sufficient to cause defection in the ranks of Henry's allies. In 1181 the emperor's army marched as far as Lübeck, which city, Henry's proudest foundation, was forced to submit. The whole region north of the Elbe followed Lübeck's example, and Henry was soon forced to confess that his cause was hopeless. He laid down his arms, and was summoned to a diet at Erfurt to learn his fate. Here he fell on his knees before Frederick, who, with tears in his eyes, raised him and kissed him in token of peace.

He was made to surrender all his possessions with the exception of Brunswick and Lüneburg. He was to go into exile, and to bind himself by an oath not to return without the emperor's permission. He soon afterwards passed over to Normandy, where he stayed for two years with his father-in-law, Henry II. He then passed over with the latter to England. *Henry banished.*

End of the stem-duchies.

Henry the Lion's fall marks an era in the constitutional history of Germany. Never again do the great stem-duchies play an important *rôle*.

Franconia had ceased to be a duchy in 939; Suabia was in the hands of the ruling dynasty. Bavaria was now given to Otto of Wittlesbach, in whose house it still remains; but, weakened as it already was by the formation of the new duchy of Austria, another duchy was now separated from it—that of Styria. The Tyrolese territory of the counts of Andech, too, was soon to become the duchy of Meran. Saxony, at the diet of Gelnhausen,[1] held in April, 1180, was divided into two parts one of which, the whole of the present Westphalia, was conferred on Philip of Cologne "with every right and jurisdiction, namely, with the county courts, with the advowsons, escort-monies, manors, vills, benefices, serving-men (ministeriales), bondsmen, and all things that pertain to that duchy." The other part, which continued to be called the duchy of Saxony, and which embraced the lands between the Weser and Elbe, was conferred on Bernard of Anhalt, son of Albrecht the Bear.

Evil results.

The mutilation of the great duchies was a measure of far-reaching importance, but it was not without disadvantageous results. Henry the Lion had inspired the Slavonians with a wholesome dread and had kept Denmark in check. His successors were unable to continue this policy. Moreover, the benefit from the subdivision of the Guelphic lands accrued not to the emperor but to the individual princes to whom he gave them. The might of these territorial lords was, in the end, to extinguish that of the central government—the members were to destroy the body; and some look upon Frederick's action as having furthered this development.

Frederick's prosperity.

The years immediately following the Congress of Venice were, strange to say, the most brilliant period of Frederick's reign. It was, after all, only his ideals that had suffered, and a time of prosperity now settled down upon the nation.

[1] See " Select Documents," p. 217.

With Alexander the emperor remained on friendly terms; but the Pope in 1181 died in exile, having been forced by the faithless Romans, as Gregory VII. had been a century before, to flee the holy city.

The peace with the Lombard towns was signed at Constance within the six years agreed upon, on June 23rd, 1183. The communal freedom for which they had fought so long was now accorded them; the emperor gave up all right to the regalia and recognized the Lombard League. His dream of becoming a second Justinian had not been realized.

Peace of Constance, 1183 A.D.

The cities received the privilege of using the woods, meadows, bridges, and mills in their immediate vicinity, and of raising revenues from them; the jurisdiction in ordinary, civil, and criminal cases; the right of making fortifications. The emperor was, to a certain extent, to be provided for when he chose to come to Italy; but he promised to make no long stay in any one town. The cities were to choose their own consuls, who were to be invested with their dignity by the emperor or his representatives. The ceremony, however, was to be performed only once in five years. In important matters where more than a certain sum was at stake, appeals to the emperor were to be allowed.

With the city of Alessandria, so long to him a thorn in the flesh, Frederick had already come to a separate agreement by consent of the League. The city was, technically, to be annihilated, and then to be refounded; it was no longer to bear the name of the Pope, but that of the emperor. Alessandria was to become Cæsarea; yet none of the inhabitants were to suffer by the change.

Alessandria becomes Cæsarea.

The treaty is extant; it provided that the people should leave the city and remain without the walls until led back by an imperial envoy. All the male inhabitants of Cæsarea were then to swear fealty to the emperor and to his son Henry VI.

The Lombard cities, from this time forward, remained true to Frederick; they even became his allies in his new struggle with the popes.

The Matilda estates. With Lucius III. efforts were made to come to an agreement regarding the Matilda estates. Frederick suggested that the Pope should formally and finally renounce them, and in return receive for himself a tenth, for his cardinals a ninth, of all the imperial revenues in Italy. This proposal was rejected, as was also one to leave the whole matter in the hands of a commission. It was finally agreed to have a personal conference between the Pope and the emperor, and the meeting took place at the end of the year 1184. But by that time new differences had arisen, and the question of the estates, important as it was, was thrust far in the background.

Frederick's plans for Henry VI. Frederick had taken a step which was to inaugurate a series of conflicts even more terrible than those which had gone before, and which were to end, more than eighty years later, with the fall of the Hohenstaufen dynasty and the execution of its last scion in the market-place of Naples.

The advancement of his son Henry VI. seems to have been the leading thought of the emperor's declining years. He had caused him to be crowned King of the Romans while still an infant; he repeatedly tried to induce the Pope to grant the boy the imperial crown. The assembly held for the purpose of solemnly girding Henry with the sword was **Brilliant assembly at Mayence, 1184 A.D.** probably the most brilliant festival of the Middle Ages. It took place at Mayence in May, 1184, and the number of knights and nobles who were for three days the emperor's guests is estimated at 70,000. Unheard of preparations had been made; a wooden palace and a wooden church had been erected for the emperor, and a sea of tents stretched in all directions. Knightly sports, and especially tournaments, filled the days, and Heinrich von Veldeke, a poet of the time, declares that the memory of all that was done at Mayence to honour Frederick will endure a hundred years; yes, to the end of the world.

Henry the Lion appeared at Mayence to cast a shadow on the festivities. He begged to be allowed to return in peace to Germany, but was ordered back into exile.

But Frederick's chief act as regarded Henry VI., the act which in future was to have such unhallowed consequences, was the affiancing of that prince to Constance, the aunt of the feeble boy-king of Sicily, and heiress of all his domains. It was this union of Sicily and Germany which threatened to destroy the power of the papacy, to enclose its territory, as it were, in a vice; and against this union pope after pope in turn invoked all powers, natural and supernatural. *Henry VI. and Constance of of Sicily.*

For the moment Frederick seemed to have gained an immeasurable triumph. He had formerly intended, after defeating the Lombard League, to proceed to the subjugation of the Norman kingdom. He had failed with the cities; but the other great goal, by the most easy and peaceful means, was now to be accomplished.

At the meeting held by agreement with Lucius III. in 1184 the Pope showed himself in no conciliatory mood. He refused absolution and reinstatement to a number of clergy who had been consecrated during the schism, and for whom the emperor now intervened; he would come to no agreement about the Matilda estates. He showed himself, finally, thoroughly lukewarm as regarded Frederick's ardent wish to have his son Henry crowned emperor of the Romans during his own lifetime. *Relations with the Pope.*

From this time on the relations between the Pope and the emperor became more and more strained. Frederick formed a defensive and offensive alliance with Milan, one clause of which treaty concerned the retention on the part of the emperor of the Matilda estates.

Of all the Lombard cities Cremona alone, Milan's rival, now held to the Pope. Her citizens were embittered by Frederick's attitudes towards Crema, which she had formerly destroyed, but which the emperor had permitted to be rebuilt. Cremona proceeded to attack the restored city, but was promptly declared in the ban of the empire.

Meanwhile the young King Henry had taken a step which drove the Pope to further acts of hostility. There had been a double election to the archbishopric of Treves and Frederick, *Henry VI. and the Pope.*

as was his undoubted right according to the Concordat of Worms, had decided which of the candidates should be accepted; the rejected one, however, a certain Folmar, had appealed to Rome. Henry VI. now proceeded to acts of violence against the supporters of Folmar, and the Pope hastened to declare the latter the lawful archbishop.

Lucius III. died in November, 1185, openly at enmity with Frederick; his last act was to enjoin that his successor should not crown Henry VI. as emperor.

Urban III.   That successor, Urban III. who had formerly been archbishop of Milan, was as hostile and unbending as Lucius could have wished. Although the old points of difference were not yet settled, new ones were constantly arising. Urban declared against the so-called regalian rights and right of spoils: the right of the emperor according to feudal law of enjoying the revenues or "temporalities" of a bishopric between the death or removal of one incumbent and the election of another, and also to be heir to a deceased bishop's movable belongings. In order to prevent Frederick from enjoying the regalian rights in the archbishopric of Milan, Urban retained that see in his own possession even after becoming pope.

The consecration of Folmar of Treves had not yet taken place, but in 1186, Urban performed this last decisive act.

Threefold coronation, 1186 A.D.   Meanwhile at Milan (January 27th, 1186), Frederick organized another grand festival such as that which he had held at Mayence. Here the marriage of Henry with Constance of Sicily was celebrated, while a three-fold coronation took place. Constance was made Queen, Frederick himself was recrowned as King of Burgundy, and Henry VI. was declared King of Italy and Cæsar.

Cæsar.   This last title was that by which the Roman emperors since Nerva had designated their successors. It was not directly the assumption of the imperial crown without the Pope's permission, although henceforward Henry ruled almost independently in Italy and occasionally signed himself "Augustus." He it was who now invested vassals with their fiefs, imposed

punishments and made donations. In fact if not in name
the imperial power was now divided between Frederick
Barbarossa and his son.

The punishment of Cremona was carried out in June, 1186;
the city was reduced to subjection and made to pay a heavy
fine. The emperor's next step was to surround Verona, where
the Pope and the newly consecrated Treves archbishop were
staying, in order to cut off the latter's return to Germany.
King Henry meanwhile led an army through the papal territory, ravaging and plundering as he went. One stronghold
after another fell into his hands ; everywhere in the Campagna
he compelled the payment of the " fodrum," and forced cities
and nobles to do him homage. According to an English
chronicler, Gervase of Canterbury, " he (Henry) proposed to
take from him (the Pope) everything."

*Chastise-
ment of the
papacy.*

Seldom before had the papacy suffered such chastisement
at the hands of a king of the Romans ; but Urban's spirit
was not broken. He raised a series of bitter complaints
against the emperor, and in the moment of his own greatest
need found an ally in Germany itself.

Philip of Heinsberg, archbishop of Cologne, now raised a
rebellion which threatened to assume such dimensions that it
caused the emperor to hurry back from Italy.

*Rebellion in
Germany.*

Philip had formerly done great services for his monarch,
and his rewards had been in proportion ; his diocese had been
increased by half the lands of Henry the Lion. But his new
position as one of the most powerful princes of the realm had
brought him into conflict with the crown. He had objected
to Frederick's plan of having Henry VI. crowned emperor ;
he was personally hostile to the young king, who had decided
against him in some disputes that came under the feudal law.

Between Verona and Cologne there had been kept up a
constant communication ; Philip was made papal legate, and
upheld the Pope in his complaints regarding the " right of
spoils " and other matters.

Philip succeeded in raising a great coalition which, however,
almost of its own accord, soon wasted into thin air. Not to

speak of Folmar of Treves and a few discontented German
bishops and nobles, Denmark, England, and, for a short time,
France, were pitted against the emperor. Henry the Lion,
too, was suspected, at least by Frederick, of having a share in
the new conspiracy.

Clergy side with Frederick.

Fortunately for the emperor the great body of the German
clergy sided with him at this crisis. At a diet at Gelnhausen
(1186) the whole matter of the conflict with the Church,
which conflict Philip had chosen as an excuse for his own
opposition, was discussed. Here Frederick in person made a
defence of his own policy and refuted the charges brought
against him. He showed that the regalian rights and the
"right of spoils" as exercised by himself were not nearly
such burdens on the churches as the necessity of providing
for pampered clergy with their horses and their retinues. He
reproached the Pope with having sown dissension among
the Lombard cities, with having consecrated Folmar of Treves,
with having retained the see of Milan.

The diet was fully won by Frederick's representations.
The bishops sent a writing to the Pope, to which all of their
seals were appended, admonishing him to make peace with
the emperor and to fulfil the latter's just demands.

Death of Urban III., 1186 A.D.

Urban III. at this time summoned Frederick before his
tribunal at Verona and declared him guilty, by default, of
the charges formerly brought against him. The Pope was
preparing to declare the emperor in the ban when the hand
of death was laid upon himself.

Philip of Cologne had raised an army, and had begun to
make hostile demonstrations but, abandoned by his allies—
Philip Augustus of France could not long remain in the same
league with Henry II. of England—and bereft of Urban's
support, finally made his submission.

Gregory VIII. and the Crusade.

Gregory VIII., Urban's successor, was as peacefully disposed
as any pope could be. He exchanged protestations of friendship with the emperor ; he addressed Henry VI., who had
desisted from his attack on the papal lands, as " Roman
Emperor elect;" he abandoned Archbishop Folmar of Treves,

and finally declared to Frederick that he could not bear the heavy burden placed upon him without the help of the worldly princes.

It was the time when a new attempt was in progress to free the Holy Land. No one grieved more than Gregory over the loss of Jerusalem, which had fallen into the hands of Saladin; the Pope was untiring in his efforts to win soldiers of the cross.

Frederick showed zeal for the undertaking ; he had himself gone on the crusade of 1147, and he now arranged for a great diet at Mayence where the matter of a new expedition should be considered.

Frederick takes the cross.

The diet (it was the same one at which Philip of Cologne made his final submission) met at Easter, 1188. Gregory VIII. had meanwhile died after a pontificate of less than two months ; but an enthusiastic summons to the crusade which he had composed before his death was read at Mayence. Here, in the midst of a scene of wild excitement, the emperor and his son, Frederick of Suabia, took the cross. Following the example of their gray-haired sovereign thousands of knights assumed the votive emblem.

Extensive preparations were now made for the expedition. The rabble that had so hampered the previous crusades was to be excluded, and only those who possessed a certain sum of money were allowed to take part. Negotiations were begun with the Greek emperor, and every effort was made to assure him that the former occurrences which had given his predecessors cause for complaint should be avoided. The King of Hungary was won by being allowed to wed his daughter to the young Frederick of Suabia.

Preparations for the crusade.

Frederick had meanwhile despatched an envoy to the great Saladin demanding that he should renounce all conquests made at the cost of the kingdom of Jerusalem, should give back the relics of the holy cross, and should pay certain damages : in case of refusal he was to know that not only the Roman Empire but the whole world was ready to make war upon him.

U

Frederick starts on the crusade. On May 11th, 1189, the crusading army started on its way; on that day the crowds assembled at Ratisbon looked for the last time on their emperor. Frederick had appointed his son Henry vicegerent in all matters pertaining to the empire, and had won a promise from Pope Clement III. that the imperial coronation should now be fulfilled; Henry the Lion had been sent anew into exile under oath not to return for three years.

His death, 1189 A.D. What need to follow the long and weary marches through the territory of the wily Greeks, and of the treacherous Sultan of Iconium? The great historical fact, the one fact of absorbing interest, is that the great leader and knightly emperor, the man who was to be worshipped as a national hero for the next eight hundred years, returned no more. In the river Saleph, not far from the Armenian town of Seleucia, he found his death while seeking refreshment in the cool waters after a hot day's march. His body was brought to land, but, although even as late as our own day the effort has been made, his ultimate place of burial has never been discovered. According to the legend so beloved in his fatherland, Frederick sits in the heart of the Kyffhäuser mountain, waiting for the time when his country shall need him. Then, like a second Messiah, he will come again.

Failure of the crusade. Barbarossa's death betokened the failure of his crusade. Many pilgrims at once returned home; a remant of the army under Frederick of Suabia was able to reach Syria, but in the summer of 1190 was decimated by the plague. The young Suabian duke himself found his death before the walls of Acre in January, 1191.

Meanwhile Germany had fallen a prey to civil war, and it might have gone hard with the land indeed had not the young king, Henry VI., shown a strength of character and a genius for ruling such as had hardly been expected from him. He knew when to strike, when to temporize, and when to yield.

CHAPTER XIX.

HENRY VI. AND RICHARD OF ENGLAND.

HENRY VI., although small of frame and delicate of constitution, was in every other way one of the strongest of the Hohenstaufens. His were the proudest ideals, his the clearest political insight, his the most fiery courage. He bade defiance, if need be, to all precedent, and occasionally, indeed, to all scruple. His reign, in proportion to its length, is more full of stirring incident than that of any German monarch who ever reigned, if we except that of the man who in our own day fought with three different countries within six years, founded a united Germany, and made a strong empire out of a weak confederation. Character of Henry VI.

Had Henry VI. lived longer, he, too, would undoubtedly have changed the character of the monarchy over which he ruled. He was as ambitious as Otto III. had been, but with less in him of the dreamer and more of the man of action. He, too, wished to rule the world from Italy as a centre; he expressly designates Apulia and Sicily as his "by ancient right of the empire." His assumption of the titles of "King of Italy" and of "Cæsar," and, above all, his marriage with Constance of Sicily, brought him nearer and nearer to the goal of his ambitions.

Hard conflicts, however, were to stand in his way. No sooner had Frederick Barbarossa started on his crusade than Henry the Lion broke his knightly word, returned from banishment, and proceeded to make a desperate fight for his former lands and possessions. He was supported by a number of Saxon princes who were discontented with the new order of Henry the Lion's return.

things. His brother-in-law, too, Richard the Lionhearted, soon to be King of England, gave him encouragement, and, as there is reason to believe, even more tangible assistance.

The Guelph had little difficulty in gaining a footing in Northern Saxony; many hastened of their own free will to join the cause of their former master, others yielded to compulsion, and thirty castles were made to surrender. Naturally, however, those who had gained by Henry's fall, proceeded to oppose him with might and main.

Henry VI. and Henry the Lion. There was no need for the new Duke Bernard to send an appeal for aid to Henry VI. The latter was aghast at the daring and at the treachery of Henry the Lion. In four weeks he was ready with his musterings and his preparations, and marched against Brunswick; but that city was more prepared to endure a winter siege than the king was to begin one, and the army finally returned to Goslar, where it disbanded. During the winter, however, Henry the Lion suffered various reverses at the hand of Saxon nobles, and in July, 1190, the rebellious prince was glad to accept the mediation of the archbishops of Mayence and Cologne, and to make peace with the king. Henry VI. was impatient to claim the crown of Sicily, and was glad enough to receive the sons of Henry the Lion as hostages, and to make to the latter certain concessions, the chief of which was that he might remain in Germany and enjoy half the revenues of Lubeck, in addition to the lands that Barbarossa had left him.

Condition of Sicily. At the time when this rebellion of Henry the Lion was at its height, the last king of Sicily, William II., had passed away, and Henry VI. and his queen were now heirs to the throne. Already, in 1184, on the occasion of the marriage with Constance, King William and his nobles had agreed that Henry VI. should be the next ruler. In 1186, at a diet in Troja, the barons had done homage to their future king and to his queen.

Tancred. But the land was torn by party dissensions, and, on the death of William II., a number of the Sicilians repented of their engagements. They chose Count Tancred of Lecce, one of the very nobles who had done homage to Henry, as their king; and he, with the approbation of the Pope, who still looked upon himself as feudal lord of Sicily, was crowned in the cathedral at Palermo.

Henry VI. had at first underrated the importance of the movement in Sicily. He had sent envoys who returned with the information that the rebellion against his authority was not serious, and could be easily quelled.

But Tancred was no mean rival; his virtues and his disinterestedness had won him the election. He now dipped into the rich treasures of the Sicilian kings, and raised and equipped a serviceable army with which he twice drove back the defenders of the German cause.

Meanwhile there had landed in Sicily, on his way to the crusade, a man who was, directly and indirectly, to have the greatest influence on German affairs. Richard of England sailed into Messina September 23rd, 1190, royally escorted and with blaring trumpets. Philip Augustus of France had made his landing a week before—far less magnificently, we are told. The two great rival kings were detained by violent storms, and were finally obliged to winter in Sicily. *Landing of Richard Lionhearted.*

The fact that Richard's sister, the widow of William II., was kept by Tancred in captivity, was cause enough for the English king to interfere in Sicilian matters. Tancred released his prisoner at once, but Richard found a pretext in some excesses of the populace, to whom the two royal visitors were far from being welcome, of continuing the hostilities. The people were made by Richard to give hostages until such time as Tancred should have fulfilled his demands.

These demands were at first high beyond all bounds; a golden throne for his sister, a golden table twelve feet long for himself, a hundred galleys equipped for two years, a silken tent in which two hundred knights might be entertained —and more of the kind. In the end Richard compromised for forty-two thousand ounces of gold, and struck an offensive and defensive alliance with Tancred, whose daughter was to *Richard and Tancred form an alliance.*

marry Arthur of Brittany, the presumptive heir to the throne of England.

Richard was impelled to make this alliance by a desire to circumvent Philip Augustus—who, loyal to Henry VI., or pretending to be so, had refused overtures of Tancred—and especially by hostility to the German emperor. The union was directed "against anyone who should attack it (Sicily) or make war against Tancred." The Pope was asked to confirm the treaty, "inasmuch as it will in future bring great gain to both kingdoms."

Richard's friendship for Henry the Lion must be borne in mind in this connection ; the son of that unruly prince appears as witness in a charter issued at la Reolle by the English king after the journey towards Sicily had already been begun. It is possible that Richard had at first intended to conquer the whole of that land. Philip Augustus was firmly convinced that such was the case, and other contemporaries give vent to the same suspicion.

Richard's motives.

Did the English king intend to help the Guelph by striking a deadly blow at Henry VI.'s influence in Southern Italy ? The chronicles leave us in darkness on the matter, but enough is known to show that Henry VI. believed the worst of Richard, and saw in him his deadliest enemy. Had the English king done nothing else, he had made common cause with a usurper whom he had induced to pour into his lap the treasures of the Norman kings.

Henry VI. and Pope Celestine III.

By this time Henry VI.'s army was on the march. The tidings of Barbarossa's death had become known in Germany, and the young king was eager first to secure the imperial coronation in Rome, and then to press on to Southern Italy. The death of Pope Clement III. took place while Henry was on his way. The new pope, Celestine III., was already eighty-five years of age, vacillating in character and given to sudden and inconsiderate outbursts of wrath. His great successor, Innocent III., in one of his letters passes severe judgment upon him.

Celestine's cardinals declared themselves no longer bound

by Clement's promise regarding the imperial coronation, and, in order not to be obliged to perform the ceremony, the Pope postponed his own consecration.

The hostility of the Romans to the town of Tusculum plays an important part at this juncture of affairs. Before accepting Celestine as Pope and head of Rome the citizens had made him promise to take their side in the matter. They now agreed to procure the imperial crown for Henry if he would make a similar convention; they demanded that the city should be left to their mercy, but promised to bestow it eventually on the Pope, thus securing his compliancy in the matter of the coronation. Thus did the rebellious Romans impose their will on the two highest powers in Christendom. Negotiations with the Romans.

When Henry had abandoned Tusculum the Pope caused himself to be consecrated, and in April, 1191, placed the crown on the head of the king and on that of his queen, Constance. Still further details are known about this coronation than about that of Barbarossa. Henry was made to promise that he would keep peace with the Church, such peace as the Lord gave to his disciples; and then to kiss, as though he were kissing a cross, the Pope's brow, mouth and chin, and his two cheeks. When Celestine accepted him as "son of the Church" he was obliged to kiss the Pope's breast. Afterwards he was submitted to a catechism; made to say the Apostles' Creed, and to promise to be reverent, chaste, sober, cheerful, and the like. Henry VI. crowned emperor, 1191 A.D.

Two days later Tusculum was in the hands of its enemies, who tore down its walls and otherwise gave vent to their hatred. Contemporary writers blame Henry severely, and consider his abandonment of a friendly city as a blot on the glory of the empire.

The new emperor now marched off joyfully from Rome to undertake the conquest of his Sicilian inheritance. He little dreamt of the series of misfortunes that were to fall upon his head. Henry VI. meets with reverses in Sicily.

The cities of Apulia were, for the most part, easily won, but before Naples Henry suffered a terrible reverse. Tancred's

admiral, Margerito, a famous seaman who went by the name
in Italy of " the second Neptune," appeared with a fleet in the
harbour. The Genoese ships that were to have aided the
Germans were belated, and the few Pisan galleys on which
they could count were glad enough to run out to sea and
escape so unequal a contest. At the same time the tropical
heat caused a deadly fever to break out among the land
forces.

Nor was this all. The young Henry, son of Henry the
Lion, who had accompanied the emperor as hostage for his
father, escaped and went over to Tancred. He aided the
Sicilian for a while and then hastened to Germany, where he
spread a report that Henry VI. had died of the fever, and
himself came forward as candidate for the throne. Henry
the Lion urged the princes to proceed with the election.

Prepares for the struggle with the Guelphs. So much was true of the young Guelph's story, that the
emperor really was seriously ill, and was forced to abandon
the siege of Naples. Nine-tenths of his army had succumbed
to the fever. His empress, Constance, too, had been betrayed
by the inhabitants of Salerno, where she had taken refuge,
and was carried off by Admiral Margerito as a captive to
Messina.

Henry VI. returned to Germany to see what he could make
out of the wreck of his fortunes. He, the Hohenstaufen,
knew well that a new and terrible conflict would have to be
fought out with the Guelphs ; again the two families stood
over against each other in fierce, unquenchable hostility.

Henry VI., directly after the treasonable flight of the young
Guelph, had sent to Germany and ordered the Archbishop of
Magdeburg to raise an army which should attack Brunswick
in the following summer. Henry the Lion, on hearing of
these preparations, sent a deputation of clergy to see if there
were no possibility of bringing about a reconciliation. The
emperor answered by frankly unfolding his programme : to
utterly annihilate the Guelphs no matter what promises they
might now make ; to return to Apulia, subject it, and then
lead back the empress with all due honour.

The younger Guelph was now declared in the ban of the empire, and Henry VI. was met at Würzburg by a number of Saxon nobles, whose lands had long been kept in a state of insecurity by Henry the Lion's acts of hostility, and who were anxious now to take part in the work of vengeance.

But at this juncture the emperor's own severity and arbitrariness not only prevented him from gaining a victory over the Guelphs, but raised up for him a new and even more dangerous class of enemies.

A whole series of episcopal sees, of which the incumbents in many cases had died in Palestine, were vacant at this time. In many of them Henry was able to secure the election of his own candidate without opposition, but in Liége it came to a schism. The majority of the cathedral chapter, influenced by the Duke of Brabant, chose the latter's brother, Albert; the minority elected a relative of Baldwin of Hennegan, a certain Albert of Retest, to whom it was thought that the emperor would be likely to be partial. Henry, when the matter was laid before him, proceeded as though no such thing as an election by the canons of the Cathedral Chapter had taken place. He rejected both candidates, and, bribed by a payment of three thousand marks of silver, gave the place to Lothar of Hochstaden.

It was a fatal act; it was a challenge flung in the face of the whole clergy, a direct breach of the Concordat of Worms. Albert of Brabant hastened to Rome to complain of Henry VI., and to cause the Pope to take measures which should prevent a recurrence of such arbitrary decisions. Celestine confirmed Albert as Bishop of Liége and threatened with the ban all who took the oath of a vassal to Lothar of Hochstaden.

Albert, on his return, applied to Archbishop Bruno of Cologne for consecration, but Bruno feigned illness, and the Archbishop of Rheims, more daring and with less to lose, performed the ceremony.

Henry VI. now appeared in Liége, and caused the houses of Albert's supporters to be broken open, their goods to be seized. The heads of the Rhenish-Lorraine nobility were

Marginal notes:

Henry VI. raises up new enemies.

Complications in the bishopric, Liége.

Murder of Albert.

summoned to appear and compelled to do homage to Lothar
of Hochstaden as their liege lord. The same demand was
made and enforced on Albert's brother, the Duke of Brabant.

Henry VI. had played the part of an oriental despot; still
more like one, if the accusations against him are true, was his
subsequent action.

Albert was visited by three German knights, who, after a
friendly reception, seized a favourable opportunity to attack
and to thrust him through with their swords. No one
doubted then, and but few can doubt now, but that Lothar
of Hochstaden's party had instigated the murder, and that
Henry was privy to it. Even the latter's supporters fail to
justify the fact that the three murderers when, later, the
nobles insisted on their expulsion from Germany, were
invested by the emperor with rich fiefs in Apulia.

League against Henry VI. The murder of Albert was the signal for a meeting of
princes, for a mighty oath of vengeance, and for a league
against Henry which, coming at the time of the Guelphic
disturbances, threatened to overwhelm him. Even the Saxon
allies who had hastened to meet him at Würzburg grew tired
of waiting for the help and the guidance that never came,
and made their peace with Henry the Lion. Only a few of
them, notably Count Adolf of Holstein, continued their own
feuds with the Guelph, and drew down on certain parts of
Saxony terrible havoc and devastation.

Denmark for the Guelphs. Henry VI. had placed his greatest hopes on Bishop
Waldemar of Schleswig, a cousin of the Danish King
Canute VI., but a renegade who had promised to bring
Denmark under German influence. In order that he might
better pursue his plans, Henry had caused him to be made
Archbishop of Bremen.

But Canute of Denmark discovered Waldemar's treasonable
plans and, embittered against the emperor, gave his support
to the Guelphs. Publicity was given to the whole intrigue
by the flight of the Archbishop to Sweden, and a contemporary
tells us that " the emperor's weakness and the duke's strength
were now apparent to all the world."

The conspiracy had by this time been joined by Duke **Henry VI. in** Ottakar of Bohemia, and had spread its meshes over a large **the greatest** part of Germany; its two great centres were Saxony and the **straits.** lower Rhine. The emperor's chief supporter was Duke Leopold of Austria who had been laid under obligations by being given the vacant duchy of Styria.

Henry VI. was in the greatest straits; the Pope had given his blessing to the league against him; the Duke of Brabant, the leader of the conspiracy, was aiming at nothing short of placing the crown on his own head.

At this time an event occurred so opportune, so unexpected, **Capture of** so pregnant with results that it well deserves the popularity **Richard** which, down to the present day it has enjoyed in works of **Lionhearted.** poetry and romance. Never have a man's enemies, if the biblical expression may be pardoned, so completely been made his footstool as at the present juncture. The capture of the English King, Richard the Lionhearted, by Duke Leopold of Austria, rescued Henry VI. from an intolerable position, and caused him to reap a perfect harvest of successes.

It is unfortunate that the details of this event which have **Two sides to** most widely obtained credence have come from the English **the question.** side. Naturally to Richard's friends his imprisonment seemed dastardly and iniquitous. The wildest tales were spread of the courageous and generous monarch being kept in dungeons and loaded with chains, of his nobles being tortured to death with inhuman cruelty. Again and again the changes are rung by the chroniclers on Henry VI.'s greed and avarice. Naturally; for the people were heavily taxed to raise the money for Richard's ransom, and even the churches were made to give up their golden chalices. Yet even among the English chroniclers themselves, voices are heard which might warn us that there are two sides to the question. William of Newbridge, although going out from the assumption that greed was Henry's only motive, declares that the emperor had concealed that motive and had known well how to veil it under a cloak of justice.

Henry VI.
and Philip
Augustus.

Let it be remembered that Richard the Lionhearted was an ardent supporter of Henry the Lion who was in open rebellion; the English king's conduct in Sicily, too, had been more than equivocal. He had made a firm alliance with Tancred, and had gone off with treasures which the emperor claimed with good right to have belonged to himself.

Is it any wonder that Henry sided with Philip Augustus of France and favoured the machinations of the latter when he returned precipitately from the crusade to work Richard's ruin? A formal treaty was drawn up between the two monarchs, and Henry promised to take Richard prisoner should he attempt to pass through his empire. An edict was issued declaring the English king a public enemy, and ordering all imperial subjects to watch for his return.

Leopold of
Austria.

No one did so more eagerly than Leopold of Austria, who had his own grounds for undying enmity. The well-known episode in Acre had occurred but shortly before. After the town had fallen, and the crusaders had entered into possession, Richard saw that Leopold had planted his own banner on one of the principal buildings. In an access of rage he had ordered the Austrian standard to be taken down and trampled in the dust. Leopold had left Palestine with Philip Augustus, vowing vengeance for his affront.

Richard's
adventures.

In returning from the crusade Richard, desiring at all hazards to avoid France, had chosen the route through Austria, intending to proceed by way of Bohemia to Saxony, and thence to England. He had been shipwrecked near Aquileija, but had escaped. While passing in disguise through the territory of the Count of Gorz, a nephew of the murdered Conrad of Montferrat, for whose death Richard was widely but unjustly believed to have been responsible, he had made an unwise display of his riches, and suspicions were aroused against one who called himself a merchant, and yet made presents of priceless value. He escaped from Gorz, but the rumour now spread of his return, and every trace was followed up which could lead to his detection. He had reached the outskirts of Vienna, and had sent his only attendant into the city to buy food ; but the Byzantine coins which the latter offered, and, finally, the rich gloves of the king which he carried at his belt, drew down suspicion on him. He was put to torture, and confessed the truth.

On December 21st, 1192, Richard, brought to bay as it were, surrendered his sword to Leopold in person. The captive was taken to the castle of Dürenstein on the Danube, and the people, as he passed, berated him as a traitor and threatened to stone him. Leopold himself, even according to English testimony, treated him with great respect ; he was guarded, however, by wardens with drawn swords. Leopold was induced to give him up to Henry VI. by the promise of half the king's ransom, and by the prospect that Richard's niece should marry his own son. He made the condition that the emperor should inflict on his captive no harm of life or limb. *Richard's treatment at Henry's hands.*

The mightiest hostage that could be desired for the good conduct of the Guelphs had fallen into Henry's hands ; the latter had secured the means, too, of inducing Philip Augustus to grant him any aid he might desire against the Rhenish princes who might be attacked now by overwhelming forces from on two sides.

It had been agreed with Leopold what conditions were to be placed on the eventual release of Richard. Besides the ransom, which was placed at 100,000 marks of silver, and which was declared to be a compensation for the money taken from Sicily, the English king was to send men and ships, and himself to aid in the conquest of the Norman kingdom. *Conditions of Richard's release.*

It was intended to terribly humble the man with the heart of a lion. He was to be asked to make war against his own ally, and to act as the vassal of his deadly enemy.

Finally he was to be retained as a pledge until the German princes who were in rebellion should promise good behaviour and submission. This last condition, which was eventually insisted upon, while that as to Richard's personal participation in the Sicilian war was modified, caused the release of

the captive to be delayed far beyond the time that had been
at first appointed.

Richard before the Diet of Spires.

Richard was now brought before a diet at Spires and made
to listen to the emperor's demands, and to a long series of
accusations. The chief charges concerned his conduct in
Sicily and the murder of Conrad of Montferrat, while the
insult to the flag of Leopold of Austria was not forgotten.
Richard was then allowed to step forward and to defend
himself in person. "He spoke royally," says his chronicler,
"with eloquent words and with a lion's courage, as if he were
sitting on his inherited throne, or in the hall of Lincoln, or
in the midst of his barons at Caen; quite forgetting his
captivity."

It was a moving scene, a scene of which we have a trustworthy account. When he had ceased speaking Richard bent
his knee before the emperor. The latter was deeply affected;
he descended from his throne, folded the king in his arms,
and kissed him, while the nobles stood around with tears in
their eyes. Henry called the English king his friend, and
promised him aid in increasing his power, and, above all, in
making peace with Philip of France. Richard's captivity was
made as bearable as possible, and later he was kept in liberal
custody at the emperor's court.

Richard does homage for England.

But on the conditions of the release Henry felt bound to
insist; he even added to them, as it seems. Richard was
allowed, indeed, to pay a sum of money instead of going to
Sicily, but he was made to do homage for England as for a
fief of the empire. He surrendered his land, and received it
back in return for a promise to pay a yearly tribute of five
thousand pounds. Later, at Winchester, at the request of
his nobles, Richard was re-crowned with the English crown
for the express purpose of revindicating his sullied honour.

Richard will not abandon Henry the Lion.

So far had Richard humbled himself before his captor;
but one demand he unconditionally rejected, although the
remission of half of his ransom had been promised in case
of compliance. After the mighty conspiracy which so
threatened Henry's throne had come to nothing, after all the

other princes had made their submission, Henry the Lion
alone remained in opposition.   Henry VI. now required that
Richard should let him fall—for all we know that he should
proceed against him in person.   Richard's refusal, while it
reflects all honour on his own chivalrous self, shows how
deeply his cause was bound up with that of the Guelphs, and
how wise, from a political point of view, the emperor had
been to take him captive.

Henry VI.'s attitude at this time was not so worthy of
admiration as that of his prisoner.   He vacillated in the end
between an English and a French alliance.   At one time his
friendship for Richard rose to such a pitch that he invested
him with the kingdom of Arles, where, indeed, in spite of all
that Frederick Barbarossa had done, his own influence was
far from secure.   But again he lent ear to the voice of Philip
of France, who offered him 150,000 marks of silver if he
would prolong Richard's captivity another year—it had already
lasted two.

Vacillation of Henry VI.

The English king, however, was set free in February, 1194,
and a month later made his entry into London.

Richard's release, 1194 A.D.

Richard's advent had indeed been a boon for the emperor
of the Romans.   It left Henry VI. master of new and vast
pecuniary resources, and at peace with almost all his enemies
in Germany.   England, in the eyes of the Germans at least,
had become a subject land; in 1198, on Henry VI.'s death,
Richard was summoned to take part in the new election as
" a distinguished member of the empire."

CHAPTER XX

The Count
Palatine as
mediator
between
Henry VI.
and Henry
the Lion.

ABOUT the time of Richard's release events occurred in
Sicily which caused the emperor to long for peace with
Henry the Lion and his party. Mediators were not wanting.
At the time of the negotiations with Philip Augustus concerning Richard's further captivity, the French king had
offered his hand to the emperor's cousin, the daughter of the
Count Palatine of the Rhine. But a romantic attachment
had long existed between the young girl and the son of
Henry the Lion, and the idea of the French marriage was
naturally looked upon by the lovers as the death-knell of all
their hopes. Their sufferings had moved the heart of the
girl's mother, who had arranged a runaway match; the pair
had been hastily wedded in the castle of Stahleck at Bacharach
on the Rhine.

At the time Henry had been furious. The Count Palatine
had no sons, so the Palatinate, which Frederick Barbarossa
had so carefully formed into a province which should be an
appanage of his house, would now eventually fall to the
Guelphs. The result of the marriage, too, had been to
incense Philip Augustus, who withdrew his offers, and to
add to the delays attendant on Richard's release.

But now that peace was so desirable the intervention of
the Count Palatine, closely connected as he was with both
parties, proved most valuable. A peace-meeting was arranged
at Tilleda, close to the Kyffhäuser, and a reconciliation was
brought about. The younger Henry was promised the succession to the Palatinate, but, in return, was to do military

service in the approaching expedition for the recovery of
Sicily. The other son, Otto, who had been named by Richard
of England one of his hostages for what had been left unpaid
of his ransom, was to remain in Germany under close super-
vision.

Henry the Lion himself was by this time well on in years,
and scarcely more to be feared. He died in 1195, after having
devoted his last days to good works, and to the collecting of
chronicles, which he caused to be copied and read aloud to
him.   He spent whole nights, we are told, in listening to them ;
perhaps a few historical truths as to the usual fate of rebels
and rebellions may have at length come home to him.

Peace was at last restored in Saxony, except for some feuds
which continued to be fought with the Archbishop of Bremen.
According to Arnold of Lubeck, a faithful observer, "Highwaymen and men of blood lamented, for their accursed harvest
was lost. Blessed be the marriage of Henry of Brunswick,
for, through this alliance, peace and joy have been wedded for
the benefit of the land ! "

In Sicily, meanwhile, even during the emperor's absence, his
cause had steadily been gaining ground. He possessed a
number of adherents there with whom he had kept in touch,
and these had managed to fill the days of Tancred with fear
and unrest. By the mediation of the Pope, the Empress
Constance, through whose intervention Celestine hoped to
make peace with Henry VI., had meanwhile been released
(June, 1192).

But these longings for a reconciliation on the Pope's part
did not last long. Celestine's character was wavering as we
have seen—he was by this time nearly ninety years of age—
and, finding that Tancred was willing to make a most favourable treaty with the Church, he proceeded to solemnly invest
him with the kingdom of Sicily, and to promise him, as feudal
lord, help against all his enemies. When the conspiracy of
German princes was formed against Henry VI., the Pope had
expressly supported the rebels and had held out hopes to the
Duke of Brabant of obtaining the imperial crown. Henry

Margin notes:
Death of
Henry the
Lion, 1195
A.D.

Sicily.

Celestine
acknow-
ledges
Tancred.

x

had retaliated by ordering the arrest of anyone in Italy who should be found on his way to Rome. The chief prelate next to the Pope, the cardinal bishop of Ostia, had been seized in accordance with this decree.

Death of Tancred and his son, 1194 A.D. Meanwhile Tancred, soon after Constance's release, caused his son Roger to be appointed co-regent in Sicily, and affianced him with the daughter of the eastern emperor, Isaak Angelos, hoping thus to gain a new ally. But within a month of each other both the rulers of Sicily, father and son alike, were carried away by sickness. A younger son, William, a mere boy, was then proclaimed king, and his mother undertook the regency.

Henry VI. called to Sicily. But the successes of the emperor's partisans in Apulia had by this time discouraged the majority of the Sicilian barons ; they sent to Henry VI. and asked him to take possession of their kingdom. Henry appeared in their midst with a splendidly equipped army which had been lavishly paid with the ransom of Richard of England. He was supported, too, by an imposing fleet, having won the Genoese by promises, which, as it turned out, he never kept. The Pisans, too, had been overwhelmed by tokens of favour ; they were to have free trade in the Norman kingdom and immense fiefs, besides certain rights in every Apulian and Sicilian city.

Attacks Salerno. One of Henry's first points of attack was Salerno which, in former days, had betrayed the Empress Constance to the followers of Tancred. Salerno, hitherto a flourishing town and especially renowned for its school of medicine, fell after a day's siege. "The city which helped the whole world with her remedies," says an Austrian chronicler, "could now find no physician to offer her a cure for her woes."

Salerno's fate intimidated the rest of Henry's enemies in Southern Italy, and the way to Sicily was soon free.

Defeats the widow of Tancred. Sibylla, the widow of Tancred, had raised an army which was defeated by the imperial troops near Catanea. The first and last great effort at resistance had failed, and one stronghold after another, last of all Palermo, fell into the hands of the Normans.

Henry VI. has been reproached with inhuman barbarity in his treatment of these Sicilian rebels, although his victims just on this occasion seem to have been very few in number. There is scarcely any doubt but that some of the ringleaders were skinned alive; but this punishment, horrible as it was, is scarcely more cruel than what was inflicted in every land of Europe during the middle ages on those guilty of high treason. In England, but a few generations later than the time of which we are writing, traitors were dragged at the tails of horses, then hung, then quartered, and their heads placed on lances in public places.

Henry VI. was determined that for the land of Sicily as a whole his advent should be that of a deliverer come to bring peace and prosperity. On the wanton destruction of property by his soldiers he placed the penalty of mutilation. In November, 1194, he held a brilliant entry into Palermo; a few days later Sibylla and her son, for whom a generous provision had been made, surrendered the royal treasure, and on Christmas Day the crown of Sicily was placed on the head of the German emperor. *Henry VI. crowned king of Sicily, 1194 A.D.*

It was not long, indeed, before a conspiracy was discovered against Henry's life, a conspiracy in which the royal family and the first magnates of Sicily were implicated. The offenders were all banished, and the queen and her children spent lonely years in Alsace, not even being allowed the solace of each other's companionship.

At this time, when Henry was firmly seated on the Sicilian throne and had once more become master of his enemies, a son was born to him, the later much-tried and too enlightened emperor Frederick II. An heir was now at hand to unite the Norman and the German claims, and the boy was christened Roger Frederick in memory of his two grandfathers. *Birth of Frederick II., 1195 A.D.*

It was with Richard of England's ransom that Henry had been able to complete the conquest of Sicily. With the accumulated treasure of the Norman kings he next proceeded in his endeavours to make himself monarch of the world. The riches of Sicily, Apulia and Calabria were now collected *Sicilian treasure carried off.*

and carried off to Germany. The country had been scoured for coined money, for gold and silver ornaments, for precious stones. The royal palaces had been stripped of their silken hangings and of their valuable furniture. Among the booty was a red silk garment which the Arabs had presented to Roger II., and into the border of which they had woven expressions of good-will towards the king. It served as a coronation mantle for the next German emperors.

Constance in Sicily. The administratration of Sicily was now conferred on the empress Constance. In the palace of her fathers at Palermo she took up her residence, and she ruled freely and almost in her own right. In her charters she speaks of " our majesty," " our fisc," " our domains," and on one of her seals which was found at Palermo she is represented as sitting crowned on her throne, the sceptre in her right hand, the imperial orb in her left. Coins have also come to light which bear on one side the name of Henry, on the other that of the empress.

For a subjected land it was a great consolation that it was to continue to be ruled by a scion of its old dynasty.

The German chronicles and letters of this time are overflowing with expressions of joy over Henry VI.'s triumphs. His former tutor, Conrad of Querfurt, is astonished at the practical lessons in geography that the emperor has taught him, and declares that men are now brought face to face with things previously only taught about in school.

Ideal of world-monarchy. Never, since Europe had separated into its different kingdoms was the ideal of a world-monarchy more nearly realized than under Henry VI. We have seen him assume, if only for the moment, the overlordship of England ; the actual rule was his of the great Apulian-Sicilian kingdom. He had intimated to the Genoese that they might reward themselves, if they wished, for their recent services at the expense of the kingdom of Arragon. He was now to turn his eyes towards France on the one hand, and towards the Greek Empire on the other.

In the summer of 1195, Henry sent a golden crown to Richard of England and urged him, in the name of the fealty sworn to himself, to press on with his war against Philip Augustus, whereby he might be sure of his, the emperor's, support. He openly declared—Pope Innocent III. is our authority —that he would compel the French King to do him homage.

Richard sent to inquire exactly on what imperial forces he could count, but a new development, an invasion of the Moors which threatened alike Navarre and Castile, the ally of England and the ally of France, caused those two warring powers to make a hasty peace against their common enemy.

The Greek Empire at this time was in a condition of super- The Greek lative weakness. In 1183, William II. of Sicily had made an empire. expedition against it, and had conquered several provinces which, however, he lost again through the treachery of his own Sicilians. In 1185, Isaak Angelos had overthrown the tyrant Andronikos, the murderer of Manuel, and had himself ascended the throne. When Henry VI. conquered Sicily, he found in Palermo the daughter of this emperor Isaak, who, it will be remembered, had married the son of Tancred. This princess he now affianced to his own brother, Philip of Hohenstaufen, who might thus eventually fall heir to the throne.

The sword of Damocles was at this time hanging over Isaak himself, and Henry VI. in a masterly manner made the most of the emperor's tribulations.

Isaak, threatened with overthrow by his own brother Henry's de-
Alexius, turned to Henry for aid. The latter consented to the mands from
levying of forces in German lands, and a number of soldiers the eastern
to whom Isaac had promised rich pay crossed over to his aid. emperor.
But Henry made this the occasion for extravagant demands; he claimed nothing less than all the provinces between Epidaurus and Thessalonica, averring that those had been the conquests of his own predecessor, William II. in 1183, and that he, as heir to the Norman crown, had a right to them. He demanded further that a Greek fleet should support the German crusaders, and that a high tribute should be paid; in case of refusal he threatened with war. As a Byzantine chronicler has it, "he came forward with his demands like the lord of lords and the king of kings."

Soon the news came that Isaak had been overthrown by Alexius and had been blinded and imprisoned. The new despot tried to win Henry's favour, but the latter considered that the time had now come for avenging the old alliance of the Greeks with the Pope against Barbarossa and the repeated ill-treatment of crusaders. He came forward now as the champion of Isaak; the latter's rights, however, now that he had been blinded, were declared to have descended on Irene, who soon afterwards actually married Philip of Hohenstaufen.

Henry VI. projects a crusade.

There was much of the wily Ulysses in the character of Henry VI. In order to carry out his plans against the Eastern Empire it was necessary to make his peace with Rome. This he did by sending to Celestine and declaring that he felt a desire and need of returning to the fatherly lap of the Pope. The inducement that he offered was nothing less than the taking of the cross in person and the sending of fifteen hundred knights, each with a squire, to the Holy Land. Their expenses were to be paid out of the treasure of Sicily.

The Pope's delight.

Celestine III., that pious, simple old man, was more than delighted. In his eyes the regaining of Palestine was the first duty of the papacy. He believed that the ill-success of the last crusade had been due wholly to the dissensions of the Christian leaders, and was far from being satisfied with the treaty which Richard the Lionhearted had closed with Saladin. That treaty, although it provided that pilgrims should be unmolested, left the land still in the hands of the heathen, and Celestine had forbidden all Christians, under pain of the Church's curse, from visiting the Holy Sepulchre.

Letter of the Pope.

We possess a letter of the Pope written to the emperor in these days. It is full of expressions of goodwill and rejoicing, and ends as follows: "Thou, most beloved son, now that thou dost see our silence broken and the bonds of our tongue loosed, receive the Apostolic greeting and blessing to the end that the whole Church may find in thee the longed-for fruits, and may fall on its knees and pray for the happy continuance of thy empire, and the prosperity of thy person; and also may the Heavenly Emperor hear the prayers of the Church and direct thy steps in the way of eternal salvation."

Henry VI.'s crusade, although Celestine did not at once perceive it, was about as worldly an undertaking as was ever put in progress. His idea was to subject Palestine, to compel the tributary states of Eastern Rome to bow to his sceptre, and then, from on all sides, to close in upon the Byzantine Empire. How grandly the religious enthusiasm of the age worked into his all-comprising plans ! Real object of the crusade.

The preparations for the crusade were zealously carried forward. In December, 1195, Henry held a diet at Worms, where for a week, the papal legate at his side, he sat several hours daily on a throne in the cathedral to receive the vows of the crusaders. The excitement was far greater than it had been even at the time of Barbarossa's expedition ; archbishops and bishops, dukes and counts hastened to take the cross .

An embassy arrived in these days from Amalrich of Lusignan, to whom Richard of England had given the throne of Cyprus, and who now offered to become the vassal of the emperor. Henry sent him a golden sceptre and a promise to crown him on his way to Jerusalem. Leo of Armenia had already done homage, having come to the conclusion that the Eastern empire was too weak to protect him.

Before leaving Germany Henry made his greatest attempt to strengthen his royal prerogative. He brought forward a law before the princes which, if it had actually passed into practice, would have fundamentally altered the constitution of the empire, and made it as much a hereditary monarchy as England and France had become. But how much more extended, how much more powerful ! Of what splendid resources would it have had the disposal ! Henry VI. proposes to make the throne hereditary.

What Henry demanded was two-fold : that the crown should be settled on his own house for ever, and that the Norman kingdom of Sicily should be consolidated with Germany. All barriers were to fall, and the Emperor of the Romans, as such, was to have undisputed sway from the North Sea to the Mediterranean.

Henry VI.'s
plans
acceded to
by the
princes.

The moment for bringing forward these proposals was well chosen. Henry was at peace with the papacy and, in bond with it, was about to fulfil the highest mission of a mediæval emperor, and to march out against the enemies of the Christian religion. Powerful inducements, too, were offered to the ecclesiastical and lay princes. The latter were promised that fiefs of the empire, which had hitherto lapsed to the crown on the death of the last male holders, might henceforth descend to daughters or go over to the nearest relatives in an indirect line. The prelates were offered the emperor's renunciation of the "right of spoils," a right, indeed, which they had never in theory acknowledged, but which had none the less been exercised to the detriment of the several sees.

At the brilliant diet of Würzburg (April, 1196) Henry's plans were, for the moment, acceded to by the princes present, who drew up charters and sealed them with their various seals. The emperor then and there proceeded to confer Thuringia on the daughter of the landgrave, Herrmann.

Henry VI.
in Italy,
1196 A.D.

Apparently at the goal of his desires, he departed for Italy in the summer of 1196, intending to superintend in Apulia the preparations for the crusade, and to procure the coronation of his son, Frederick II., at the hand of the Pope.

The Lombard cities, which had not been on the best of terms of late with Henry VI., feared at this time that it was intended to turn the crusading forces against themselves. The representatives of thirteen towns took an oath to uphold against anyone and everyone the rights granted by the peace of Constance.

But Henry had larger prey in view. He left the cities to their own dissensions, which kept them fully occupied.

Philip of
Hohen-
staufen.

In Tuscany, which had been given as a fief to Philip of Hohenstaufen, the power of the empire was fully established. Philip entitled himself "Duke of Tuscany and lord of all lands of the late Countess Matilda." But the Pope had begun to feel the inconvenience of having so proud and influential a neighbour; he was becoming aware, too, of the true import of Henry's crusading zeal. He entered into negotiations now, for his own part, with the Greek Emperor.

Henry's servants were able to intercept messengers of Alexius to the Pope and to possess themselves of the letters which they bore. It came to mutual reproaches now between Celestine and the emperor; the former's principal animadversions were directed against reported misdeeds and oppressions of Philip of Hohenstaufen. The ban of the Church was laid, in a general way however, on the originators of all acts of violence in Tuscany.

Henry VI. instead, as the Pope wished, of entering into a discussion of the evils that were laid to his charge, now demanded the coronation and at the same time the baptism of his son. This coronation, performed on one who had not been elected by the German princes, would have betokened the papal recognition of the heredity of the crown, and an acceptance of Henry's plan of constitutional reform. Of the union of Sicily and Germany too, for the candidate on whom Celestine was asked to place the German crown was the undoubted heir to the Norman kingdom. *Henry VI. and Celestine III.*

Celestine mustered up courage enough to refuse; he insisted moreover that Henry should take the oath of allegiance to himself for his Sicilian possessions. The negotiations lasted three months and at the end of that time the Pope still remained unbending; it must be taken as a sign of his pacific disposition that he did not threaten the emperor with the curse of Rome.

Meanwhile the princes of Germany had been occupying themselves with Henry's plan of reform, against which a violent opposition has declared itself. The right of electing a king was a much cherished privilege which no one was willing to renounce, certainly not for the compensations that had been offered. There was no princely family either that might not eventually hope to see one of its own members on the throne of the empire. Could that throne at any price be allowed to become hereditary in the house of Suabia? *The princes oppose Henry's cherished plan.*

Henry VI. now showed his greatness and his diplomatic *Henry abandons it.*

skill. He saw clearly that his other designs would be frustrated if he were to insist on the carrying through of this one. He retracted his proposition altogether; he did it with such a good grace that those who had been most violently venting their wrath against him now voluntarily chose his son Frederick as his successor. The principle had been rejected, the result for the moment was to be the same.

Henry now laid the question before his nobles whether he should in person proceed to the Holy Land, or whether he should remain in Apulia and direct the undertaking; nothing could have induced him to take this step save his dread of leaving Italy at a time when the Pope was at enmity with him. The nobles answered of course as the emperor had intended, and soon enough it became evident how much his presence was needed.

League of the Pope, the Lombards, and the Sicilians. Henry VI.'s character, as has been seen often enough, was none too gentle. He had, in the first place, injured the national feeling of the Italians by trying to incorporate their land with Germany; he had offended the Lombards in various ways, and he was looked upon with dislike and suspicion by the Sicilians. A harsh judgment passed upon the Count of Acerra at Christmas, 1196, did not mend matters. The count was drawn at the tail of a horse and then hung head downwards from a gallows while the court fool put a stone in the mouth of the dying man to amuse the emperor who was looking on. The Sicilians, the Pope, and the Lombards now formed a league, and the Empress Constance, touched by the complaints of her own people, sided with her husband's enemies. How far she sympathized with the revolt which now broke out in Sicily and with the plan to murder Henry and put up a new ruler is a matter which is not made clear by any of the writers of her time.

Terrible punishments inflicted on the rebels. Henry VI. mastered this rebellion as he had the others; he captured the chief conspirators, and now, in truth, outdid himself in the infliction of severe punishments. Strange to say, such were the sentiments of the times that we owe the recital of these penalties, not to his enemies, but to those among his chroniclers who were his warmest friends and admirers; nor have they a word of blame or even of excuse for their stern master. Yet some of the prisoners were sawn in pieces, others covered with pitch and ignited, others impaled alive. The principal conspirator, the governor of the fortress of San Giovanni, whom it had been intended to make king, was crowned with a red hot crown which was fastened to his head with nails. The Empress Constance was forced to be present at this barbarous scene, the only punishment, so far as is known, that was ever inflicted upon her.

At last Henry VI. was free to pursue his plans for the conquest of the Orient. The Greek emperor was now induced to pay an enormous tribute in order to raise which he tried to impose the so-called "German tax" on all his provinces. This measure raised such opposition that Alexius desisted. He then thought to raise the money by confiscating the holy utensils of the churches, but involved himself thereby in a terrible conflict with his clergy. As a last resort the graves of the former emperors were sacked and the corpses plundered of their gold ornaments. Even the last resting-place of the great Constantine was not spared, although Alexius found in this case that thieves had been there before him and had carried off all that there was of value. *The Greek emperor pays tribute.*

The great crusade started from Apulia in the summer of 1197. Henry had brought together a much greater army even than that which had accompanied Barbarossa. The numbers are placed at 60,000. The emperor had been untiring in his efforts to raise supplies and to remove all hindrances. For the Teutonic order, which had been founded in 1190, and which was likely to prove a valuable ally, he had already gained the confirmation of Clement III., he now himself granted to the new foundation lands and privileges in Italy and Sicily. The brothers were to be allowed to enter Palermo without paying toll; their grain was to be ground free in royal mills; they might exercise the priest's prerogative and extend the last unction to all dying Germans. It was but a year later than this that an assembly of German nobles and *Starting of the great expedition, 1197 A.D.*

of the clergy and barons of Jerusalem solemnly raised the Teutonic brotherhood to be an order of knights which should stand on equal ground with the Templars and the knights of St. John.

Henry VI. at the summit of his glory.

We have reached the period of Henry VI.'s greatest power and glory. Shortly before the Poet Peter of Ebola had exclaimed in his enthusiasm : " Thou wilt once more elevate to the stars the structure of the church and of the empire, and, when there is no enemy remaining thou wilt lay thy bed next to Jove ! "

His death, 1197 A.D.

Henry's ships were now hurrying over the sea to glean him, as he hoped, a new harvest of triumphs. He was master for the moment of all his enemies. Of all but one ; on the fevers of Italy he had not counted. The cold dews of night after a hot day's hunting did more than numerous conspiracies had been able to accomplish. The great emperor, only thirty-two years of age at the end of his eventful life, was laid to rest in the cathedral of Palermo, where one may still stand and muse beside his porphyry sarcophagus.

Failure of the crusade.

The crusade was in the end a failure. The knights of St. John and the Templars had banded together, and even conspired with the infidels against the Germans. The latter, indeed, had made important conquests, notably that of Beirout —but demoralization and dissension had already begun to do their work among them when the news of Henry's death arrived. Many princes at once set sail for home, anxious to secure their lands and their dignities.

Henry VI.'s will.

A few months after the death of the world-monarch a world-pope was enthroned on the chair of Peter, and Henry VI.'s widow did him homage, and allowed appeals to Rome as well as the introduction of papal legates, and the final decision over disputed elections of bishops. She drove all Germans from the court and, finally, on her death-bed made the Pope the guardian of the Norman kingdom and of its youthful heir. In this, indeed, she did not run counter to the intentions of her husband, for Henry VI. had left a will, the terms of which were long kept secret, which pointed to the Pope as the

proper refuge, and which offered him great inducements in
Italy if he would espouse the cause of the young Frederick.

Innocent III. was the counterpart of Henry VI., but the
success of the Pope's plans necessarily betokened the fall and
the ruin of the whole fabric which the ambition of the
emperor had raised.   One of his first steps was to revoke the
privileges granted to the Teutonic order in Sicily.

The power of Innocent III.

Innocent was soon to rule over Tuscany as well as over the
Norman kingdom; over Arragon and Hungary, and over the
new Latin empire in the east, that dream of Henry VI. which
was now actually to be fulfilled.   He, too, was to have
England laid at his feet as a fief, and, more fortunate than
the emperors, he and his successors for nearly a century were
to receive her yearly tribute.

CHAPTER XXI.

Long civil war in Germany.

SELDOM has the loss of any one man affected a country as that of Henry VI. did Germany. The highest pitch of prosperity seemed about to be reached when there came the most utter and entire reaction. Philip of Hohenstaufen later wrote to Innocent III.: "It was astonishing and pitiful, the condition of wild confusion into which the empire came after Henry VI.'s death; how it was torn in pieces, and so shaken in all its parts and boundaries that far-sighted men could doubt with good reason whether in our day it could ever be brought back to its former condition . . . . All Germany was like to a sea lashed by every wind."

The prophecy of the "far-sighted men" was to be only too truly realized. An era of civil war now broke in upon the nation; it was to last, with due interval, for the next twenty years. The cities of Lombardy, Tuscany, and Romagna threw off the German yoke, and began to grasp in all directions for the territory about them that had belonged to the empire.

Italy no longer submissive.

It was at this time—a sure token of regained confidence and audacity—that Cæsarea dropped the name which had been imposed upon her in 1183, and reassumed the old name of Alessandria. The church, too, began energetically to make annexations, and in Tuscany the Papal legates were the prime movers in a series of revolts. A Tuscan League was formed which enjoyed the warm support of Innocent III., while Conrad of Spoleto was induced to resign that duchy in favour of the Church and to return to Germany.

Soon after Henry VI.'s death it became evident that the rule of the Hohenstaufen dynasty had rested more upon the fear than upon the love of its subjects. The young Frederick II., who had been elected but not crowned, had his upholders, it is true; chief among them was his uncle, Philip of Suabia, the most powerful, the richest, the most respected of the princes. But Philip was soon forced by circumstances to abandon the ward for whom he had at first so eagerly entered the lists. He found that a large party, headed by Archbishop Adolph of Cologne, was determined at any and every risk to set aside the youthful Frederick. The Church could not endure the thought of the Sicilian king becoming emperor of the Romans; Frederick, too, was a mere infant, and every one saw that a strong hand was needed at the head of affairs.

Abandonment of Frederick II.

Philip then came forward in his own person as candidate for the throne. He was himself still very young, probably not more than eighteen years of age. He possessed the best qualities of his race, although no opportunity was ever given him of unfolding them. Fair-haired, handsome, and brave, his gentleness and friendliness, as well as his gay disposition, are praised by contemporaries. Walter of the Vogelweid who, like all true poets, was fond of saying much in few words, calls him nothing short of "a sweet young man."

Philip of Hohenstaufen.

Adolph of Cologne, richly endowed as his see had been by Frederick Barbarossa, and many as were the bishoprics under his jurisdiction, was at this time doubly influential as being the representative of the Archbishop of Mayence, who was still absent on the crusade. He was bound, moreover, by ties of friendship to Richard of England; in fact English influence was strongly felt in many ways in Cologne, for between that city and England a busy commerce had begun to be developed. Adolph's attitude with regard to the election of 1198 seems to have been dictated by the purest greed and selfishness. His mind was made up on two points; no Hohenstaufen was to be elected, and any prince who should be chosen must pay dearly for the honour conferred upon him.

Adolph of Cologne.

He offered the crown to Bernard of Saxony, who, however, refused it.

Otto IV.

Adolph's final candidate, and one on whom he was sure that the English king would look with the greatest favour, was to be none other than Otto, the younger son of Henry the Lion—the elder son, Henry of the Rhine Palatinate, was still in Palestine. Once more Guelph was to be pitted against Hohenstaufen, and all the political miseries which that enmity entailed were to be conjured up anew. The fight, indeed, was to be a fiercer one than ever, and its different stages were to be marked as usual by the curses of Rome. Double elections, so common with the papacy, had been known but twice in the history of the empire; they were to be frequent enough in the century that was about to begin. What reckless squandering of territory and riches they were to lead to; how insatiable was to be the greed of the allies sought for by either party!

Philip's election.

Philip of Suabia's election was put through at an assembly held in Thuringia in March, 1198; that prince had not been backward with presents and promises. He was first chosen regent or defender of the kingdom, with powers which were to become void so soon as Frederick II. should appear in the land; but the nobles present came to the conclusion that a stronger title was needed if anything was to be gained, and he was soon in possession of the full royal prerogative.

On the news of these proceedings the followers of Adolph of Cologne were in despair. Having no candidate at hand, as the younger Guelph was still in France, they began negotiations with Duke Berthold of Zäringen. A regular bartering took place for the crown, an unworthy haggling for a few marks of silver more or less. Berthold at last found the sum of the outlays that he was expected to make altogether too high, and, although he had once accepted, finally withdrew. He was soon won by promises from Philip of Hohenstaufen, and acknowledged the latter as king.

Otto's election.

Otto of Brunswick was then chosen by the Cologne party, but not until three months had passed in delays and negotiations.

Otto, only sixteen years old at this time, was scarcely to be called a German at all. Henry the Lion, it will be remembered, had married the sister of King Richard, and this son had been brought up chiefly at the English court. Richard always bore Otto the greatest affection, and had named him Count of Poictou. The uncle and nephew, indeed, were surprisingly similar in character, alike powerful of frame and fond of knightly sports. Richard was now Otto's warmest supporter; he loaded him with riches, as to the amount of which contemporaries tell fabulous tales. English gold was thus pitted against the treasures which Henry VI. had amassed, and which had fallen to Philip of Hohenstaufen.

In 1197, immediately after the death of the great emperor, Pope Celestine III. had formally placed Philip in the ban on account of his proceedings in Tuscany. Innocent III. had offered to absolve him if he would release the Archbishop of Salerno and other Sicilian prisoners who had been carried off to Germany. Innocent's legate, the Bishop of Sutri, performed the absolution before Philip had fulfilled all the necessary conditions, a proceeding for which he atoned on his return to Rome by lifelong imprisonment in a monastery. *Philip loosed from the ban.*

Philip is declared by one of the chroniclers to have been "too tame and benevolent" in the matter of opposing the party of Adolph of Cologne. Why did he not disperse the assembly that met to elect another king? Why did he not wrest recognition of his own claims at the edge of the sword instead of allowing the schemings and deliberations to be uninterrupted during all the ten weeks between his own and Otto's election?

Whatever his grounds for delay, this inactivity cost him dear, for Otto's first step was to take Aix, the old coronation seat of the empire. On the first day after its seizure the antiking affianced himself with the daughter of the Duke of Brabant; on the second he caused himself, at the hand of Adolph of Cologne, to be crowned and anointed—a ceremony which was not performed in Philip's case until some months later. *Otto seizes Aix.*

Y

Otto
squanders
the rights of
the empire.

Otto now possessed a considerable following, chiefly composed of holders of the secular and ecclesiastical dependencies of the see of Cologne; he proceeded to increase it by an almost wanton squandering of the rights and privileges of the empire. Archbishop Adolph, especially, was richly rewarded, and Otto was obliged to swear that he would never try to regain the lands taken from his father and given to Cologne by Frederick Barbarossa. He furthermore renounced the right of spoils, that right which Henry VI. had offered to give up in return for the heredity of the crown.

But his chief concessions were with regard to Italy; he hoped thus to gain the support of Innocent III. He acknowledged all the rights of the Church to the patrimony of Peter, to the Matilda estates, the exarchate of Ravenna, the Pentapolis, the March of Ancona, and the duchy of Spoleto, and offered to aid in recovering and maintaining them. He agreed to act according to the Pope's advice in the matter of the Tuscan and Lombard leagues, and, finally, expressly recognized the Church's suzerainty over the kingdom of Sicily.

Innocent
takes no
part.

Innocent was in no hurry to accept these offers; it remained to be seen if Otto was capable of carrying them into effect. But the deed which was drawn up concerning them on the day of Otto's election was later pointed to as proof positive of the validity of this or that pontifical claim.

One by one the nobles who had been on the crusade reached home and took sides with one or other of the rival claimants. Otto thus gained the support of his brother Henry, Count Palatine of the Rhine, of the Duke of Brabant, and of Landgrave Herrmann of Thuringia.

The war
between
Philip and
Otto.

Philip's following was, on the whole, far more numerous than that of his opponent and, indeed, for the next two years he maintained the ascendancy. No great battle was fought, but Philip burnt Bonn, Remagen, and Andernach, and devastated the Palatinate, while Otto took the imperial city of Nordhausen, and conferred it on Hermann of Thuringia.

The death of Richard of England in 1199 was a great blow to Otto's cause, for although the English king left him heir to

all his jewels and to three-fourths of his treasure, the legacy
was not paid till many years later.   In 1200 King John Lack-
land bound himself in a treaty with France to let his nephew
fall, and it was not till 1208 that he energetically and openly
took his part.   He made agreements with him at different
times, it is true, but they did not signify much more than did
that dead letter compact which Philip entered into with Philip
Augustus in 1198, and which was directed against Richard of
England, " Count Otto," Adolph of Cologne, and other enemies
of the Hohenstaufen king.   And yet these treaties are interesting as showing the effort to carry a German war far out
over the boundaries of Germany.   A few years later that
effort was to succeed, and one single battle was to affect the
fate of the three chief European powers.

Meanwhile Otto's fortunes were at their lowest ebb. Philip   **Otto loses**
had gained the support of the imperial *ministeriales*, of which   **ground.**
new and weighty factor in German politics we shall speak in
another connection.   He had under him, moreover, the
greatest commander of the age, Henry of Kalden, who had
just returned from the crusade.   Strasburg, whose bishop
held to Otto, was forced to surrender, and the landgrave of
Thuringia was induced by Philip, at the cost indeed of
imperial fiefs which Otto had promised but had not been able
to give, to desert the young Guelph.   Even the Archbishop of
Cologne, whose lands had been repeatedly devastated, and who
had been obliged to pawn the treasures of his church, began
to waver.

Innocent III. had not yet taken part for either candidate.   **Represen-**
In May, 1200, forty-eight German princes sent a writing to   **tations to**
the Pope informing him that Philip of Hohenstaufen had been   **Innocent.**
lawfully elected, and warning him to respect the rights of the
empire.   They declared that they were about to lead Philip to
Rome and to procure for him the imperial crown.   Philip
himself also sent envoys.   Innocent expressed to the latter his
satisfaction at their advent; he declared that the final decision in such matters rested of course with the Church.   Had
not the Popes transferred the empire from the east to the

west, and had they not the bestowal of the crown of that empire in their power? There was no Barbarossa now to take offence at such utterances, or at a writing drawn up at this time in which Innocent speaks of the empire as though it were plainly a fief of the papacy.

Innocent for Otto IV.

The only result of the representations made by Philip's followers to Innocent was to induce the latter to declare more openly for Otto. If there was one thing that the Pope dreaded, it was the appearance of another Hohenstaufen in Italy. He sent a writing to those princes whom he considered most influential in Germany, and weighed in the balance the two candidates for his favour. He showed how Philip had been elected in the wrong place and crowned by the wrong bishop; how he had broken his oath of allegiance to the young Frederick, and how at the time of his election he had been in the ban of the church. He depicted the dangers of a new attempt on the part of the Hohenstaufens to found a hereditary monarchy: "if brother should now succeed to brother as son formerly succeeded to father, inasmuch as he would have obtained the kingdom not by their election, but rather by succession, the liberty of the princes would perish." To the announcement of the princes that they would lead Philip to Rome to assume the imperial crown, Innocent answered that he would *summon the lawful king* to his coronation.

Innocent openly takes Otto's part.

In March, 1201, Innocent formally recognized Otto IV. as king and future emperor, bade the clergy of Germany do the like, and promised to absolve the princes from any inconvenient oath in the matter that they might previously have taken. Philip of Hohenstaufen and his upholders were then declared in the ban.

Innocent now unfolded an immense activity in the interests of his pretendant. John of England was ordered to give up the legacy left by Richard, and every effort was made to win over Philip of France. Letter after letter was sent to Germany to this prince or to that; the Duke of Saxony, the Archbishop of Madgeburg and others were promised in the

Pope's own name that Otto would not endeavour to recover the lands of Henry the Lion.

Innocent shows a surprising knowledge of German affairs; he knew just what weakness to appeal to in the case of each particular man of power. A papal legate, Guido of Præneste, was despatched to Germany to confirm Otto's election, and to work in his interests; also to settle the matter of a double election in the archbishopric of Mayence where each of the two great parties had put in its own candidate.

The conflict between the two rival kings had now become a conflict between Church and State. Those of the bishops who still remained faithful to Philip had now to renounce the Pope or at least openly to disobey him. During the next few years Innocent caused many of them to be called to account and managed at every vacancy to secure the election of such men as would be friendly to the Guelphic cause. *Innocent turns the scale in Otto's favour.*

This one man alone, with all the apostles and saints behind him, it is true, and with all the terrors of hell and joys of heaven at his disposal, was able to turn the whole current in Otto's favour. The latter wrote to him later: " My kingship would have dissolved in dust and ashes had not your hand, or rather the authority of the Apostolic chair, weighed the scale in my favour."

Nothing seems to have been holy to Otto except his own personal advancement. In the hope of securing the friendship of the King of Denmark, a friendship which helped him little in the end, he quietly looked on while the Danes wrested Holstein from its duke. He consented to this plundering of the empire as he had formerly consented to renounce Italy. Slowly but surely, however, he made himself master of all the north-western part of Germany, of the land from the North Sea to the Mosel and Werra, and from the French boundary to the Elbe and the Harz. *Successes of Otto IV.*

The upholders of Philip, in the year 1202, sent a stirring protest to Rome: " When have you popes ever read, when have you cardinals ever heard that your predecessors or their envoys have interfered in the elections of the Roman *Protest sent to Rome.*

kings, have played the *rôle* of electors, or have weighed the electoral votes as judges over the election ? We believe you will find no answer."

Innocent deigned to reply to the protesting princes, but, entrenched as he was behind a wall of Biblical quotations and assumptions of almost divine rights, gave them little satisfaction. It was not in the nature of a Pope, of this Pope especially, to give a plain answer to arguments against his own real or fancied prerogatives.

Otto at the height of his power.

Otto stood now at the height of his power. John of England, having just been bereft of his French fiefs for not having appeared to answer the charge of murder, was seized with an excess of great friendliness for his nephew. The partizanship of Ottokar of Bohemia, too, whom Innocent had at last induced to desert Philip, gave Otto an immense advantage. Ottokar did homage to his new liege lord and caused himself to be recrowned at his hands, the papal legate giving him the consecration and the assurance that Innocent would now recognize his royal title, which he had previously disputed. Philip's campaign in Thuringia, in 1203, was not successful; he was unable to hold his own against the landgrave, aided as the latter was by the Count Palatine and the Bohemian king.

The tide turns.

But the tide of Otto's fortunes was at its flood ; all his hard-won acquisitions were now to ebb away.

To those who have followed the splendid struggle made by Barbarossa and his son to uphold the rights of the empire, this civil war in Germany is indeed a sad sight. More disloyalty and baser motives come to the surface than we have yet had to deal with.

Otto IV.'s own brother Henry now deserted him and did homage to Philip. By holding to Otto, Henry had lost the Palatinate, where, as was natural, the sympathies of the people were for the Hohehstaufen. As a recompense he had demanded Brunswick, which was Otto's chief inheritance from Henry the Lion. Otto refused, and the result was Henry's defection from his cause.

Philip now again prepared to subdue Thuringia and marched into the land at the head of such forces that the King of Bohemia, who had prepared to oppose him, was completely intimidated and fled before him. The Thuringian landgrave was compelled to make his submission. He was obliged to listen to contemptuous utterances from Philip, and reflections on the character of a man who had four times changed his party. Lands formerly conceded him were now withdrawn, and his son was retained as a hostage for his good behaviour.

Philip's power in the ascendant.

Ottokar of Bohemia now sought peace of his own accord, and was made to pay a penalty of 7,000 pounds of silver. In the course of a few months Philip regained all that he had lost in the three years that had passed since his enemies had first been induced to rally against him by Innocent III.

One by one Otto's friends deserted him. His greatest loss was Adolph of Cologne, the citizens of whose capital, indeed, still remained true to the Guelph. Innocent, foreseeing what was about to happen, had admonished the faithful burghers in most moving terms : " Can the mother, too, forget her child ? Ye must not abandon this king, your son, as it were, with respect to his kingship. Ye have planted him, now show yourselves careful gardeners." Cologne, indeed, was now the last remaining stronghold of the Guelph.

Otto deserted by his friends.

Adolph himself was to be moved by no representations. He adopted Philip's cause fully and freely, and agreed to make good the one deficiency in the Hohenstaufen's title, and to crown him in the chapel of Charles the Great.

Philip crowned at Aix, 1205 A.D.

This ceremony was performed in January, 1205. Philip laid aside his former crown and submitted to a new election by the princes. He was recrowned by Adolph with the crown of his predecessors. Walter of the Vogelweid declared that it fitted him as though made for him, and that its principal gem, which seems to have been famous under the name of the " orphan," would now be a guiding star to all the princes.

Innocent
bans Otto's
faithless
followers.

Innocent III. hurled the ban at Otto's renegade brother
and at the Duke of Brabant, while Adolph of Cologne was
declared deposed, and a new archbishop, who, however, only
found adherents in the city itself, was set up in his place.
The Pope regarded Adolph as a traitor to himself, "For," as
he said in one of his letters, "in the question concerning the
empire *he* did not follow our judgment but *we* his; he won
us, not we him for Otto, whom he now gives up of his own
accord."

One sees how baneful this interference of the Pope in German
matters had been. For years Innocent III. had fed the
flames of civil war, and had furthered every kind of schism
and disunity; it must not be forgotten that he was the same
relentless and terribly consistent man who a few years later
was to lay waste, and finally to cause the depopulation of
Southern France, the home of the Albigensian heresy.

Philip
defeats Otto,
1205 and 1206
A.D.

King Philip proceeded in person against Cologne and Otto,
who made a sally from behind the walls, was wounded and
driven back. In the next year (1206) the latter determined
to try his fate in the open field, but was defeated near Wassen-
berg; he fled to Brunswick, where he continued for a while to
play the *rôle* of a king, without supporters and without land.

Cologne, from which all supplies had been cut off, was
soon compelled to surrender and to promise fealty to Philip.

Innocent
III. changes
policy.

Innocent III. was too wise a man to try and hold a position which had at last become fully untenable. He now sent
legates to Germany to loose Philip from the ban. That king,
indeed, was obliged to swear the usual oath to the effect that,
as to all the grounds of his excommunication he would implicitly obey the commands of the Pope; but, as the chief
ground had been his wearing of the crown, it will be seen
that the oath was a mere formality.

Both Philip and Otto were induced to leave the decision as
to who should be king in the hands of Innocent; it was no
longer doubtful, however, how that decision would turn out.
It is not even known if it was ever formally rendered. Philip,
none the less, now raised the largest army that had ever stood

at his disposal, intending to attack Otto in Brunswick. The latter had promise of aid from the Danish king and from his uncle, King John. His one idea seems to have been to die like a king at the head of an army ; Denmark and England might see to it from where that army was to come.

Negotiatiations with Innocent had meanwhile been carried on through envoys. The Pope agreed to renounce all lands of the empire in Italy that had been unlawfully appropriated by the Church at Henry VI.'s death. A marriage was furthermore arranged between a nephew of the Pope and a daughter of Philip; the bridegroom was to be invested with Tuscany as a fief. Innocent promised, finally, to crown the Hohenstaufen with the imperial crown as soon as he should come to Italy.

Innocent promises to crown Philip.

How sudden was that change of destiny which now made of Otto IV., instead of a forsaken pretendant preparing to defend his last stronghold, the sole and undisputed ruler of Germany and the emperor of the Romans !

Philip's murder, 1208 A.D.

Philip of Hohenstaufen had, on the morning of June 21st, 1208, attended at Bamberg the marriage of his niece Beatrice with Duke Otto of Meran. In the afternoon he was resting in the archbishop's palace when the count palatine of Bavaria, Otto of Wittlesbach, asked for and obtained admission. Otto had often amused the king with exhibitions of his skill as a swordsman ; for once, however, Philip declared that he was in no mood for such play. " This time it shall be no play " was the fierce answer, and Otto turned his sword against the unsuspecting monarch. " He made a little wound in the neck of the king," says a chronicler, " but he severed the one vital vein."

Philip of Hohenstaufen was slain by no political enemy, by no envoy of the rival king. It was a family difference that brought about the catastrophe, a difference which began with a refusal on Philip's part, in spite of a promise previously given, to allow one of his nieces to become the Wittlesbach's bride.

Philip murdered by a private enemy.

The murderous blow fell upon the king at the moment

when fate seemed at last about to be kind to him; for eight years he had been obliged to fight his way inch by inch to recognition. In the midst of his triumph, when the imperial crown was already within his reach, he was struck down.

Philip's murderer.

According to the custom of the time the nearest relative of a murdered man had to appear in open court and demand vengeahce for the blood that had been shed. In November, 1208, at a diet held by Otto IV. in Frankfort, Philip's eldest daughter was led forward by the bishop of Spires, who had witnessed the crime. Otto of Wittlesbach, as no doubt existed concerning his guilt, was at once condemned and proscribed. He was eventually seized by Henry of Kalden, once the commander of Philip's forces and now the marshal of the empire, who gave him his death with his own hand. The Wittlesbach possessions were given to two of the Guelph's supporters.

CHAPTER XXII.

OTTO IV. AND FREDERICK II.

IMMEDIATELY after Philip's death we see the princes who had been on his side turning one by one to Otto. The latter showed himself only too ready to come to terms with them, to confirm their old privileges and to grant them new ones. In the lands of the influential archbishop of Magdeburg, for instance, he agreed never to erect new mints or to impose new tolls, and never to encamp there without the archbishop's consent. Acknowledgment of Otto IV.

Innocent III. looked upon Philip's death as a righteous judgment of God. He had made his peace with the king, it is true, and had been about to crown him Emperor of the Romans; but that was only because the desertion of Otto by all of his allies had left him no other course. The bishops of Germany were now threatened with the ban and with deposition should they favour the election of any other king than him whom they had so recently abandoned. The secular princes received a similar admonition, and even the citizens of Cologne were not forgotten by the zealous and ever-active Pope.

Otto himself was given a lesson in the difficult art of ruling: "Show good will and condescension, oh dearest son," wrote Innocent, "show honour and favour to all and refrain from hard words and from violent deeds. Do not be backward with making concessions, do not be sparing of promises but also keep them faithfully. . . . Thou must educate thyself to the dignity and the bearing of a king." Innocent and Otto.

During the negotiations in Rome between Innocent and

the envoys of Philip and Otto the question had been broached
of settling the differences between the Guelph and the Hohenstaufen by means of a marriage alliance. Otto himself was
to have wedded Philip's eldest daughter Beatrice.

This plan was now eagerly taken up by Innocent, who
added to his already enormous duties as a correspondent by
writing to the mother of the princess in question, to the
marshal of the empire, Henry of Kalden, and also to those
who had been Philip's representatives in Rome.

It was not to be supposed that Otto's irregular election in
1198 could be simply made binding now on the whole nation.
It was decided, accordingly, that in form at least an entirely
new election should be held.

England and France. Meanwhile England and France began to interest themselves in German affairs as they never had done before.
King John had at last come to the conviction that Otto's
success was a necessary adjunct to his own hoped-for triumph
over Philip of France. The latter king seems to have shared
John's view of the subject; he first wrote and urged Innocent
to prevent Otto's election, and then, having failed to win the
Pope, commenced treating with Philip's widow, in common
with whom he induced the Duke of Brabant to come forward
as candidate for the throne. A candidate almost without a
supporter in Germany, it is true; and even the widow of
Philip could lend him no aid, for she died before the
election.

Otto's election and betrothal. That election, which took place at Frankfort in November,
1208, was a unanimous one; it is interesting to note that
Otto, from now on, when speaking of his dead rival, no
longer refuses him the title of king, although he continues
to date from 1198 as the beginning of his own reign.

At Frankfort the princes urged Otto to complete his reconciliation with the past by wedding Philip's daughter; at
Würzburg in May, 1209, the betrothal was celebrated with
all due form, the Pope having granted a dispensation, as Otto
was distantly related to his young bride.

Innocent's conditions. Innocent III. was ill when the message from Otto concerning his successful and unanimous election arrived; he afterwards declared that the news had made him well. Legates were despatched to Germany to treat of the imperial coronation and to bring forward the conditions which the Pope meant to attach to the performance of that ceremony. Innocent himself wrote to Otto : " Inasmuch as, by the grace of God, true peace and firm concord now exist between the Church and the empire, we have thought best, O dearest son, in order to remove all matter for future dissension and suspicion, to ask certain things of thee which thou altogether must grant without making difficulty; for they accord with reason and with thy salvation."

The requests which Innocent made and which Otto granted were the renewed renunciation of the right of spoils and the recognition of the papal acquisitions in Italy as well as the Pope's suzerainty over the Sicilian kingdom. More than this, Otto swore to help in rooting out heresy, to allow appeals from the tribunal of any bishop in Germany to that of Rome, and to give up all influence over episcopal elections—even that influence which the Church, in the Concordat of Worms of 1122, had acknowledged as rightly belonging to the German king. *Otto's renunciations.*

The only excuse for Otto's consenting to allow Rome to control the rich German sees with their lands and jurisdictions is that he probably never meant to, as he never did, keep his promises in this regard. What he wanted now was the imperial crown ; that crown once gained he did not trouble himself greatly about his promises towards Innocent.

In the summer of 1209 Otto crossed the Brenner, about to begin that strange progress through Italy which was finally to result in the practical loss of his German crown. In Viterbo he met the Pope, who received him as a son and folded him in his arms, but who soon left him to return to Rome and prepare for the coronation. *Otto's progress through Italy, 1209 A.D.*

This ceremony took place October 4th, 1209 ; the usual conflict with the Romans, who were offended because Otto had not negotiated with them and had granted them no new *The coronation, 1209 A.D.*

privileges, cast its shadow on the day. The new emperor found the streets of the city so insecure that he refused the Pope's invitation to the usual coronation banquet, and carried Innocent off to his own camp without the walls, where he caused a feast to be prepared. When they separated after this friendly meal it was for ever. In more senses than in one their ways were henceforward to lie apart.

Europe too small for a pope and an emperor.

The history of the last years of the mediæval German Empire shows most clearly that there was not room in Europe for two such claimants to world rule as the Pope of Rome and the ʃholy Roman Emperor. Beginning with Frederick Barbarossa three successive German monarchs had been placed in the ban—Henry VI. not openly so, indeed, during his lifetime, but at his death Celestine III. had declared that by taking captive a crusader, Richard of England, he had *ipse facto* fallen under the curse. Celestine had long refused to have Henry buried in consecrated ground.

We shall now see how the very men who had been the Church's creatures, as it were—Otto IV. and Frederick II.—were each in turn to find it impossible to satisfy that Church's claims, and to live with it on a peaceful footing.

Otto comes into conflict with Innocent.

During the months which followed his coronation, Otto devoted himself to the bringing of order into the affairs of Northern and Central Italy.

He travelled from city to city settling disputes and reclaiming the rights and estates of the empire. His object was the restoration of things to the state in which they had been at the death of Henry VI. in 1197. In Ferrara he fulfilled one at least of his engagements towards the Pope by banning the heretics there, and decreeing the confiscation of their goods.

The break with Innocent came when Otto made common cause with Count Dipold of Acerra, who for twelve years had combatted the Pope's influence in the kingdom of Sicily. Dipold was given Spoleto, and was allowed to call himself "grand captain" of Apulia and Calabria. If such a title was to be given it was the prerogative of Frederick of Sicily, and

of him alone, to give it.   Innocent now accused Otto of
stretching out his hand for the Sicilian crown, as well as for
the patrimony of Peter.

Otto did in truth now proceed to the conquest of lands
claimed by the Papacy on the borders of Tuscany—lands to
which indeed the empire had an equally good title.   Radi-
cofani and Montefiascone fell into his hands.

He prepared, too, for the expedition into Southern Italy
so dreaded by the Pope.   Pisa, in return for a promise of aid
against Genoa, engaged to supply him with forty galleys at
her own expense, and as many more as he might choose to
pay for.

By the end of the year 1210 the emperor had proceeded as
far as Capua, where he entered into winter quarters.   Innocent
III. at this time seems to have been utterly helpless ; he implied as much himself in a letter to the consuls of Terracina,
in which he spoke of a rushing torrent that he was unable to
stem.   All the same he wrote to Otto : " If thou dost continue
in thine obstinacy we cannot help but punish thee with the
anathema."

Innocent
helpless.

On the news that Otto had crossed the boundaries of the
Sicilian kingdom Innocent carried his threat into execution ;
one more emperor was declared accursed, and his subjects
freed from their oath of allegiance.

The ban
against
Otto IV.,
1210 A.D.

Innocent, with his usual political forethought, began at
once to raise up for himself friends in the struggle that had
thus broken out.   He became reconciled to the deposed
Adolph of Cologne ; he made overtures to Philip Augustus,
who had long been in the ban on account of steps taken to
divorce his queen, Ingeborg.

The Pope now begged the King of France for forces and
money to be used in Apulia, and especially did he urge him
to manipulate the German princes, and to raise up such a
rebellion amongst them as should compel Otto to leave
Italy.

The Pope
and the king
of France.

With respect to the latter of these commissions Philip was
able to answer : " Know that we think to have already seen

to this well and thoroughly." As to the former he proposed that Innocent should force the clergy of France to contribute a third of their income, and offered for his own part to give up a third of the amount due from the clergy to the crown.

Otto and John of England.

King John of England had meanwhile been in constant communication with Otto; it was evident that when the struggle came it would not be between the Pope and the emperor alone. The first question of general European importance had arisen; it was the birth time of really great alliances.

Innocent to the German princes.

Innocent III. wrote to the German princes giving the grounds upon which he had placed Otto in the ban; chief among them was the attack on Sicily. He declared that the emperor, in having commenced this attack without seeking the advice of his nobles, was threatening the very foundations of princely power. "Should he accomplish his purpose in this regard he will then crush you down into a condition such as that to which the English barons have been reduced by his relatives. Brought up in England he will do his utmost to introduce also into the empire the customs of that land."

Innocent went on to say that he had been deceived in Otto as God Himself had once been deceived in Saul—indeed this comparing of himself to the Divinity was not uncommon with this supremest of supreme pontiffs.

Otto against Frederick II.

Otto's expedition against the Sicilian kingdom was so successful that in a few months almost all the mainland provinces had fallen into his power, and the young King Frederick's days of royalty seemed numbered. The latter is said to have kept a galley moored in the harbour of Palermo always ready to carry him at a moment's notice to the shores of Africa.

It was to the church that Frederick owed his deliverance; he was later often enough reproached with ingratitude to that institution which had indeed preserved to him his throne.

Rebellion in Italy and Germany.

Innocent succeeded in his efforts to raise up a rebellion in Germany; its heads were Archbishop Siegfried of Mayence,

King Ottokar of Bohemia, and Landgrave Herrmann of Thuringia—that eager and industrious changer of parties.

In Italy already, in various ways, the Pope had induced or compelled a number of cities to renounce the emperor. Bologna, for instance, had been threatened not only with ban and interdict but with the closing of her famous university.

Innocent finally issued a manifesto to the princes of the empire in which he exhorted them to proceed to the election of a new ruler. He showed them how God had reproved Saul and had substituted one younger than he, who had obtained the kingdom and held it.

Under this "one younger than he" Innocent meant beyond a doubt King Frederick of Sicily. To be sure he was one of the hated race of Hohenstaufen; the dreaded union, too, of the Sicilian and German crowns in one hand would now take place. But Frederick had already taken the oath of allegiance for Sicily, and before procuring his election to the German throne it was possible to hamper him with every kind of condition that the heart of the Pope might desire. *Frederick II. called to the German throne, 1211 A.D.*

Towards the end of February, 1211, those of the German princes who were in rebellion met at Nuremberg and decided to offer the crown of the empire to him who, as seems to have been expressly emphasized, had already once previously received their oath of allegiance. All the former merits and services of the Hohenstaufens were now recalled to memory. Envoys were despatched to Frederick to invite him to come to Germany; each prince, writing individually, assured him that he would at once be formally elected king.

Frederick of Hohenstaufen, worthy in many ways to be compared with his noble grandfather Frederick Barbarossa, was at this time seventeen years of age, and had already married, in 1209, the widowed ex-queen of Hungary, Constance of Arragon. This union had been the work of Innocent III. *Frederick's youth.*

Frederick's youth had been passed in Sicily in the midst of constant wars and party intrigues. Of immense influence on his character, and on his whole career, had been his contact with those Saracens who had settled in Sicily and who had re-

z

mained, in spite of occasional persecutions, on friendly terms with the Norman kings.

Saracen influence.

All around Palermo were Moorish palaces and country houses with their parks and gardens, while in the town itself a number of merchants traded peaceably with the Christian inhabitants. Many of the court servants were Mohammedans, as were also some of the young king's teachers, and Frederick always more or less retained his oriental surroundings. His morals and his religious orthodoxy alike suffered from this intercourse, for he continued to keep a harem almost to the end of his days, and Pope Gregory IX. was able at the last to give a goodly list of his heretical acts and utterances.

The great service that the Saracen culture did for Frederick was to train his mind in the appreciation of art, science, and literature, and to give him broad views of philosophy and of the duties of a monarch. Was it not he who declared that persons who continued to believe in the ordeals or judgments of God were not so much to be corrected as to be laughed at ?

Frederick's character and personality.

Frederick tells us himself in one of his numerous letters that he spent all his spare moments in reading and in acquiring knowledge. A record still remains of his having sent to the university of Bologna "various compilations from Aristotle and other philosophers formerly published in Greek and Arabic and relating to controversial and mathematical subjects."

In person Frederick, like his immediate ancestors, was not imposing. According to one account he was "red, bald, and shortsighted," and he is known to have been small of stature. A Mohammedan historian, who described him at the time of his crusade (1228-9) is of the opinion that as a slave he would not have brought two hundred drachmæ.

Otto IV. returns to Germany.

Otto IV. was on the point of crossing over to Sicily when the tidings of the rebellion and of the danger to his throne reached him. "He was struck by grief of heart," as an annalist tells us. His first thought was to continue on his way and to try and overcome Frederick before the latter could leave Sicily. But the representations of the German and Lombard envoys who had brought him the news caused him to change his mind. He returned to Germany, stopping however to settle disputes and to make changes in the administration of those cities in northern Italy on the allegiance of which he could still count. Chief among these was Milan. By the middle of March, 1212, he was in Frankfort. Otto's mere presence in Germany, representing as he did the only legal and legitimate power, was enough to influence in his favour many wavering elements that would otherwise have joined his enemies. The opposition was soon confined to Mayence, Bohemia, and Thuringia.

The emperor thought now to further his influence with the friends and supporters of the Hohenstaufens by at last consummating his union with the daughter of Philip of Suabia. The marriage ceremony was performed at Nordhausen in July, 1212, in the midst of the tumult of war ; Otto was engaged at the time in devastating the lands and besieging the castles of Landgrave Herrmann of Thuringia. *Marriage of Otto with Beatrice of Hohenstaufen, 1212 A.D.*

The campaign was progressing favourably, all the plans of the Guelphic monarch seemed about to meet with success, when once more his good fortune suddenly and unaccountably turned her back upon him—this time for ever.

Otto's young bride died suddenly within three weeks after her wedding day ; the news came that Frederick of Sicily was about to appear in Germany, and those Suabians, whom regard for the daughter of Philip of Hohenstaufen had thus far caused to hold to Otto, left his camp in a body. *General defection from Otto.*

The Bavarians followed suit, and the imperial army dwindled so rapidly that Otto was obliged to give up the siege of Weissensee, although that stronghold was almost on the point of capitulating. He marched off to the south to meet and turn back if possible the approaching danger.

Frederick of Sicily had hesitated long before accepting the invitation of the German princes ; but at last he found that he had scarcely an alternative. It must be remembered that his own lands of Apulia and Calabria were already in the hands of Otto who, on leaving Italy, had by no means given *Frederick II. leaves Sicily.*

up his conquests; on the contrary, he had taken every means to permanently secure them. So soon as Otto should make peace with or subdue the rebels in Germany he would be free to continue his previous policy and to wrest from Frederick what remained of his kingdom.

Frederick does homage to the Pope. Before embarking on his new undertaking, Frederick renewed his oath of allegiance to the Pope and did homage to him, at the same time confirming the concordat drawn up between the Church and the Empress Constance in 1198. Finally, at Innocent's command, Frederick's infant son Henry was crowned King of Sicily which was to be his special and only heritage. Everything in human power had been done to prevent the union in one hand of Germany, and the Sicilian kingdom.

Frederick at this time was full of real devotion to Innocent. He names himself King of Sicily and Emperor Elect of the Romans " by the grace of God and of the Pope." Innocent is said to have spoken of him as " the Church's son."

Frederick comes to Germany. His adventures. Frederick's journey through Lombardy was full of danger and adventure. Cremona, head of the one faction among the cities, was friendly to him; her rival, Milan, hostile. On one occasion he only escaped falling into the hands of the Milanese by swimming across a river on an unsaddled horse; " he washed his trousers in the Lambro," to use the derisive words of a Milan chronicler.

Frederick finally entered Germany over the Rhætian Alps and by way of Coire, having purposely, without army as he was, avoided the greater Alpine passes. Ecclesiastical princes such as the Bishop of Coire, the Abbot of St. Gall and, after some hesitation, the Bishop of Constance, furnished him escort. He was soon in Suabia, in the land of his ancestors and the home of his strongest adherents.

Here, from the very first, Otto had been unpopular; he had seemed to the Suabians harsh and unbending, and even his conscientious attempts to administer justice had been looked upon as acts of tyranny.

Frederick's following grew from day to day; he was obliged,

however, to pay his supporters by liberal promises of lands
and of rights that belonged to the empire.

Frederick soon discovered how much of Otto's strength lay
in the alliance with John of England, and how important it
was for himself to secure the friendship of Philip of France.
With this end in view he had a meeting with the heir to the
French throne at Toul in November, 1212. For his own part
he promised to make peace neither with Otto nor with the
English king without Philip's knowledge. The latter at
this time placed large sums at the disposal of his ally, and
Frederick distributed these new resources with so free a hand
that the fame of his liberality proved one of his strongest
advocates with the German princes.

Frederick and Philip of France.

A few weeks later Frederick was formally elected king at
Frankfort and crowned at Mayence by Archbishop Siegfried.
The rightful insignia were in Otto's possession, but others
were made in imitation of them.

Frederick elected king, 1212 A.D.

The princes took oath that even should Frederick die they
would never again acknowledge Otto.

The factors that had raised Frederick on the throne were
the authority of the papacy, the influence of France, the
satisfaction of the demands of the princes, the prestige of his
race and, finally, his own personality. To add to his triumph
Henry of the Palatinate, who for his own part remained true
to his brother Otto, was obliged by the sentiments of his subjects to renounce his principality in favour of his son whom
he allowed to do homage to the Hohenstaufen.

The one unfortunate part of Frederick's elevation was that
he had been obliged to hamper himself with promises to the
Church. He now, in a charter drawn up at Eger and signed
with a golden seal, agreed to all the renunciations in Italy
that Otto had made, gave up the right of spoils and the
royal influence on episcopal elections, and acknowledged
without reserve the right of the German bishops to make
appeals to Rome.

Frederick's promises to the Church.

The great significance of the charter of Eger lies in the
fact that its engagements were not merely personal as they

The Charter of Eger.

had been in the case of the grants made by Otto IV., but that
they were made with the consent of the princes and under
their witness; a fact which Innocent caused to be especially
emphasized in the final version of the document. Each
prince, too, was made to declare in a separate charter that he
had agreed to and signed the chief instrument.

The empire was now bound as firmly as possible so far as
these promises to the Church were concerned. The Pope had
at last a legal claim to vast territories in central Italy and
especially to the Matilda estates. The renunciation of the
influence over episcopal elections changed the character on
the one hand of the ecclesiastical principalities, on the other
of the German monarchy itself. The bishops were now completely under the influence of Rome, while their sees became
more and more independent of the empire to which they
nominally belonged. The crown was obliged to look round
for new props to sustain its power.

**Otto's re-
treat to
Brunswick.**
Otto IV., all this time, had not been idle, as the fearful
desolation in Thuringia and in parts of Saxony could best
bear witness. The English king had kept him supplied with
funds, and he was able to prevent a diet at Merseburg which
Frederick had intended to hold.

Otto was finally obliged, however, to retreat to his old
refuge of Brunswick; his opponents had intended to seek
him out here, but were so long detained by the siege of
Quedlinburg that the cold weather put an end to the
campaign.

**England and
France.**
Otto had not yet given up hope, but he had determined
that the conflict should be fought out on another field of
war. He had sent to John of England urging him to attack
France, and announcing to him that not only he himself, but
also the Dukes of Flanders and Limburg and the Counts
of Holland and Boulogne, were ready to aid in such an
enterprise.

Philip of France, for his part, was preparing for an invasion
of England, an expedition which he was able to look upon as
undertaken in a holy cause. In January, 1213, he was ex-

pressly admonished on the part of the Pope to carry into execution the ban that had been laid upon the luckless King John. Philip was able to comfort himself with the thought that his enemies were the enemies of the Church, and that God's curse rested on them.

Innocent, indeed, soon changed his policy, accepted the complete surrender that John, in dread of his barons, made to him, and became feudal lord of England. It was now in his interest to prevent the French war that he had done his best to bring about, but it was too late. Large armies had been raised on both sides, and Philip Augustus proceeded to lay waste the lands of the Count of Flanders, intending then to cross the Channel. His fleet was attacked and destroyed by the English, and he himself was obliged to retreat and to abandon his Flemish conquests. *French defeat.*

At the end of the year 1213 the English-Guelphic coalition was so in the ascendant that it was decided to strike a final and decisive blow at France; it was intended to annihilate the latter Power as a state organization. Otto considered that it would be a light matter then to strike down the opposition in Germany and to make his peace with Rome. *Invasion of France.*

In the winter of 1214 John crossed with his army from Portsmouth to La Rochelle. He was able for a time to occupy Poitou, but was driven out by the French crown prince.

Otto IV. was meanwhile approaching from Aix-la-Chapelle; on his course he had managed to gain over the Duke of Brabant, who was the French king's son-in-law. He now became the emperor's father-in-law, for Otto wedded that same Maria who had been affianced to him in 1198. No priest dared to bless this union with one who was in the Church's ban, and the Duke of Holland gave the bride to her imperial husband.

The climax of the struggle between the rival claimants in Germany, as well as of that between France and England, had now been reached. Otto had the advantage of numbers, but his army was composed of adventurers, and was practically under many commanders. The soldiers of Philip Augustus were fighting for their own altars and their hearths and were under their one royal leader.

The crash of the opposing forces came at Bouvines, not far from Tournay (July 27th, 1214) ; the attack was begun by the allies and the battle raged for hours with terrible severity. But at last the day—the greatest single day in the history of the Middle Ages—turned in favour of the French. Otto fled from the field of battle, but only when all hope was over. His army was all but annihilated and his ally, the Duke of Flanders, was taken prisoner.

Now and henceforward King John of England left Otto to his fate, and closed a six year truce with Philip Augustus.

The battle of Bouvines is particularly memorable as having been the birthday of France's greatness. Her king had not only conquered his great German enemy, not only reduced his old foe of England to sue for peace, but he had, with the forces of the French communes, become master of his own vassals, many of whom, like the Count of Boulogne, had fought on Otto's side.

Philip Augustus sent the gilded imperial eagle that he had captured on the field of battle to Frederick II., having first caused its broken wings to be mended. A highly symbolical gift, for Frederick had indeed only the French king to thank for the boon of the royal power.

The Hohenstaufen himself was at this time engaged in raising and mustering an army, but the decisive blow had been struck before he was ready with his preparations. He now marched first against Aix-la-Chapelle, which he was unable to take, and then against the Dukes of Brabant and of Limburg, who were reduced to subjection. The Counts of Cleves and Juliers and other allies of Otto were also induced to make their peace.

Aix, Cologne—where he had taken refuge—and the smaller towns of Landskron and Kaiserswerth were Otto's only remaining strongholds, and everywhere the voice of the people had turned against him. He lived on pittances sent him from England, while, to add to his misfortunes, his wife,

Maria of Brabant, developed an uncontrollable passion for gaming. There are memoranda of accounts still remaining to show that he had to pay debts for her to no inconsiderable amount, and that, too, with borrowed money.

Everywhere new friends rallied to Frederick; Burgundy, Friaul, and Istria declared for him, as did also the King of Denmark, who seized or devastated the lands of Otto's northern followers.

Frederick II. and Denmark.

King Waldemar, indeed, was paid as the Pope had been by a renunciation on a large scale to possessions of the empire. At a diet at Metz, Frederick and his princes surrendered the lands that Denmark had just conquered; in fact, all the imperial territory beyond the Elbe and the Eider.

Frederick must not be too harshly blamed for this transaction; he was not in a position to prevent the Danes from claiming what they wished. It was better for him to have them as friends than as enemies. He felt the shame of the compact, indeed, and later was glad enough to seize an opportunity for rendering it null and void.

Frederick's next triumphs were the subjection of Aix-la-Chapelle and the taking of Kaiserswerth. In the former town, the usual coronation place, he was now crowned king by Siegfried of Mayence, July 25th, 1215. His contemporaries consider this the real beginning of his reign.

Frederick's triumphs.

Here at Aix Frederick, in the enthusiasm of the moment, took a step which, more than he himself or any one else could have dreamed, was to influence the whole future course of his life. He allowed one of the crusade preachers present to affix the cross to his shoulder; he vowed a vow upon the fulfilment of which the Church was to insist with iron inflexibility. For the next thirteen years Frederick was to be like a man with a millstone tied around his neck.

Frederick takes the Cross.

From Aix Frederick proceeded against Cologne, which, although in spite of the papal interdict it had held faithfully to Otto for seventeen months, was now glad enough to rid itself of its dangerous guest, even allowing him to depart with his debts unpaid, and giving him money to help him on

Cologne receives Frederick.

his way. The empress, in order to be the more thoroughly secure from recognition, donned the garb of a pilgrim.

Cologne received Frederick in its midst and promised to do him homage; its submission betokens the completion of that change which brought the burghers of Germany over to the side of him who had been essentially the chosen of the princes. Even now these two opposing political factors, the cities and the princes, were not to continue long in perfect harmony.

Otto IV. was left to depend on the lands of his house in Saxony and on the help of the Ascanian dukes—those descendants of Albrecht the Bear who were to be the ancestors of the later Hohenzollerns and Wettiners. In Lombardy and Tuscany, too, a few cities remained faithful to him until the day of his death.

Culmination of the power of Innocent III. If the year 1215 marks the ebbing of Otto's power it marks the culmination of that of Innocent III.; nothing could now happen in any part of Europe without his claiming and exercising the right of interference. France, England, and Germany were submissive to his will. He had summoned a great council to be held in the Lateran at Rome; and Milan and Piacenza, Cremona and Pavia had promised to send representatives who should witness the final settlement of the dispute concerning the throne of the empire.

Innocent had gone his way steadily gaining power for the Church. His courage had been broken by no reverses. He had been obliged to declare first for, then against Otto of Brunswick; first against and then for Philip of Suabia. He had been forced to consent to a far closer union than he had wished of Germany and Sicily. But he was now to preside over the stateliest assembly of the century, and to render the last verdict in the strife that had gone on for generations between the Guelphs and the Hohenstaufens.

The Lateran Council of 1215 A.D. Seventy-one primates and archbishops—among them the German patriarch of Constantinople and the patriarch of Jerusalem—more than four hundred bishops and eight hundred abbots and priors met together in the palace of the

Lateran ; eight kings and countless princes and cities had sent envoys. Various matters were at issue, among them the bettering of the Church organization and the announcement of a crusade ; seventy canons on these matters were drawn up to Innocent's satisfaction.

When the question of the conflict concerning the German throne came up an effort was made by the supporters of Otto to win the members of the council over to the latter's side. A writing was published at this time which advocated appealing to the council as a whole from the decrees of a pope who was not " Innocentius " but " Nocentius," not " Apostolicus " but " Apostaticus."

It was too late for such an attempt as this ; one of the last proceedings of the assembly was to renew the deposition and banning of Otto, and to confirm the election of Frederick as future emperor. *Council confirms Frederick II.'s election.*

It was among the last acts of Innocent III., too, to promulgate these decrees ; he died of a fever in July, 1216. His successor was Honorius III., known to be a person with no great force of character and one not likely to make himself greatly feared.

Otto IV. now occupied himself, with the help of his allies, the Margrave of Brandenburg and the Duke of Saxony, in ravaging the lands of the Archbishop of Magdeburg. Frederick hastened to the latter's aid and drove Otto once more to retreat to Brunswick. Magdeburg had suffered severely from the Guelph's devastations; it was a common saying of the time that an Emperor Otto and an Archbishop Albrecht had been the founders alike and the destroyers of the see. *End of Otto IV.*

But Otto's unhallowed and disastrous course was at length run ; he died in Harzburg from an overdose of a remedy to which he was partial. It healed the ill from which he most suffered, that of having lived too long.

On his death-bed a Cistercian monk loosed him from the ban, gave him the last unction and the Holy Eucharist. He seems to have been seized with a fury of repentance ; again and again he confessed his sins against the Church, and *Dies as an emperor.*

priests were told to scourge him until the blood should flow. Against their will they applied the rod, a *miserere* being chanted the while.

In the midst of his self-abnegation, of his rendings of the heart, Otto never gave up the claim of being rightful emperor. Even while promising implicit submission to the will of the Pope he emphasized the fact that he had been lawfully and with due solemnity crowned and that nothing had happened which could deprive him of his throne.

In making his will he enjoined on his brother not to hand out the insignia of the empire either to him who should in future be chosen, or "to him who is now elected" until twenty weeks after his own death. He wanted it to seem as though no compulsion had been exercised upon him.

Is buried as one. He passed away on the 19th of May, 1218, and was buried in the church of St. Blasius in Brunswick. According as he himself had provided he was laid to rest in royal garments, a crown on his head, the sceptre in his right hand, the imperial orb in his left; a sword was at his side.

Otto may have taken pleasure at the last in knowing that his rank would be thus asserted; the Germans of to-day can only look with sadness and regret on his fatal attempts to reign. How often had those attempts been renewed in these twenty dark years of German history

CHAPTER XXIII.

FREDERICK II.'S CRUSADE.

HENRY of Brunswick, the brother of Otto IV., only too Otto's brother delivers up the insignia. faithfully carried out the latter's last wishes as to the insignia of the empire. The twenty weeks and more passed away, and they still remained in his possession.

Not that he for a moment thought of renewing the claim of the Guelphs to the crown; he wished, however, to set a price on the insignia, and Otto had once enjoined him to see if he could not rescue some of the lands that had belonged to Henry the Lion. But the duchy of Saxony, as well as Henry of Brunswick's former principality, the Rhine Palatinate, were now in the hands respectively of the Ascanians and Wittlesbachs, whom Frederick had no wish to offend. Henry finally, after having at Frederick's request been threatened with the ban by Pope Honorius, compromised for a large sum of money, 14,000 marks, and for the title of imperial vicar for the territory between the Elbe and the Weser, and delivered up those emblems the symbolical importance of which made them worth so much more than their own intrinsic value.

The matters of greatest interest in the history of Frederick II. are his relations to the Popes and to the Lombard cities, and his pacification and administration of the kingdom of Sicily. To this last topic, affecting as it does only indirectly the history of Germany we shall by no means be able to do justice.

The war with the popes, which was to reach its climax Frederick's struggle with the popes. under Gregory IX. and Innocent IV., was to be the death struggle of the empire, so far as that empire could claim to be universal. An empire, still called "holy" and "Roman," was to emerge again after the general anarchy which immediately preceded, and which followed upon Frederick's death; but it was to have far other aims and objects than the world-monarchy of a Henry VI. Italy, the goal that had lured so many German emperors and so many German armies to their ruin, was to play no part in the new order of affairs.

Frederick's vow, taken in a moment of enthusiasm at the time of his coronation in 1215, was the pretext for an unlimited interference on the part of Honorius III. and his successors in the matter of the movements of that monarch. To them the crusade was his holiest and chief duty, while to him one complication after another seemed to require his more immediate attention.

Honorius III, becomes uneasy. First and foremost it was necessary to provide for the administration of Germany, so recently full of turmoil, during an absence of its head which might last no one knew how long.

The young king of Sicily, Henry VII., had at Frederick's command been brought by his mother to Germany, and invested with the duchy of Suabia. However unpleasant such a proceeding must have seemed to the Pope, Honorius had made no objection. Frederick now proposed that his son should be elected king of the Romans and should rule in his own stead, under proper guardians, while he was away from Germany.

The Pope became uneasy; would not the dreaded union of the two crowns in one hand thus become an accomplished fact? Frederick had given a promise in 1216 to the effect that, when he himself should become emperor, all connection with Sicily should cease; that promise was now about to become meaningless and void.

Frederick assured Honorius that his only object was to further the cause of the crusade by providing for the peace of Germany, and that nothing would be changed in the relations of Sicily to the papal chair. This Hohenstaufen was so immeasurably superior to the Pope in diplomatic talent, and in the clearness of perception that prevented him from ever losing sight of any desired goal, that he was able in this matter to put through his will without giving Honorius any really valid excuse for objecting to the young Henry's election.

That election took place in April, 1220, the princes of their own accord having come to the conclusion that the only way to avoid a new season of anarchy was to have a fitting representative for Frederick. The latter was able to tell the Pope that he himself had scarcely been consulted in the matter and that he should not consider Henry's elevation valid until he, Honorius, should have given his consent. Election of Frederick's son, 1220 A.D.

The princes thus took upon themselves the whole responsibility in the matter ; they deputed one of their number to go to Rome and to bring Honorius a written assurance, sealed with their own seals, to the effect that the empire would claim no jurisdisdiction or right of interference in Sicily.

The embassy was, for various reasons, delayed, and Honorius was beginning to be offended at not receiving the official announcement of so important a matter as the election when Frederick despatched a comprehensive statement drawn up by himself of all that had taken place. He succeeded in pacifying the Pope ; the more so as he himself had just made, in all due form, a most important grant of privileges to the ecclesiastical princes of Germany. By it the absolute right of bishops to will away their property had been acknowledged ; should they die intestate, their successors were to inherit their movable goods. The king had further agreed henceforward to found no new toll-centres and no new mints in territory under the jurisdiction of ecclesiastics and to receive no one in his cities who, bound to such princes by ties of dependency, should have tried to escape from their jurisdiction. New grant to the Church.

Frederick had undertaken, finally, to place in the ban of the empire all persons who for more than six weeks should be under the Church's curse. The excommunication would indeed have become a dreaded weapon in the hands of the bishops had this clause of the agreement been rigorously

carried into effect.   But it never was; and King Rudolph of
Hapsburg later, while confirming Frederick's charter of privileges as a whole, left it out entirely.

Frederick's policy in Germany.

Frederick had been obliged to deed away right and left the
prerogatives of the empire, but the blame for his so doing
attaches more to his predecessors than to himself.   The
princes had tasted the joys of independence, it was no longer
possible to hold them back.   Times had changed since a
Charlemagne or even since a Frederick Barbarossa could impose his will upon them.   They were to proceed now slowly
but uninterruptedly on their way to absolute sovereignty; by
the fifteenth century the map of Germany was to assume that
kaleidoscopic form which it was to retain until the beginning
of our own generation.

As to Frederick II., he gave to the nobles and clergy
of Germany almost everything that they demanded, and then
to a large extent left the land to its fate.   There is no doubt
but that he, "the child of Apulia" as he had been called at his
first coming, preferred his southern kingdom, and devoted his
best energies to its interests.

Frederick's crusade delayed.

The vow concerning the crusade, much as it was later to
hamper Frederick, proved at first a means of gaining the
Pope's consent to various measures.   One of these had been
the election of Henry VII. as king of the Romans; another
was the coronation as emperor of Frederick himself.

The crusade had already been planned and postponed several
times.   The Pope had seen the necessity for the delays, and
had on the whole been very patient, although he had hinted at
the necessity for excommunicating those who did not keep
their vows.   In 1220 Frederick did penance and allowed
himself to be absolved as one who actually had fallen under
the ban.

Preparations for the imperial coronation.

As to the imperial coronation, which caused a still further
delay, the Pope himself was as anxious as Frederick that
it should be performed, and it was as a welcome guest that the
latter appeared in Italy.

In Lombardy, Frederick's envoys had carefully prepared the

way, and as he passed through on his march to Rome all the cities did him homage. His measures were most conciliatory ; he had declared beforehand that he considered the peace of Constance of 1183 as the legal basis for the relations to the empire. His strongest ally was Cremona, which was the leader of a strong coalition opposed to that headed by Milan.

Before Honorius would crown him, Frederick was obliged to repeat his assurances that Germany and Sicily would never be consolidated. He declared expressly that he had received Sicily, not as an inheritance from his forerunners, the German emperors, but as a fief of the Roman Church through his mother, Constance. He promised to appoint only native officials in this, his southern kingdom, to employ for it a special and separate seal, and to do nothing to infringe on the final right of ownership which pertained to the Church.

As a counter-concession, his son Henry being occupied in Germany, Frederick was allowed to continue to retain for his own person the royal dignity in Sicily, in spite of his former promise to abandon it the moment the imperial crown should be placed upon his head.

The coronation, the last one that was to take place for nearly a hundred years, was performed in St. Peter's on November 22nd, 1220 ; the ritual observed was much the same as in former cases, and Queen Constance, too, was included in the ceremony, *The coronation ceremony, 1220 A.D.*

As soon as Frederick had been invested with his new dignity he renewed the taking of the cross ; he took it at the hands of that same cardinal of Ostia who, as Pope Gregory IX., was to be more than inexorable in demanding the fulfilment of his vow.

At this same time Frederick granted a series of new privileges to the Church. The clergy were not to be made to appear before secular tribunals either in criminal or in civil matters. Heretics, chiefly those of certain sects, which were named, were to be condemned to perpetual infamy, to banish- *Frederick against heretics.*

A A

ment and loss of goods; their children, even, were to be deprived of their inheritance. Should any temporal lords delay to cleanse their lands from heresy, the "orthodox" were to take the matter into their own hands.

Italy, where the sects mentioned in Frederick's charter had mainly established themselves, was the land most affected by these regulations. The heretics there had formed themselves into regular communities, had gained for themselves in many cases the acknowledgment of their rights as burghers, and had even been allowed to open public schools, It was a great misfortune for them now that Frederick's political needs compelled him to be very gracious, very generous towards the Pope, and to do what he demanded.

It has not been proved that Frederick's own shortcomings in the matter of the faith were as yet sufficiently suspected to cause him to cloak them with zeal against the heretics. Later, indeed, this charge might safely be preferred; for his persecuting ardour can be proved to have varied at times in direct ratio to the accusations of unorthodoxy that were brought against him.

Laws passed by Frederick at his coronation. The laws passed by Frederick at his coronation concerned themselves, besides the matters mentioned, with the safety of pilgrims and with the treatment of shipwrecked mariners. The latter, hitherto, together with whatever of their possessions might happen to be rescued, had been treated as lawful spoils of fortune; they had been frequently sold as slaves.

Honorius III. confirmed Frederick's new laws and spoke the ban against all who should infringe them; they were considered of so great importance that they were incorporated in the law books of the Bologna School, and the professor of that institution instructed their scholars in these new decrees as well as in the *corpus juris* of Justinian.

Administration of Sicily. His coronation over, Frederick turned to the ordering of affairs in his kingdom of Sicily. Sicilian nobles had appeared in Rome, and there already we find Frederick demanding back crown lands and settling disputes as to the possession of this or that piece of territory.

In December, 1220, Frederick held an assembly at Capua, and here an assize was published ordering that all privileges conferred since the death of the last Norman king in 1189 should now be brought forward for confirmation.

In justifying these measures to the Pope, Frederick wrote that "the emperor Henry gave away much that he ought to have kept; after his death, moreover, many privileges were forged under his seal, and so the greater part of the royal domain was flung away." In his own, Frederick's, youth, finally, the various men in power had managed matters in the same way to the ruin of the kingdom.

All the former estates, rights and privileges of the crown, **Laws of** to which a good title could not be shown, were now reclaimed, **Capua.** and laws passed regulating feudal services, protecting fiefs in their integrity, and ordering the destruction of fortresses and towers erected without permission. Lands were not to remain in mortmain; religious foundations were to regrant their newly acquired territory within a year.

These laws of Capua were the beginning of Frederick's immense legislative activity for his kingdom of Sicily— Germany, alas, was not ripe for such orderly and wholesome measures.

It is an interesting sight, this reorganization of a kingdom **Reorganiza-** that had so long been in a state of chaos; to it Frederick **tion of** devoted himself heart and soul. We find him promulgating **Sicily.** edict upon edict, arranging in person what taxes were to be imposed, sending his envoys all through the land to see that his laws were observed. He placed the sea-coasts in a state of defence, caused fleets to be built, and passed measures intended to further Sicily's commercial interests. The predominating influence of the Pisan and Genoese merchants was done away with, and every encouragement given to home industries.

All these administrative cares demanded time, the more so **Crusade** as the Mohammedans in the interior of Sicily had broken into **again post-** open revolt. It proved impossible for Frederick to be ready **poned.** at the time fixed upon for the crusade.

Honorius, fortunately, still showed himself reasonable and patient. He saw how useful the resources of Sicily were likely to prove in the attempt to regain the Holy Land, and he allowed Frederick again and again to postpone his going. The latter's zeal was as yet unimpeachable; day and night, as he wrote to the Pope, the crusade was on his mind. He prepared numerous galleys and ships of transport and placed them at the disposal of those pilgrims who had made themselves ready for the voyage.

Unfortunate expedition against Egypt, 1221 A.D. In April, 1221, an expedition started for Damietta, which had been a Christian stronghold for two years, an expedition the movements of which Frederick had done all in his power to further. He had published a manifesto to all his German subjects: "Forward, ye true champions of the kingdom, and seize the weapons of Christian knighthood; for already the eagles of the Roman Empire have gone on in front!"

The attack on Egypt, which was to be undertaken from Damietta, was intended as an unexpected blow in the flank of the Mohammedans; had it succeeded it is possible that the papacy would have found it less necessary to enter into its conflict with the head of the empire who had remained at home. But it failed miserably; the army became involved in the Delta of the Nile at the season of the floods, and the Egyptians managed to cut off from it all supplies. The Christians were finally obliged to capitulate, to give up Damietta, and to enter into an eight years' truce, which, however, it was agreed that a crowned head of Europe, should he come in person, might put an end to.

New term for the crusade. Honorius III. blamed Frederick for the loss of Damietta, but, although holding before him the terrors of the ban, still kept on good terms with him, knowing that he alone could retrieve the disaster, if retrieval were still possible. He held a friendly meeting with the emperor in the spring of 1222, and it was agreed that the final term for Frederick's departure should be settled at a congress to be held in Verona. This congress did not take place, as illness kept the Pope, a renewed Saracen revolt the emperor, from attending. At a

brilliant assembly held in Ferentino in March, 1223, however, June 24th, 1225, was fixed upon for the starting of the
great crusade.

There was still no doubt of the emperor's eagerness to do The crown of
all in his power for the rescue of the Holy Land. He showed Jerusalem.
this by his ready consent to the plan of a marriage on his
part—the Empress Constance had died in 1222—with Iolanthe,
the heiress to the throne of Jerusalem.   Honorius had
furthered the union, hoping thus to engage Frederick heart
and soul in the cause of the crusade.

The crown of Jerusalem, indeed, which was nominally to
remain in the hands of the German emperors even as late as
the time of Charles V., was an illusory possession; but the
Pope and the cardinals offered to assist Frederick in regaining
it by imposing a tax for three years on every hearth in
Christendom.

The marriage took place at Brindisi in November, 1225.
Iolanthe's father, John of Brienne, had practically consented
to renounce his claims in her favour, but Frederick's rough
insistance on a formal abdication soon turned his father-in-
law from a friend into an enemy.

The new date fixed upon for the crusade approached, and Saracen
Frederick still found it impossible to proceed to the fulfilment revolt in
of his vow.   In his kingdom of Sicily, indeed, his power had Sicily.
come to be almost absolute.   He had put down a stubborn
insurrection of the Apulian nobleman, Count Thomas of
Molise, and had, after four years of warring, reduced the
Saracens to entire subjection.   One of their fortresses after
another had fallen into his hands, and by the autumn of 1225
all opposition was at an end.

A large number of the Saracens were made to cross over Saracen
to the mainland, and a colony of them formed at Luceria colony at
enjoyed, during all the rest of his reign, Frederick's special Luceria.
care and protection.   The colonists were allowed to till their
fields, to practise their handicrafts, and to exercise in peace
their religious rites.   Frederick seems to have preferred that
they should remain Islamites, although in 1223 he allowed

Pope Gregory IX. to send Dominican monks to them as missionary preachers. Later, when the Church had entirely broken with the emperor, the latter was bitterly reproached with having unduly favoured the Saracens and with having committed unhallowed acts in common with them.

It was from Luceria that Frederick drew his best and most faithful troops, the kernel of his army.

Further postponement of crusade.

What prevented Frederick from starting in 1225 was the ill-success that the crusading preachers had met with in France and England as well as Germany. For a century and a quarter Europe had been sending her nobles and people to water the Orient with their blood; the time for great and overwhelming expeditions had passed. Continued ill-success, ending with the loss of Damietta, had chilled the fervour of the once so devoted Christendom. It had proved impossible, too, to raise the tax that had been decreed at Ferentino, and Frederick was compelled to ask for a further delay of two years. Honorius was momentarily not in a position to refuse it, although other causes of complaint, chiefly concerning the Sicilian bishoprics, had begun to embitter him against his dilatory champion. As a matter of fact, the Pope was at this time an exile from Rome and in no wise capable of entering into a final struggle with a powerful emperor.

Treaty with the Pope, 1225 A.D.

By the treaty of San Germano, drawn up in July, 1225, Frederick bound himself to the Pope by promises more definite than any he had yet given. He agreed to cross in August, 1227, with a thousand knights, a hundred transport ships and fifty galleys, and to maintain these forces for a period of two years. He was, in addition, to have ships ready for two thousand knights, each with three horses; also to make payment of one hundred thousand ounces of gold (about eleven million francs of modern coin) at five different terms to John of Brienne and the patriarch of Jerusalem, and to the grandmaster of the Teutonic order. This money, however, was again to be placed at his own disposal when he should once really have crossed the sea.

Should Frederick fail to cross, should he not take with

him the thousand knights, or should he not remit the sums agreed, he was to consider himself *ipse facto* under sentence of the ban. For the fulfilment of his promises, finally, the pledge was to be the kingdom of Sicily.

Frederick had now taken a series of new responsibilities upon his shoulders; his crusade was no longer to be international, but entirely his own affair, and Sicily was to bear the burden of it in case he himself should die.

The recovery of the Holy Land became almost more of political than of religious importance, and the undertaking began to assume much the aspect of the expedition once planned by Henry VI.

One of the first uses to which Frederick put the new respite that had been granted him was to try and bring order into the affairs of Northern Italy. In January, 1226, he summoned all his Sicilian vassals to do service against the Lombard cities. His programme was the readjustment of the relations to the empire, the restoration of peace between different towns that were at war with each other, the uprooting of heresy, and, in general, the furthering of the crusade. A diet was summoned to meet at Cremona.

Frederick and the Lombard cities.

Honorius III. was horrified at the preparations for a possible war against Lombardy, preparations, too, which were being made without his consent being asked in the matter. He was more than incensed when Frederick began levying troops in papal territory. He wrote and reminded the emperor of the humiliations that his grandfather Barbarossa had been made to suffer on account of his enmity to the Holy See. He brought Barbarossa's sudden death, as well as the fate that in turn overtook both Henry VI. and Philip of Hohenstaufen, into connection with their hostility to the papacy. "Take care that God do not annihilate thee and wipe out thy race; We, indeed, if thou dost insist on thy ruinous course, shall not omit to chasten thee with the ban."

The Pope's anger.

For the first time the rooting out of the whole Hohenstaufen stem was laid down as a possible necessity for the Church; it was to become that Church's holiest aim and object.

Renewal of the Lombard league.

The result of Frederick's interference in Northern Italy was that Milan, induced probably more than by anything else by the emperor's partiality for Cremona, renewed the Lombard League, in which twenty cities were soon enrolled. Frederick could reckon on the goodwill and support only of Cremona, Pavia, Parma, Modena, and Asti. As the emperor approached, accompanied only by inconsiderable forces from Sicily, the allied cities assumed a more and more hostile attitude. They began to exert pressure on towns which remained neutral, stopping all commerce with them ; their own members were forbidden under heavy penalties to even communicate with the emperor. The passes near Verona were occupied, so as to prevent the approach of King Henry and the German princes.

The League thought itself strong enough to impose its own conditions on the emperor. He was to promise not to place in the ban of the empire any of the cities belonging to it ; he was to dismiss his own armed followers, and the escort of his son was not to exceed twelve hundred horsemen.

Frederick bans the cities of the league.

Frederick scornfully rejected all such propositions, and with the approval of an assembly of nobles and bishops, laid the ban upon all the cities of the League. Bishop Conrad of Hildesheim had already excommunicated them and laid them under the interdict.

All privileges were now withdrawn from the cities and the Constance treaty was declared no longer binding. Intercourse with the burghers was forbidden, their civic constitutions declared null and void ; even their institutions of learning were ordered to be closed.

The new complications with the Lombard League threatened ruin to the whole crusading project. This Honorius saw ; he knew that what he felt to be his chief object in life was likely to remain unfulfilled should the quarrel between the emperor and the cities be pushed to extremes. He sent a conciliatory embassy to Frederick, and finally induced the latter to consent to submit the whole matter to papal arbitration if the Lombards would do the same.

The cities of the League, after some difficulties and delays —on one occasion it was declared that the draft of the peace sent from Rome had fallen into the water and become illegible, and all negotiations had to cease till a new copy could be procured—were at last brought to agree to this arrangement, and both parties finally accepted the Pope's decision.   The emperor was to revoke all his hostile decrees; the cities to furnish him with four hundred knights for the crusade, and to observe the canons passed at the Lateran council of 1215 as well as the laws against heretics.

Temporary peace with the Lombards.

It will be seen that the decision of Honorius was extremely one-sided, that no mention was made of the imperial rights as opposed to the cities, and that the Church alone reaped all the advantage of the peace.   Frederick, true to his agreement, was obliged to accept that peace; but by it the conflict with the Lombards was only postponed, not terminated.

Honorius had shown himself from first to last conciliatory; Frederick had responded in kind.   The death of the Pope, however, in March, 1227, brought to the Chair of Peter a man who was determined to have his due, no matter what the cost might be to the empire.

Death of Honorius, 1227 A.D.

The shadows deepen now all along the scene.   The almost comedy-like trifling between the heads of Christendom ceases, and the first dark episodes of the greatest of all mediæval tragedies begin.   What fate-drama of classic times can show a plot equal in incident to the history of the downfall of the Hohenstaufen?   The popes play the part of the avenging furies; unrelenting, always on the alert, they pursue their prey through three generations.   They raise up friends for themselves by squandering their stock of heavenly rewards, and by playing fast and loose with the superstitions and the greedy desires of mankind.   They are able at last to dispose of the kingdom of Sicily as if it were a trinket or a bauble.   The old mythological twilight of the gods seems descending upon the earth, and the whole original structure of the mediæval empire falls to the ground in a heap of ruins.

The shadows deepen.

Pope Gregory IX., 1227-1241.

Gregory IX., the new Pope, was the nephew of Innocent III., and heir to that pontiff's ambitious hopes and world-embracing plans. In the notification of his election which he sent to Frederick, he reminded the latter of his crusading vow, and of the ban that was in store should that vow not be fulfilled. "Do not bring us and thyself," he wrote, "into that position of dire need, out of which we could not easily free thee even if we would."

Frederick meanwhile had been doing his best to raise a crusading army, and at last, by dint of pecuniary and other gifts had succeeded. Louis of Thuringia, for instance, the husband of that Elizabeth of Hungary who was afterwards canonized for her good works, was offered five thousand marks of silver and the succession to the margravate of Meissen.

Frederick had offered to furnish ships for the transport of all crusaders without respect to person, and the number that finally came together surpassed all expectations.

The crusaders at Brindisi.

The ships had been collected at Brindisi, and here the crusaders assembled in August, 1227. Unfortunately the heat of the summer, and the poor food and insufficient accommodation, brought on a pestilence to which thousands fell victims. Strange that Pope Honorius and the emperor alike had been so blind to the dangers of the Italian climate as to set such a term for the departure of the pilgrims!

Many of the German leaders, among them the landgrave of Thuringia, died, and the emperor himself was seized with the malady. He bore up under it for a time, and saw in person to the sending out of one detachment of ships after another. As he felt the sickness gaining on him he held a council of war at Otranto, at which the Patriarch of Jerusalem and the Grand Master Herrmann of Salza were present. He laid the question before the assembly as to whether or not he should continue the journey. By general advice, and in view of the evils which his possible death would bring upon his two monarchies, he decided to postpone his departure until the following May. He then hastened to the baths of Pozzuoli to seek a cure for his illness.

Gregory IX. and his partisans always stoutly maintained **Frederick in the ban.** that Frederick's illness was feigned, and the Pope would listen to no justification whatever. He at once declared the emperor in the ban, and sent an encyclic letter to the bishops of Western Europe heaping one accusation after another on his head. The capitulation of the Christian army in Egypt, and the consequent loss of Damietta, were again laid to his charge; the plague at Brindisi, too, was declared to have been owing to his faulty arrangements and preparations.

Frederick himself never maintained that the Pope did not have a formal right, based on the treaty with Honorius, to excommunicate him. He even went so far as to accept the sentence and ask for absolution, bringing forward evidence to prove the baselessness of most of the charges against him. He published a justification of himself, of which many copies were distributed through Italy and Germany.

But Gregory IX. had given full rein to his wrath, and **Gregory's wrath.** nothing could make him relent.

The emperor had declared his intention of still going on his expedition to the Holy Land; he now prepared to execute this threat, for as threat Gregory regarded it. The Pope had no interest in a crusade to be conducted by one who was in the ban; he absolved all crusaders from their vow.

Frederick had friends even in Rome; when the Pope in March, 1228, repeated the promulgation of the ban, and ordered the clergy of Sicily to place under the interdict any spot where the emperor might tarry, he found himself attacked by a mob in the very church of St. Peter's itself. He was obliged to flee the city, and finally to take refuge in Perugia. His misfortunes did not dishearten him, however, for we soon find him preparing to send an army into Sicily, where he had already forbidden the payment of the taxes which Frederick had imposed. He also loosed all the latter's subjects from their oath of allegiance, and spoke of him as the " so-called " emperor, and as a servant of Mahomet.

Frederick undertook his crusade with absurdly small forces, **Frederick's crusade.**

and directly in the face of the Papal anathema. The irony
of fate willed it to be the most successful expedition that had
taken place for many a long year.

A civil war that had broken out among the heirs of the
great Saladin gave the emperor a splendid opportunity of
playing off one faction of the Mohammedans against the
other. One of Saladin's sons, the Sultan of Egypt, had
actually sought an alliance with Frederick, and offered him in
return Jerusalem and the Coast of Syria.

After declaring the Duke of Spoleto his representative in
Sicily, and arranging that, in case of his death, the young
King Henry should succeed him both in that kingdom and in
Germany, Frederick set sail from Brindisi with only forty
galleys (June, 1228). He landed in Acre in September, and
found there ten thousand pilgrims and about eight hundred
knights.

Two Franciscan monks had followed in the wake of Frederick's expedition bearing a command of the Pope that no
obedience should be shown to the excommunicated emperor.
The Patriarch, the Knights of St. John, the Knights Templars,
and others, gave ear to this injunction.

Christian
hostility in
Jerusalem.
The Templars even tried to betray Frederick into the hands
of his own ally, the Egyptian Sultan, El Kamel, who straightway sent to the emperor the letters containing the treacherous
proposals. In spite of the fact that Frederick's forces were
neither formidable on the one hand, nor likely to prove of
great assistance on the other, El Kamel continued to treat
with him. Not only self-interest, but a personal friendship
and admiration soon bound him to the emperor; he was filled
with wonder at the latter's learning as well as at his religious
tolerance.

Gregory IX., according to the assertion of Frederick himself, who declared ten years later that he still had the inter-
cepted letter in his hands, wrote to El Kamel, and urged him
not to surrender to the emperor the Holy Land, and the right
to the crown of Jerusalem. So far did implacable hatred
lead even the Vicar of the Prince of Peace!

By the treaty with El Kamel, which was finally signed in February, 1229, Jerusalem, as well as all the land between it and the coast, was ceded to the Christians. Bethlehem, Joppa, Nazareth, and Sidon were among the towns acquired, and it was expressly stipulated that the walls of Jerusalem, Joppa, Cæsarea, Sidon, and Castle Montfort might be rebuilt. Two churches in Jerusalem were to remain in the hands of the Mohammedans. *The treaty with El Kamel, 1229 A.D.*

When signing this treaty El Kamel promised to observe it under penalty of having to acknowledge the Father, Son, and Holy Ghost. Frederick swore that, rather than infringe it, he would eat his left hand.

Since the time of the first crusade all the vaunted courage of European kings and princes, and all the immense outlays on the part of Christian subjects, had achieved no such successes as these. The patriarch of Jerusalem, however, sent a very garbled account of the treaty to the Pope, mentioning for the most part only the points of it that were favourable to the Saracens.

Frederick took possession of Jerusalem on the 17th of March and, on the 18th, in the church of the Holy Sepulchre, in the presence of the archbishops of Palermo and Capua, and surrounded by a crowd of pilgrims, placed the crown of Jerusalem on his own head. On the 19th the Archbishop of Cæsarea, commissioned by the patriarch, laid under the interdict the church where this ceremony had taken place, as well as the other sacred places in the city. The patriarch insisted, moreover, that the treaty entered into with the Sultan of Egypt was no real peace, and that the true possessor of Jerusalem was the Sultan of Damascus. *Frederick in Jerusalem.*

Frederick retaliated against his Christian enemies by decreeing that all foreign crusaders should leave the Holy Land, that the patriarch and those who refused to obey should be kept prisoner in their own houses, and that no Knight Templar should be allowed to enter Jerusalem, the gates of which city were to be kept guarded.

Meanwhile in Italy events were happening the tidings of which, when they reached him, caused Frederick at once to *Gregory's invasion of Sicily.*

return home. On the very day of the coronation in Jerusalem the papal troops, the *clavigeri* or " key-bearers " as they were called, had attacked and defeated his chief commander near Monte Cassino. Almost all of the mainland provinces of the Silician kingdom had then fallen into their hands. Gregory IX.'s plans seem to have included the utter ruin and destruction of the emperor. At this same time in Germany his legate was raising up sedition, and trying to induce the only remaining male descendant of the Guelphs, Otto of Luneburg, to dethrone the young Henry VII. and place the crown on his own head.

Frederick routs the papal troops. Frederick set sail from Acre on May 1, 1229 ; on the 10th of June he landed in Apulia. He hastily raised such forces as he could, his army consisting chiefly of German crusaders, and of Saracens from Luceria. In September he appeared before Capua, and within a few weeks the Papal troops had been routed, and the whole land, with the exception of Monte Cassino and a few fortresses, had been recovered.

Frederick used his victory with moderation ; indeed, all through this conflict with the Pope he had shown himself singularly patient and long-suffering. He now urged Gregory to make peace, and the latter was no longer in a position to refuse. The Emperor promised immunity from punishment to all those who had fought against him and, in return, in August, 1230, was loosed from the ban. Gregory, a year later, acknowledged him as king of Jerusalem, and officially called him by that name. He also confirmed the treaty which Frederick had entered into with El Kamel, and enjoined obedience to the emperor on the Templars and the Knights of St. John.

CHAPTER XXIV.

RENEWED STRUGGLE BETWEEN FREDERICK II. AND GREGORY IX.

DURING Frederick's absence in Italy and Palestine, an absence which lasted in all twelve years, the young King Henry had been under the control first of Archbishop Engelbert of Cologne, and then of Louis of Bavaria. Engelbert kept such peace in Germany that his administration could be likened by a contemporary chronicler to the reign of Augustus.

Germany during Frederick's absence.

But, in 1225, Engelbert was murdered by a personal enemy, and Germany became a prey to the greatest disorder; the young king came under the influence of evil advisers, and his path began to separate from that of his father. Sunk in selfish pleasures he troubled himself little about the duties of government.

The chief incident of importance during this time had been the capture of King Waldemar of Denmark and his son by Count Henry of Schwerin. This was in 1223, and Count Henry's motives had been of a private nature, he being a vassal of the Danish monarch, and having received harsh treatment at his hands. It soon became evident, however, that the episode might become politically important in the same way, if in a less degree, than the famous capture of King Richard of England.

Capture of King Waldemar of Denmark, 1223 A.D.

Waldemar, it will be remembered, had been allowed by Frederick II. to keep, as the price of his friendship, certain German provinces lying between the Eider and the Elbe. It was now arranged that the Count of Schwerin should give over his prisoner to the empire for a sum of money, and that the Danish king should be made to pay a ransom, and to surrender the recently acquired lands.

A treaty was actually drawn up with Waldemar in 1225, by which he was to pay 45,000 marks of silver, and to give back the territory between the Elbe and the Eider as well as the Slavic lands, with the exception of Rügen. Waldemar was then set free, but did not keep his agreement, and the princes of North Germany resorted to arms. They defeated the Danes at Bornhövede in 1227; Waldemar was compelled to renew his treaty, and to surrender Holstein and Lubeck, Hamburg, Mecklenburg, and Pomerania—provinces which Denmark never regained.

Frederick's Sicilian constitutions. Frederick II., after the peace of San Germano, under which name the treaty concluded with Gregory IX. is known in history, applied himself with all energy to the completion and working out of his administrative system in Sicily. The result was that that state soon became a wonder among mediæval governments; it became what the kingdom of Jerusalem might have been had its rulers been more capable.

The constitutions of Melfi, drawn up in 1231, crystallized, so to speak, all of Frederick's former measures. The monarchy was now absolute in all respects; the princes had little or no influence on the government. Frederick claimed to hold his power from God alone; he chose his advisers from among those of his subjects whom he knew to be most capable, showing a preference for those skilled in the law.

A great code for Sicily. It was a great code that Frederick caused to be published at Melfi, a code that embodied the decrees of his Norman predecessors as well as the new ones promulgated by himself. One is astonished at the advanced ideas of government that are here brought forward. The feudal system is made to retreat before the power of the throne; the aristocracy no longer hold all the offices of state; they lose the right of fortifying their castles, and no longer have jurisdiction over their subjects in criminal matters. They are obliged to swear allegiance to the king, and may not even marry without his consent.

On the other hand, their daughters and collateral relatives are allowed to inherit their fiefs, which thus remain in the family even in default of direct male heirs.

The administration of justice and the care of the finances are the concern of the crown ; Frederick greatly increased his revenues by establishing monopolies in salt, iron, copper, steel, and raw silk.

The prelates are made to submit in certain questions to the decisions of the temporal courts ; no one is allowed to sell property to any church or religious order, or to any of the clergy.

One would willingly dwell longer on these Sicilian reforms, on the forbiddal of judicial combat, on the laws against quacks and poisoners, and against those who administered love-potions. On the measures for the improvement of commerce, too, on the abolition of serfdom, the establishment of model farms, the encouragement of agriculture, and the introduction of strange plants, such as indigo, cotton, and sugar-cane.

The decrees of Melfi did not at all please Pope Gregory IX. **The Pope's displeasure at Sicilian reforms.** " We have learned," he wrote in the beginning to the emperor, " that thou, whether of thy own accord, or seduced by the thoughtless counsel of ungodly men, dost intend to publish new constitutions which will necessarily gain thee the title of a persecutor of the Church and a destroyer of the public liberty."

A glance at Frederick's activity in Sicily was needful in order to show the contrast of the policy which he pursued in Germany. Here his allies and supporters had been the prelates and princes ; he could not now turn round and try to subject them or crush them down.

Frederick's son Henry, indeed, who after 1230 became **Opposite views of Frederick and his son.** practically independent, held a different view of the matter, and tried to stem the growing independence of the German aristocracy by leaning on the cities, which were fast becoming powerful. When a town desired privileges, as opposed to its lay or ecclesiastical lord, Henry granted them; he favoured the adoption of municipal constitutions and the formation of leagues or alliances.

In order to protect the interests of the princes, whose power was thus being undermined by the actions of his own son, Frederick in 1230 restored the office of grand chancellor of the empire, which had been vacant since 1224, and chose Bishop Siegfried of Ratisbon to that position. At a diet held at Worms early in 1231, Siegfried, in the emperor's name, forbade leagues of every kind among the cities, and declared all such as had been already entered into to be dissolved. No permission to renew such unions was to be given in future by the princes without the emperor, or the emperor without the princes.

The territorial lords. Henry VII. was forced soon afterwards by his father to issue a so-called golden bull, which was for the princes a practical charter of independence. For the first time they were officially given the title of *domini terræ* or lords of their territory. All privileges and jurisdictions were to be theirs absolutely, all the counts or administrators of the hundreds or lesser districts were to hold office directly from them. The only restriction laid upon them was that they should not change the laws of their land without consulting their nobles. The duchies, margravates, and bishoprics were fast becoming states within a state.

Frederick's bull went on to strike at the fundamental hindrance to princely progress, the power and prosperity of the cities. These were no longer to be allowed to confer upon the people of the faubourgs (Pfahlburgher) the rights and privileges of citizens which had hitherto enabled them to escape fulfilling their duties to their lords.

Insubordination of Henry VII. The young Henry had by this time given signs of open insubordination. Frederick had called a diet at Ravenna in 1231, for the purpose of restoring peace with the Lombards who were in rebellion and who had raised an army of 10,000 men. He had summoned his son to the diet, but Henry failed to appear. The young king did, however, come to a second assembly at Aquileija, where he swore to adopt the emperor's policy and to obey his commands. He promised to treat the German princes with especial favour, and it was agreed that should he act counter to his engagements those princes might consider themselves absolved from their oath of allegiance. Frederick took this occasion to confirm the privileges granted at Worms in the previous year. Henry's submission at Aquileija was but a lull in the storm that had commenced to rise. On his return to Germany he continued to favour the cities as before, and to take their part against the lords.

It was a time for the empire of terrible disorders, of political anarchy, and of religious oppression. Germany was torn by internal feuds; the King of Bohemia was at war with Austria and Bavaria, the Archbishop of Cologne was fighting against his Westphalian vassals, the Count of Limburg against the Bishop of Münster. *Internal disorders.*

It was a time, too, when the Inquisition was girding itself for its work, and the Franciscans and Dominicans, or "dogs of the Pope," were beginning to scour the land in search of their prey. *The Inquisition in Germany.*

In 1231 the land saw burnings innumerable, and every other kind of persecution. The common people, driven wild by superstitious fears, joined hands with Conrad Dorso and other monks, and helped them in their search for heretics. The lords of suspected persons were rendered more pliable and well-wishing towards the persecutors by being allowed to keep the confiscated lands of victims. The inquisitors, to whom Frederick was obliged, out of deference to the Pope, to grant his imperial protection, went on the principle, as the trustworthy annals of Worms tell us, that they would rather burn a hundred innocent persons than let one guilty one escape.

To Master Conrad of Marburg, a Hessian, Gregory IX. gave extended powers for the rooting out of heresy. Conrad was told to preach a crusade against the guilty, and to promise forgiveness of sins to those who would hunt them down. Even murderers were to be absolved if they would help in so godly a work. *Conrad of Marburg.*

The inquisitors grew so courageous in time, that they ventured to accuse even venerable preachers and prelates; the young king himself finally became an object of their suspicion. Against Count Henry of Sayn they brought charges that remind one strongly of those advanced in the later trials for witchcraft. One was that he had been seen to ride upon a crab.

The count in question caused King Henry and the Archbishop of Mayence to call an assembly where he confronted his accuser and justified himself; but Conrad of Marburg still insisted on his charge. The Count of Sayn then appealed to Rome, and with his messengers went envoys from many of the German nobles.

Conrad's murder. Gregory IX. seemed surprised at the dimensions which the matter had assumed, and was about to send an answer favourable to the princes, when the news came that the German people had found a way of helping themselves. Conrad of Marburg was murdered, as were also some of his aiders and abettors.

Diet of Frankfort, 1234 A.D. Gregory IX., infuriated by what had taken place, made further efforts to inflame the masses against the heretics; but a reaction had already set in. The diet of Frankfort, held in February, 1234, set bounds to the excesses of religious fanaticism by decreeing that offences against the faith should be tried in the secular courts, and according to regular judicial procedure. The decisions were to be according to equity. In order that such cases should the sooner be brought to a termination, King Henry agreed himself to hold a court on four days in each month.

In spite of measures like these it was possible for the Inquisition to gain a great and lasting triumph.

Annihilation of the Stedingers. Gerard, Archbishop of Bremen and Count of Oldenburg, had long since announced that his particular enemies the Frisian Stedingers, a tribe of peasants numbering about 11,000 souls, were guilty of heresy inasmuch as they scorned the sacraments and teachings of the Church and occupied themselves with works of darkness. In 1229 Gerard had induced the Pope to empower the bishops of Minden, Lubeck, and Ratzeburg to preach a crusade against the Stedingers. An army had been raised in this way, but the sturdy Frisians had held their own. In 1234, however, 40,000 " crusaders " came together under the leadership of the counts of Oldenburg, Cleves, and Holland, and of the Duke of Brabant. Thousands of the Stedingers were slain, the tribe as such being fairly annihilated.

The emperor disapproved of his son Henry's attitude in the matter of the heretics ; exactly on what grounds has never been made clear. Frederick's wrath was also aroused by news of a feud which the young king carried on against Bavaria, likewise by Henry's treatment of two Suabian princes who were known to be loyal to his father. The cleft grew wider and wider. *Coolness of Frederick with Henry VII.*

In September, 1234, Henry took the decisive step of issuing a manifesto to the German princes recalling his own services to the emperor and declaring that the latter was trying to diminish powers once freely granted. He complained of having been threatened with excommunication—the Pope and the emperor were at this time in accord.

While continuing to adopt a tone of injured innocence Henry prepared openly for rebellion. He held a meeting at Boppard where the final arrangements were made, the aim and object of the revolt was to be the separation of Germany from Italy. An alliance, to be valid for ten years, was now entered into with the Lombard League ; it was expressly directed against the emperor. Henry also tried to win the support of Louis IX. of France, but here his overtures met with a repulse. *Rebellion of Henry VII.*

Henry made an attack on Worms—whose citizens, as the local annals tell us, did not swerve from their loyalty to the emperor as much as "a bean's breadth "—with an army of 5,000 men, but was beaten back. It was his first and last undertaking, for Frederick was already on the march, and the effect of his presence in Germany was to show the weakness of Henry's following and the utter foolishness of his revolt.

Frederick had no army to speak of, but considerable pecuniary resources were at his disposal. He was at one, too, with the Pope and with England and France.

Life-long imprison-ment of Henry VII.

Henry sent envoys to Nuremberg to try and appease his father's wrath ; he was ordered to appear in person at Worms, where Frederick had arranged to celebrate his wedding with Isabella of England—Iolanthe, the heiress of Jerusalem, had died just before the anomalous crusade of 1228.

Henry might have gained his father's forgiveness, although not his own reinstatement in power, had he submitted uncon-ditionally. He is said, however, to have refused to give up the castle of Trifels which had come into his power and to have tried, after having consented to appear there, to escape from Worms.

He was taken prisoner, and never again recovered his liberty. He died in 1241, and was honourably buried in Cosenza, memorial services being held for him throughout all the kingdom of Sicily. Frederick mourned him sincerely ; he was, as he declared himself, neither the first nor the last father who had suffered harm from a disobedient son, and yet had wept at his grave.

The Diet of Mayence, 1235 A.D.

Frederick's marriage was celebrated at Worms with great magnificence, the English princess bringing him an immense dowry. A brilliant diet was soon afterwards held at Mayence ; no such assembly had been seen since the great festival held by Barbarossa in 1184.

This diet of Mayence marks an important epoch in the legal and constitutional history of Germany. Not only was a resident chief-justice appointed for the empire, but regulations were passed concerning tolls and coinage, and especially con-cerning the peace of the land. Robbers and brigands were to be systematically pursued ; the right of carrying on feuds was confined to cases of self-protection or to cases where justice had been denied. Even then a formal challenge was declared necessary.

It is not surprising that Frederick, in view of recent events, passed a law against sons who were disobedient and disloyal to their fathers. They were to be utterly disinherited.

An attempt was made at Mayence to fix the legal customs and usages and to codify the laws already existing in the empire; for the first time such laws were now published in the German tongue.

Laws of 1235 A.D.

It was at this same diet that the last possible sparks of future discord between the Guelphs and Hohenstaufens were extinguished. Otto of Luneburg, Henry the Lion's only remaining male descendant, promised to renounce all the hatred and enmity that had existed between his own and the emperor's forefathers, and gave up the allodial possessions of his family, receiving them back as a fief of the empire. A new duchy was formed from these lands and conferred on Otto and his male and female heirs.

Last in the measures passed at Mayence, but not least in its consequences, which were dire enough, was the declaration of war against the Lombard League. Frederick had already had a number of differences with this organization, and now it had dared to join his son in rebellion against himself.

War against the Lombard League.

With this war we enter on the last act of the Hohenstaufen tragedy. At the beginning of that act Frederick is seen to be prosperous and successful enough, but the Pope soon enters upon the scene and begins the work of extermination which his successor was to carry out so well.

As regarded the differences that had arisen with the Lombards previous to their making common cause with King Henry, Frederick had consented, upon quitting Italy in 1235, to leave the decision to the Pope. Matters were changed now in so far as the emperor thought no more of arbitration but of a retributive war.

Gregory was by no means pleased at this change of policy; he wrote to the German princes, pictured the harm that the struggle would do to the cause of the Holy Land, and begged them to induce the emperor to accept his mediation. Frederick consented that the negotiations should proceed for a time, and sent Herrmann of Salza to Rome to look after his interests.

Gregory IX. and the Lombard war.

The deputies of the Lombards, however, failed to put in an appearance at the date appointed, and Herrmann was recalled.

There was all the less chance of a compromise as the Lombards had already taken steps towards opening hostilities. They had renewed their league and had sworn to let none of the Germans or their allies pass through their territory. They had tried to take Verona, which was in a measure the key to Italy, from Frederick's commander Ezzelino da Romano.

Herrmann of Salza, after leaving Rome, held an assembly at Piacenza of deputies from a number of Ghibelline cities. Gregory IX. raised a loud outcry, declared that the Lombard League was ready to submit to arbitration, and requested that Herrmann be empowered to reopen the negotiations.

Frederick and Gregory. It was too late. By the summer of 1236, Frederick was already in Verona at the head of 3,000 knights. A somewhat bitter correspondence had meanwhile been carried on with the Pope. Gregory had accused the emperor of robbing churches, restricting freedom of elections, doing violence to the persons of clergy, furthering heresy and favouring the Mohammedans. Frederick had answered calmly and with dignity: "You bring up against us whatever, during our absence, has been done amiss by our officials in our kingdom of Sicily; as if we, from Germany, could oversee everything with the eyes of a lynx and make ourselves heard with a voice of thunder!"

Frederick II. in Austria. Frederick, for his part, after a not very brilliant campaign in Northern Italy, was obliged hastily to return to Germany. Duke Frederick the Warlike of Austria had assumed an equivocal attitude at the time of King Henry's rebellion. To answer this and other charges he had been summoned to two diets in succession, but had failed to appear. He had then been placed under the ban of the empire, the carrying into execution of which had been entrusted to Bohemia, Bavaria, Passau, Frising, and Bamberg.

The complications in Austria became so serious as to demand the emperor's presence. The duke had been bereft of his lands but had regained them after engaging in separate conflicts with each of his enemies in turn.

Frederick II. now reduced to subjection Austria, Styria, and Carinthia, and in 1237 held a court in Vienna, where his nine year old son, Conrad, was chosen King of the Romans, his election being confirmed soon afterwards by a diet at Spires.

Frederick II. remained but a short time in Germany, and hurried back to Italy. The first decided success of the Lombard war, which, interrupted by vain attempts at negotiation, dragged on for years, was the battle of Cortenuova, fought in November, 1237. If the emperor's own statement can be believed, the League lost 10,000 men. The caroccio of Milan fell into Frederick's hands, and he presented it to the Romans who, much to Pope Gregory's disgust, placed it on exhibition, elevated on columns, in their Capitol. A Latin inscription regarding it still exists: "This illustrious booty, taken from the Milanese, comes (to Rome) to show the triumphs of the emperor."

Battle of Cortenuova, 1237 A.D.

Negotiations were entered into after this defeat at Cortenuova, but Frederick would have nothing but unconditional surrender, and for this the Lombards were not prepared.

Frederick had meanwhile given the Pope a tangible cause of offence by wedding his own illegitimate son Enzio to Adelasia the heiress of Sardinia, and by naming Enzio king of that land. The new monarch now proceeded to take possession of some of the principal cities. Sardinia, as Frederick himself had acknowledged, was a fief of the see of Rome; the breach with the Pope was now complete.

Enzio, king of Sardinia.

Gregory now made up his mind to use his last great weapon; to close the doors of Heaven and flaunt the keys in the emperor's face.

Banning and deposition of Frederick II., 1239 A.D.

On Maundy Thursday, in the presence of a great assembly at Rome, the sentence of excommunication was solemnly pronounced. The emperor's body was given over to Satan in order that his soul might be saved at the day of Judgment; his subjects were loosed from their allegiance, every place that he should enter declared under the interdict.

The bull deposing Frederick, which was sent to the different

countries of Europe, contained numerous charges and ended
up with the remark that as the emperor was universally
accused of irreligion, the Pope intended to have him legally
tried for heresy.

Frederick's
letter to the
princes of
Europe.
Both Frederick and the Pope issued manifestoes which
leave nothing to be desired in the way of venom and bitterness.   We cannot read them to-day without a feeling of
breathless excitement; they are the ponderous blows of a
deadly struggle.

Frederick's letter was directed to the sovereigns, prelates,
and nobles of Europe: "Cast your eyes around you and
open your ears, oh, children of men. . . . . Princes, take
heed; people, listen to what is your own cause; may your eyes
be opened to the light and your decision be inspired by the
Lord Himself!" Frederick goes on to enumerate the wrongs
he has received at the hand of the Pope, to accuse the latter
of prevarication and to show the dangers that threaten all
other monarchs should he himself fall a victim: "Run for
water for the protection of your own house when that of your
neighbour burns; . . . . for a certainty he will think it easy
to cast down the other princes if he once succeeds in crushing
the head of the empire."

Gregory's
letter.
Gregory's letter is a masterpiece of invective: "A furious
beast has come up from the sea; her feet are those of a bear,
her teeth those of a lion, in her members she resembles the
leopard; she only opens her throat to blaspheme the name of
the Lord, to attack the divine tabernacle and the saints who
inhabit the heavens.   Formerly she laid secret ambushes for
the Church, now she attacks it openly with her nails and her
teeth of iron."

Gregory repeats the old story of the Church having been a
mother to Frederick and he having heaped ingratitude upon
her.   All the old griefs are brought up: the plague that
broke out in Apulia at the time of the crusade, Frederick's
vow so often deferred, his feigned sickness, his having allowed
the Saracens to worship in the temple at Jerusalem.   The
Pope calls the emperor the precursor of Antichrist, and

finally works himself up to the most terrific of all his accusa- **The three**
tions: "This king, enthroned on the seat of pestilence, **impostors.**
maintains, to use his own words, that the whole world has
been deceived by three impostors, Moses, Mahomet, and
Christ; of whom two died honourably, the third on the cross.
Furthermore he has dared to aver, or rather to say falsely,
that all those are fools who believe that Almighty God, the
Creator of heaven and earth, was born of a virgin. This
heresy he bases on the assertion that no one can be born
without the previous union of a man with a woman, and that
there is no need to believe anything at all that cannot be
proved by reason and by natural means."

Terrible charges these at a time when on far less grounds **Frederick's**
men were often sent to the stake. The charges, too, if not **unortho-**
literally true were undoubtedly so in substance; all that we **doxy.**
know of Frederick makes it highly probable that he gave
utterance to these or similar remarks.

The emperor, in a letter to the cardinals, did his utmost to
clear himself, and made a formal and explicit profession of
faith. He declared that Mahomet's soul was delivered up to
the flames of hell, while Moses was the friend and favourite
of God. In this same letter he broke forth in further attacks
upon the Pope, calling him the father of discord not of mercy,
of desolation not of consolation. "He is himself the Antichrist of whom he calls us the precursor; the great dragon,
the false prophet, the angel of darkness who fills with rancour
the earth and the sky."

This war of words was but the prelude to a war of deeds. **Failure of**
Before the end of the year Gregory tried to induce the nobles **Gregory's**
of Germany to proceed to the election of a new ruler and his **plot.**
agent, a certain Albert de Behaim, did cause the King of
Bohemia, the Duke of Austria and others to try and elect the
son of the Danish King. The plot failed, much to the disgust
of the agent, who in his report to the Pope calls the chief
promoter of it "rex Blasphemiæ" instead of "Bohemiæ."

The princes as a whole had refused to be concerned in the
movement, implying to the Pope that he was meddling with

matters which were none of his affair and that, although he
might invest the elect of the people with the imperial ornaments, he had no right to withdraw them.

Gregory's unceasing hostility. Gregory next turned to Louis IX. of France, proposing to
give the empire to the latter's brother, the Count of Artois,
whom he offered to support with the treasures and influence
of the Church.   Louis, too, refused to be the Pope's instrument of vengeance.

Meanwhile the mendicant monks were going from hamlet
to hamlet in Italy, inciting the people to rebellion against the
emperor, and carrying the promise of indulgences to those who
would embrace the papal cause.   Frederick for his part
hastened to raise a strong army of mercenaries, to equip his
fleet and to put his fortresses in order.

Gregory left no stone unturned to gain adherents in his
new struggle; those who had already taken the cross were
first allowed, then compelled, to buy absolution from their
vows; being warned at the same time that Frederick was
likely to cast into irons and condemn to horrible punishments
those crusaders who might fall into his hands.

Frederick's successes in Italy. In Italy, as was natural, the Pope's efforts met with more
success than elsewhere; here he raised up a wasting war that
kept the emperor busy for the next two years.   In the Tuscan
cities Frederick found allies against the Lombard League; in
Florence, although Guelphs and Ghibellines were fighting
between themselves, both parties were as yet friendly to the
empire.

There is no need to follow the details of the war, or to
dwell on the defection of Frederick's allies, Azzo of Este, and
Alberic, brother of Ezzelino da Romano.   The emperor was
aided by his illegitimate son Enzio, who was already king
over a large part of Sardinia, and who was now made imperial
legate for the whole of Italy.   Enzio's later misfortunes
helped to break the heart of his father.

On the whole Frederick was not unsuccessful in these days.
He wrested nearly the whole of Spoleto and the March of
Ancona from the power of the papacy, and was able to occupy

Viterbo. He took Ravenna and, after a long siege, Faenza (April, 1241). The papal army answered the fall of the latter by an unsuccessful inroad into Sicily.

In 1240 the princes of Germany had sent to Rome the grandmaster Conrad of Thuringia, successor of Herrmann of Salza to negotiate a peace between the emperor and the Pope. The negotiations had failed as Gregory had insisted on including the Lombards in the agreement. Gregory calls a Council, 1240 A.D.

Gregory, meanwhile, had evolved a plan of his own for giving back to Christendom its much needed rest. He had determined to hold a general council of the Church at Rome, to submit to the representatives of the different parts of the Christian world his grievances against Frederick and to obtain of them his enemy's condemnation.

Easter-day 1241 was the term fixed for the assembly, and Frederick was asked to grant the prelates attending a safe conduct, and to suspend hostilies so long as the council should be in session.

Frederick was not for a moment in doubt as to what attitude an ecclesiastical assembly under the headship of his own bitter enemy would take towards himself. He wrote to the princes of Germany denouncing the hypocrisy of the Pope in the matter of the council, and declaring that Gregory only wanted him to make truce with the Lombards in order that the latter might procure for themselves reinforcements. He forbade those of his subjects who had been summoned to the council to attend it, and refused roundly to grant a safe conduct to any of the prelates. Frederick will not grant safe-conduct to the prelates.

That Gregory was in truth seeking the ruin of the emperor seems proven by the fact that even after summoning the council he continued to try and induce the Count of Artois to come forward as candidate for the throne of the empire.

Meanwhile there had begun to make itself heard on Germany's eastern boundary the roar of a torrent which, as it seemed for a time, threatened to engulf the empire and the papacy alike, and with it the whole civilivation of western Europe. The Tartar invasion.

During the early part of the century the Mongols, or Tartars, under their leader Temuchin or Gengis-Khan, had conquered the greater part of the celestial empire, the Corea, the mountains of Thibet, parts of Hindostan and Persia, and the lands bordering on the Caspian Sea. Gengis died in 1226, and his descendants continued his conquests.

Batou-Khan. It was his grandson, Batou-Khan, who now threatened Germany from the direction of Hungary. Parts of his army had at the same time been sent against Poland, Bohemia, and North Germany. At Liegnitz, in 1241, Duke Henry of Silesia was defeated by the tenfold more numerous army of the Mongols, but only after such a resistance that the victors had learned to dread their opponents and hurried off to join their leader in Hungary. Here they ravaged the country with a mercilessness that had not been equalled since the days of the Huns. King Bela, who had suffered a great defeat in March, fled to an island of the Adriatic, and sent wild calls for aid to the Pope and to the emperor. He offered, if Frederick would only aid him, to submit to becoming a vassal of the empire.

Frederick and the Tartars. The young King of the Romans, Conrad, the King of Bohemia, and other princes sent to Italy to urge the extremity of the danger, and to beg that a peace might at once be brought about between the heads of Christendom.

Frederick probably estimated the actual danger from the Mongols more truly than the alarmed princes. He contented himself with giving, through messengers, advice and directions as to how to war with the new enemy. He caused a decree to be issued ordering every one of his German male subjects with an income of more than three marks of silver to take to arms. He warned the generals not to engage in battle in the open plains; he gave suggestions as to the collecting of supplies and as to the economical use of barley and wheat, which were not to be employed for brewing beer or any other drinks whatever.

Satirical writings. The invasion of the Tartars, and the attitude of the Pope and of the emperor towards it, gave rise to a number of satirical and polemical writings. An anecdote went the rounds to the effect that Batou had offered Frederick, if he would lay down his arms, a lucrative employment at the Mongol court. Frederick was declared to have answered that he knew a good deal about ¡birds—on which subject, as it happens, a treatise of his has come down to us—and would like the position of falconer.

A forged letter, purporting to have been written by a Tartar general, was circulated throughout Europe and asserted that the object of the Khan's coming was to make peace at last between the empire and the papacy.

In one of these writings Frederick, who was called the worthy rival of Satan, was accused of having called in the Tartars to destroy the Christian faith, and to gain for himself the rule of the world.

Gregory maintained that Frederick had taken pains to exaggerate the whole danger, so that a large army might be brought together which could then be used against the papacy.

Frederick himself was sure, as he wrote to the princes, that if he were to leave Italy at this juncture of affairs the Pope would at once fall like a vulture upon the kingdom of Sicily. His absence from Germany did not in the end prevent the greatest and most successful preparations from being made there. A general crusade was preached against the invaders, and a universal peace proclaimed for the land. *Frederick cannot leave Italy.*

It was in these days that the emperor made his most bold and successful move against the Pope, after which he hastened to descend upon the estates of the Church, and prepared to end the struggle by taking Rome itself. *The capture of a hundred prelates, 1241 A.D.*

In naval combat, assisted by the Pisan fleet, King Enzio secured for his father one of the strangest prizes that ever fell to the lot of monarch. Frederick had always warned the prelates summoned by Gregory to attend the council that they would do so at the greatest peril to themselves. He had written special letters to this effect to the kings of France and England.

None the less, a large number of prelates embarked from Genoa in April, 1241, thinking to escape the emperor on the high seas. Vain hope! Between the islands of Giglio and Monte Cristo they were attacked by Enzio and overcome. Two thousand men in all, among them the Archbishop of Besançon, found their death in the waves. About one hundred cardinals, bishops, abbots, and deputies from Lombard cities were taken captive and brought to the emperor at Gaeta. At his command they were incarcerated at Naples and at Melfi, and it was long before they regained their liberty.

Gregory's indignation. Gregory's grief and indignation may be imagined; he sent a pathetic letter of condolence to the prisoners declaring, to comfort them, that the ship of Peter, now on a rock, would soon be sailing in smoother waters. He wrote to the kings of Europe, the Doge of Venice, and the heads of the Italian Republics, urging them to come to his aid against the tyrant and oppressor of the Church.

Frederick in a similar manifesto announced that he gave thanks to God whose powerful hand had laid low the abettors of the Pope.

Gregory's death, 1241 A.D. The emperor was already at the gates of Rome; he had taken Tivoli and stormed the fortifications of the monastery of Farfa, when he learned that the pontiff against whom all these hostilities were directed had gone the way of all flesh. In order to show that he was warring against the head of the Church as a man, and not against that institution itself, he immediately withdrew his army.

CHAPTER XXV.

FREDERICK II. AND INNOCENT IV.

MEANWHILE the great danger from the Tartars dis- Celestine appeared as quickly as it had come. Wenceslaus of IV. Bohemia defeated a strong detachment of them at Olmütz, and the death of the grand khan or head of the Mongol empire drew them away from Hungary and back to the Russian steppes.

In Rome the cardinals, among whom were two captured by Frederick, who released them temporarily and conditionally for the occasion, proceeded to the election of a new pope. They chose Celestine IV., a man who, had he lived, would in all likelihood have proved friendly to the emperor. But he died even before he could be consecrated, and disturbances in Rome, as well as the dread of the plague which was raging there, prevented the cardinals from making a new choice for the next twenty-one months. Frederick's two prisoners returned to their confinement.

Meanwhile in Germany Gregory IX.'s influence for evil Efforts to had made itself felt far out over his grave. His agent, that raise anti-king. same Albert of Behaim who had previously tried to raise up an antiking, resumed his activity. He entered into relations with Siegfried of Mayence, archchancellor of the empire and regent for the young Conrad, and with the new Archbishop of Cologne, the warlike Conrad of Hochstaden. They were soon joined by Arnold of Treves, by Bremen, Strasburg, and Liége.

The majority of the cities of the empire, however, held firmly to Frederick, who was obliged, indeed, to extend their privileges.

C C

The goal of the insurgents was the election of a new king, and the man on whom they had intended to bestow this dangerous honour was landgrave Henry Raspe of Thuringia. But Frederick made a flying visit to Germany, deposed Siegfried of Mayence from his position as vicegerent, and gave that office to none other than his own proposed rival, the landgrave.

Frederick tries to hasten papal election. Leaving King Conrad in the field against Siegfried of Mayence, and the Duke of Brabant and the Count of Juliers against the Archbishop of Cologne, whom they soon overcame, Frederick returned to Italy to hasten, if possible, the election of a pope. He wrote a letter to the cardinals and reminded them of their duty in forcible terms: "Like serpents you cling to the earth instead of raising yourselves to the skies. Each of you is aiming at the tiara, and no one of you is willing to leave it to the other. Renounce the spirit of faction and of discord! Let the college of cardinals give by unanimous choice to Christendom a pope who will satisfy us and the empire, and whose election will be for the universal good."

Frederick's disgust at the delays to which he was subjected caused him to use ever stronger and stronger terms. He calls the cardinals "sons of Belial," "troop of perdition," "the laughed-at of nations." At the same time he gave emphasis to his words by recommencing his ravagings in the neighbourhood of Rome, while Enzio devastated the territory of Piacenza, Milan, and Brescia.

Frederick and the vacant chair of Peter. Meanwhile the affairs of the Church, without a head as it was, had come into a state of almost irretrievable confusion. A pamphlet was written at this time, the author of which was supposed to be the emperor's chancellor, Peter de la Vigne, and which seems to have advocated doing away altogether with the papacy. Its language is somewhat enigmatical: "If the pontifical unction has ceased to be performed, if a pope anointed and consecrated is not to be found, are you not afraid that another holy of holies will arise? And what will it be?"

It was even hinted in certain circles that Frederick would like the position of pope for himself, and Louis IX. of France, in a letter to the cardinals, speaks of a "prince who would fain at the same time be king and priest." The French clergy, for their own part, are said to have been on the point of electing a pope for themselves.

At last, in June, 1243, an end was put to this anomalous state of affairs, and Sinibald Fiesco, a Genoese, was raised to the papal throne. He took the name of Innocent IV. As cardinal he had been on the best of terms with the emperor, who, however, did not build great hopes on his elevation, declaring that no pope could ever be a Ghibelline. He wrote, nevertheless, in a most conciliatory spirit to the new pontiff: " We have learned with extreme joy that our old friend has become our father; we believe that your elevation to the papacy will put an end to all our discords." ·

Innocent IV., 1243-1254.

The ambassadors who brought this message of congratulation were not admitted into the presence of the new pope, being envoys of a prince who was in the ban. It was an ill omen for the success of the necessary negotiations.

These negotiations were soon entered into by the Pope, who sent the Archbishop of Rouen and two other prelates to the emperor at Melfi. Innocent's demands were as follows : Frederick was to release the remainder of those who had been taken captive in the great naval battle of 1241—a number of them had already been set at liberty. He was to restore all the lands taken from the Church, and to make peace with the Lombards. The complaints of the emperor against the Church, and of the Church against the emperor, were to be submitted to a tribunal of kings, princes, and prelates.

Negotiations with Innocent.

Frederick, for his part, was willing enough to give up all the lands in question on condition that he should receive them back as a fief of the papacy, paying tribute for their use. He offered, further, to give the Pope a sum of money, and to undertake a new expedition to the Holy Land. Disturbances in Viterbo, where the inhabitants drove out the imperial garrison and called in the Guelphs, as the partisans of the

Pope had now come to be called, to their assistance, jeopardized for some time the success of the negotiations.

The
drawing-up
of a peace.
Frederick had spent three months before the town, which had received pecuniary assistance from the Pope, and was preparing to bring about its utter destruction, when the representations of the German princes, on the one hand, and of Louis IX. and the Count of Toulouse on the other, induced both Pope and emperor to consent to the drawing up of a preliminary peace. The captives were to be released, and the Church lands given back, while all those who had taken the Pope's part were to be pardoned.

The Pope and the cardinals were to be arbiters in the Lombard question; Frederick, finally, was to declare to the princes of Europe that in not submitting to the papal ban, he had not intended to scorn the Pope's authority, but that, as a matter of fact, he had never been properly notified of the sentence. To show his regret for all that had taken place, he was to fast and to give alms, to found monasteries and hospitals, and to place knights at the disposal of the Pope.

The peace
broken.
The peace had been signed and sworn to by the imperial plenipotentiaries, the Pope had spoken publicly of Frederick as a devoted Catholic prince and son of the Church, when difficulties and differences of interpretation arose, which altogether prevented a reconciliation.

Frederick wanted the Lombards to take an oath of fealty to himself before the liberation of their delegates who were among the captives; Innocent insisted that the latter should be freed at once, and that the whole question at issue between the League and the Empire should be subjected unconditionally to his own decision. The Pope furthermore demanded that the restitution of the Church lands should be made without reserve, Frederick that certain rights of his own should be regarded. A grave question arose as to whether the emperor should be absolved from the ban before or after making his restitutions.

The rejoicings that followed on Frederick's signing of the peace were of short duration. Before a month had passed

Innocent despatched a writing to Germany to the effect that the emperor preferred breaking his oath rather than to obey the commands which he, the Pope, had laid upon him.

Innocent had begun to feel that Rome was no longer a safe place for him; he was anxious, too, to hold a general council, but not in Italy. He knew that no more foreign prelates could be induced to lay themselves open to capture by the emperor. Flight of Innocent IV., 1244 A.D.

While still carrying on negotiations with Frederick, and while not refusing the latter's invitation to a personal interview, the Pope prepared for flight. His three nephews met him with a fleet at Civita Vecchia; by July, 1244, he was in Genoa, by December in Lyons, whence he wrote his general summons to the long-projected council: " In order that the Church," so ran the document, " may, through the assistance of her faithful ones, gain the honour and adornment that belongs to her; in order that relief may be brought as soon as possible to the ill-fate of the Holy Land, and to the sorely tried empire; also that a means of riddance may be found against the Tartars and other betrayers of the faith and persecutors of Christendom; finally, because of the conflict at issue between the prince and the Church, we have decided to call together the kings, prelates, and other princes of the world." Summons to Council of Lyons.

The missive goes on to say that " the prince " mentioned has been summoned to appear before the council either personally or through emissaries.

The mishap to the Holy Land, to which Innocent referred, had been caused by the fact that the Sultan of Egypt, irritated by the dealings of the Jerusalem barons with his own enemies, had called in the Charismian Turks, who had visited the Holy city with havoc and devastation. A Christian army, raised to avenge this proceeding, had been defeated and dispersed. The Holy Land.

Shortly after Innocent had issued his summons to the council the three heads of his party in Germany, the Archbishops of Mayence and Cologne and Albert de Behaim, now Archdeacon of Passau, came to Lyons. They engaged themselves, should the Pope see fit to proceed to Frederick's deposition, to themselves undertake the election of a new king. They returned to Germany to carry out this plan, for the furtherance of which Innocent soon sent a special legate, Philip of Ferrara.

The Council, 1245 A.D. That the council of Lyons was not universal, and could not be so in the absence of almost all the German bishops, was a foregone conclusion. Frederick sent his two great legists, Thaddeus of Suessa and William of Ocra, to appeal from whatever decisions should be made to a future pope, and to a proper council.

At the assembly, which was opened in June, 1245, there were present about 150 prelates, mostly from France, Spain, and Italy. The question at issue with Frederick II. was at once taken up, and Innocent proceeded to heap one accusation after another upon his enemy. Among the crimes mentioned were the establishment of the Saracen colony at Luceria, Frederick's oriental habits and customs, his astrological superstitions, his scorn of the Christian religion, his friendship with the Sultan of Egypt, the permanent violation of all his promises.

Deposition of Frederick. At the third session of the council, held three weeks after its opening, Frederick's condemnation was passed, and he was declared deposed from the throne of the empire. Innocent, in his boundless self-partiality, asserted later that he could remember no case which had ever been more carefully and deliberately tried by experienced and holy men. To use his own words, "Some of our brethren undertook for him [the emperor] in secret session the *rôle* of defenders, others that of accusers, in order that through thesis and antithesis, according to the method of the customary disputations in the schools, the truth might be most thoroughly proven."

The secret sessions. What went on in those secret sessions is not difficult to conjecture from the public acts of accusation which were drawn up for the benefit of the whole asssembly. Frederick is called the prince of tyranny, the effacer of the Church's dogma, the master of cruelty, the destroyer of the universe, the hammer of the whole earth, and more of the kind. "For

inasmuch as four times and more he has committed the
crime of high treason, and through all the crimes mentioned
and many others, has so robbed himself of all imperial and
royal power, that a new election must be gone through with
by the princes: see to it that one so vicious and unrepentant
do not again arise to the shame of the princes and to the ruin
of the world.   Rather, as a warning to these same mighty
princes, give over this man, drunk with the blood of so many
saints, to everlasting ignominy.   Wipe out the name and the
offspring of this Babylonian; let his name be forgotten,
inasmuch as he is boundlessly unmerciful and cruel."

After the final decree of condemnation had been read, after
all who were bound in any way to the emperor had been loosed
from their oaths, and all who should in any way assist him had
been declared excommunicate, Thaddeus of Suessa, Frederick's
representative, rose in solemn protest.   At the beginning of
the session he had declared again that the council was not
universal, and had been told that it was as much so as the
ambushes of the emperor would allow.   He now exclaimed, if
Matthew Paris can be believed, "This is the day of wrath, of
misery, and of anguish," and foretold the end of all things.
The Pope answered: "I have done what I was bound to do,
may God fulfil it according to His will."   The clergy lowered
their torches to the ground to the sound of the " Te Deum."

Protest of Frederick's envoy.

Frederick, after his deposition, wrote circular letters to the
princes and prelates of Europe.   He declared that no law,
divine or human, had conferred on the Pope the right to
dispose of empires, or to punish princes by depriving them of
their temporal dignities.   He denounced the whole manner of
procedure of the council, and, finally, attacked the corruption
and greed of the clergy and the abuse which they made of
their power.   "Devoured with ambition they hope that the
whole Jordan will flow into their mouths. . . . If you reach
them your hand they will take your arm all the way up to the
elbow. . . . Join yourselves to us and we will look to it
together that they lose what is superfluous, that they serve
the Lord henceforward and content themselves with little."

Frederick to the princes of Europe.

Innocent's letter.

Frederick had often declared that his own cause was the cause of the kings and princes to whom he was writing. Innocent wisely undertook to refute this assertion, arguing that there was a difference between a king whose throne was hereditary and an emperor who had been chosen by the princes and consecrated at Rome. At the same time he made a strong defence of his own almost god-like prerogatives : " As to the imperial dignity, was it not the papacy which transferred it from the Greeks to the Romans and from Constantinople to Rome ? . . . Can the successor of the Apostle not judge kings ? Has it not been said to him, ' Behold, I have set thee over kings and kingdoms to the end that thou shouldst uproot and plant ? ' . . . It is not only a sacerdotal rule but a royal domination that Christ has founded."

Hostile utterances.

The war between the empire and the papacy was now more than ever a conflict of irreconcilable principles ; in passing sentence upon Frederick the Pope had declared : " we and our brothers the cardinals will maintain the struggle for the cause of God and of the Church until our last breath." Frederick, for his part, gave the world to understand that hitherto he had played the part of anvil, but that now he was determined to undertake the *rôle* of hammer.

An effort was made by Louis IX. of France to bring about a peace between the two great adversaries, and Innocent IV. and twelve cardinals spent a week with the French monarch at Cluny ; but neither then nor through the correspondence that followed was any result achieved.

The war in Italy.

In various parts of Italy hostilities were now resumed ; Frederick was efficiently aided by Ezzelino da Romano, by King Enzio, and by Count Thomas of Savoy. No great action took place, but, on the whole, the emperor's cause was in the ascendant. Before the end of the year 1246, he seemed on the point of being able to bring the Pope to terms. Enzio joined him in Western Lombardy, and in the spring of 1247 all was ready for a combined undertaking against Innocent. But at this juncture the loss of Parma, which was important as dominating the way to Tuscany, and which had been

counted on as a sure Ghibelline stronghold, caused Frederick
to hasten and attempt its recovery.

At this time a conspiracy in which those of his own house- **Conspiracy**
hold were concerned, was made against the emperor's life. It **against**
was headed by Tibald Francesco, a former Podesta of Parma, **life.**
who is said to have been won by the promise of the Sicilian
crown. The subjects of the latter land had already been
specially exhorted by the Pope to throw off the yoke of " the
second Nero, the master of lies, the corrupter of the world,
despiser of the faith, and persecutor of the Church."

The conspiracy was discovered by Frederick in time; many
of its leaders, together with the garrisons of the fortresses
Scala and Capaccio, where they had taken refuge, were
blinded, mutilated, and killed. One hundred and fifty persons
perished in this way, and twenty-two women were sentenced
to life-long imprisonment.

In a circular letter addressed to the sovereigns of Europe **The Pope**
Frederick accused Innocent of having sharpened the sword **favours the**
that had been intended for himself. The Pope was unwise **assassins.**
enough soon to give colour to these charges by heaping
rewards on those who had been engaged in the conspiracy and
who had escaped Frederick's wrath. The deed of gift to a
certain ringleader, Pandulf Fasanella—or rather the copy of
it that the Pope kept in his own registry—is still extant.

For his own part the Pope raised a countercharge of intended
murder against the emperor, and is declared by Matthew
Paris, who has recently been convicted, however, of a tendency
to invent romantic details, never to have left his palace unless
attended by a bodyguard of men-at-arms.

Meanwhile in Germany the efforts of the papal party had **Henry**
been successful, and Henry Raspe, landgrave of Thuringia, **Raspe as**
had been elected king and future emperor. **antiking.**

The election took place in May, 1246; already a month
beforehand Innocent had been able to write to the princes
that the landgrave "was ready to take upon himself the
burden of the empire for the honour of God and of the Church,
and for the protection of the Christian religion."

The Pope had displayed an immense activity in the matter; his messengers had gone from end to end of Europe. Even the citizens of Lübeck had received a special writing exhorting them to take the side of Henry. Nor did Innocent shrink from expense ; immediately after the election he sent the anti-king ten thousand marks of silver, later he forwarded fifteen thousand more. He ordered that a crusade should be preached against Frederick by the Archbishop of Mayence, but the latter had already anticipated the command. The souls of those who fought in the good cause were to be freed from all sin.

The German princes. It was fortunate for the Hohenstaufens that many of the German princes showed indifference to and took no part in the struggle while others declared against Henry Raspe. The emperor failed indeed in his efforts to win Frederick the War-like of Austria by raising that duchy to a kingdom and by offering·his own hand to the Austrian duke's niece and pro-spective heiress. The prince in question, however, died in these days.

Otto of Bavaria. The man whose partizanship proved most decisive and availing for the emperor was Otto of Bavaria, a prince whose policy was chiefly prompted by jealousy of the King of Bohemia. The latter's son married that same daughter of Frederick the Warlike whom the emperor had sought as his own bride, and the Bohemian hoped in this way to gain for his house the rich Austrian heritage. But the Wittlesbach, Otto, was unwilling to have so powerful a neighbour on his boundary, and he declared for Frederick, to whose son, Conrad, he wedded his own daughter Elizabeth. The ceremony took place in all haste, September 1st, 1246.

Henry Raspe's success. The one great and only success of Henry Raspe's short reign was a battle fought at Frankfort, where he had determined to hold a diet, with the young King Conrad, who had tried to prevent the assembly. Conrad was deserted after the fighting had already commenced by a part of his Suabian nobles who had been bribed by the Pope. One sees that there was no depth to which the successor of Peter would not descend for the sake of ruining the race to which he bore so intense a hatred.

The victory of the antiking was complete; many of Conrad's followers were killed, six hundred knights were carried away captive.

Henry held his diet after the battle and at it, in obedience to the papal injunctions, the Archbishops of Salzburg and Bremen, ten bishops and five abbots were excommunicated for having remained true to the Hohenstaufens. The majority of those thus punished, however, later submitted to Innocent.

Frederick II., at the news of the progress which the rival king was making, determined to return with an army from Italy, and to conduct the war in person ; but there was no need. Conrad recovered from the blow that he had received, and, supported by Bavaria, was soon able to hold his own.

Henry Raspe prepared for a winter campaign in Suabia. **Death of** He held a diet at Nuremburg, and then, towards the end of **Henry** January, besieged Ulm. After a few days he was compelled **Raspe.** by want of provender, and by an illness which befell himself, to raise the siege and to return to Thuringia. A fall from his horse increased his malady, and he died in the Wartburg February 16th, 1247. At the news of this misfortune the papal party became so demoralized for the moment that the legate, Philip, first concealed himself, and then hastily fled from the land.

Henry Raspe has generally been represented as a coward and a weakling ; his conduct during the few months that he reigned shows nothing to justify such accusations. It is impossible to say whether or not he was capable of accomplishing great things had a longer rule been granted to him.

Innocent IV. showed no intention of ceasing from his perse- **Innocent** cution of the house of Hohenstaufen. His party employed **IV. does not** the short period of quiet that ensued on Henry's death in **desist.** preparing new forces, and in finding a new candidate for the throne.

In May, 1247, Innocent published the sharpest edict that a Pope had yet invented against an emperor. Those who

still remained faithful to Frederick were not to be admitted
to give testimony in court, or to perform any other legal
functions; should they be pursued for crimes, and have fled
to a church, they were to be denied the ordinary right of
asylum. No one, under pain of anathema and interdict, was
to have any intercourse or in any way to carry on trade with
the emperor's supporters.

William of Holland. The crown of the empire was offered now to various princes,
to the Count of Gelders, the Duke of Brabant, Richard of
Cornwall—who all, however, refused. It was finally accepted
by William of Holland, a youth of twenty, who was elected
at Worringen, October 3rd, 1247. The assembly which chose
him consisted chiefly of prelates, and of Rhenish and Westphalian nobles. But one prince of importance was present,
the Duke of Brabant.

Innocent at this time again caused the cross to be preached
against Frederick, and gave his legate a general permission
to change the objects of vows already taken against the
heathen if Palestine had not been expressly mentioned by
name. In William's hereditary lands even this feeble exception
was omitted.

In this way William was able to raise a considerable army;
in the lower Rhenish provinces, and in the land between the
Maas and the Ems, he soon gained recognition.

His greatest acquisition was Cologne; the city closed a
treaty which was full, indeed, on his part, of the unworthiest
concessions. The Pope sent his thanks to " the glorious, and
as it were, the only city of Germany; which surpasses all
others in size, fame, and power."

Aix besieged. It was expected that Aix would follow Cologne's example,
and a diet was summoned to meet there. But the city
proved refractory, as did also Kaiserswerth, and William
spent the whole winter in preparing to besiege these two
strongholds. It was almost a year before he was able to
enter the old coronation city, and to have that ceremony performed. The true crown being still in the hands of the
Hohenstaufens a new one was prepared.

William of Holland's elevation to the throne was only of
interest to a small part of the empire.   It did little to stem
the anarchy that was at this time rampant all over Germany
as well as in Italy.   Guelph was fighting Ghibelline in every
corner of the one country as of the other.   There were feuds
and wars in Bavaria and Franconia, and on the Suabian,
Austrian, and Bohemian boundaries ; a few sieges more or
less made little difference.

CHAPTER XXVI

THE star of the Hohenstaufens was sinking beneath a threatening horizon, and over a political sea that had already began to rage violently. The young King Conrad made what efforts he could to better the state of affairs, but, in the main, was obliged to keep on the defensive. He had neither strong allies nor pecuniary resources.

Siege of Parma by Frederick II. The emperor meanwhile had been engaged in besieging Parma. That city had been wrested from the Ghibellines by a number of its own Guelphic exiles, assisted by partisans of Innocent from neighbouring towns. Frederick had been obliged to give up an intended expedition into Burgundy for the purpose of attacking the Pope in Lyons.

Parma, as has been said, was particularly important from its position ; Frederick had reason to fear, too, that if it were not recovered other Italian communes would fall into the hands of the papal party. The siege was carried on with vigour, but the defence was courageous and determined.

Frederick caused his camp to be laid out in the form of a city, with streets, houses, and churches; he intended that Parma, once in his power, should be given over to destruction, and that the inhabitants should settle in his new foundation, to which, confidant as he was of success, he gave the name Vittoria.

The taking of Vittoria. By February, 1248, Parma had been almost reduced to subjection, and for three months no supplies had entered the city. But all at once the carelessness of the besiegers altogether reversed the order of affairs. The emperor had gone on a hunting expedition, leaving Vittoria with but a scanty

garrison, when the Parmesans made a quick sally from their
city, and possessed themselves of the new settlement. They
set fire to its wooden houses, reducing the town to a heap of
ashes. Fifteen hundred of the enemy, among them Thaddeus
of Suessa, are reported to have been killed, three thousand to
have been taken prisoner.

Frederick returned from the hunt to find the work of
months undone ; he gathered together the débris of his army
and retreated to Cremona. His sceptre, crown, and seal, as
well as his harem, remained in the hands of the victors.

The result of the events at Parma was to greatly encourage
the followers of Innocent, to whose side Ravenna and almost
all the cities of the Romagna now passed over.

During the next two years Frederick regained much of his
influence, but it was a hard up-hill fight that he fought; the **Peter de la**
more so as treason was once more found to lurk in his imme- **Vigne.**
diate vicinity. Peter de la Vigne had been the emperor's
cherished friend and counsellor as well as the judge of the
royal court; he had been sent, too, on many an important
and confidential mission. How much Frederick thought of
him may be gathered from the fact that in the palace at
Capua one painting represented the emperor together with
de la Vigne and with Thaddeus of Suessa, another the emperor
on his throne and Peter in his judicial chair.

Whether Frederick's suspicions were well-founded or not is
a matter of dispute, but at Cremona in February, 1249, he
had Peter de la Vigne arrested on a charge of having attempted
to poison him. According to one account a physician bribed
by Peter, according to another Peter himself, had presented
the emperor with a deadly potion. Frederick maintained
that the chief responsibility for the intended crime rested
with the Pope.

Peter de la Vigne, after almost falling a victim to the rage **Death of**
of the inhabitants of Cremona, was carried to Borgo San **Peter de la**
Donnino, where he was judged by a number of commissioners. **Vigne.**
He was then taken to San Miniato, where his eyes were burnt
out with red hot irons. At Pisa, on the way to Sicily, where

it was intended that he should pass the rest of his days, he put an end to his own life by dashing his brains out against the stone pillar of a church.

Enzio's captivity.

A misfortune even more severe than the treason and death of his once faithful adviser was still reserved for Frederick. At the time of de la Vigne's arrest the young king Enzio had been wedded at Cremona to a niece of Ezzelino da Romano. A few months afterwards he, the emperor's favourite son and most devoted adherent, was taken prisoner by the Bolognese in an insignificant skirmish at Fossalta. A number of his followers were likewise captured.

Frederick did his utmost to procure his son's release, but all his efforts were in vain. For the next twenty-three years the unfortunate prince languished in confinement. Death at last put an end to his sorrows in the year 1272.

In spite of all his trials Frederick's position in 1250 was by no means desperate. The Pope's prestige had received a severe blow through the failure of the crusade of Louis of France and, on the whole, the balance of power in the Italian cities was with the imperialists. In Germany, too, Conrad's cause was slightly in the ascendant, and he had made successful ravaging expeditions against the territory of his opponents.

Frederick's death, 1250 A.D.

But the emperor's chequered career was now at an end. He fell a victim to dysentery while on the march from Foggia to Luceria, December 13th, 1250. At the last the Archbishop of Palermo removed the church's ban, and Frederick was buried in the Cathedral at Palermo where his magnificent porphyry mausoleum still stands.

In 1781, during some repairs to the cathedral, this tomb was opened by order of the government. It was discovered that two other bodies had later been placed with Frederick, the one that of Peter of Arragon, who died in 1346, the other that of a person unknown. The great emperor's remains were found to be in a perfect state of preservation except for the fact that the weight of these bodies superimposed upon him had somewhat flattened his features.

His head, which lay on a leather cushion, bore a crown; the garments in which he was attired are supposed to have been those worn at his imperial consecration.

The imperial orb was there but, contrary to usage, was surmounted by no cross. A cross sewn on to his cloak, however, served as a reminder that the dead monarch had once been a crusader.

According to Frederick II.'s will King Conrad IV. and, in the event of the latter's death another son, Henry, was to succeed to the throne in Sicily. As a last possibility, Manfred, whose birth had been legitimatized shortly before the emperor's death, was to uphold the honour of the Hohenstaufens.

Conrad, whose reign thus far had been one of continual hardships and trials—on one occasion he had barely escaped falling victim to an attempt upon his life—now gave up the struggle in Germany and hastened to claim his Sicilian inheritance. In January, 1252, he joined his brother Manfred, who had been occupied in the meantime in mastering various uprisings in Southern Italy.

Innocent IV. steadily refused all overtures made to him by the young king, against whom he caused a crusade to be preached. He sent special writings to many princes, and an encyclical writing to all the cities of Germany in favour of William of Holland. William came in person to Lyons where he remained with Innocent several days. On the occasion of a great public function he held the stirrup of the papal charger.

In order to provide himself with a strong ally, Innocent induced the Lombard cities to renew their league. He offered Sicily in turn to Richard Cornwallis, brother of Henry III. of England, to Charles of Anjou, and to Henry III.'s son, the youthful Edmund, who finally accepted. His father raised the enormous sums which the Pope demanded, and in March, 1254, Edmund was invested by a papal legate with Sicily as a fief of the Roman see. He never took possession of the land, however, and Henry III. soon had need of the monies he had raised for his own wars with France.

Conrad IV., 1250-1254.

D D

Conrad IV.'s death.

At this time Conrad IV., who had raised an army of 20,000 men, prepared to strike a decisive blow. He was carried away, however, by a fever contracted while besieging Naples.

Conrad had always intended, after subjecting Italy, to return and take up the struggle in Germany. He had left his queen there and she, in 1252, had borne him a son—Conradino as the Italians called him. The guardianship of this son, Conrad on dying gave to his own arch-enemy Innocent IV. It was an experiment that had once worked well for the Hohenstaufens in the case of Frederick II., but this time, although Innocent IV. had first accepted the charge, it was destined not to succeed.

Manfred.

Conrad IV. and his brother Manfred had, at the last, no longer been on good terms with each other. The one was German at heart, the other Italian. Manfred finally became reconciled to the Pope, accepted the office of lieutenant of the kingdom of Sicily, and, shortly before Innocent's death, which occurred in December, 1256, held the bridle of the latter's palfrey at Naples. He soon tired of his position as papal vassal, however, and hurried to Lucera, where the Saracens received him with open arms. He gained a victory at Foggia over the papal troops, and caused Alexander IV., the successor of Innocent, to flee from Naples.

Manfred then proceeded to take possession of one province after another, and, in August, 1258, to the exclusion of the rights of the young Conradino, caused himself to be crowned at Palermo as King of Sicily.

His reign proved rather a boon than otherwise for the land, but, in February, 1265, Pope Clement IV. signed a treaty with Charles of Anjou, brother of the King of France, transferring to him all rights over the Sicilian kingdom.

Charles of Anjou.

Charles of Anjou, whose rule of oppression was to form the prelude to the cruel Sicilian Vespers, entered Italy at the head of a brilliant army. The Pope greeted him as "a Charles the Great, son of Pippin." He was crowned at Rome, in the church of St. Peter's, by five cardinals, the Pope himself not being able to enter the city because of debts which the Holy See had contracted, and for which he was held personally responsible.

The great reckoning with Manfred took place at Benevento in February, 1266. That unfortunate prince, after making a brave resistance, fell in the thickest of the fight. The French knights, his victors, are said, as a token of homage to his valour, to have each carried a stone to the place where he was buried, near the bridge of Benevento. He was soon exhumed from his honourable place of rest by order of the papal legate, and his remains were thrown in the Volturno. *Manfred's death, 1266 A.D.*

There remained one scion of the great race whose destinies have concerned us so long. The young Conradino, who had been brought up at Constance by his uncles, the Count Palatine and the Duke of Bavaria, was now fifteen years of age. After the death of Manfred, fugitives from Benevento came to offer him the crown of Sicily, and the prospect of eventually becoming emperor. *Conradino.*

A proclamation was now issued in Germany protesting against the rule of Charles of Anjou over Sicily, and calling for knights to join the young Hohenstaufen. With an army of 6,000 men Conradino crossed the Brenner in October, 1267, being received at Pisa as the liberator of Italy. Rome outdid herself in bidding him welcome, and one of her senators proclaimed him emperor in the Capitol.

None the less, as Clement IV. is said to have remarked, Conradino was going "like a lamb to the slaughter." *The battle of Tagliacozzo, 1268 A.D.*

Tagliacozzo, near the Abruzzian Mountains, was the scene of the final effort of a Hohenstaufen to regain the lands of his fathers. The battle at first went against the French, but a sudden charge of Charles of Anjou and a thousand of his best knights changed the fortunes of the day.

Conradino escaped from the field and fled first to Rome, and from there to the sea coast, where one of the Frangipani, a former Ghibelline, to whom he incautiously revealed his identity, gave him up to Charles. He was taken to Naples, and, together with his faithful friend, Frederick of Austria, was publicly beheaded in the market place. *Conradino's death.*

Many details were later invented concerning this tragic scene, the more so as it became a favourite theme for the troubadours. All that is really known is that the boy of seventeen showed the courage of his race, and met his death with calmness.

William of Holland.

How little William of Holland's kingship signified for Germany, to turn back to the affairs of that land, may be gathered from the fact that he was able to spend nearly two years (February, 1253, to January, 1255) in the Netherlands, where he was engaged for the most part in a feud with the Countess of Flanders. He had somewhat strengthened his cause, indeed, by marrying, in 1252, the daughter of Otto of Brunswick, the descendant of Henry the Lion. He had also been recognized by the Duke of Saxony and the Margrave of Brandenburg.

The Rhine Confederation.

Of great importance for William was the formation of a large and well-organized confederation of the Rhine cities, which, after Conrad's death, placed itself at his disposal. It was soon joined by the cities of Westphalia. The avowed object of the confederation was to gain protection for its members against violence and against unjust tolls; its ideal was to found a general peace. It gave itself a military organization, and prepared to form a large fleet which should protect its interests on the Rhine.

Had William of Holland not received assurances of fidelity and support from the newly-founded league, it is more than probable that he would have resigned his crown in favour of Ottokar of Bohemia. He was surrounded everywhere by powerful enemies. The Archbishop of Cologne went so far in his hostility as to set fire to the house in which the king was having a conference with the papal legate, and the august pair barely escaped with their lives.

It is interesting to note that while joining his cause to that of the league, William did not confirm the latter as an already existing power, but pretended, as it were, to be its founder. His object was to represent the organization as one not independent of, but subject to the central power; and he ignored those acts which had taken place before the league had won his own sanction.

William held a diet at Worms in January, 1255, at which, for the first time in the history of the empire, deputies from a large number of cities were present.

William of Holland lost his life in an expedition against his hereditary enemies the Frisians, January, 1256. His reign had embraced one of the most dreary periods in the whole of German history, yet his death was a misfortune, for he was beginning to restore peace and order to a part at least of the land. *William's death, 1256 A.D.*

Germany was now to suffer the greatest shame that had yet befallen her; no worthy candidate from her own princes now came forward for her vacant throne. She became the spoil of foreigners, who desired the possession of her royal title as a means to the conquest of Italy.

It was the Rhenish cities which at this time seemed about to enter the lists successfully for the preservation of law and order. They declared that the princes must proceed at once to a proper election; should two or more kings be chosen, they, the cities, would refuse to acknowledge any one of the candidates—they would lend him no money nor would they allow him to enter their precincts. Would that the cities had remained firm in the patriotic attitude which they had assumed. But differences made themselves felt, and dissensions crept in among them. Those especially which were under the rule of bishops, like Cologne, Mayence, Spires, and Worms, were soon following the selfish and disjointed policy of their masters.

Two foreigners, Alphonse of Castile and Richard Cornwallis came forward and vied for the throne. Alphonse had already caused himself to be elected Roman king and emperor by Pisa, and king by the town of Marseilles—vain and empty ceremonies, the significance of which is hard to comprehend.

The great importance of the election of 1257 lies in the fact that here, for the first time, the electoral college, with its *The rise of the electoral college.*

seven members, appeared as a complete and exclusive organization with power to choose whom it would. Seven princes
had risen so in power and influence above their fellows,
that to them alone belonged the right to give a head to their
nation.

It is one of the unsolved problems of German history to
know exactly how this change came about. In the elections
of Henry VII., of Conrad IV., of Henry Raspe and of William
of Holland, a number of lesser princes had been concerned;
they were now suddenly thrust in the background.

Already in the Sachsenspiegel, the great law-book which
was published about 1230, the theory had been advanced that
the chief votes in the election belonged to six princes; the
archbishops of Mayence, Cologne, and Treves, the Count Palatine, the Duke of Saxony, and the Margrave of Brandenburg.
The reason for mentioning these men and not others seems to
have been that they actually were already the representatives
of their fellow princes at the ceremony of the coronation.

The provision of the Sachsenspiegel remained merely a
theory for nearly a generation, but it is highly probable that
after William of Holland's death and after two or more fruitless diets had been held concerning a new election, the method
there proposed was adopted by consent of the princes.

The seven electors. To the original six members mentioned in the Sachsenspiegel came as a seventh the King of Bohemia, who claimed
his position as being chief steward of the empire. His vote
was at first disputed, but the Pope upheld him and the
German people soon came to look upon him as an elector. In
the double election that now took place his vote was eagerly
sought after by both parties, there being three votes for each
candidate.

The double election of 1257. The Archbishops of Mayence and Cologne and the Count
Palatine, who shared his vote with his brother, Henry of
Bavaria, declared for Richard Cornwallis; the Archbishop of
Treves, the Duke of Saxony, and the Margrave of Branden-
burg for Alphonse of Castile.

The King of Bohemia, strange as it may seem, gave his vote

to both candidates. It is probable that his envoy used the unlimited powers conferred upon him in favour of the one, while the king himself was gained over personally for the other. It is also probable that even had Bohemia acted otherwise, the schism would still have taken place; for Richard's electors were determined, if need be, to count as two the votes of the Count Palatine and his brother.

Richard Cornwallis came to Aix-la-Chapelle and was crowned there with great pomp and circumstance. The expenses of the ceremony as well as the enormous sums with which, as previously stipulated, he was obliged to reward his electors, caused him to draw heavily on his resources. "Foolish England," exclaims a Hamburg chronicler of the time, "which has deprived itself voluntarily of so many pence! Foolish princes of Germany who have sold for money their noble prerogative!"

One result of the double election was the practical dissolu- **End of** tion of the Rhine Confederation; the cities now took sides **Rhine Con-** with the one king or the other. Aix-la-Chapelle had set the **federation.** example by receiving Richard within its walls. A number of other cities such as Frankfort, Nuremburg, Wetzlar, and Gelnhausen followed suit and acknowledged the English prince in return for privileges which made them almost independent of the empire. Richard was obliged to promise, too, to absolve the citizens from their oath of fealty should his own election not be ratified by the Pope, and should a king who should be generally recognized as lawful be raised up against him.

One remarkable feature of the history of Germany at this time is the lack of interest that the nation as a whole took in the matter of the king and the antiking. No one seems to have known on the whole which was which, and no one cared enough to take to arms for the cause of either. No German annalist concerns himself with these affairs at all, and we are dependent for most of our information on English chroniclers and on papal letters.

Alphonse of Castile, occupied as he was with the affairs of **Alphonse of Castile.**

his Spanish kingdom and with his wars against the Moors, never once appeared in Germany. At the beginning he had fully intended to do so and, like Richard, had squandered large sums of money. But in the end he came to look upon his German dignity as the merest honorary title, a necessary preliminary to the longed for imperial crown.

Many of the great nobles, indeed, on Germany's western boundary considered themselves vassals of Alphonse, and went to Spain to be invested with their fiefs. As a matter of fact they were practically their own masters, and troubled themselves little about their distant suzerain.

Richard Cornwallis. Richard Cornwallis tried for a time to do his duty to the land over which he had become king, but possessing as he did no crown estates in Germany, and entangled as he was in the disputes between the crown and the nobles in England, he accomplished nothing. He returned after a year and a half to the land of his birth, where he henceforth passed by far the greater part of his time.

The empire meanwhile was left to its own dissensions. Each prince was striving to develop into an independent territorial lord, and constant disputes arose as to the proper boundaries between one neighbour and another. The land was full of petty feuds and jealousies innumerable.

The imperial crown. Neither Richard Cornwallis nor his rival was crowned emperor at Rome; great efforts, indeed, had been made in this direction, but without success. The popes remained neutral until a process which had been instituted in the matter at Rome, but which had dragged on for years, should have been decided. Urban IV. went so far as to address both kings in turn as " elected king of the Romans," and Clement IV.'s plan was that both kings should abdicate and a third person should be elected. After Manfred's death the prospect of having once more a really German king in Conradino seems to have met with general approval among the princes, but we have seen the outcome of the young Hohenstaufen's prior undertaking against Charles of Anjou.

After Conradino's execution efforts were made to bring forward Frederick III., as he was called, a son of Frederick II.'s daughter Margaret and of the Margrave of Meissen. The majority of the princes, however, saw plainly that nothing was to be gained by such a proceeding—instead of two there would have been three nominal heads of Germany.

With the accession of Gregory X. to the pontifical throne, in 1272, the process concerning the German throne seemed likely to be brought at last to a conclusion. But a higher power stepped in and rendered the continuance of that process unnecessary. The news came of Richard's illness and death, and no one troubled themselves any more about Alphonse of Castile. **Richard's death.**

Alphonse, indeed, now demanded from the Pope the imperial consecration and coronation as his own undoubted right, but he found no favour in the eyes of Gregory X. **End of the interregnum**

The latter proceeded to take a step that was to be the salvation of Germany. He fairly commanded the electors to hasten and make a new choice; in case of refusal he threatened that he and his cardinals would give the empire a head.

The so-called interregnum, which had lasted since 1250, was at an end; the fearful time of anarchy was over and a new order of things began.

One of the first proceedings of the new ruler, Rudolph of Hapsburg, was to annul, with consent of the electors, all public measures that had been passed by the kings who had reigned since the deposition of Frederick II.

CHAPTER XXVII.

INTERNAL CHANGES AND DEVELOPMENTS IN THE TWELFTH AND THIRTEENTH CENTURIES.

Colonization of Slavic lands by Germans.

DURING all the years in which the Hohenstaufens had been occupied with their bitter wars against the papacy, Germany of her own accord had been making wonderful progress in social, agricultural, and intellectual matters. In the eleventh century she possessed little more than the lands between the Elbe, Rhine, and Danube; by the fourteenth she had doubled her territory, had extended her bounds to the Baltic and the river Vistula, and had peopled Bohemia, Silesia, and even Transylvania with her colonists.

A new field of activity had been discovered, and in working it, all the experience of past generations was brought to bear. Peasants and citizens, knights and clergy from all parts of Germany wandered out to the Slavic lands in the north and in the east. Their new settlements were unhampered by old traditions; their mode of life became more free and democratic.

System of land-holding in the villages.

Various causes tended to induce men to leave their homes and seek their fortunes elsewhere. Chief among them, for cultivators at least, was lack of space in their native villages.

All through the Middle Ages the unit of landed possession for the village communities was the manse or *hufe*, which comprised room for house and garden, the right of using the common village pastures and also a certain number of parcels of agricultural land. These parcels were distributed among the three fields, or three greater divisions of land, one of which was to lie idle each year in order that the soil might improve.   As a rule about thirty acres of agricultural land would generally fall to the share of each possessor, whose parcels, however, being assigned by lot, did not necessarily adjoin each other.

By the twelfth century the inconveniences of this system had come to make themselves widely felt.   To reach one of his own lots or plots the farmer had to cross his neighbour's land ; it was necessary, therefore, in order to avoid spoiling crops already sown, for all to plough, sow, and harvest at the same time.   This was, naturally, a great hardship for active men who had to accommodate themselves to the ways of their slower neighbours. *Better system in the new districts.*

The great attraction for those who emigrated and became colonists was that in the new districts to which they were invited, or in which they arranged with the lord of the land to become settlers, the different parcels of land were no longer scattered.   A long central street was usually laid out and from this each man's allotment ran backward in a long strip, if necessary over hill and dale.

The new manse, too—the *mansus regalis* as this measurement was usually called—was almost invariably double the size of the old.

The thinly populated Slavic lands in North-eastern Germany, in Silesia, and in Transylvania were rich in marshy districts, in moorlands, and in uncut forests that were altogether uninhabited.   The methods of agriculture of the Slavs were far more primitive than those of the Germans ; the process of reclaiming lands, so familiar already to the Dutch and to the Flemings, was to them entirely unknown. Many of the Slavic land-owners now called in the Germans as settlers and divided their districts among them on the new system that was everywhere coming into vogue. *Germans called in by Slavs themselves.*

It was with four great groups of Slavs that the German colonists came, peacefully or otherwise, into contact ; the Tschecks and Moravians, the Poles, the Baltic tribes, and the Sorbs. *Different groups of Slavs.*

The Tschecks were settled in the present Bohemia, and

the Moravians, as now, adjoined them on the east and spoke their language. The Poles possessed at this time an immense stretch of territory, and were destined to play a large part in German as well as in Swedish and Russian history. The Baltic Slavs consisted of the Pomeranians, Liutitians, and Abodrites; their land was flourishing, and Danzig and Wollin had already been founded, the one at the mouth of the Vistula, the other of the Oder. The Sorbs, whose descendants in the Spreewald, about fifty miles from Berlin, still keep their language and their quaint costume, had settlements at that time which extended over a large part of the present kingdom of Saxony.

Peculiarities of Slavic villages.
The Slavs, as has been intimated, possessed no really practical method of agriculture. They had established themselves wherever the land seemed easy to cultivate. Their villages were of a circular form, and did not admit of being enlarged; it accordingly frequently became necessary to found new ones.

In Bohemia and Silesia there were villages under the protection of Slavic princes, where the inhabitants all pursued one trade or occupation; Tscheckish names still exist to remind us of such places. Kolodéja, for instance, was once the village of the wheel-makers, as the word itself implies; Mydlovary, in like manner, has perpetuated the memory of those who were engaged in boiling soap.

The Slavs along the Elbe were in a lower state of civilization than those in Bohemia; it was against them that the Ottos had fought, that Meissen had been founded, and that the Billungs had won their laurels.

Henry the Lion and Albrecht the Bear against the Slavs.
It is with Henry the Lion and Albrecht the Bear that the great increase of the empire's boundaries at the expense of the Slavs may be said to have begun. Albrecht, originally possessed of lands in the present Anhalt, where his descendants still rule, was given the North Mark by the Emperor Lothar in 1134. This embraced the present Altmark and the tongue of land between the Elbe and the Havel. Albrecht's chief goal was the incorporation of the Slavic territories of

Havelberg and Brandenburg into his new dominions. This
he accomplished in the one case by violence, in the other by
a treaty, Brandenburg falling to him by inheritance after the
death of its prince, Pribislav Henry, in 1150.

Both Albrecht and Henry the Lion took part in the crusade
of 1147 against the Wends ; the results of the undertaking
were small, but the terrible devastation and depopulation of
the land prepared the way for the calling in of German
colonists.

Count Adolf II. of Holstein, a vassal of Henry the Lion,
had in the meantime been doing much to carry German
culture into Slavic lands. He it was who, in 1143, having
called in Flemish, Dutch, Westphalian, and Frisian colonists,
began the building of Lubeck, which in both senses was to
be the first German city on the Baltic.

For his own part Henry the Lion had at first found it to **Henry the**
his advantage to favour the Slavic princes on his borders and **Lion's con-**
to accept their tribute. In 1160, however, he determined to **quests.**
conquer the land of the Abodrites in spite of the fact that
its prince, Niklot, had been his friend and ally. Niklot fell
after a heroic resistance, but in 1164 his son defeated the
Saxons and regained for himself the land of his father.
As a fief of the empire, however, with which he remained on terms of peace. He was the founder of the two
modern duchies of Mecklenburg Strelitz and Mecklenburg
Schwerin.

Henry the Lion next proceeded to attempt the conquest
of Pomerania and Rügen. As regards the latter place the
Danes were before him, and founded a rule which lasted
until the time of the Reformation. In Pomerania Henry was
more fortunate. In common with Albrecht's successor, Otto
of Brandenburg, he reduced the land to subjection.

It was, on the whole, the Dutch and the Flemings that **Dutch and**
proved most successful in the matter of colonizing conquered **Flemish**
lands. Accustomed as they were to low moorland, they **settlers.**
undertook the cultivation of tracts that had hitherto seemed
worthless. To them was due the credit of reclaiming the

marshes around Bremen, and their methods were largely adopted by other German settlers.

Discovery of silver mines. The territory around the Erzgebirge on the eastern border of the present Saxony was settled in feverish haste, not by farmers, but by miners. Here, near Freiberg, silver was discovered about the year 1160, and a rush was made for the place. By 1225 Freiberg had come to have no less than five different churches and parishes. Tin and copper were also found in the neighbourhood, and around each promising centre German settlements arose.

Colonization of Brandenburg. About 1160 began the systematic colonization of Brandenburg by Albrecht the Bear. He had but shortly before suppressed a Slavic rebellion, and seems now to have adopted the principle that the Slavs had no longer right or title to the lands which had so long been theirs. They were given away right and left to the followers of the margrave and to the new settlers. The former owners took refuge in the forests or founded miserable hamlets on the seashore. Only a few remnants of them can be traced in the following centuries; we know, for instance, that as late as 1752, in Lüchow, near Hanover, sermons were preached in the Slavic tongue.

The Slavs were treated by the Germans much as the later redskins by their American conquerors; in certain districts the war against them was one of extermination. In the county of Schwerin, about the year 1170, we hear of an order being given that every Slav who could not answer certain inquiries about himself should be strung up to the nearest tree.

Influence of the Church. The influence of the Church must not be forgotten in connection with this work of Germanizing Slavic lands. In the wake of the farmers followed the clergy, and churches and chapels soon dotted the landscape. In Meissen to-day, in the former land of the Sorbs, remains of this early colonial architecture are still to be seen.

The monkish orders. The monkish orders were especially active in furthering colonization. The first to take the field were the Premonstratensians, founded by Norbert, Archbishop of Magdeburg from 1126 to 1134.   By 1150 they had already established themselves as far north as the island of Usedom.   After 1170 their influence yielded to that of the Cistercians, whose order had been founded by Bernard of Clairvaux.

The Cistercian monasteries, founded one after the other in rough uncultivated districts, proved very oases in the desert, and worked their civilizing influence in every direction.   Their monks took the matter of colonizing the reclaimed lands into their own hands, and called in Dutch and other settlers as occasion demanded.

The Teutonic Order proved in the end the most successful **The Teutonic Order.** of all civilizing and Germanizing agents.   The knights were called in to Transylvania at the beginning of the thirteenth century by King Andreas II. of Hungary.   They undertook the defence of the boundary against the Kumani, a tribe of plunderers.

The rapid progress which the Order made, and the independent power which it seemed about to found soon awakened the fears of King Andreas, and, after fourteen years, the knights were banished.   The Order was transplanted to Prussia, where an immense field of activity awaited it.

The Prussians, a people who were divided into many stems **The Prussians.** and tribes, lived in the land between the Vistula and the Memel.   They were about on a level of civilization with the Germans of the time of Tacitus; their priests sacrificed to the gods and tended a never-dying flame.

It was at the hands of the Prussians that St. Adalbert, the friend of Otto III., had met his death ; since then there had been various attempts at conversion, some of which had met with no small success.   About 1215, however, there was a terrible uprising against the new teachings, and the heathen raged so furiously that a crusade was preached against them in Poland and Germany.   The failure of this crusade showed the necessity for more radical measures ; Herrmann of Salza, friend alike of Frederick II. and of the Popes who opposed him, procured permission for his Order to undertake the difficult task and to take possession of a large tract of land.   It

was expressly stipulated that the Order should be independent
of the Polish Church, and that its land as well as its future
conquests should form a separate principality of the Holy
Roman Empire.

Conquests of the Teutonic Order. This was in 1226; by 1231 the knights had crossed the
Vistula and founded the town of Thorn, and already a year
later the whole bank of the river between Thorn and Kulm
had come into their possession. In 1233 Marienwerder was
begun, by 1237 the mouth of the Vistula had been reached.
Colonists followed everywhere in the wake of the conquerors;
not only peasants and burghers, but nobles as well. In 1236
a grant of thousands of acres near Marienwerder was made
to the Noble Lord Dietrich of Tiefenau.

The knights continued their conquests along the Baltic.
They were assisted by the "Brothers of the Sword," an order
which had been founded in Livonia at the beginning of the
century, and which now gladly amalgamated itself with the
Teutons. The next task was to conquer the land which
separated the former seats of this new branch from those of
the rest of the Teutons. The work was rapidly accomplished;
in 1251 Memelburg was founded, in 1254 the important town
of Königsberg.

The Order now ruled over Prussia, Courland, Livonia, and
the land of the Lettes.

Struggles of the Order. Terrible revolts of the subjected peoples were still to be
met and put down. The next years were full of bloodshed,
and the real struggle was found to have only commenced.
The Prussians attempted to massacre all the Christians in the
land; in the end they themselves were all killed, enslaved, or
driven away.

Several times the Order had been on the verge of destruction, but in the end it conquered. By 1283 the struggle was
over, and there was no more opposition to be feared. The
Teutons were soon able to extend their influence into Poland
and Pomerellen, to which latter land the Margrave of Brandenburg was induced in 1308 to abandon all claim.

Marienburg. In 1309 Marienburg was founded at the Delta of the

Vistula, and became the capital as it were for the whole order. The ruins of this mighty fortress are to-day among the finest in all Europe.

The land of the Teutonic Order came to be the best governed state of the later Middle Ages; it was divided up into districts, each with its own directory, and with a fortress for its central point. The officials were all chosen from among the brothers, and there existed an admirable system of control. Every year there was a general calling to account, and the grand master, with the advice of the chapter, could depose, advance, or transfer according as he saw fit. **Administration of the land of the Order.**

By the efforts of the Order a strong bastion to the north-east of Germany had now been formed against the Slavs; in the south Silesia was strong enough to fear no ordinary attacks. Between the two that part of the Polish kingdom which comprises the present province of Posen made a great indentation to the westward, and touched the confines of Brandenburg. It was the task of the Brandenburg margraves to secure and extend their boundaries in this direction, and well did they succeed. By the time of the interregnum Brandenburg was one of the largest provinces of the entire empire, and fifty years later one of its margraves, Waldemar, became candidate for that empire's throne. **Extension of Brandenburg's boundaries.**

We have followed far enough the growth of Germany as regards the acquisition and colonization of new territory. In another direction a great inward development was going on quietly the while, and results no less remarkable were being obtained. A population formerly scattered over a large extent of territory began to concentrate itself at different points; we have reached the period of the rise of great towns. **Growth of cities in Germany.**

We may define a city in the Middle Ages as a place privileged to hold markets, with immunity from the jurisdiction of the king's officials, and governing itself by means of a corporation.

No connection remained with the old Roman cities that had existed on German ground; if new settlers occupied the sites where those cities once had been, as was the case with

E E

Cologne, they adopted nothing of the old Roman municipal institutions.   For centuries the counts and centenars ruled over such incipient towns as over any other part of their county or hundred.

Markets.   What gave the impulse to a new growth or a new founding of cities was the establishment of markets and the bestowal of privileges in connection with them.   Markets might be founded at first only by express permission of the kings, who received in return certain tolls or taxes.   A large symbol, usually a cross that was erected at the time of each yearly or weekly market, signified to all that the gathering was under the king's especial peace.

Such markets were held already in Carolingian times, towards the end of which period, too, the places where they were held were often granted immunities.   The people within certain limits were not to be subject to the usual financial burdens, but were to enjoy for themselves the revenues accruing from their pastures and fields, and from judicial fines and penalties.   They were to be exempt, too, from the jurisdiction of the count or centenar and to have their own official, the advocatus or defensor.

The only duties which these and other districts enjoying immunity were obliged to fulfil were hospitality to the king when he came in their midst, the building of fortresses and the keeping of watch and ward, the building of streets and bridges, and the obeying of a summons to the army.

Markets the nucleus of towns.   It is no mere chance that the market place in all older German towns occupies so important a position.   It was the nucleus of the city which spread out from it in all directions. Mints and other necessary institutions were established in the neighbourhood ; fortifications were erected so that the place should not be disturbed ; merchants, and especially Jews, began to settle themselves comfortably round their place of exchange.   Judicial courts that began with settling differences relating to market affairs, and that were under a special market judge, developed into the chief judicial bodies of the cities.

The land, for which a small rent was paid to the lord of the

town, was already by the end of the eleventh century technically free, and could be willed away or sold. At first the
administration as a whole was in the hands of the community
in general, and records remain, for Magdeburg, for instance,
to show that mass meetings were called for the transacting of
ordinary affairs. A chosen few naturally soon gained the
ascendancy, and the institution of city councils was evolved.

The old market cross, which was erected and taken down **Market
crosses.**
as occasion demanded, was replaced in the twelfth century by
a monumental stone cross, to which often a glove, a hat, a
sword, or a shield was attached as symbol of the king's protection. This protection implied that offences committed
during market time were to be punished with the royal ban of
sixty shillings in addition to the usual penalty. In the fourteenth century the stone crosses gave place in many towns to
the Rolands—huge stone figures bearing the sword of justice.

Already in the tenth century Mayence, the *Aurea Maguntia* **The Rhine
cities.**
as it was called, had begun to be an important centre. One
by one the cities along the Rhine now rose into prominence.
In the eleventh and twelfth centuries Cologne possessed the
commercial supremacy, carrying on a large trade with England
and other countries.

The twelfth century, as a result of the constant intercourse **Increase of
commerce.**
kept up with the Orient by crusaders, saw a vast increase of
commerce all over Europe. Eastern wares were landed on
the English and Flemish coasts, and were transferred from
there to all parts of Germany, especially to the coasts of the
North Sea and the Baltic. Bremen and Lubeck quickly
became large and flourishing.

The needs of commerce had meanwhile given rise to those **Gilds of
merchants.**
great and important associations, the Merchant Gilds. Trade
was originally carried on by wandering merchants who went
with their wares from place to place, and bought, sold, or
exchanged at the different markets. For their own protection
on the way, a number of traders would unite themselves into
caravans. Rich and poor, men of high degree and men of
low united into such societies, and chose a leader or alderman

for themselves, whose duty it was to arrange for the safety of the expedition.

Such temporary associations for mutual convenience soon led to more lasting unions. The Gild took a name to itself, chose a patron saint, and arranged festivals and banquets. The actual meaning of the word gild is a sacrificial feast—*convivium* was the common translation for it later in Saxony —and this social and festal element was never wanting.

Gilds manage trade.
The earlier alderman becomes a regular official; a number of gild brothers form an advisory committee. The gilds undertook the improvement of intercourse between commercial centres, introduced new scales and weights, and developed new codes of commercial usage. They strove for and obtained the monopoly of trade in certain branches, and they formed sub-gilds in far-off places, thus assuring their members of a good reception and of proper protection. Cologne had a gild in London, Groningen had gilds in Cologne and in Utrecht.

Pre-eminence of gild merchants.
In the cities of the twelfth and thirteenth centuries there were thus three factors, the gilds, the city councils, and the lesser or local tradesmen, if we may call them so. The gilds themselves became more and more associations of greater merchants, who in many towns formed a regular oligarchy, securing for their members the chief positions in the city council. They often came into conflict with the other members of the community, but the great struggles between the classes and the masses belong to the history of the fourteenth and fifteenth centuries.

The cities were now proud corporations with a great sense of their own importance, their inhabitants are addressed even in royal charters as " distinguished citizens." More and more did they strive for freedom and for complete emancipation from the rule of the lords to whose territory they belonged.

The lords of the cities.
By the end of the Hohenstaufen period there were comparatively few of these market cities still remaining under the direct jurisdiction of the crown. They had for the most part been deeded away to great nobles, to bishops and abbots.

It was Otto I. who had commenced making such grants of markets and of the jurisdiction over them; by the time of Henry IV. nine-tenths of the markets were subject in the last instance to members of the clergy.

When the markets developed into regular cities, which they did chiefly in the eleventh century, the princes to whom they had been granted retained their authority, drew their revenues from taxes and judicial fines, coined their own money, and saw to the maintenance of peace.

It was not long, however, before the cities tried to throw off the authority of their lords. Already, under Henry IV. and in his favour, Cologne had risen against the Archbishop Anno; many other cities, too, took the part of the unfortunate king, who rewarded them with grants of tolls and jurisdictions. *Revolt against these lords.*

Later, as we have seen, the territorial princes, supported by Frederick II., made strenuous efforts to prevent the growing autonomy of the cities; a decree of 1231 categorically forbade them to elect their own authorities. The result was a fiercer conflict than ever; the laws passed were disregarded, and in the end the burghers had their way. The cities gradually became little republics, drew the inhabitants of the surrounding districts under their influence and made leagues and confederations with each other.

In the struggle between the Hohenstaufens and the anti-king, Henry Raspe, the cities played an important part—all the more so as the greater lay princes maintained an unworthy neutrality. Sought after by both parties they drew all the profit possible from the condition of affairs. Frederick II. and Conrad IV. were not chary in promising privileges, and were able to win over Aix, Treves, Augsburg, Worms, Ulm, and many other towns. *Cities grow more and more independent.*

The Archbishop of Mayence, on the other hand, gained over for himself his own capital by granting it practical autonomy; the Bishop of Strasburg followed suit, while Cologne accepted favours from the papal as well as the Hohenstaufen side and remained neutral.

The disorders consequent upon the fall of the Hohenstaufens gave the cities an opportunity to complete their emancipation. Already in 1254, as we have seen, it had become possible for an organization like the Rhine Confederation to spring into being and to become for a moment the most important political factor in the land.

Growth of feudal system.

At the time when the colonization of the Slavic lands by the Germans was making such progress and the German cities were growing so rapidly in importance, in wealth, and in independence, another development was reaching its climax, a development no less interesting and wonderful.

The twelfth and thirteenth centuries are the period when the feudal system flourished in Germany in its greatest completeness. This system may be said to have begun at the time when Charles Martel confiscated the lands of the Church, and parcelled them out among his nobles. His object was to enable the latter to support the heavier expenses of military duty contingent on the extension of the use of cavalry.

The "Benefices" of Charles Martel.

In distributing these lands among his followers Charles Martel stipulated that the holders should pay a certain rent to the especial church to which the property belonged—a stipulation which was confirmed and repeated under Pippin.

The "benefices," as they were called, proved for the Carolingian kings a powerful factor in controlling their nobles. Whoever fell under the royal displeasure was likely to forfeit lands which had been given him, not only as a reward for past services but as a pledge for services to come.

Subdivision of benefices.

The services in question were mostly of a military nature, and the man to whom the land was lent was obliged to subdivide a certain part of it and lend it in turn to those who were willing to be his followers in the army. What the kings did on a large scale they, the nobles, were compelled to do on a smaller one.

Homage.

Those to whom they sub-granted their land were obliged to swear loyalty or fealty, and this oath, or homage as it was called, came to be incumbent on the original holders themselves as regarded the king. They became his vassals, and aided him with an army of sub-vassals of their own. These holders-in-chief, or *seigneurs*, were the men who, towards the end of the Carolingian period, answered the call to arms, and not, as up to the time of Charlemagne, the whole body of freemen.

The feudal system gradually invaded the whole of Europe, although in Germany especially, in addition to fiefs, there were always private landed possessions or allods. These latter, indeed, in order to fit them into the prevalent scheme of land-holding, were often designated as " fiefs of the sun ! "   *Feudal system invades Europe.*

For centuries, fiefs were not hereditary. They lapsed to the crown at the death of every holder; at every change of monarch or of lord there had to be a renewal of the grant. When the time came, as it did in the thirteenth century, that they could descend regularly from a father to his son, or daughter, or even to his collateral relations, the power of the king as a feudal monarch was at an end.   *Heredity of fiefs.*

Not only land, but offices and privileges could be granted out as fiefs in return for certain services. These, too, were at first withdrawable at the will of the crown and in time became hereditary.

The result of the spread of vassalage was to ruin the state in its old form. The land became subject to many masters, the monarch wasted the greater part of his time in reckoning with this or that aspiring noble. We no longer find kings issuing general laws or capitularies for all of their subjects just as we no longer find them directly commanding those subjects to fight their battles.   *Results of the spread of vassalage.*

By the twelfth century, feudalism had invaded everything ; even the episcopal sees were looked upon as fiefs which were to be withdrawn and held for a while after every vacancy. Rulers of foreign lands hastened to become vassals of the emperors and also of the popes ; Henry VI. and Innocent III. claimed homage from nearly all the kings of Europe.

Among the vassals of the higher nobles in Germany the so-called *ministeriales* or serving men came to form a class of high   *The "Minis-teriales."*

importance, a class by themselves of men who, originally not
free and without land of their own, raised themselves in rank
and formed a sort of lesser nobility. In a royal charter of
1134 they are spoken of as the *ordo equestris minor*. Their
advancement was owing to the fact that the services demanded
of them were of a military nature, and that they could thus
make themselves indispensable on occasion. Many free
knights, seeing the rewards that the *ministeriales* were entitled to, voluntarily gave up their own rank and privileges
and entered into this connection.

It was the *ministeriales* who made up the kernel of the
armies of the Hohenstaufens; they it was who helped those
kings in their struggles with the princes, with the popes and
with the Lombards.

**The knights
a distinct
class.**

By the time at which we have arrived the knights themselves, *ordo equestris major*, had come to form a class so distinct and so exclusive that no outsiders could enter it except
in the course of three generations or by special decree of the
king. Only to those whose fathers and grandfathers were of
knightly origin could fiefs now be granted; only such could
engage in judicial combat, in knightly sports, and above all
in the tournament or joust.

**Duties of a
knight.**

One of the chief duties of a blameless knight was to be a
true vassal to his liege lord, and at once to repair to that
lord's court when summoned, even if the object were only to
assist at festivities. He was to be ready to aid in the administration of justice or to take part if need be in a war or
a feud. He was obliged to swear on receiving his fief to be
"faithful, devoted and willing;" he laid his hands in the
hands of his master, and in many cases sealed the compact
with a kiss.

Feudalism did much to awaken a moral sentiment; fidelity,
truth, and sincerity were the presuppositions upon which the
whole system rested, and a great solidarity of interests came
to exist between the lord and his vassals. The latter might
bring no public charges against their master in matters affecting his life, limb, or honour; on three grand occasions, in

case of captivity, the knighting of his son, the marriage of his daughter, they were obliged to furnish him with pecuniary aid.

Knightly honour and knightly graces come in the twelfth century to be a matter of fashion and custom; a new and important element, too, the adoration of woman, is introduced. A whole literature arises that has to do almost exclusively with knightly prowess and with knightly love. Altogether we see the dawn of a new social life. Money begins to circulate more freely, we find an increased luxury in the matter of clothing and of household arrangements. The streets become more secure and more passable, and visitors move to and fro from one castle to another. A number of minor courts begin to flourish besides that of the king; the Wartburg, for instance, becomes a centre for the musical and intellectual life of the times. A regular code was finally established of the rules of conduct considered suitable and becoming; the German words "hübsch" (from höfisch = courtly) and "höflich" are a legacy of these days, and serve to remind us of what was considered good style in such courtly circles.

Knightly etiquette.

Just as certain classes of society to-day adopt by preference the garb and the customs of a foreign country, so already in the twelfth century French influence made itself felt in Germany in many directions. The names that refer to the tourney and to knightly sports at this time are all French, so are those which refer to the more elaborate dishes at the table. In fact everything that had to do with festivities or with luxury in general seems to have been taken from France. We have French names for dress-materials, for the costumes themselves, for various dances, and the love-poems of the time are overflowing with French expressions.

French influence.

The formalism and etiquette, too, of German chivalry was a direct legacy from France. Men troubled themselves about their manners as in other ages they did about their sins; great stress, for instance, is laid on the forms to be observed when entering or when leaving a room, when addressing persons or when parting from them. Godfrey of Strassburg weaves a

French formalism.

long discussion into his "Tristan" concerning the different ways of greeting; should one only bow, or should one speak?

A conventionalism not only of action and expression, but also of feeling, developed itself. It became the custom to sink oneself in one's love, to discuss and to analyze the emotions of the soul.

CHAPTER XXVIII.

THE LITERATURE OF THE HOHENSTAUFEN TIMES.

WE learn of the tendencies described in the last chapter from the literature, and especially from the poetry of the time. Almost the whole literature of the twelfth and thirteenth centuries, for that matter, was poetry; but a poetry which was accepted as a means of chronicling real facts. No one, because they happened to be written in verse, doubted the adventures of Æneas or the possibility of the tranformations of Ovid. The most impossible details were woven into the poems of the day, and it was the fashion not to question their truth. *The poetry of the time.*

It was the hey-day of love-poetry, the most flourishing period for the minnesingers or wandering minstrels. The nobles, too, commence not only to find pleasure in the songs of others, but also to take the pen into their own hands.

A manuscript still exists which was written in the fourteenth century, and which contains the poems of 140 minnesingers who had written during the previous two hundred years. It is headed by songs of the emperor Henry VI. and of the unfortunate young Conradino. The whole is a series of pictures taken from the knightly life of the times; they deal with war and peace, with love and play, with tournaments and crusades. *The Minnesingers.*

Among all the writings of the time none can be more amusing than the memoirs of the poet-knight Ulrich von Lichtenstein, who describes his own love-adventures from 1222 to 1255. He inserts the songs that he composed on each occasion of especial tenderness. His hopes and his dis- *Ulrich von Lichtenstein.*

appointments are all reproduced, and his work, more than
any other, shows the extent to which the worship of woman
could be carried. He, a married man and father of several
children, has an operation performed on his mouth because
its expression does not suit the chosen object of his devotion.
He cuts his finger off because his lady had been told that he
had lost it for her sake in a tournament, and is surprised to
find that that was not the case.

Devotion to Woman.   These fair ladies who were thus loved and fought for held,
for the most part, the far-off, half-deified, position that
Beatrice did to Dante. Reinmar of Zweter, a contemporary
of Ulrich von Lichtenstein, compares a beautiful woman to
the holy grail; he who would win her must remain pure as
that grail's guardians.

Reinmar of Hagenau drove sickly sentimentality and un-
satisfied longing fairly into the ground. Those who read his
poems at last began to laugh at him, and to ask how old the
lady might be whose praises he had been singing for such an
eternity.

There were not wanting those among the poets themselves
who made themselves merry over the devotion of their fellows.
A certain Tannhuser, who lived until about 1270, ridicules the
onerous services which the ladies demand from their adorers.
His dame wants him, he says, to stop the Rhine from flowing
by Coblenz, to take its reflection from the moon, and to
capture her a salamander from the fire. It was Tannhuser
who declared that he had spent his whole fortune on fair
women, good living, and baths twice a week.

Walter of the Vogelweid.   The greatest master of lyric poetry in this period—indeed
the greatest lyric poet who lived before the time of Goethe—
was Walter of the Vogelweid. We can trace his career from
1198 to 1227, during which time he was continually wandering from court to court. He sang for Philip of Suabia, for
Otto IV., and for Frederick II., and some of his poems have
to do with the affairs of the nation. He was looked upon by
many as a dangerous man who led the people astray, and it
was declared by one of the Italian clergy that with a single

poem he could bewitch thousands, and make them disobedient
to God and to the Pope.

In truth, Walter was anything but pleased with the doings
of the court of Rome. He was essentially a German patriot,
loving and admiring his own country. "He who wishes to
look for virtue and for true love," he exclaims, "shall come
to our land; there delight is to be found in plenty—oh, that
I may live long therein!" He objects to German gold finding its way to Rome, and calls the Pope a new Judas, and a
servant of the devil.

Although unchurchly to the last degree, Walter's system of
ethics was highly admirable. He is an apostle of humanity
and toleration, and declares that Christians, Jews, and
heathen serve one and the same God. He is most severe on
himself because there are some of his enemies whom he can
not bring himself to love. He insists on moderation in all
things, and on self-restraint. He sings the praise of friendship, and esteems it higher than blood relationship. "Let a
friend's smile," he urges, "be true and without guile, pure as
the evening glow that presages a beautiful day." *Walter's ethics.*

In attacking the Pope for continually demanding money
for new crusades, Walter, whose rhetorical turns and artifices
are nothing if not original, apostrophizes the collection-box:
"Tell me, collection-box, has the Pope sent you to us that you
should make him rich, and plunder the Germans?" He
draws a graphic picture of the Pope sitting among his Italians,
and expressing his contempt for the Teuton. "Eat fowls,"
cries his holiness, "and drink wine, ye priests, and let them
fast, the German ——." (A word so strong, apparently, that
it has been omitted in all the manuscripts that have come
down to us.) *Walter and the Church.*

Witty allusions crop up even in Walter's tender love-songs.
In praising his fair one he likens her body to a garment that
covers her true personality, and takes occasion at the same
time to mock at the custom of rewarding minstrels by gifts of
cast-off clothing: "Garments that have been worn I have
hitherto never accepted: this I would willingly accept for life; *Walter's wit.*

for this an emperor might turn minstrel. There, emperor, begin thy lay! No, emperor, somewhere else!"

Walter's character. In summing up Walter of the Vogelweide's character, Scherer, our chief modern authority in such matters, draws the following attractive picture: "The best representation that he gives is that of himself—a man such as one would like to have for a friend, so bright in all his being, so gentle; for all his light and pleasing form, so inwardly earnest and firm; merry with the gay, sad with mourners; full of hope from childhood on, and unwearying in striving after high goals; fresh and cheerful even in time of need, thankful for good fortune. Somewhat gloomy, indeed, in old age, and with good cause, for spring and summer were over for the minnesingers, and Walter foresaw the approach of autumn."

So much for lyric poetry; simultaneously with it epic poetry had reached a high development in Germany.

The "Nibelungenlied." Between 1190 and 1208 was composed the "Nibelungenlied," or "Song of the Nibelungs." It is an open question whether one hand or many wrote this great work, some parts of which are dull and lifeless, while others rise to the greatest heights of tragic art.

The poem relates how Siegfried, the great hero, the son of Siegmund, comes to Worms, to the capital of the Burgundians. He has heard of the beauty of Kriemhilde, the sister of Gunther and Gernot. At first he appears as a would-be conqueror and destroyer of the Burgundian kingdom, but soon his wrath is appeased, and he becomes Gunther's friend and ally, the winner of all his battles.

Siegfried and Brunhilda. Gunther sends him to tame, on his behalf, Brunhilda, Queen of the Isenstein beyond the seas; it is necessary to combat with her to win her love; the reward for Siegfried is to be Kriemhilde.

Siegfried, disguised in the *tarnkappe*, or magic mantle, which he had once captured from the dwarf Alberich, subdues Brunhilda, whom he had formerly known, and makes her believe that her conqueror is Gunther. Brunhilda is brought to Worms, Siegfried and Kriemhilde are wedded.

Brunhilda will not submit to Gunther, and Siegfried, in his *tarnkappe*, is again called in. Once more he subdues Brunhilda, and this time takes from her a ring and her girdle.

Later Siegfried and his bride, who had departed for Norway where the great hero ruled over the land of the Nibelungs, and where he possessed a rich treasure, return to Worms to visit Gunther and Brunhilda. A quarrel ensues between Brunhilda and Kriemhilde, the latter having boasted too highly of her husband's prowess. In the excitement of the moment Kriemhilde shows the ring and girdle that Brunhilda had been forced to surrender to Siegfried. Brunhilda complains to Gunther that Siegfried is falsely assuming the honour of having subdued her, and Gunther is filled with hatred against the friend who has betrayed his secret.

Brunhilda's grief rouses Hagen, Gunther's faithful follower, to take vengeance on Siegfried. He draws from Kriemhilde the information that, when Siegfried had slain a dragon, and was bathing in its blood to make himself invulnerable, the leaf of a linden-tree had fallen between his shoulders and left an unprotected spot. **Siegfried's death.**

Hagen arranges a hunt, and Siegfried, who has shown his fearlessness and boyish spirits in various conflicts with wild beasts, at last is weary, and bends at a fountain to drink. Hagen pierces him through the back; Siegfried dies and is carried home on his shield, and placed in a coffin before Kriemhilde's door. Kriemhilde comes out on her way to early mass, sees the coffin, and has it opened. She raises with her white hand the head of the dead man and covers it with kisses. Her eye falls on Siegfried's shield. She sees that there are no clefts in it, that there has been no combat, and that he must have been murdered. She and Siegfried's father, Siegmund, plan to take a terrible vengeance.

The second half of the poem is devoted to unfolding the progress of this work of retribution. Kriemhilde gives her hand to Attila, the fierce king of the Huns; Gunther, Gernot, Hagen, and all the flower of the Burgundian nobility, **Kriemhilde's vengeance.**

are bidden to a feast at Attila's court. A massacre ensues, and all are either killed or taken captive.

The end of the Burgundians.

The last canto of the "Nibelungenlied," which describes this tragic end of the Burgundians is about the finest production of mediæval poetry. The catastrophe is splendidly described with all its boundless horror, with here and there a striking episode of individual heroism.

Hagen and Gunther are among the captives, and are brought in chains to Kriemhilde, who demands from the former the treasure of the Nibelungs, of which he had possessed himself after Siegfried's death. He refuses so long as Gunther and Gernot shall live. Kriemhilde then has Gunther put to death, and shows his head to Hagen. Gernot in the meantime had already fallen. Hagen still refuses, and Kriemhilde slays him with Siegfried's sword. She is then struck down herself by the hand of one of Attila's guests.

Other epic poems.

The "Nibelungenlied" is not the only great literary product of the late twelfth and early thirteenth century. The epics "Wolfdietrich" and "Gudrun" each lead us through two generations of loving, faithful, and sorely tried personages. Henry of Veldecke wrote an Æneid based on a French translation of Virgil's work; so highly was it valued that a Thuringian noble stole the manuscript while still incomplete from the bride of the landgrave to whom Henry had lent it. It was nine years before the poet could regain his property and complete his work.

In the poems of this time we find foreign legends taken up by German writers, and worked over in their own especial style. So it was with the story of King Arthur and the Knights of the Round Table which, first recorded by the British chronicler, Geoffrey of Monmouth, soon became the common property of Europe. So it was with the legend of Tristan and Isolde, so also with that of Parsifal and the search for the holy grail.

Tristan and Isolde.

Godfrey of Strassburg, who died about 1210, worked the Tristan legend into its completest form, and surrounded it with picturesque details. He represents Tristan as an ideal knight, possessed of every virtue. Tristan has been brought up at the court of his uncle Marke in Cornwall, in whose service he performs the bravest deeds. He conquers Morold of Ireland, and frees Cornwall from a shameful tribute. He then makes peace between the two lands, and wooes the Irish princess Isolde for his uncle. On the ship which carries the bride to her intended husband Tristan and Isolde drink by mistake a love potion originally intended for Isolde and Marke. Love makes Tristan forget all his duties and all the ties which have bound him to his liege lord. Remorse, however, soon makes him flee from Isolde and take service in a foreign land. Here he meets and marries a second Isolde— Isolde Whitehand. He cannot forget his first love, however, and he succeeds in making his new bride miserable, and in turning her affection to hatred and jealousy.

Tristan is wounded, and the first Isolde is secretly called in to heal him. The second Isolde prevents her coming until too late; the Irish princess arrives to find Tristan dead, and breathes out her own life over his corpse.

Mediæval epic poetry reached its height in Germany under Wolfram of Eschenbach; his own contemporaries were foremost in singing his praises. "Never did mouth of layman speak better," says one enthusiastic poet, and indeed Wolfram's works seem to have been universally considered as second only to the Bible and the writings of the Church fathers. He was master of his own language as no one before him had been, and yet personally he could neither read nor write. Everything had to be read aloud to him, and he dictated all his verses. His eloquence has been likened to the rushing of a torrent which art had done nothing to stem.

Wolfram of Eschenbach.

"Parsifal" is Wolfram's greatest poem, a poem with a religious background, and full of deep ethical teachings. Parsifal is the son of Gahmuret, a Christian prince of Anjou, who had long lived peacefully among the Saracens, but who had deserted his Moorish wife, Belakane, after the latter had already borne him a son, Feirefiss. Gahmuret had later won

Parsifal.

F F

the hand of Queen Herzeloide of Valois, having defeated her other suitors in a tournament. From this union Parsifal had sprung.

Parsifal and Feirefiss. One of the later episodes of the poem shows us how the two brothers, strangers to each other, meet in deadly combat; how Parsifal's sword breaks of its own accord, and how Feirefiss not only spares his brother's life, but shows him during the rest of his days a faithfulness as great as that of any Christian, even though, as the poet explains, it was through Christ that faithfulness was first brought into the world. Feirefiss finally is baptized and carries Christianity to India.

The Holy Grail. Wolfram introduces us in his poem to the Holy Grail. According to the heathen legends this was a vessel or receptacle which gave forth food and drink; according to the Christian version it was the cup used by the Saviour at the Last Supper, and in which His blood had been collected by Joseph of Arimathea.

Wolfram understands under the Grail is a costly jewel which has fallen from Heaven, and which has been given over to a religious order of knights to guard. It is a symbol of eternal life; he who looks upon it does not die, but remains for ever young. It is kept in the wild mountain of Monsalvat, where none can enter save those who are specially called and chosen. Its votaries must renounce earthly love, and only the king of the order may take to himself a wife.

The Order of the Grail. The Order of the Grail is represented as comprising a large congregation of men and women, knights and squires, priests and laymen; it is mystical and secret, and receives its commands direct from Heaven. The dignity of king represents the highest office to which mortal is capable of attaining; his power is far above that of the Pope.

It is to this dignity of king that Parsifal is destined, but he has first to go through a process of purification in order to throw off his load of sin. The fundamental idea of Wolfram's poem is to find out how to obtain the needed perfection; it is much the same problem that Goethe has worked out in his "Faust." Wolfram comes to the conclusion that by steadfastness and fidelity a man may reach the highest of all goals.

Parsifal's career is unfolded before us, and he is seen conquering one by one the evil influences that are brought to bear upon him, and being benefited by the good ones. His mother wants to keep him from the warlike pursuits of those of his own rank, and has him brought up in a lonely wood. He meets by chance, however, with knights who inflame his chivalrous nature by tales of King Arthur and his followers.

Parsifal's career.

Parsifal bursts away from his mother, who dies of grief at parting from him; he comes to King Arthur's court clad in the garb of a fool, and utterly without knightly training. Gurnemauz, at home in all the external forms and proprieties of worldly knighthood, but without spiritual insight, undertakes to teach him what is suitable and becoming. He warns him, among other things, against asking questions.

Parsifal comes to the aid of the oppressed queen Condwiramurs, and finally marries her, but leaves her in search of adventure. He is admitted to an assembly of the knights of the Holy Grail. He sees King Amfortas in mortal pain; he sees a bloody lance brought in, at the sight of which there is general wailing. He receives a sword from Amfortas who alludes in connection with it to his own deadly suffering; but as Gurnemauz has taught him to ask no question, Parsifal refrains from sympathy and is silent. The poet intended to show how the knightly etiquette and stiff conventionalism of the time stood in the way of the common feelings of humanity.

Parsifal and Amfortas.

The word of human compassion which Parsifal failed to utter would, according to the decree of the Grail, have cured the pain of Amfortas, and would have raised Parsifal to the throne. The latter, having failed to perform the chief duty of a really chivalrous soul, leaves Monsalvat in disgrace and is received by King Arthur among the knights of his Round

Parsifal's want of compassion.

Table. Here Kundry, a messenger of the Grail, informs him reproachfully of the evil which he has unwittingly done.

Parsifal's despair. He insists on his innocence ; he renounces the God who could have allowed such shame to fall upon him. He will be true to his wife and strong in battle, but declares that from God he expects nothing more. He starts at once in search of the Grail, and wanders disconsolate for five long years.

Parsifal's purification. On a Good Friday a pilgrim meets him, induces him to search his own soul, and brings him to a pious hermit, Trevizent. Here he learns humility and submission to the will of God. He meets and conquers the knight Gawan, and the conflict typifies the higher, spiritualized chivalry as opposed to that which is lower and more earthly. The child of God fights and overcomes the child of the world.

Parsifal is finally sufficiently chastened to be recalled to the Grail. He asks the question and expresses the sympathy on which so much depends, is made king, and is joined by his queen Condwiramurs and by his two sons.

Lohengrin. Lohengrin, one of the sons of Parsifal, is the hero of another legend that was made use of by various poets. Wolfram, at the conclusion of his Parsifal, speaks of the Knight of the Grail who, drawn by a swan, comes to Antwerp and weds the Princess of Brabant. Lohengrin makes the condition that she shall not question him about his origin ; she disobeys and he leaves her, being borne homeward by a swan. The theme was greatly elaborated by a Bavarian poet who wrote about 1290 ; and other characters, such as King Henry, and Frederick, Count of Telramund, were introduced.

Asceticism kills romance. Enough has been said to show how rich the early thirteenth century was in literary works of thrilling interest. Before the century had waned Dominican and Franciscan monks, inquisitors and papal legates, had invaded Germany and had entirely altered the direction of men's thoughts. The Franciscans especially had thundered forth their powerful sermons against tournaments, fine garments, and every other luxury ; against minstrels and against dancing, against singing secular songs and reading books that were written in the German tongue.

Chivalry itself was to go down eventually before the more practical needs of the day; social and political life was to undergo a radical change. The knights were to degenerate into highwaymen and robbers. In the time of the Reformation we see them make one last attempt to maintain their position as a class; they then sink for ever in the ruins of a civilization that had passed away.